CREATING **COOL**™
HTML 4
WEB PAGES

CREATING COOL™
HTML 4
WEB PAGES

Dave Taylor

IDG Books Worldwide, Inc
An International Data Group Company

Foster City, CA ♦ Chicago, IL ♦ Indianapolis, IN ♦ Southlake, TX

Creating Cool™ HTML 4 Web Pages
Published by
IDG Books Worldwide, Inc.
An International Data Group Company
919 E. Hillsdale Blvd., Suite 400
Foster City, CA 94404
www.idgbooks.com (IDG Books Worldwide Web site)

Library of Congress Catalog Card No.: 97-78211

ISBN: 0-7645-3201-4

Printed in the United States of America

10 9 8 7 6 5 4 3 2

1DD/SS/QV/ZY/IN

Distributed in the United States by IDG Books Worldwide, Inc.

Distributed by Macmillan Canada for Canada; by Transworld Publishers Limited in the United Kingdom; by IDG Norge Books for Norway; by IDG Sweden Books for Sweden; by Woodslane Pty. Ltd. for Australia; by Woodslane Enterprises Ltd. for New Zealand; by Longman Singapore Publishers Ltd. for Singapore, Malaysia, Thailand, and Indonesia; by Simron Pty. Ltd. for South Africa; by Toppan Company Ltd. for Japan; by Distribuidora Cuspide for Argentina; by Livraria Cultura for Brazil; by Ediciencia S.A. for Ecuador; by Addison-Wesley Publishing Company for Korea; by Ediciones ZETA S.C.R. Ltda. for Peru; by WS Computer Publishing Corporation, Inc., for the Philippines; by Unalis Corporation for Taiwan; by Contemporanea de Ediciones for Venezuela; by Computer Book & Magazine Store for Puerto Rico; by Express Computer Distributors for the Caribbean and West Indies. Authorized Sales Agent: Anthony Rudkin Associates for the Middle East and North Africa.

For general information on IDG Books Worldwide's books in the U.S., please call our Consumer Customer Service department at 800-762-2974. For reseller information, including discounts and premium sales, please call our Reseller Customer Service department at 800-434-3422.

For information on where to purchase IDG Books Worldwide's books outside the U.S., please contact our International Sales department at 650-655-3200 or fax 650-655-3295.

For information on foreign language translations, please contact our Foreign & Subsidiary Rights department at 650-655-3021 or fax 650-655-3281.

For sales inquiries and special prices for bulk quantities, please contact our Sales department at 650-655-3200 or write to the address above.

For information on using IDG Books Worldwide's books in the classroom or for ordering examination copies, please contact our Educational Sales department at 800-434-2086 or fax 817-251-8174.

For press review copies, author interviews, or other publicity information, please contact our Public Relations department at 650-655-3000 or fax 650-655-3299.

For authorization to photocopy items for corporate, personal, or educational use, please contact Copyright Clearance Center, 222 Rosewood Drive, Danvers, MA 01923, or fax 978-750-4470.

ABOUT IDG BOOKS WORLDWIDE

Welcome to the world of IDG Books Worldwide.

IDG Books Worldwide, Inc., is a subsidiary of International Data Group, the world's largest publisher of computer-related information and the leading global provider of information services on information technology. IDG was founded more than 25 years ago and now employs more than 8,500 people worldwide. IDG publishes more than 275 computer publications in over 75 countries (see listing below). More than 60 million people read one or more IDG publications each month.

Launched in 1990, IDG Books Worldwide is today the #1 publisher of best-selling computer books in the United States. We are proud to have received eight awards from the Computer Press Association in recognition of editorial excellence and three from *Computer Currents'* First Annual Readers' Choice Awards. Our best-selling *...For Dummies®* series has more than 30 million copies in print with translations in 30 languages. IDG Books Worldwide, through a joint venture with IDG's Hi-Tech Beijing, became the first U.S. publisher to publish a computer book in the People's Republic of China. In record time, IDG Books Worldwide has become the first choice for millions of readers around the world who want to learn how to better manage their businesses.

Our mission is simple: Every one of our books is designed to bring extra value and skill-building instructions to the reader. Our books are written by experts who understand and care about our readers. The knowledge base of our editorial staff comes from years of experience in publishing, education, and journalism — experience we use to produce books for the '90s. In short, we care about books, so we attract the best people. We devote special attention to details such as audience, interior design, use of icons, and illustrations. And because we use an efficient process of authoring, editing, and desktop publishing our books electronically, we can spend more time ensuring superior content and spend less time on the technicalities of making books.

You can count on our commitment to deliver high-quality books at competitive prices on topics you want to read about. At IDG Books Worldwide, we continue in the IDG tradition of delivering quality for more than 25 years. You'll find no better book on a subject than one from IDG Books Worldwide.

John Kilcullen
CEO
IDG Books Worldwide, Inc.

Steven Berkowitz
President and Publisher
IDG Books Worldwide, Inc.

Eighth Annual Computer Press Awards ≥1992

Ninth Annual Computer Press Awards ≥1993

Tenth Annual Computer Press Awards ≥1994

Eleventh Annual Computer Press Awards ≥1995

IDG Books Worldwide, Inc., is a subsidiary of International Data Group, the world's largest publisher of computer-related information and the leading global provider of information services on information technology. International Data Group publishes over 275 computer publications in over 75 countries. Sixty million people read one or more International Data Group publications each month. International Data Group's publications include: **ARGENTINA:** Buyer's Guide, Computerworld Argentina, PC World Argentina; **AUSTRALIA:** Australian Macworld, Australian PC World, Australian Reseller News, Computerworld, IT Casebook, Network World, Publish, Webmaster; **AUSTRIA:** Computerwelt Österreich, Networks Austria, PC Tip Austria; **BANGLADESH:** PC World Bangladesh; **BELARUS:** PC World Belarus; **BELGIUM:** Data News; **BRAZIL:** Annuário de Informática, Computerworld, Connections, Macworld, PC Player, PC World, Publish, Reseller News, Supergamepower; **BULGARIA:** Computerworld Bulgaria, Network World Bulgaria, PC & MacWorld Bulgaria; **CANADA:** CIO Canada, Client/Server World, ComputerWorld Canada, InfoWorld Canada, NetworkWorld Canada, WebWorld; **CHILE:** Computerworld Chile, PC World Chile; **COLOMBIA:** Computerworld Colombia, PC World Colombia; **COSTA RICA:** PC World Centro America; **THE CZECH AND SLOVAK REPUBLICS:** Computerworld Czechoslovakia, Macworld Czech Republic, PC World Czechoslovakia; **DENMARK:** Communications World Danmark, Computerworld Danmark, Macworld Danmark, PC World Danmark, Techworld Denmark; **DOMINICAN REPUBLIC:** PC World Republica Dominicana; **ECUADOR:** PC World Ecuador; **EGYPT:** Computerworld Middle East, PC World Middle East; **EL SALVADOR:** PC World Centro America; **FINLAND:** MikroPC, Tietoverkko, Tietoviikko; **FRANCE:** Distributique, Hebdo, Info PC, Le Monde Informatique, Macworld, Reseaux & Telecoms, WebMaster France; **GERMANY:** Computer Partner, Computerwoche, Computerwoche Extra, Computerwoche FOCUS, Global Online, Macwelt, PC Welt; **GREECE:** Amiga Computing, GamePro Greece, Multimedia World; **GUATEMALA:** PC World Centro America; **HONDURAS:** PC World Centro America; **HONG KONG:** Computerworld Hong Kong, PC World Hong Kong, Publish in Asia; **HUNGARY:** ABCD CD-ROM, Computerworld Szamitastechnika, Internetto online Magazine, PC World Hungary, PC-X Magazin Hungary; **ICELAND:** Tolvuheimur PC World Island; **INDIA:** Information Communications World, Information Systems Computerworld, PC World India, Publish in Asia; **INDONESIA:** InfoKomputer PC World, Komputek Computerworld, Publish in Asia; **IRELAND:** ComputerScope, PC Live!; **ISRAEL:** Macworld Israel, People & Computers/Computerworld; **ITALY:** Computerworld Italia, Macworld Italia, Networking Italia, PC World Italia; **JAPAN:** DTP World, Macworld Japan, Nikkei Personal Computing, OS/2 World Japan, SunWorld Japan, Windows NT World, Windows World Japan; **KENYA:** PC World East African; **KOREA:** Hi-Tech Information, Macworld Korea, PC World Korea; **MACEDONIA:** PC World Macedonia; **MALAYSIA:** Computerworld Malaysia, PC World Malaysia, Publish in Asia; **MALTA:** PC World Malta; **MEXICO:** Computerworld Mexico, PC World Mexico; **MYANMAR:** PC World Myanmar; **NETHERLANDS:** Computer! Totaal, LAN Internetworking Magazine, LAN World Buyers Guide, Macworld Netherlands, Net, WebWereld; **NEW ZEALAND:** Absolute Beginners Guide and Plain & Simple Series, Computer Buyer, Computer Industry Directory, Computerworld New Zealand, MTB, Network World, PC World New Zealand; **NICARAGUA:** PC World Centro America; **NORWAY:** Computerworld Norge, CW Rapport, Datamagasinet, Financial Rapport, Kursguide Norge, Macworld Norge, Multimediaworld Norge, PC World Ekspress Norge, PC World Nettverk, PC World Norge, PC World ProduktGuide Norge; **PAKISTAN:** Computerworld Pakistan; **PANAMA:** PC World Panama; **PEOPLE'S REPUBLIC OF CHINA:** China Computer Users, China Computerworld, China InfoWorld, China Telecom World Weekly, Computer & Communication, Electronic Design China, Electronics Today, Electronics Weekly, Game Software, PC World China, Popular Computer Week, Software Weekly, Software World, Telecom World; **PERU:** Computerworld Peru, PC World Profesional Peru, PC World SoHo Peru; **PHILIPPINES:** Click!, Computerworld Philippines, PC World Philippines, Publish in Asia; **POLAND:** Computerworld Poland, Computerworld Special Report Poland, Cyber, Macworld Poland, Networld Poland, PC World Komputer; **PORTUGAL:** Cerebro/PC World, Computerworld/Correio Informático, Dealer World Portugal, Mac*In/PC*In Portugal, Multimedia World; **PUERTO RICO:** PC World Puerto Rico; **ROMANIA:** Computerworld Romania, PC World Romania, Telecom Romania; **RUSSIA:** Computerworld Russia, Mir PK, Publish, Seti; **SINGAPORE:** Computerworld Singapore, PC World Singapore, Publish in Asia; **SLOVENIA:** Monitor; **SOUTH AFRICA:** Computing SA, Network World SA, Software World SA; **SPAIN:** Communicaciones World España, Computerworld España, Dealer World España, Macworld España, PC World España; **SRI LANKA:** Infolink PC World; **SWEDEN:** CAP&Design, Computer Sweden, Corporate Computing Sweden, Internetworld Sweden, it branschen, Macworld Sweden, MaxiData Sweden, MikroDatorn, Nätverk & Kommunikation, PC World Sweden, PCaktiv, Windows World Sweden; **SWITZERLAND:** Computerworld Schweiz, Macworld Schweiz, PCtip; **TAIWAN:** Computerworld Taiwan, Macworld Taiwan, NEW ViSiON/Publish, PC World Taiwan, Windows World Taiwan; **THAILAND:** Publish in Asia, Thai Computerworld; **TURKEY:** Computerworld Turkiye, Macworld Turkiye, Network World Turkiye, PC World Turkiye; **UKRAINE:** Computerworld Kiev, Multimedia World Ukraine, PC World Ukraine; **UNITED KINGDOM:** Acorn User UK, Amiga Action UK, Amiga Computing UK, Apple Talk UK, Computing, Macworld, Parents and Computers UK, PC Advisor, PC Home, PSX Pro, The WEB; **UNITED STATES:** Cable in the Classroom, CIO Magazine, Computerworld, DOS World, Federal Computer Week, GamePro Magazine, InfoWorld, I-Way, Macworld, Network World, PC Games, PC World, Publish, Video Event, THE WEB Magazine, and WebMaster; online webzines: JavaWorld, NetscapeWorld, and SunWorld Online; **URUGUAY:** InfoWorld Uruguay; **VENEZUELA:** Computerworld Venezuela, PC World Venezuela; and **VIETNAM:** PC World Vietnam. 3/24/97

Credits

Acquisitions Editor
Greg Croy

Development Editor
Matthew E. Lusher

Copy Editor
Tracy Brown

Technical Editor
Tamra Heathershaw-Hart

Production Coordinator
Susan Parini

Graphics and Production Specialists
Mario F. Amador
Christopher Pimentel

Proofreader
Jennifer K. Overmyer

Quality Control Specialist
Mark Schumann

Indexer
C^2 Editorial Services

About the Author

Dave Taylor has been involved with the Internet since 1980, when he first logged in as an undergraduate student at the University of California, San Diego. Since then, he's been a research scientist at Hewlett-Packard Laboratories in Palo Alto, California, a software and hardware reviews editor for *SunWorld* magazine, and an interface design consultant. He's the President of Intuitive Systems of Los Gatos, California, and Chief Technology Officer of The Internet Mall, Inc., of Los Gatos, California.

So far, Dave has designed over 1,000 Web pages. He has published more than 800 articles on the Internet, UNIX, Macintosh, and interface design topics. His books include *Global Software, Teach Yourself UNIX in a Week,* and *Teach Yourself UNIX in 24 Hours.* He coauthored *The Internet Business Guide,* and is well known as the author of the popular Elm Mail System and, more recently, the Embot mail autoresponder program.

He holds a Masters degree in Educational Computing from Purdue University and an undergraduate degree in Computer Science from the University of California at San Diego.

On the Web, Dave has created a number of award-winning sites, including the top-25-rated Internet Mall™, the Purdue Online Writing Laboratory, Trivial.Net (which is geeky nerd trivia central!), The Custer Battlefield Historical and Museum Society, and much more. He serves as a Web design consultant for a variety of organizations, including the State of California.

You can find Dave Taylor online just about any time at http://www.intuitive.com/ or you can send him electronic mail at taylor@intuitive.com.

To my favorite little angel, Ashley Elizabeth

Preface

Who should buy this book? What's covered? How do I read this book? Why should I read this book? Why not just use a Web page editor? Who am I?

Welcome!

"Wow! Another Web book. What makes this one different?"

That's a fair question. I wrote this preface to answer that question. I want you to be confident that *Creating Cool HTML 4 Web Pages* will meet your needs as well as provide fun and interesting reading.

What This Book Is About

In a nutshell, *Creating Cool HTML 4 Web Pages* is an introduction to HTML. HTML stands for *HyperText Markup Language*, and it is the markup language that enables you to create and publish your own multimedia documents on the World Wide Web. Millions of users on the Internet and online services such as America Online, CompuServe, and the Microsoft Network are using the visually exciting World Wide Web from within Internet Explorer, Netscape Communicator and Navigator, Mosaic, and a variety of other programs.

Using HTML, you can create attractive documents that are on the cutting edge of interactive publishing. That's why I went through the pain of learning HTML in 1994, the very dawn of the Web era. For me, learning was hit–or–miss, because the only references I could find were confusing online documents written by programmers and computer types. For you, it will be easier. By reading this book and experimenting with the software and samples included, you can learn not only the nuts and bolts of HTML, but also how to design and create useful, attractive Web documents and spread the word about them on the Net.

To make things even more fun in this book, I show you some of the award-winning sites I've created, list the HTML underneath, and explain what's going on and why I implemented pages one way and not another. In the end, cool Web documents aren't necessarily those that have extensive or pretty graphics, lots of animated Java applets, or thousands of links. With a little verve and some witty prose, you'll see how you can present purely textual information via the Web in a way that's interesting, visually engaging, helpful, and fun — in other words, cool.

Before you delve into this book, you should know the basics of what the Internet is, how to get on it, and how to use your Web browser. If you seek detailed information on these topics, you can find many interesting and useful books from IDG Books Worldwide, Inc. `http://www.idgbooks.com/` and elsewhere. Once your have this basic knowledge at habd, you'll find that *Creating Cool HTML 4 Web Pages* is a fun introduction to the art and science of creating interesting Web documents that you'll be proud of — and that other users will want to visit and explore.

Why Not Just Use A Web Page Builder?

If you've already flipped through this book to see what's covered, you've seen a ton of different example listings with lots and lots of "<" and ">" instructions. Yet the advertisements in every single computer magazine you read doubtless are telling you that you don't need to get your hands dirty with HTML when you can use a Web page editor!

The problem is every single Web page editor I've seen is designed to create pages for a particular Web browser and has only a limited understanding of the rich, complex, evolving language that HTML is today. Use Microsoft Front Page and your site will invariably look better in Internet Explorer (a Microsoft product) than it will in Netscape Communicator. Use Adobe Page Mill or Claris Home Page, and you'll have the opposite problem; they'll be more accurate to your design if users are using Communicator.

It's a subtle but insidious problem. One clue to this lurking problem is that surveys of Web developers invariably show the vast majority of the top award-winning Web sites on the net are coded by hand, not with page builders.

A development company that I occasionally help with online design recently sent me a pleading message as they encountered this inconsistency of browser presentation themselves:

```
Dave. Help!  Everything looks different in the different
browsers!! This is turning out to be a nightmare!  How
much effect do different browsers have on the appearance
of the site? My customer is using AOL and from the e-mail
she sent me, things are a mess. When I look at the site,
it pretty much is ok. There are a few modifications to
make - font, bold - but what's going on?
```

That's one of the greatest frustrations for all Web site designers: Not only do different versions of Web browsers support different versions of HTML, but the exact formatting that results from a given HTML tag varies by Web browser, too. It's why the mantra of all good Web designers is "test, test, test."

In fact, if you're going to get serious about Web development, I would suggest that you consider a setup like I have: Before you officially say that you're done with a project, check all the pages with the two most recent major releases of the two biggest Web browsers on both a Mac and Windows 95 system. (That's a total of eight different browsers. Right now I have Internet Explorer 3 and 4, Navigator 3 and Communicator 4 on both of my computers.)

Text Conventions Used in This Book

Stuff you type appears in bold, like this: **something you actually type**.

Filenames, names of machines on the Net, and directories appear in a special typeface, like the following address for the White House Guest Book Web site, where visitors can sign a White House guest book:

```
http://www.whitehouse.gov/WH/html/Guest_Book.html
```

HTML-formatted text appears in the same special typeface, like this:

```
<HTML>
<TITLE>How to Write Cool Web Pages</TITLE>
<IMG SRC="intro.gif" ALT="How To Write Cool Web Pages">
```

I use three icons in this book:

Tip icons point out expert advice on tricks and techniques.

 Caution icons alert you to information that may help you avoid trouble.

 Note icons point out details that may deserve special attention in the long term.

Who Should Read This Book

Even if you don't have a connection to the Internet, you can use this book and software to learn HTML and the techniques of creating cool Web pages. All you need is a simple text editor, such as Notepad (which comes with Windows) or SimpleText (which is part of the Macintosh operating system), and a Web browser (the two most popular are on the CD-ROM included with this book). If you have itchy fingers and are raring to go, stop reading the preface and pop back to Appendix A to see a step-by-step demonstration of how to use these simple (free!) tools to create a dynamite Web page.

If you're already online and have a Web browser installed on your own computer, you can easily explore all the local files included on the CD-ROM and then log on to explore the many fascinating examples of Web page design on the Internet itself.

A Sneak Peek at Some Actual HTML

Are you curious about how this HTML stuff looks? The following figure shows a simple HTML document, as seen in Internet Explorer.

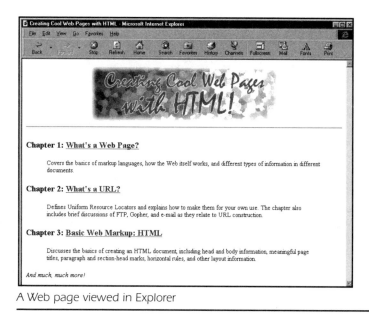

A Web page viewed in Explorer

The following is the raw HTML document that lurks behind the figure:

```
<HTML>
<HEAD>
<TITLE>Creating Cool Web Pages with HTML!</TITLE>
</HEAD><BODY BGCOLOR=#FFFFFF>
<IMG SRC=intro.gif ALT="Creating Cool Web Pages with
HTML!">
<HR>
<H2>Chapter 1: <A HREF=chap1.html>What's a Web
Page?</A></H2>
Covers the basics of markup languages, how the Web itself
works, and different types of information in different
documents.
<H2>Chapter 2: <A HREF=chap2.html>What's a URL?</A></H2>
Defines Uniform Resource Locators and explains how to make
them for
your own use. The chapter also includes brief discussions
of FTP, Gopher, and e-mail as they relate to URL
construction.
<H2>Chapter 3: <A HREF=chap3.html>Basic Web Markup:
```

(continued)

```
HTML</A></H2>
Discusses the basics of creating an HTML document,
including head and body information, meaningful page
titles, paragraph and section-head marks, horizontal
rules, and other layout information.
<P>
<I>And much, much more!</I>
</BODY>
</HTML>
```

By the time you're halfway through this book, you'll be able to whip up the kind of material in the figure yourself, guaranteed. And by the time you finish this book, you'll know other ways to organize information to make creating Web versions of print material easy. You'll also learn why the particular HTML layout seen in the figure isn't necessarily the best way to present information in a hyperlinked environment such as the Web.

Want to contact the author? Send e-mail to taylor@intuitive.com or visit my home page on the Web at

```
http://www.intuitive.com/taylor/
```

The home page for this book is

```
http://www.intuitive.com/coolweb/
```

If you're ready, let's go!

Acknowledgments

No writing project can be done while the author is locked in a room, though if there's a good Net connection, we can probably negotiate something! Seriously, a number of Internet folk have proven invaluable as I've written the different editions of this book, some for their direct help and others for simply having produced some wickedly cool Web pages that helped inspire me when things were moving a bit slowly.

Chief among those is the almost omniscient James Armstrong, who has continued to help me through the different editions, verifying the internal details of the more obscure HTML tags, and technical editor Tamra Heathershaw-Hart, who helped keep me honest herein. My editorial team at IDG Books Worldwide, particularly Matt Lusher, has been dynamite, and the gangsta team of Kevin Savetz, Rick Tracewell, Tai Jin, and Marv Raab also helped with their insight on page design and Web page layout, as well as suggestions for cool sites not to miss. Thanks also go to Scott Wild for his help configuring my spiffo Pentium system, and to Power Computing for my rockin' PowerWave Mac compatible. I'll miss ya, Power Computing.

Adobe Systems, Macromedia, Auto F/X, Pixar, and Brøderbund were most generous with their assistance; most of the graphics presented in this book were created in Photoshop — particularly with the Alien Skin Software add-on "Eye Candy" — and other top-notch commercial applications. Screen shots were done with HiJaak Capture on the PC and Captivate Select on the Macintosh. Most of the book was written on my decked-out Power Computing PowerWave 132 (I have to admit, I'm a Mac guy at heart) and the Windows work was all done on my fast Tangent 166 Windows 95 box.

Finally, warm hugs to Linda, Jasmine, Karma, and, of course, the newest member of my family, Ashley Elizabeth, for ensuring that I took sufficient breaks to avoid carpal tunnel syndrome or any of the other hazards of overly intense typing. The time off would be a lot less fun without ya!

Contents at a Glance

Table of Contents

What's a Web Page? What's a Browser?

This chapter will get you started by covering the basics of the Web, showing how information pointers help organize information, and illustrating how Web browsers can simplify file transfer, Gopher, and other Internet services. It also introduces you to the Netscape Navigator and Microsoft Internet Explorer programs, both freely available on the Internet (and on the included cross-platform CD-ROM, too!).

It's important for you to have a basic understanding of what a "web" of information is all about right off the bat. Before we look at the basics of creating your own cool Web pages, therefore, take a close look at what the Web is, how it works, and what HTML itself is all about. I promise to be brief!

What Is the Web Anyway?

To understand the World Wide Web, it's a good idea to consider first how information is organized in print media. Print media, I think, is a fair model for the Web and how it's organized, though others may feel that adventure games, movies, TV, or other information-publishing media are better suited for comparison to the Web.

Linear media

Think about the physical and organizational characteristics of this book for a second. What is most notable? The book has discrete units of information: pages. The pages are conceptually organized into chapters. The chapters are bound together to comprise the book itself. In some sense, what you have in your hands is a collection of pages organized in a format conducive to your reading them from first page to last. However, there's no reason why you can't riffle through the pages and create your own strategy for navigating this information.

Are you still with me? I call the book example *linear information organization.* Like movies, most books, including this one, are organized with the expectation that you'll start at the beginning and end at the end.

Hypermedia

Now imagine that instead of physically turning the page, you can simply touch a spot at the bottom of each page — a forward arrow — to flip to the next page. Touching a different spot — a back arrow — moves you to the preceding page. Further, imagine that when you look at the table of contents, you can touch the description of a chapter to flip directly to the page where the chapter begins. Touch a third spot — a small picture of a dictionary — and move to another book entirely.

Such a model is called *hypermedia* or *hypertext,* terms coined by mid-twentieth century computer visionaries, most notably Ted Nelson in his book *Computer Lib.* Some benefits to the reader become apparent in this more dynamic approach to information organization. One immediate boon is that the topical index becomes *really* helpful: by being able to touch an item of interest, whether explanatory narrative or descriptive reference material, you can use the same book as a reference work in addition to the linearly organized tutorial that it's intended to offer. It's like the best of two worlds — the linear flow of an audio or video tape, and the instant access of a music CD.

Another benefit of hypertext involves footnotes. Footnote text doesn't have to clutter up the bottom of the page; with hypertext, you merely touch the asterisk or footnote number in the text, and a tiny page pops up to display the footnote.

One more idea: You can touch an illustration to zoom into a larger version of that illustration or maybe even convert the illustration to an animated sequence or 3D space, within which you can cruise around and examine the item from a variety of vantage points.

Obviously, what I'm talking about here are Web pages. But there's an additional capability of the Web that makes things much more fun and interesting: the pages of information can reside on systems throughout the world. The pages themselves can be quite complex (and, ideally, cool and attractive) documents. Imagine: Instead of writing "You can see the White House Web page to learn more," leaving everyone stranded and unsure of how to proceed, Web documents enable direct *links,* so readers can click the highlighted words in the sentence — or a picture of the building — and immediately zoom to the White House site.

Cool spots on the Web

Figure 1-1 shows a typical text-only Web document that you'll explore later in the book. Notice particularly the underlined words, each of which actually is a link to another Web document elsewhere on the Internet.

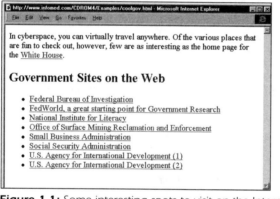

Figure 1-1: Some interesting spots to visit on the Internet

If you're on the Internet and you click the phrase *National Institute for Literacy,* you travel (electronically) to the center in Washington, D.C., as shown in Figure 1-2.

What do I mean by "click"? I'm sure you already know. Clicking is "touching" a spot on the screen with the mouse pointer; place the mouse pointer over a word or picture and then press the mouse button. Clicking works whether you're running on a Macintosh, a Windows machine, a UNIX workstation running X Windows, or even a handheld Windows CE or Newton.

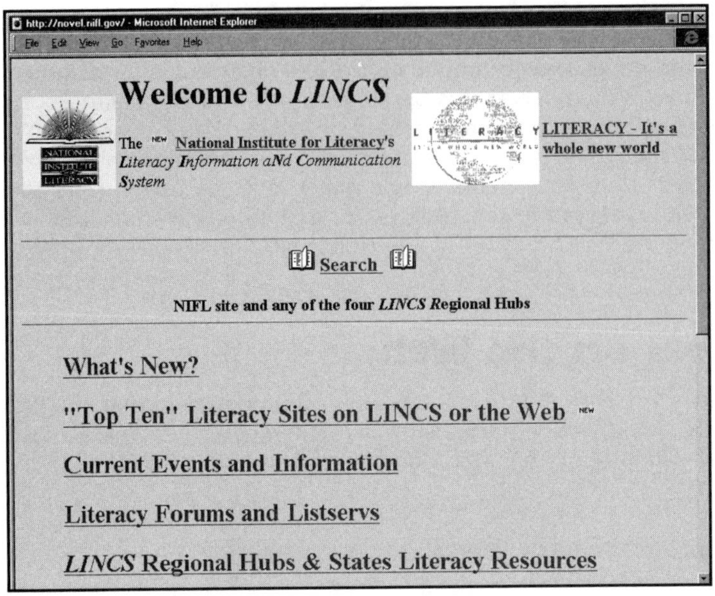

Figure 1-2: The National Institute for Literacy

What makes all this so compelling for me (and for millions of other users) is the fact that there aren't thousands or tens of thousands of Web documents, there are *millions* of them — so many, in fact, that no one has ever visited them all. So many documents are available that finding information is perhaps the single greatest challenge on the Internet. (Whew! — I almost wrote *on the information highway.* I'll try to avoid that cliché, even though the metaphor actually can be helpful in considering traffic patterns, connection speeds, and various other arcana.)

Non-HTML Web Information

Although it's certainly true that much of the information on the World Wide Web consists of rich multimedia documents written in HTML specifically for the enjoyment of Web readers, a surprising number of documents actually come from other types of information-publishing services on the Internet. These documents are presented in the most attractive formats possible within the Web browsers themselves.

FTP

The simplest of the different information services on the Internet is FTP (File Transfer Protocol). FTP is a mechanism for letting you access remote hard disks to list folders and directly access specific files. It's been around for a long time — long before the Web was envisioned. Traditionally, working with FTP is a pain, and the interface has always been only a tiny step away from programming the computer directly. For example, from a UNIX host, you would have to type the following sequence of steps to connect to the Digital Equipment Corporation FTP archive called gatekeeper.dec.com (user input is in boldface):

```
% ftp gatekeeper.dec.com
Connected to gatekeeper.dec.com.
220 gatekeeper.dec.com FTP server (Version 5.97 Fri May 6
14:44:16 PDT 1996) ready.
Name (gatekeeper.dec.com:taylor): anonymous
331 Guest login ok, send ident as password.
Password:taylor@intuitive.com
230 Guest login ok, access restrictions apply.
ftp> dir hypertext
200 PORT command successful.
150 Opening ASCII mode data connection for /bin/ls.
total 11
dr-xr-xr-x 2 root    system    512 Dec 28 12:57 docs
-r-r-r- 1 root    system    2435 Feb 8 00:26
gatekeeper.home.html
-r-r-r- 1 root    system    455 Dec 29 22:17
gatekeeper.temphome.html
lrwxr-xr-x 1 root    system    20 Feb 8 00:20 home.html -
> gatekeeper.home.html
dr-xr-xr-x 2 root    system    512 Feb 8 23:13 includes
dr-xr-xr-x 2 root    system    512 Feb 8 00:35 info
dr-xr-xr-x 2 root    system    512 Feb 8 00:35 orgs
dr-xr-xr-x 2 root    system    512 Dec 29 22:05 pics
dr-xr-xr-x 2 root    system    512 Dec 28 12:57 util
226 Transfer complete.
remote: hypertext
619 bytes received in 0.28 seconds (2.2 Kbytes/s)
ftp>
```

Calling such a procedure complex would be an understatement. FTP is fast and easy to use after you learn all the magic, of course, but the point of working with computers is that you should be able to focus on *what* you want to accomplish, not on *how* you need to accomplish it.

Compare the preceding example with the following procedure for using Microsoft Internet Explorer to access the same archive directly (see Figure 1-3). Instead of typing all that information, you simply open location `ftp://gatekeeper.dec.com/hypertext` by typing that into the box displayed when you choose Open Location from the File menu. In this example, `ftp` indicates what kind of service is available, the `://` part is some fancy (if mysterious) notation, and `gatekeeper.dec.com/hypertext` is the name of the computer and the directory to view. Then you just press Enter.

```
ftp://gatekeeper.dec.com/hypertext - Microsoft Internet Explorer      _ □ ×
 File  Edit  View  Go  Favorites  Help

 FTP directory /hypertext at gatekeeper.dec.com
 ─────────────────────────────────────────────────────────

 Up to higher level directory

 01/18/96 12:00AM              0 .upd15027
 04/14/95 12:00AM      Directory docs
 09/19/97 10:24AM          3,358 gatekeeper.home.html
 04/14/95 12:00AM             20 home.html
 09/19/97 11:04AM      Directory includes
 09/19/97 11:04AM      Directory info
 04/14/95 12:00AM      Directory orgs
 02/26/96 12:00AM      Directory pics
 04/14/95 12:00AM      Directory util
```

Figure 1-3: Microsoft Internet Explorer visits DEC's Gatekeeper FTP archive.

The location format (`ftp://gatekeeper.dec.com/hypertext`) is called a *Uniform Resource Locator* (URL).

Ready to visit a listed directory or folder? Click it, and you'll move to that spot. Ready to grab a file? Just click the file, and Explorer automatically figures out the file type, asks what you want to call the file on your PC, and transfers it across. No fuss, no hassle.

Throughout this book I'll use PC to refer generally to any personal computer. I'm actually writing this book on a Macintosh and double-checking things on a Windows 95 system.

Easy FTP isn't a unique feature of Explorer, but a capability of *all* Web browser packages, including the ever-popular Netscape Navigator. Figure 1-4 shows the same place (the Digital FTP site) in Navigator.

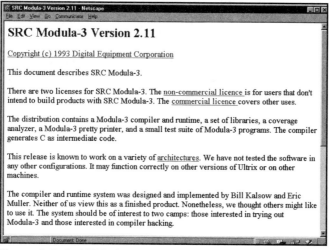

Figure 1-4: Navigator visits DEC's Gatekeeper FTP archive.

Here's where the difference between the *paper* and the *words* becomes important: The type of service that you can connect with is what I call the *information transfer system,* and the actual information presented is the *content.* By analogy, the Web is the information transfer system, and *hypertext markup language* — HTML — is the format used for content. Some of the HTML documents available on the Internet aren't available within the Web itself, but are accessible directly via FTP. Figure 1-5 shows an example of this: the first portion of a Web page that is accessible only with an FTP program or, of course, with your Web browser reading FTP information.

Figure 1-5: An HTML document via FTP

Gopher and telnet

Web browsers also can traverse *Gopher* information space and help you telnet to other computers. To see how helpful those capabilities can be, consider how things were done in the days before the Web took a stab at unifying the various interfaces. Figure 1-6 shows a screen from the Windows program HGopher. The application is easy to use, but it can't help you with FTP, Web documents, or anything else.

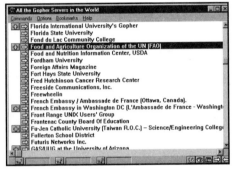

Figure 1-6: HGopher is a limited alternative to Web browsers.

Telnet is also fairly easy to use; from your UNIX host, you just type the word **telnet** followed by the name of the computer to which you want to connect. Note that you'll need an account on the remote computer to be able to log in. But there's the rub: How do you remember all the computer names? The capability to be an easy, unified starting point for the different Internet services is a real selling point for a Web browser.

Figure 1-7 shows a Web page in which the links actually are pointers to different types of Internet services. Using this Web page, you don't have to remember the name of the remote computer or how to get to the place.

As you learn how to design and create Web documents, you also learn how to choose among the various services on the Net and how to use them.

Click here to continue. (Just kidding.)

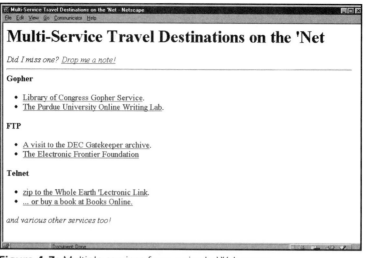

Figure 1-7: Multiple services from a single Web page

Introduction to Netscape Navigator

Two events were the highlight of 1995 from an Internet perspective: The massive hype surrounding the introduction of Microsoft Windows 95, and the initial public offering of stock in a small startup company called Netscape Communications. Netscape exploded onto the scene and quickly became one of the highest valued small companies in the U.S. What really excited everyone about Netscape was Navigator, the cutting-edge Web browser that the company was freely distributing to the Internet community, a Web browser that had been born as NCSA Mosaic and rapidly took on a life of its own.

Fast forward more than two years and Netscape continues to lead the pack, retaining its reputation as the leader of the Web business with its powerful server software and the ever-improving Netscape Navigator application. In fact, the browser is evolving fast — very fast — so fast that at any given time, the company has a formal release version of Navigator, a beta release of the next version, and a early beta release of the version after the next for developers. There's a major release about every six months, which means that it's a constant effort to maintain.

If you've not heard of the Communicator package, it's a bundle of Netscape Navigator with a bunch of other programs, including a video conferencing package, and more. If you're like me, you'll only want their browser so the rest is superfluous, though there is one application worth exploring: Composer. Composer is Netscape's Web page builder, which enables you to build decent pages without fussing with the HTML codes. However, the results you'll be able to produce by the time you're done with this book will be far superior!

Don't feel left out, however, because Navigator includes lots of fun stuff, too, including a chat system, a net-based telephone package and more. What isn't included with either Navigator or Communicator is a way to plug into the network or a dialup connection to the Net.

The nuts and bolts of a dialup network connection are a bit beyond the scope of this book, but suffice it to say that if you can connect to the Internet from your PC, odds are very good that you'll be running something called *Point-to-Point Protocol* (PPP). If you consider a telephone and how you get that to work, PPP is the equivalent of the language your phone speaks so that your computer can talk with the wire coming out of the wall. Of course, you can't use a phone without a phone service, and a phone from Europe, for example, might not understand the signals sent on a phone wire in Japan, so indeed, it's a combination of all three — phone, signal standards, and phone service — that gives you a dial tone and calling service.

In exactly the same fashion, the pieces for you to have Internet connectivity are the dial tone (a dialup line from an access provider such as America Online, Netcom, or Best Internet Communications), a shared signal standard (in this case, PPP), and a software "telephone" (a Web browser such as Navigator or Internet Explorer).

Launching Netscape Navigator

You're reading this book, so odds are pretty good you've already spent some time exploring the Web and are ready to publish your own material online. If you haven't, you'll be glad to find out that it is quite easy to become an expert "surfer" — once you have a network connection, of course — and that even with the differences between Navigator and Internet Explorer, the basic functionality is quite similar.

At any given time, you're looking at a document on your screen that has static information (text, graphics), active information (animation, audio, video), and links to other pages. To jump to another page, you move your mouse over the hot link (either text or a graphic) and left click (well, if you're using a Mac, you don't have to worry about distinguishing between left and right: just click).

As you travel about, the browser remembers where you've been, so the Back button becomes a quick way to zoom to a previous page you visited so you're not forced to always be moving ever forward (see Figure 1-10). It's the equivalent of being able to shift your car into reverse on the highway, but without the screech of other cars and danger involved!

Navigator works identically if you're surfing a set of Web documents that is on your local disk as it does for remote pages from around the world; just lots faster off your disk or CD-ROM drive. Because of this capability, Navigator — and Internet Explorer — are invaluable aids as you develop your own Web pages on your computer, as you'll see.

Find Navigator on the enclosed CD-ROM, or on your computer if you've already installed it, and launch it by double-clicking the icon or filename. Odds are it will immediately try to connect via the network to the Netscape home page (`www.home/netscape.com/`). Instead, you want to open one of the HTML files on the included CD so you can explore each of the examples in this book as you read along. To do that, choose Open File from the File menu in Navigator. You should see a dialog box similar to Figure 1-8.

Open	? X
Look in:	Cdrom

Examples
Graphics
Navigate
coolweb.html
examples.html
index.html
mac-shareware.html
Win95-shareware.html

File name: examples.html   Open
Files of type: HTML Files   Cancel

Figure 1-8: Find the file Coolweb.html and click Open.

If the browser insists on using a network connection that you might not have (which is perfectly okay; you'll still be able to work with all the Web pages in this book and build your own), then you may need to cancel out of the connection dialog before you can open a local file in Navigator.

Once you've successfully moved to the CD-ROM drive and found the file Coolweb.html, you should see some fun graphics that appear as a more colorful version of Figure 1-9. The toolbar display on your screen may vary slightly from what I have here in the book — in particular, you may have more stuff on your toolbar — but that's easy for you to change from the Options menu ("show toolbar," "show location," and "show directory buttons" can switch on or off: Try it!).

Throughout this book, I use Netscape Navigator 4.1 for my Navigator examples. By the time you read this book there may well have been a few more releases along the way. You can always get the most up-to-date copy of Navigator from Netscape's Web site at `http://home.netscape.com/`. Be warned: The last release I downloaded was over 13 MB, so it takes quite a while to transfer!

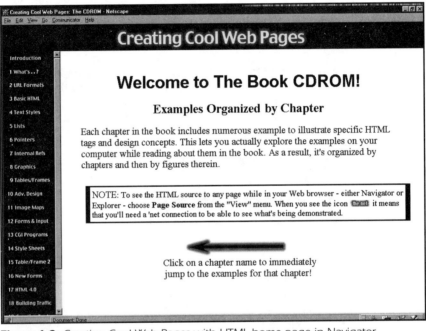

Figure 1-9: Creating Cool Web Pages with HTML home page in Navigator

If you have the toolbar selected with Navigator, then you'll see a set of buttons along the top of your window, either with or without one-word text descriptions underneath (it's a preference setting you can change from the Edit / Preferences dialog; choose Appearance from the list on the left side).

From left to right, the standard toolbar buttons in version 4.0 are

➡ Back — Click this and you'll jump to the page prior to the one you're currently viewing. You can go back quite a ways if you've been exploring for a while. Even more cool: Click and hold down the mouse button if you're on a Mac and you'll suddenly see a pop-up menu of the last bunch of sites you've visited. Move to a specific site and you'll go back instantly.

➡ Forward — If you've gone back too far, forward will move you ahead on your list of visited pages. On the Mac, it's also a secret pop-up button, so click and hold down the mouse button to see how it can help you directly to the page you seek.

➡ Reload — Many pages on the Web update frequently to reflect visitor activity, system activity, or perhaps just changes in weather maps or stock values. With your own pages, as you develop them, you might want to continually refresh the browser page. Clicking the reload button allows you to request an up-to-date copy of the current Web page.

 The Reload button recreates the page you're on, but it might be a cached page, a copy that's been saved on your local PC to speed up your Web interaction. To force a new copy of the actual page — and bypass the cache — use Shift-Reload (on the PC) or Option-Reload (on the Macintosh).

➡ Home — A quick shortcut to get to the default page. You'll see how to change that to your favorite Web site or HTML file later in this chapter.

➡ Search — Navigator enables you to specify a default search site for your browser sessions, and one click on the flashlight and you'll be there instantly. There are, of course, quite a few choices for search engines, though I tend to use Yahoo! myself. (Earlier versions show a pair of binoculars and call this "Find," but it's the same button.)

➡ Guide — If your search site doesn't help you find what you seek, the Netscape guides might help a lot. Click this button and you'll have direct access to a variety of different information resources.

➡ Images — On a slow network connection, you might find it considerably faster to surf the Web if you opt not to automatically download and display the graphics on a Web page. Many times this can cause confusion because most page designers don't take into account nongraphical users, but if you're exploring, it can speed things up quite a bit. After you find a page that looks interesting, a click of the Images button will request all the graphics and build a complete page for you. If you don't see this button, don't worry; if you have automatic image loading set in your preferences, this button is superfluous and isn't displayed onscreen.

➡ Print — Ready to keep a hard copy of the page you're viewing? Click the printer icon and it'll come out beautifully.

➡ Security — Wondering if the page you're currently viewing is secure or not? One click and you'll get an informative summary of the security status of the page you're viewing. Don't be worried if 99 percent of the pages online are listed as "insecure;" however, this is really only important when it's highly confidential information being displayed — information like your social security number, your bank statement for online banking, or a credit card charge.

➡ Stop — When you're waiting and waiting for a page to finish downloading, it's nice to know that you can tell Navigator "Okay, I've seen enough" by clicking the Stop button.

Figure 1-10 shows the Netscape Navigator buttons just described.

Figure 1-10: Navigator basic toolbar buttons

Changing the default page

One thing you might find very helpful as you read through this book is to change the default page in Netscape Navigator so that you start right up with the Coolweb.html file rather than have to find it on your system each time. It's pretty straightforward and involves four steps:

1. Open Navigator and move to the Coolweb.html file as explained earlier.

2. Choose Preferences from the Edit menu.

   Click "Navigation" from the list on the left side, and you should see a bunch of options that look like Figure 1-11. In the middle of the dialog box is an option called Home Page.

Figure 1-11: Changing the default home page in Netscape Navigator

3. Click the Use Current Page button.

4. Click OK and you've done it!

Now that you know how to change your default home page, you can modify it at will — perhaps to point to your own page on the Web once you get it created or to start at any of the variety of great pages online.

Introduction to Internet Explorer

You'd have to live under a rock not to catch the hoopla surrounding the unveiling of Windows 95 in 1995. Windows 95 is much more than just an operating system; it's a whole new environment for PC users — an environment that is focused on making the computer easier to use and the interface more seamless and consistent.

Just like Netscape's constant revisions to its browser, Microsoft has been on an aggressive upgrade path with major releases distributed as fast as the company can complete them. What's surprising is that Microsoft seems to be pulling ahead. The first version of Microsoft Internet Explorer, included with the Windows 95 Plus Pack, was okay, but lacked many of the best features of Navigator. As of this writing, the 4.0 release of both browsers had remarkably similar features; the differences revolve around the add-on pieces such as group conferencing (Microsoft has a better design, Netscape has a better implementation), Net-based telephony (Microsoft has a better system), and interactive chat (they're about even). There are almost no HTML tags that are only available in one browser, unlike the first generation of these applications, which is good; very sophisticated Web page designs work for both with just a few exceptions, which I'll talk about later in the book. A version of Internet Explorer will be included in Windows 98, too, so it will be easier to find this Web browser on computers you use.

Launching Internet Explorer

Once you're ready to start browsing the Web — or even just the files I've included with this book — you need to find and launch either Explorer or Navigator. You can most easily do so by double-clicking the Internet icon on your desktop, launching the application from within your Program Manager, or launching the application from the ubiquitous Start button in Windows 95.

The first time you start Explorer, it's going to try to connect to the Microsoft home page on the World Wide Web, which could be a problem if you don't already have your Internet connection up and running. If that happens, don't worry; just choose Cancel when it either pops up a dialog box asking for a phone number or otherwise indicates that it's waiting for a Net connection. You'll end up looking at a blank page, but all the controls will be there. Now, from the File menu, choose Open File (or use the Ctrl+O keyboard shortcut). That will bring up the Open Local File dialog box, as shown in Figure 1-12.

Figure 1-12: Find the file Coolweb.html and click Open.

Now you're getting somewhere! Internet Explorer should promptly open up the file and the associated graphics, displaying it all in one neat window. You might have different toolbars shown on your screen, by the way, but it's easy to change back and forth from the Preferences settings. Figure 1-13 shows how the *Creating Cool Web Pages* Web page should look on your screen.

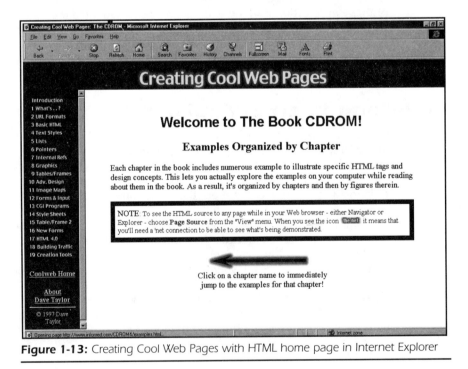

Figure 1-13: Creating Cool Web Pages with HTML home page in Internet Explorer

If you have the toolbar selected, you'll see a set of small buttons that can help you move your way around the Web. From the left, they let you move backward and forward in the set of pages you've viewed, stop the transfer of a slow page, refresh the current page (that is, get a new copy of the page and rewrite the screen; this will prove a huge help to you as you develop your own Web pages), and instantly zip back to your home — or default — page. The globe icon with the magnifying glass lets you pop straight to your favorite Web search engine, the mailbox jumps you to the way-cool Microsoft Internet Mail and News program (included with Explorer) enabling you to send and receive electronic mail (e-mail), and the newspaper icon lets you participate in any of the thousands of online Usenet discussion groups. The folder icon with the star in the center enables you to open your list of favorite sites; you might have heard this called your "bookmark list," too. A cool feature that's unique to Internet Explorer is represented by the next button: The capital A with the small up and down arrows will enlarge, or shrink, all the type on the current Web page (up for larger, down for smaller). That is, if you look at a Web page and the text is just too tiny to read comfortably, click the Larger button to make all the text larger. Figure 1-14 shows the Internet Explorer toolbar buttons.

Figure 1-14: Handy Internet Explorer shortcuts from the toolbar

Changing the default page

Now that you have the program running, one useful trick before you begin your exploration of HTML and the mysteries and adventure of building cool Web pages: Change your default page to the Cool Web page you currently should have on your screen. When you're done learning how to write cool Web pages, you can then change it to your own page, or perhaps to a useful site on the Internet itself.

To change your default page, click the Preferences button from the toolbar or choose Preferences from the View menu. One of the options you'll now notice is labeled Home/Search, and that's the one you want. Choose it and now you should see something remarkably like Figure 1-15.

Because you're currently viewing the page that you want to make your default, you'll want to click in the "Location:" area of the browser, select the entire URL, and then paste it into the "Address" box in the Home Page area of this dialog box.

Figure 1-15: Changing your default start page

That's all there is to it. Now the next time you start up the Internet Explorer, you'll find the cheery Creating Cool Web Pages with HTML page conveniently accessible.

An ironic note: In version 3.0 of Navigator and Explorer, Explorer had a nice "Use Current" button in the preferences area to set your home page quite easily. Navigator didn't. Now, in version 4.0, the two have reversed their position on this useful feature. Which will have it in their 5.0 release? Stay tuned and we'll find out together!

Take a few minutes now to scroll around and click the Examples button to see how I've laid out the hundreds of example files so that they parallel what's shown in this book. Remember that you can always use the back arrow on the toolbar to go back to the preceding page you were viewing.

Summary

In this chapter, you quickly toured some of the sites available on the Net and saw how you can use Web pointers to access more than just HTML documents. You learned that you can use Web browsers to transfer files via FTP, search Gopher sites, and jump to other machines on the Internet via telnet. In Chapter 2, I delve into the mysteries of constructing the URLs that are the heart of the Web information-linking scheme.

URLs: What They Are and How to Use Them

Are you itching to start writing your own HTML documents and creating a world of information on the Web? Take heart — when you've mastered the concepts in this chapter, you'll be ready to start tackling the fun stuff! This chapter discusses the various types of URLs — where they came from, what they're all about, and how to make them for your own use. It includes brief discussions of FTP, telnet, and e-mail as they relate to URL construction. Once we're done here, I promise that in the next chapter, we'll start exploring the nuts and bolts of Web page creation!

Finding Information in the Flood of Data

As our society has made the transition from products to information, we have seen the rapid acceleration of an age-old problem: identifying needed resources. Finding and obtaining resources have been important themes of world history, whether it be spices, fuel, raw materials, or information.

Today, it would seem that computers should make searching *easier*. After all, aren't computers supposed to be experts at sifting through large bodies of data to find what you seek? Well, yes and no.

First, I should differentiate between data and information. Data is "stuff"— an all-encompassing body including every iota of digital memory and space on hard disks and backup tapes. Information, on the other hand, is the data that is relevant to and valuable for your specific interests. If you're interested in Beat poets of the '60s, for example, information on other topics such as municipal drainage systems or needlepoint isn't informative at all, but rather is clutter.

Computers have tremendously expanded the proliferation of data. As a result, separating out information from the massive flood of data is one of the fundamental challenges of the age of information. I can only imagine how much worse the situation will get in the next decade, as more and more data flows down the wires.

When considered in this light, the Internet has a big problem. Because it has no central authority or organization, the Net's vast stores of data are not laid out in any meaningful or intuitive fashion. You are just as likely to find information on Beat poets on a machine run by a German embassy as you are to find it on a small liberal arts school's computer in San Francisco.

URLs to the Rescue

CERN is a high-energy physics research facility in Switzerland that created the underlying technology of the World Wide Web. When Tim Berners-Lee and his team at CERN began to create a common mechanism for uniquely identifying information in dataspace, they realized the need for a scheme that would neatly encapsulate the various parts and that could be extended to include a wide variety of Internet services. The result was the URL.

To state the case succinctly, a URL is a unique descriptor that can identify any document (plain or hypertext), graphic, Gopher menu or item, Usenet article, computer, or even an archive of files anywhere on the Internet or your machine. That's what makes URLs so tremendously valuable, although their format seems a bit puzzling and cryptic at first.

The name URL can be something of a misnomer. Many times, jotting down URLs as you surf the Web only helps you find resources the *second* time, serving as a sort of memo service for your Internet travels. Resource location — finding information for the *first* time on the Internet and the World Wide Web — is a problem I explore later in this book. For now, think of URLs as business cards for specific resources on the network.

Reading a URL

On the plus side, the format for specifying a URL is consistent throughout the many services that the URL encompasses, including Usenet news, Gopher, Web documents, and FTP archives. As a general rule, a URL is composed of the following elements:

```
service    ://    hostname: port    /    directory-path
```

Not all of these components appear in each URL, as you will see when you learn about the different types of URLs for different services. But the preceding template is a good general guide.

Consider the following example:

```
http://www.intuitive.com/taylor/index.html
```

In this example, the service is identified as `http:` (HTTP stands for *HyperText Transfer Protocol*, the method by which Web documents are transferred across the Internet). By using `http:`, you indicate to the *client* program — the program, such as Explorer or Navigator, that you use on your computer to browse the Web — that you're connecting to a Web document. The host computer that offers the information you seek is `www.intuitive.com`. The `com` (called the *zone*) tells you that the site is a commercial site; `intuitive` is the domain or host; and `www` is the name of the Web server, a particular computer. Usually, as is the case here, you don't have to specify a *port* (ports are sort of like TV channels) because most servers use standard, default port numbers. On the server, we want the file `index.html` from the `taylor` directory. It is, in fact, my personal home page.

The following URL is a slightly more complex example:

```
ftp://ftp.cts.com/pub/wallst/
```

The URL identifies a file archive for the firm Wall Street Direct (I just happen to know this). You can see that the URL points to an archive by its service identifier (`ftp`, which stands for *File Transfer Protocol*, the way files are copied over the Net). The server and host in question is `ftp.cts.com`. Notice that this URL specifies that upon connecting to the FTP server, the browser program should change to the `/pub/wallst/` directory and display the files therein.

Here's one more example:

```
news:alt.internet.services
```

The preceding URL enables a browser to read the Usenet newsgroup `alt.internet.services`, and you will notice that it is quite different from the other URL examples. For one thing, it doesn't specify a host. When you set up your browser program (the details differ from browser to browser), you indicate in a preferences or configuration file which host you can use to access Usenet. Usually, the host is the news server at your Internet provider. As a result, no slashes are required in the URL because the browser already has that information. URLs for news resources, therefore, boil down to simply the service and newsgroup name.

You can specify a variety of Internet information-publishing services with URLs. The actual meanings of the URL components differ subtly, depending on which type of service is being specified. In the following sections, I examine URLs for each service in more detail.

FTP via URL

If you are familiar with the historical roots of the Internet and its predecessor networks (notably ARPANET), you already know that one of the earliest uses of the system was to transfer files quickly between hosts at different sites. The standard mechanism for accomplishing file transfers was and still is FTP. But while computers have acquired friendlier interfaces, FTP has remained in the Stone Age. Many users still use clunky command-line interfaces for this vital function.

 FTP via a Web browser is much nicer than via a command-line interface.

Anonymous FTP

Millions of files are accessible throughout the Net via FTP. At a majority of hosts, you don't even need an account to download the files you seek. That's because a standard Net practice called *anonymous FTP* enables any user to log in to an FTP host using the name *anonymous*. If asked for a password, you type in your e-mail address. Among other uses, you can use anonymous FTP to acquire new programs for your computer.

FTP was one of the first services addressed in the URL specification developed at CERN. An FTP URL takes the following form:

```
ftp://host/directory-path
```

The URL `ftp://gatekeeper.dec.com/pub`, for example, uniquely specifies the `pub` directory of files available via FTP at the host `gatekeeper` at Digital Equipment Corporation.

 In fact, the URL `ftp://gatekeeper.dec.com/pub` specifies more, if only by omission. By not including a user name and password, the URL tells you that the site is accessible by anonymous FTP.

Nonanonymous FTP

Although most Web browser FTPing is done anonymously, FTP URLs can include the user name and password for a specific account. If I had the account *coolweb* on DEC's machine, and the password was *xyzxyz*, I could modify the URL to allow other people to connect to that account, as in the following example:

```
ftp://coolweb:xyzxyz@gatekeeper.dec.com/pub
```

Ports

Things can get even more complex when you start dealing with ports. FTP, like other programs on Internet servers, may be listening to ports other than the default port for its type of service.

Let me explain: Imagine that each computer on the Internet is like a TV station/TV set. It doesn't broadcast and receive all data across all possible frequencies; it aims specific types of data, formatted in prescribed manners, at individual frequencies or channels. On the Internet, those channels are called ports. If you want to watch your local ABC affiliate, for example, you may know that the station comes in on Channel 7 and not on Channel 4. By the same token, if you want to connect to the mail server on a specific computer, you may know that the mail server has a *default port* of 25. Some sites, however, opt to change these default port numbers (don't ask why; it's usually ugly). In such cases, you need to identify the special port within the URL.

What if a site decides to offer anonymous FTP for public use, but uses port 494 instead of the default FTP port? Then you have to specify that channel number in the URL, as in the following example:

```
ftp://gatekeeper.dec.com:494/pub
```

The preceding URL makes a browser connect to channel 494, look for the FTP server, and then show you the contents of the pub directory thereon.

If you want to use your own account and password simultaneously, put together the URL that contains all the necessary information, as follows:

```
ftp://coolweb:xyzxyz@gatekeeper.dec.com:494/pub
```

Fortunately, you're unlikely to see anything so complex with an FTP URL. In fact, this is unquestionably a worst-case URL!

Using FTP URLs

The most valuable thing about FTP URLs is that, if you specify a directory, most Web browsers list the files in that directory, and with a click, you can either transfer the files you want or move into other directories to continue browsing. If you specify a file within the URL, the browser connects to the server and transfers the file directly to your computer.

The following example is a URL containing all the information you need to obtain a copy of the HTML 3.0 specification document, should you for some strange reason want to read this highly complex and lengthy technical description:

```
ftp://ftp.w3.org/pub/doc/html_30.tar.Z
```

Are you curious about what else is in that directory? To find out, use the same URL, except omit the actual file name at the end, as in:

```
ftp://ftp.w3.org/pub/doc/
```

Translating spaces in URLs

URLs have a couple of subtle limitations, things that took me quite a while to realize through hit-and-miss. Fortunately, you have my book! Of the limitations, the most important is the fact that a URL cannot contain spaces.

 Repeat: URLs cannot contain spaces.

This no-spaces limitation caused me much consternation and some lengthy debugging sessions when I started working with Web servers. The other limitation is that URLs are case-sensitive, even on machines that are otherwise case-insensitive for filenames.

If you have a space in a filename, for example, you have to translate each space into a special character that is understood to represent a space within a URL. You can't use the underscore character (_), however. That character may be used to mean something else in some systems, and automatically translating it into a space would likely break many programs. You wouldn't want to do that.

Instead, the URL specification allows any character to be specified as — ready for this? — *a hexadecimal equivalent prefaced by a percent sign (%)*. To use `test server` in a URL, for example, replace the space with its hexadecimal equivalent (20), resulting in `test%20server`.

Hexadecimal (base 16) numbers range not from 0 to 9, as in the decimal (base 10) system, but from 0 to 15. Actually, here are the hexadecimal numerals: 0, 1, 2, 3, 4, 5, 6, 7, 8, 9, A, B, C, D, E, F. The hexadecimal letters, A-F, represent the decimal numbers, 10-15.

To compute the decimal equivalent of a hexadecimal number, multiply each number by the base raised to the appropriate power. Hex 20, therefore, would be 2 x 16 + 0 x 1, or 32 decimal. (Don't worry if this doesn't make sense; you'll probably never need to figure this out. Just remember to check Table 2-1 for the most common hex equivalents.)

Table 2-1 shows the special URL forms of some common characters that you may encounter while building URL specifications. Notice especially that you also need to codify any use of the percent sign itself so the Web browser program doesn't get confused. Almost perverse, eh?

Table 2-1	URL Coding for Common Characters	
Character	Hex Value	Equivalent URL Coding
Space	20	%20
Tab	09	%09
Enter	0A	%0A
Line feed	0D	%0D
Percent	25	%25

Gopher URLs

Now that you've learned more than you ever wanted to know about the nuances of having spaces and the like in URLs, you're ready to look at some Gopher URLs! The good news is that the majority of Gopher URLs don't look much different from their FTP cousins, as the following example shows:

```
gopher://newsgopher.uns.purdue.edu/
```

The preceding example is the simplest possible Gopher URL. The URL specifies the Gopher service (`gopher:`) and the name of the server system (`newsgopher.uns.purdue.edu/`). In this case, the system is the University News Service server at Purdue University (my alma mater).

Here is another example:

```
gopher://gopher.uchicago.edu:70/1
```

That URL specifies the main information Gopher for the University of Chicago. Instead of using the default Gopher port, though, the site specifies port 70 (which turns out to be the default port for Gopher anyway). After the port, the URL indicates that the first thing the user will see is a directory, specified in a Gopher URL by inserting /1. When no *specific* directory is indicated in the URL, the preceding URL actually accomplishes exactly the same thing as the slightly simpler.

```
gopher://gopher.uchicago.edu:70/
```

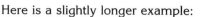
Here is a slightly longer example:

```
gopher://boombox.micro.umn.edu:70/00/internet-kit/Windows-
Internet-kit/winsock.dll
```

That URL loads an executable file (`winsock.dll`) that is available through the University of Minnesota Gopher server. Winsock.dll, for those on a regular Windows machine (not Windows95), is a valuable program that lets you add PPP networking to your PC.

E-Mail via URL

URLs for e-mail are quite simple, fortunately, and require minimal explanation. You can specify any e-mail address as a URL simply by prefacing the snippet `mailto:` as the service name, as in the following example:

```
mailto:taylor@intuitive.com
```

Again, make sure that you don't use spaces in the URL.

Note that you can send e-mail in a URL, but you cannot retrieve it.

 Some browsers, such as Mosaic, launch a separate e-mail program to handle e-mail services. Others, such as Navigator and Explorer, handle e-mail directly. A box pops up that allows you to compose and send mail (albeit with somewhat less control of the final content when compared to a full-blown electronic mail package like Eudora).

Telnet via URL

Transferring files through FTP is unquestionably valuable (hence, its status as one of the original Internet services). Another service that caused Internet use to explode is *telnet*. Telnet gives everyone on the Net the ability to log in to other computers on the Net, just as though they were connected to that machine directly. Not all Internet computers support telnet, but many do.

Telnet, you will be glad to know, is easy to specify in URLs: You simply specify the service and the host to which you want to connect. For example, to log in to the *Massachusetts Institute of Technology's* (MIT's) media laboratory, use the following URL:

```
telnet://media.mit.edu/
```

When you use telnet URLs, your Web browser program actually tries to launch a separate, external telnet program to negotiate the telnet connection, which means that nothing happens unless you've already installed and configured a separate telnet program (such as NCSA Telnet). Netscape Navigator, Internet Explorer, Mosaic, and similar programs aren't designed to allow you to directly interact with the remote computer from within the browser.

Usenet News via URL

Working with Usenet news is somewhat tricky because you must find an existing server that will allow you access. Many systems don't give you that access, even if you pay for a regular dialup account. A list of *public* Usenet hosts — which means hosts that attempt to provide news free of charge to all comers — is available on the Net, but in my experience only about 5 percent of them actually allow you to connect.

 To see the list of public Usenet sites for yourself, visit the URL
`http://www.freenewsgroups.com/`

If you already have access to a server that offers access to NetNews, you should be able to configure your browser to access it. Alternatively, check your account settings for an NNTP server — a computer that can usually be used to access news from your Web browser, too.

Building a news URL is a straightforward process. Simply type *news:* followed by the exact name of the newsgroup. No slashes are needed (or allowed), and there's not yet a standard approach for specifying individual articles. Here are a couple of examples:

```
news:news.answers
news:comp.sys.ibm-pc.announce
```

The Heart of the Web: HTTP URLs

Although all the services listed earlier in this chapter are valuable and interesting when used via a Web browser, the capability to connect with other Web servers via *HyperText Transfer Protocol* (HTTP) is what *really* makes the Web revolutionary.

The general format for HTTP references is the same as in the FTP references earlier in this chapter. Following is a typical HTTP URL:

```
http://www.halcyon.com/normg/shn/index.html
```

That particular URL is for the *Seattle Hometown News*. You can see the secret: The file lives within what's very likely to be the directory of a user called `normg`. The format of the preceding URL should be quite familiar to you by this point: the service name, a colon, the double slash, the host name, a slash, some specific options (in this case, the directory `normg`), and the name of a specific file with the Web standard `html` filename extension to denote an HTML markup file.

If you're on a PC running Windows 3.*x*, you already know that it's unable to cope with four-letter filename suffixes. Windows simply chops off the fourth character in the extension, making it .htm instead. Throughout the net, all files you see with the .htm suffix are exactly the same as .html files.

As it turns out, many times you don't even need to specify a filename if you'd rather not do so. Following is another example of a URL, this time for the *Palo Alto Weekly* in Palo Alto, California:

```
http://www.service.com/paw/
```

Note that the URL contains a default directory (paw). But because the URL doesn't specify a filename, the Web program is savvy enough to choose the default file — probably `index.html`, as configured on each server. If your system doesn't recognize `index.html`, then try `default.html` or `Welcome.html`, or ask your administrator for the secret filename!

If the HTTP server is on a nonstandard port, of course, that fact can be specified, as follows:

```
http://www.book.uci.edu:80/
```

The preceding URL is one way to get to the University of California at Irvine bookstore. Instead of using the default port for an HTTP server, the site opted for port 80. If you wanted to create a URL that contained both the port and a specific filename, you could do so, as in the following example:

```
http://www.book.uci.edu:80/Books/Techno/techno.html
```

Actually, port 80 is the default port for Web servers. UCI used to have its server running on port 8042, which would be specified exactly as shown above.

Theoretically, you can specify an unlimited number of different URL types (although you probably don't want to know that at this point). The vast majority of the URLs that you'll see, however, are in the http, ftp, telnet, gopher, mailto, and news formats, as demonstrated in this chapter.

Summary

A great deal of information was jammed into this chapter, so don't be too nervous if you feel a bit lost. The main point of this chapter was to give you a passing familiarity with what URLs are, how they're built, and how different types of services require different URL formats. In a few chapters, you wil learn how to tie URLs into your own Web documents. After that, the material in this chapter will doubtless crystallize and make much more sense. Chapter 3 begins the fun part of this book (indeed, the heart of the book): How to write cool Web documents!

Basic HTML

In This Chapter

Learning the basics of HTML layout

Breaking at lines and paragraphs

Breaking your document into sections

Using headers and footers

Defining section heads

Using horizontal rules to aid visual organization

Okay — it's time to get going and learn HTML! In this chapter, you go from 0 to 60 in no time flat, and by the end of it, you'll be able to create attractive Web pages. This chapter covers the basics of creating an HTML document, including head and body information, meaningful page titles, paragraph and section head marks, horizontal rules, and other, miscellaneous layout information and data.

Basics of HTML Layout

What is HTML? At its most fundamental, *HyperText Markup Language* (HTML) is a set of special codes that you embed in text to add formatting and linking information. HTML is based on *Standard Generalized Markup Language* (SGML). By convention, all HTML information begins with an open angle bracket (<) and ends with a close angle bracket (>) — for example, <HTML>. That *tag* — or *HTML tag*, as it's also known — tells an HTML *interpreter* (browser) that the document is written and marked up in standard HTML. An example of an HTML interpreter would be Microsoft's Internet Explorer, the Web browser included with both Microsoft Plus! for Windows 95 and Apple's Internet Connection Kit (and available for free off the Microsoft Web site, too; pop over to http://www.microsoft.com/ to get your copy).

HTML, like any other markup language, has some problems. Suppose, for example, you want to have the word *<HTML>* — including angle brackets — in a document. You need some way to prevent that word from being interpreted as an HTML tag. Later in this book, you'll learn how to include such tricky information within your documents. For now, keep an eye open for this kind of problem as you read along.

HTML and browsers

What happens if a program that interprets HTML, such as Internet Explorer, reads a file that doesn't contain any HTML tags? Suppose that you recently created the file not-yet.html, but haven't had a chance to add HTML tags. Your file looks something like this:

```
Dave's Desk
Somewhere in Cyberspace


Dear Reader,

   Thank you for connecting to my Web server, but I
regret to tell you
that things aren't up and running yet!
They will be _soon_, but they aren't today.

                 Sincerely,

                 Dave Taylor
```

Looks reasonable, although some of the lines seem to be shorter than you're used to when you read such notes. Figure 3-1 shows what the file looks like when it's read into the Explorer browser.

Figure 3-1 is clearly not at all what you wanted and probably would be quite puzzling to a viewer. Notice also that, although placing an underscore before and after a word is a clue in some systems that the word should be underlined (*soon*), that's *not* part of HTML, so the underscores are left untouched, whether or not they make sense to the viewer.

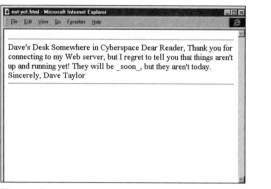

Figure 3-1: The file not-yet.html, without any HTML, in Explorer

What the document shown in Figure 3-1 needs are some HTML tags — some information that Web browser programs can use to lay out and format the information therein. The implied formatting information contained in not-yet.html works for humans visually, but Web browsers would ignore it because it's not in HTML. In other words, to you or me, seeing a tab as the first character of a sentence is a good clue that the sentence is the beginning of a new paragraph, but as you can clearly see in Figure 3-1, that just isn't the case with World Wide Web browsers.

The example shown in Figure 3-1 may seem a little silly right now. But as you work with HTML, I'm sure you'll discover that when you think you set up a document in a certain way, from time to time you'll find that the document looks dramatically different from within a Web browser than you expected.

Always test your HTML documents by viewing them through one or more Web browser programs to ensure that everything looks correct. Also, if you do encounter a problem where the browser is showing you all the formatting tags, rather than interpreting them, a likely culprit is that you have the file named with a ".txt" suffix, rather than a ".html" suffix. Web browsers are dumb; give them a text file and they'll display it exactly as is. To fix this, simply rename the file.

If you open it, close it

Although many HTML tags are stand-alone units, some are *paired,* with beginning and end tags. The beginning tag is called the *open* tag, and the end tag is called the *close* tag.

The most basic of all tags is the one shown earlier: ⟨HTML⟩, which indicates that the information that follows it is written in HTML. The ⟨HTML⟩ tag is a paired tag, however, so you need to add a close tag at the end of the document, which is the same as the open tag with the addition of a slash: ⟨/HTML⟩. By the same token, if you begin an italic phrase with ⟨I⟩ (the italics tag), you must end it with ⟨/I⟩. Everything between the open and close tags receives the particular attribute of that tag (the procedure of surrounding what you want to format is what I call *section-block notation*).

If you get confused and specify, for example, a backslash instead of a slash, as in ⟨\HTML⟩, or some other variant, the browser program doesn't understand and simply ignores the close tag, and the attributes in the open tag continue past the point where you meant them to stop. In the case of the ⟨HTML⟩ tag, because ⟨/HTML⟩ should appear at the end of the document, the problem probably isn't significant because there would be nothing after it to mess up. But some systems on the Net are very picky and can show some peculiar results for HTML tags that aren't closed.

Certainly, remembering to close any tags that you open is a good habit.

What do you think would happen if you included quotation marks around the tags — for example, if you used "⟨HTML⟩" at the beginning of your document rather than ⟨HTML⟩? If you guessed that just the quotes would be displayed, you're right. Let me emphasize that Web browsers are very simpleminded in their interpretation of HTML. Anything that varies from the specific characters in the HTML-language specification results in a layout other than the one you want or your formatting requests being ignored completely.

Breaking at Paragraphs and Lines

The most important markup tags you will learn — and probably the tags that you'll use most often — specify that you want a *paragraph break* or a *line break*. Several variants of these tags exist, but you can create readable and useful Web documents by using only the two tags ⟨P⟩ and ⟨BR⟩.

To specify that you want a paragraph break, use the tag ⟨P⟩. (The tag is mnemonic: P for paragraph.) The following example adds some ⟨P⟩ tags to the not-yet.html file shown in Figure 3-1 and also wraps the file in the ⟨HTML⟩ and ⟨/HTML⟩ tags:

```
<HTML>
Dave's Desk
Somewhere in Cyberspace
<P>
Dear Reader,
<P>
   Thank you for connecting to my Web server, but I
regret to tell you
that things aren't up and running yet!
They will be _soon_, but they aren't today.
<P>
                    Sincerely,
<P>
                    Dave Taylor
</HTML>
```

Figure 3-2 shows what the preceding HTML text looks like in a browser.

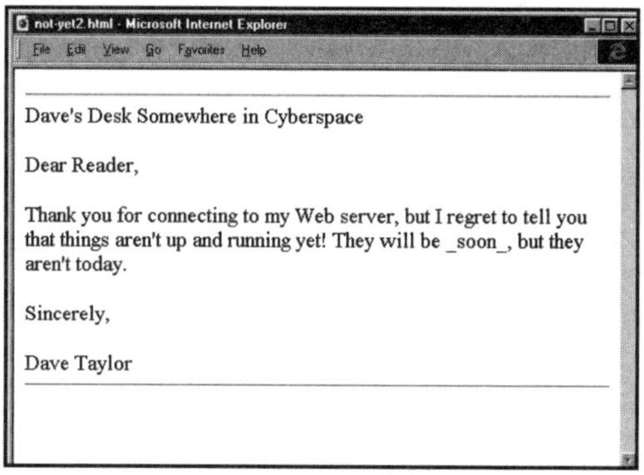

Figure 3-2: Paragraph breaks in not-yet.html

Figure 3-2's version of the file is a huge improvement over Figure 3-1's, but some problems still exist, not the least of which is the fact that the first few lines don't look right. In their zeal to organize the text neatly, Web browsers, by default, fill as many words into each line as they can manage. Filling the lines is okay for the main paragraph of the file, but the first few lines would be closer to what you want if you indicated that the browser should break the line between items, rather than fill it all in.

The way to break lines in HTML is to use the *break* tag: <BR>. Like any tag, the break tag can appear anywhere in the text, including at the end of the line you want to break. HTML tags are also case-insensitive, meaning that <BR> and
 (and <bR>) are all exactly the same. Following is the HTML file when the break tag is used:

```
<HTML>
Dave's Desk<BR>
Somewhere in Cyberspace
<P>
Dear Reader,
<P>
   Thank you for connecting to my Web server, but I
regret to tell you
that things aren't up and running yet!
They will be _soon_, but they aren't today.
<P>
                  Sincerely,
<P>
                  Dave Taylor
</HTML>
```

From a stylistic perspective, you should try to have a consistent scheme for your tags, particularly because you may have to go into fairly complex files and figure out what's wrong. As a result, I suggest that you place all line breaks at the end of text lines and all paragraph marks in lines of their own. This book uses that style throughout.

Figure 3-3 shows the output of the not-yet.html file when <BR> is used.

Figure 3-3: The break tag in not-yet.html

One remaining problem with the layout is the signature information is intended to be shifted to the right a few inches, as in a standard business note, but in the browser, it stays at the left edge of the document.

To remedy the problem, you can use the *preformatted information* tag: `<PRE>`. The `<PRE>` tag is also a paired tag, so it works across as many lines as needed, without any fuss, and must end with `</PRE>`. The following example shows how `<PRE>` preserves all character and line spacing. I've changed the last few lines of the not-yet.html file to reflect the use of this tag:

```
<HTML>
Dave's Desk<BR>
Somewhere in Cyberspace
<P>
Dear Reader,
<P>
   Thank you for connecting to my Web server, but I
regret to tell you
that things aren't up and running yet!
They will be _soon_, but they aren't today.
<PRE>

                    Sincerely,

              Dave Taylor

</PRE>
</HTML>
```

After adding the `<PRE>` tags, you achieve the desired formatting, but now another problem has cropped up: The text in the preformatted block (the stuff between `<PRE>` and `</PRE>`) appears in a different, monospace typeface! You can see the difference in Figure 3-4, if you look closely.

Typefaces refer to a particular style of letters in a variety of sizes. A font, by contrast, is a typeface in a specific size and style. Helvetica is a typeface, but 12-point Helvetica italic is a font. A monospace typeface is one where every letter has exactly the same width. Ten lowercase 'i' characters (iiiiiiiiii), for example, end up exactly as wide as ten lowercase 'm' characters (mmmmmmmmmm). In this book, we're using a proportional typeface for this note so you can clearly see that the ten 'i' characters are considerably narrower than the ten 'm' characters.

Dave's Desk
Somewhere in Cyberspace

Dear Reader,

Thank you for connecting to my Web server, but I regret to tell you that
things aren't up and running yet! They will be _soon_, but they aren't today.

                                        Sincerely,

                                        Dave Taylor

Figure 3-4: Format is correct, but typeface is new.

The reason Explorer changed the typeface in Figure 3-4 is because the
browser assumed that the preformatted text was a code listing or other
technical information. That's the most common context for the <PRE> tag.
So it worked, sort of, but it's not quite what you wanted. (You can use
<PRE> to your advantage in other situations, however, as you'll see later in
this chapter.) For now, just leave the salutation and my name at the left
edge of the screen by removing the <PRE> tags and replacing the <P>
paragraph breaks.

Wait a minute! Where do I type this stuff? Any editor that enables you to
save regular ASCII-text files will work fine. On my PC, I use NotePad, a
program that is included free with Windows 95, and on my Macintosh,
SimpleText, also free. Just make sure that you save the file as a text-only
format and that you use the ".html" filename suffix so that when you open
your test file in a Web browser, it'll be interpreted as a web page. Appendix
A is a step-by-step demonstration of creating a simple Web page: If you're
dying of curiosity, leap ahead and read through it.

Breaking Your Document into Sections

If you take a close look at a fully specified HTML document, you'll find that
it's divided into two sections: what I call the stationery section (the information that would be printed on the pad if the file were a physical note), and
the body of the message itself. Think of the information you typically find
at the top of a memo:

```
M E M O R A N D U M
To:                                              Date:
From:                                            Subject:
```

Those are the most common items of information at the beginning of a memo, and then there's usually a *rule* (a line) followed by blank space in which you write the actual content of the memo.

Similarly, for the sake of organization, HTML files are commonly broken into two sections: the *head* (or header) that contains the introductory page-formatting information, and the *body*. You use the paired tags <HEAD> </HEAD> and <BODY> </BODY> to surround each section. The following example shows how the not-yet.html file looks when these tags are added:

```
<HTML>
<HEAD></HEAD>
<BODY>
Dave's Desk<BR>
Somewhere in Cyberspace
<P>
Dear Reader,
<P>
   Thank you for connecting to my Web server, but I
regret to tell you
that things aren't up and running yet!
They will be _soon_, but they aren't today.
<P>
                    Sincerely,
<P>
                    Dave Taylor

</BODY>
</HTML>
```

The <HEAD> </HEAD> and <BODY> </BODY> formatting information doesn't add anything to the display, I admit. Also, the document doesn't contain any introductory HTML-formatting information yet, so the HEAD area is empty. If you were to view the preceding HTML text in a Web browser, it would look identical to Figure 3-3. Later, when you start learning some of the more complex parts of HTML, you'll see why section-block notation (for example, <HEAD></HEAD>) can be a boon.

What do you think would happen if I fed the following information to a Web browser?

```
<HTML><HEAD></HEAD><BODY>Dave's Desk<BR>Somewhere in
Cyberspace
<P>Dear Reader,<P>Thank you for connecting to
my Web server, but I regret to tell you that
things aren't up and running yet!
They will be _soon_, but they aren't today.
<P>Sincerely,<P>Dave Taylor</BODY></HTML>
```

If you guessed that the screen output of the preceding example would look exactly like the carefully spaced material shown earlier (see Figure 3-3), you're correct.

 Remember that Web browsers ignore carriage returns, tabs, and multiple spaces when the document is reformatted for display. That suggests that you can save a great deal of space — and display a great deal more of your document source onscreen — simply by skipping all the extra returns; *but I strongly recommend against such a strategy.* Why? In a nutshell, writing your Web documents with the markup tags in logical places makes the document easier to work with later. I've written and had to debug more than a thousand HTML documents, and I can assure you that the more things are jammed together, the less sense they make a few weeks later, when you find you have to add some information or modify the content.

Title Your Page

One of the subtle (but simple) things you can do to make your Web page look smart is give it a good title with the <TITLE> tag. The title usually appears in the top border of the window displayed on the user's computer. Go back and look at the information in the header of Figure 3-4: The browser shows the name of the file, which is remarkably dull.

The <TITLE> tag enables you to define the exact title you want in the document. It is a paired tag and appears within the <HEAD> </HEAD> block of information, as follows:

```
<HEAD>
<TITLE>This is the title</TITLE>
</HEAD>
```

For the document you've been developing in this chapter, not-yet.html, a nice title would be one that reinforces the message in the file itself, as in the following example:

```
<HTML>
<HEAD>
<TITLE>Not Ready for Prime Time!</TITLE>
</HEAD>
```

Figure 3-5 shows how the new title text would look within the Explorer browser. Notice particularly the change in the top window border (also known as the title bar).

Figure 3-5: The <TITLE> tag produces an appropriate title for the browser window.

The <TITLE> tag has one limitation: Some Web browsers don't display titled windows, so the <TITLE> information isn't displayed for folks using those browsers. On the other hand, the text in <TITLE> is also used as the link info when a user saves a Web document into a *bookmark* or *hotlist* (compiled URLs for sites you've visited and want to remember). So, a meaningful <TITLE> for each page you create can be very helpful to your readers.

Common Footer Material

Just as you commonly see certain information, such as the title, in the header of a Web document, certain other information is commonly placed at the foot of the document. On the Web, you usually find copyright information and contact data for the creator of the page at the bottom of documents.

The tag used for such contact info is usually <ADDRESS>. It's a paired tag (<ADDRESS> address information </ADDRESS>). The following example shows this tag added to the not-yet.html document:

```
<HTML>
<HEAD>
<TITLE>Not Yet Ready for Prime Time!</TITLE>
</HEAD>
<BODY>
Dave's Desk<BR>
Somewhere in Cyberspace
<P>
Dear Reader,
<P>
Thank you for connecting to my Web server, but I
regret to tell you
that things aren't up and running yet!
They will be _soon_, but they aren't today.
<P>
                    Sincerely,
<P>
                    Dave Taylor
<ADDRESS>
Page Design by Dave Taylor (taylor@intuitive.com)
</ADDRESS>
</BODY>
</HTML>
```

Do you have to use the <ADDRESS> tag? Nope. Like various other items that appear in HTML pages, it can be used or skipped. (In Web pages I create, I tend not to include address information, but many people like to have that information at the bottom of pages.) That's why I call tags like <ADDRESS> quasi-standard — it's useful, but not always present. As you can see in Figure 3-6, the address stuff is presented in italics, which can look quite attractive for certain Web pages.

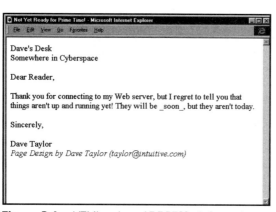

Figure 3-6: <HTML> plus <ADDRESS> information

Defining Section Heads

The formatting information discussed so far in this chapter enables you to create attractive text. But what if your Web page should be organized in sections or even subsections? The various levels of *header-format* tags handle that situation.

Each header-format level has an open and close tag. The highest-level header-format tag is <H1>; the lowest (the smallest and least important subsection) is <H6>. To specify a top-level header, use <H1>First Header</H1>.

Header-format tags would be best illustrated in a different HTML page than not-yet.html, because that document doesn't need headers and is already attractive. The following is the beginning of a table of contents or outline for a movie information Web site:

```
<HTML>
<HEAD>
<TITLE>The Cool Web Movie Database</TITLE>
</HEAD>
<BODY>
Welcome to the Cool Web Movie Database. So far we offer
information on the many brilliant films of David Lean;
soon, a lot more will be online.
<H1>The Early Years</H1>
<H2>In Which We Serve (1942)</H2>
```

(continued)

```
(continued)
<H2>This Happy Breed (1944)</H2>
<H1>Films with Sam Spiegel Productions</H1>
<H2>The Bridge on the River Kwai (1957)</H2>
<H2>Lawrence of Arabia (1962)</H2>
<H1>The Later Years</H1>
<H2>Doctor Zhivago (1965)</H2>
<H2>Ryan's Daughter (1970)</H2>
<ADDRESS>
This information maintained by Dave Taylor
</ADDRESS>
</BODY>
</HTML>
```

Figure 3-7 shows how the preceding text appears in a Web browser:

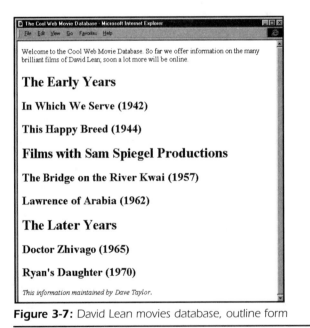

Figure 3-7: David Lean movies database, outline form

Most Web pages that you design probably won't have *quite* as many headers as the example in Figure 3-7.

The following example adds a little more information about some of the films to show the value of different headers:

```
<HTML>
<HEAD>
<TITLE>The Cool Web Movie Database</TITLE>
</HEAD>
<BODY>Welcome to the Cool Web Movie Database. So far we
offer
information on the many brilliant films of David Lean;
soon, a lot more will be online.<H1>The Early Years</H1>
<H2>In Which We Serve (1942)</H2>
Co-directed and produced by Noel Coward, this film also
starred
Noel Coward as Captain Kinross and Celia Johnson as Mrs.
Kinross.
<H2>This Happy Breed (1944)</H2>
Based on the play by Noel Coward, this starred Robert
Newton and
again featured Celia Johnson.
<H1>Films with Sam Spiegel Productions</H1>
<H2>The Bridge on the River Kwai (1957)</H2>
Produced by Sam Spiegel, this film was the first of the
Lean blockbuster
movies and featured a young Alec Guinness, William Holden,
and a
brilliant performance from Sessue Hayakawa.
<H2>Lawrence of Arabia (1962)</H2>
One of my personal all-time favorite movies, this epic
adventure
really established Lean as the creator of sweeping
panoramas.
```

When the preceding example is viewed in a browser, the different headers appear in different size type, and information that is not part of the header appears in a nonbold, roman typeface (see Figure 3-8).

 One thing to remember about HTML is that the actual fonts, sizes, and layout of the final presentation can be altered by users based on the preferences they set in their browsers. I contend, however, that precious few people actually alter their preference settings, so if your page looks good with the default values, you should be okay. If the default values look a little weird, as may well be the case with Explorer in particular, by all means experiment with the settings.

Figure 3-8: Movie database with some text

The Horizontal Rule

A very useful tag for organizing your document visually is the *horizontal rule* tag: <HR>. Dropped anywhere in a Web document, it produces a skinny line across the page. The following example shows the movie-information page with the <HR> tag added:

```
<HTML>
<HEAD>
<TITLE>The Cool Web Movie Database</TITLE>
</HEAD>
<BODY>
Welcome to the Cool Web Movie Database. So far we offer
information on the many brilliant films of David Lean;
soon, more will be online.
<HR>
<H1>The Early Years</H1>
<H2>In Which We Serve (1942)</H2>
Co-directed and produced by Noel Coward, this film also
starred
Noel Coward as Captain Kinross and Celia Johnson as Mrs.
```

```
Kinross.
<H2>This Happy Breed (1944)</H2>
Based on the play by Noel Coward, this film starred Robert
Newton and
again featured Celia Johnson.
<HR>
<H1>Films with Sam Spiegel Productions</H1>
<H2>The Bridge on the River Kwai (1957)</H2>
Produced by Sam Spiegel, this was the first of the Lean
blockbuster
movies and featured a young Alec Guinness, William Holden,
and a
brilliant performance from Sessue Hayakawa.
```

You *can* overuse the horizontal rule, as well as any other formatting and design element, in a Web document. Used judiciously, though, the <HR> tag is tremendously helpful in creating cool pages. Figure 3-9 shows the browser view.

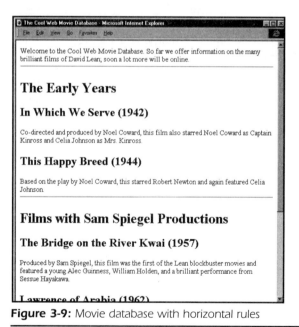

Figure 3-9: Movie database with horizontal rules

Table 3-1 contains a summary of the HTML tags covered in this chapter.

Table 3-1	Summary of Tags in This Chapter	
HTML Tag	**Close Tag**	**Meaning**
`<ADDRESS>`	`</ADDRESS>`	Address and creator information
`<BODY>`	`</BODY>`	Body of the HTML page
` `		Line break
`<HEAD>`	`</HEAD>`	HTML-formatting information
`<Hn>`	`</Hn>`	Document header level (n = 1-6)
`<HR>`		Horizontal rule
`<HTML>`	`</HTML>`	Defines a Web-formatted file
`<P>`		Paragraph breaks
`<PRE>`	`</PRE>`	Preformatted information

Summary

A great deal of information was presented here. You've learned most of the basics of HTML and are about ready to start creating your own Web pages. Already, you should be able to reproduce formatted information (like this chapter of this book, to pick the most immediate example) in an attractive format for users on the World Wide Web. Chapter 4 continues to explore HTML by explaining how to use boldface and italic formatting, how to add other types of emphasis to text, and how to make various other changes within sentences and paragraphs.

Text Styles

Helping readers navigate with boldface and italics

Changing text with underlining, monospace, and other typefaces

Using font sizes, colors, and faces

Applying logical styles

Pulling it all together

This chapter explores some of the nuts and bolts of text presentation and information layout. By *text styles,* I mean specification of boldface, italics, and other changes that can be made in text. The preceding chapter showed you all the basics of HTML document layout in the proverbial fell swoop. But there's much more to creating cool Web pages.

When you were given your first box of crayons, you probably went wild and tried to use all the colors on each picture that you colored. Eventually, however, it dawned on you (unless you were a young Peter Max) that a subset of colors can be much more useful and attractive. The same holds true for the various formatting commands in HTML: You can use all the commands all over the place, but a better strategy is to use them only when they are most appropriate. Many Web pages already tend to be cluttered, and using too much italicization or boldface makes the clutter even worse.

Nevertheless, there will be times when you'll want to highlight certain words, phrases, titles, names, or other information. You'll learn how to do that using HTML before you finish this chapter.

First, a Little History

Page design and layout have been around for thousands of years — since the beginning of writing. In Egyptian hieroglyphs, for example, vertical lines separate columns of glyphs to make them easier to read. Before the year A.D. 1000, scribes all over the world were using various techniques of presenting information on a page, including illumination (adding gold or silver to the ink, or including other illustrations in the margins or twined around the letters), illustration, and other devices.

By the time Johann Gutenberg introduced his printing press in the fifteenth century, with its revolutionary movable type supplanting etched- or engraved-plate printing, designers and artists were codifying various approaches to page design. A glance at the Gutenberg Bible reveals that it foreshadows many aspects of modern text design, including italicized and boldface text.

Why am I rambling on about the history of page layout? Well, it's important to realize that italics and boldface text have commonly accepted standard meanings. You don't have to follow the rules to the letter, but if your goal is to help people breeze through your Web material and quickly find what they seek, then keeping the guidelines in mind can be quite valuable.

Helping Readers Navigate with Bold and Italic

In the examples in Chapter 3, I mentioned that some standard computer notation for underlining doesn't work. In Figure 3-1, I included the example _soon_, hoping that when read by a browser, the word would be italicized, underlined, or otherwise presented in a manner that would emphasize it.

One of the most important characteristics of any document layout — on the Web or in print — is the use of different fonts and various styles to help the reader navigate the material. For example, imagine this page without any spacing, paragraph breaks, headings, italics, or boldface words; it would look boring. More important, it would be more difficult to skim the page for information or to glance at it quickly to gain a sense of what's being discussed.

I like to remember the different text treatments by imagining that I'm reading the material to an audience. Italicized words or phrases are those that I *emphasize* in my speech. Words or phrases in boldface I imagine to be *anchors* — items that help me skim the material and find specific spots. Apply this practice to text, and you see why section headings are in bold rather than italic: Headings would be harder to find if they didn't stand out. The same reasoning applies to text size; larger words stand out from smaller adjacent text.

Now take a look at how bold and italic work in Web page design. Italic and boldface formatting require paired tags.

➡ The italic formatting tag is <I>, which is paired with </I>.

➡ The boldface formatting tag is <B>, and its partner is </B>.

Here's how a brief HTML passage looks with both bold and italics text:

```
It turns out <B>Starbucks</B>, the popular and
fast-growing coffee chain, got its name from the
coffee-loving first mate in Melville's classic
tale of pursuit and revenge <I>Moby Dick< /I >,
although few people realize it.
```

Figure 4-1 shows how the preceding information looks in a Web browser. Notice I made a slight mistake in the coding: The name of the book, *Moby Dick*, has an open italics tag, but I incorrectly added spaces within its partner, the close italics tag. As a result, the request to end the italics passage doesn't end when the title of the book is complete. Also, if you view this exact same snippet in Explorer or Navigator, you'll find that each has a slightly different way of dealing with an error of this form. Another good reason to double-check your Web pages in multiple browsers!

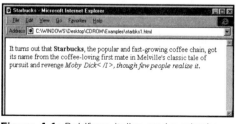

Figure 4-1: Boldface, italics, and a mistake

You must always follow the opening angle bracket of an HTML formatting tag with the format code immediately; no spaces are allowed.

Underlining, Monospace, and Other Text Changes

A number of other formatting options are available within Web documents:

- The underline formatting tag is <U>, which is paired with </U>.
- The monospace tag is <TT>, which is paired with </TT>.
- Superscripts are denoted by ^{and}, subscripts by _{and}.
- Text can be crossed out using <STRIKE>, which ends with </STRIKE>.

Monospace is so named because each letter in a monospace typeface occupies exactly the same width, even if the letter itself is quite narrow. Monospace type typically looks like the product of a typewriter. `This is a monospace typeface`. Proportional typefaces are more common. The text you are reading now is a proportional typeface. Note that it varies the width of the letters for easier reading; five occurrences of the letter *i*, for example (iiiii) aren't as long as five occurrences of *m* (mmmmm).

You may not want to use the <U> and <TT> tags too often because of the possible problems. Mosaic, for example, doesn't understand the <TT> format at all, and some versions of Netscape Navigator ignore <U> formats. Also, when you create a Web document that contains links to other documents, the links are displayed in a different color — usually blue. To make links stand out more, however, and to ensure that people with gray-scale or black-and-white displays can recognize links, links also appear with an underscore. Therein lies the problem with the <U> formatting tag: If you use it on a Web page, which underlined words or phrases are links, and which are just underlined text? Figure 4-2 demonstrates this underlining problem more clearly.

Figure 4-2: Links or underlined text?

You can't tell by looking at Figure 4-2, but the word *Starbucks* is a pointer to another document on the World Wide Web, whereas the book title, *Moby Dick*, is just an underlined word. As you can see, using underscores in Web pages can be confusing, and as a result, it's not used on pages very often.

Monospace is often more useful than underlining, but it's not used extensively in Web pages either. If you want to simulate computer input or output, for example, you might display that text in monospace, as in the following:

```
Rather than typing <B><TT>DIR</TT></B> to find out what
files you have in your Unix account, you'll instead
want to type <B><TT>ls</TT></B>, as shown:
<PRE>
% <B>ls</B>
this      that      the-other
</PRE>
```

The preceding example demonstrates that the preformatted text tag <PRE> also produces text in monospace typeface, but it also preserves the original line breaks and extra spacing between words.

You can combine some HTML tags to produce exactly the output that you seek. In Figure 4-3, the terms *DIR* and *ls* appear in bold monospace text.

Figure 4-3: <B> and <TT> together produce bold monospace.

If you're working with mathematical formulas or otherwise have reason to use superscripts and subscripts on your Web pages, there are two tags that offer easy formatting, as shown here:

```
<H2>If you could double the amount of water on the
planet - essentially H<SUB>2</SUB>O<SUP>2</SUP> - you'd
never have to worry about mowing the lawn again; it'd be
under the ocean!</H2>
```

The resulting format is very attractive and lends itself to slick formulas and instant math, as you can see in Figure 4-4.

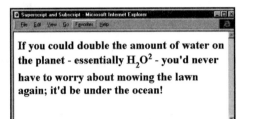

Figure 4-4: Superscript and subscript format tags at work.

Note a trick here: To make the text stand out, I've enclosed the entire passage in `<H2>` header tags. It will automatically make the text larger and bold. There's an easier way to accomplish this task, however, as you'll see later in this chapter.

Finally, sometimes you want to be able to show a change in text to someone visiting your page and so being able to cross out the text, while still having it displayed, can be quite useful. You can do that — in most Web browsers — with the `<STRIKE>` strikethrough tag. Here's how it would look as source code:

```
<H2>If you could double the amount of water on the
planet - essentially H<SUB>2</SUB>O<SUP>2</SUP> - you'd
never have to worry about <STRIKE>watering the lawn again:
everything would be
under the ocean!</STRIKE>buying a dryer: everything would
be permanently wet!</H2>
```

The strikethrough formatting works well in this case — as you can see in Figure 4-5 — because the text is fairly large (remember, I'm using the <H2> trick to accomplish that), but if the text were smaller, the strikethrough line could make it unreadable. Be sure you carefully preview any <STRIKE> text before you unleash it on the world, for just that reason.

Depending on the Web browser you're using, some HTML tags can be combined, and others can't. Combining bold and italics in some cases doesn't work, but either format works when combined with <TT>.

If you could double the amount of water on the planet - essentially H_2O^2 - you'd never have to worry about ~~watering the lawn again: everything would be under the ocean!~~ buying a dryer: everything would be permanently wet!

Figure 4-5: Corrections onscreen with <STRIKE> formatting

Using Font Sizes, Colors, and Faces

One recent addition to HTML is also one of the most entertaining: the capability to change font sizes, colors, and faces. HTML–font sizes range from size 1 to size 7, with 1 being the smallest and 7 the largest. It's the opposite of the numbering of header tags, unfortunately, where header 1 is the largest and header 6 the smallest.

All font changes are modifications to the <FONT> tag, and it's the first tag we've encountered where the tag itself includes specific attributes. HTML tags that can have attributes typically specify them as name=value pairs. The <FONT> tag is a fine example: To change the size of a passage of text, you use the formatting:

```
<FONT SIZE=7>some important text</FONT>
```

In this example, the words "some important text" would be displayed at the largest possible size in the browser.

Notice the closing tag `</FONT>` needn't include the attributes of the opening tag: You didn't need to use `</FONT SIZE=7>` to end the larger text. This is an important nuance and a great time–saver as you start to explore more complex formatting.

Font sizes can be specified absolutely as in the previous example, or they can be relative size changes. Here's the HTML to make a particular word one font size larger than the text surrounding it:

```
This is a <FONT SIZE=+1>very</FONT> important issue to us.
```

The default font size in most browsers is `SIZE=3`, but in Microsoft Internet Explorer, you can change the default size on the page by using the font size buttons on the toolbar (see Chapter 1 for details). Relative changes can't go below `SIZE=1` or above `SIZE=7`, so if you have a default size of 3 and add 10 to it, with a tag like `<FONT SIZE=+10>`, it'll be identical in function to `<FONT SIZE=7>` or `<FONT SIZE=+4>`.

Color can be specified for a range of text in a very similar manner by using a different `<FONT>` attribute. The logical name is "color," and that's just what you can use: `<FONT COLOR=BLUE>I'm blue</FONT>` will display the specified passage of text in the specified color. There is a wide variety of colors that can be specified by name and you can have even finer resolution of color control by using RGB hexadecimal values (I explain the red-green-blue color identification technique in Chapter 10), but for basic colors, you'll find that you can work without worrying about the RGB values and instead just specify them by name.

When you have these HTML tags that let you specify attributes, a nice feature of the markup language is that you can have multiple attributes in the same tag. If you wanted big red text, for example, you could do that with `<FONT SIZE=6 COLOR=red>Big Red</FONT>`. It doesn't matter what order you specify the name=value pairs, so `<FONT COLOR=red SIZE=6>` would be exactly identical to `<FONT SIZE=6 COLOR=red>` to the browser.

The third possible attribute for the `<FONT>` tag is the typeface specifier `FACE`. This is a tricky one, however, because you need to specify the exact typeface name on the user's system, and typefaces have different names on different platforms. For example, on my Macintosh, the standard typeface is "Times," but in Windows 95, the equivalent typeface is called "Times Roman." Many typefaces are included on computers nowadays, but again, there's no standardization on typeface name.

The long and short of it: You specify typefaces with the FACE attribute to the <FONT> tag, and you can specify a list of typefaces as the value. If you wanted to ensure that you got either Arial (a popular typeface on Windows) or Chicago (a popular face on the Macintosh), you would specify:

```
<font face="Arial,Chicago">special text</font>
```

The browser, upon receiving this HTML instruction, will look for Arial, and if found, use it to display 'special text' on the screen. If Arial isn't available, then it'll use Chicago. If that's also not available, the text will be displayed in the default proportional typeface.

You should really get into the habit of using quotes for the list of typeface names, because many typefaces have multiple-word names. A more complex example is:

```
<FONT SIZE=4 COLOR=blue FACE="Helvetica Narrow,Arial
Narrow">Skinny Text</FONT>
```

Again, this would display in Helvetica Narrow, if available, or Arial Narrow, or regular text.

One final tag and you'll have an example that demonstrates all of these modifications: To change the default size of all text on a page, you could use <FONT SIZE=4> or similar at the very top of the document, but, in fact, there's a specialized tag for just this purpose called <BASEFONT>. It's use is demonstrated as follows:

```
<BASEFONT SIZE=4>
<FONT SIZE=7 FACE=Arial>Common Foods of the French
Quarter</FONT><BR>
You can visit <FONT SIZE=+1>New Orleans</FONT> and have a
great time without ever leaving
the picturesque and partyin' French Quarter area,
particularly if you partake of some of these
fabulous local foods:
<UL>
<LI><FONT COLOR=RED>Beignets</FONT> - small deep-fried
donuts in powdered sugar. Best with
a steaming fresh <FONT SIZE=+1>cup of coffee</FONT>.
<LI><FONT COLOR=GREEN>Seafood Gumbo</FONT> - a stew-like
soup that's delicious.
Typically served with a side of white rice
```

(continued)

```
(continued)
that's best dumped into the soup directly. Skip the
chicken gumbo some
places serve too: the seafood is definitely better!
<LI><FONT COLOR=ORANGE SIZE=+2>Jambalaya</FONT> - the best
of all possible dinners. You'll just have
to order it so you can find out what it's about.
<LI><FONT SIZE=2 COLOR=BLUE>alcohol</FONT> - it's the
grease on the wheels of the tourist experience in the
French Quarter, but I'm not convinced it's as necessary
for a good time as the bars suggest…
</UL>
Whatever you do, make sure you have <FONT
SIZE=+1>F</FONT><FONT SIZE=+2>U</FONT>
<FONT SIZE=+3>N</FONT>!
```

In this example, the screen is full of fun and interesting text in a variety of sizes and colors (see Figure 4-6).

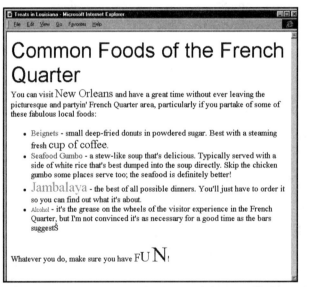

Figure 4-6: A wide variety of colors and sizes specified by using <FONT> tag attributes

Applying Logical Styles

The style directives discussed up to this point are easy to understand. The HTML language also supports what are called logical styles. Logical styles enable readers (and their software) to define emphasis.

The most common logical styles are ⟨EM⟩⟨/EM⟩ for emphasis and ⟨STRONG⟩⟨/STRONG⟩ for stronger emphasis. Figure 4-7 shows an example of these tags:

I'd like to make two points during this presentation: *Things are okay* and **Things are getting better!**.

This is a kbd key. *this is a citation.*

Figure 4-7: Logical styles in HTML

In the example shown in Figure 4-7, the first point (shown in italics) is specified as ⟨EM⟩Things are okay ⟨/EM⟩, and the second point (boldfaced) is specified as ⟨STRONG⟩Things are getting better!⟨/STRONG⟩.

NOTE
I have to admit I don't particularly like the logical tags and never use them myself. I have no way of knowing if a particular browser will think ⟨EM⟩ should be in bold or italics, and the two have very different meanings in layout, as discussed at the beginning of this chapter. You are free to make your own decision about the use of these tags, of course, but I avoid them myself.

Many other logical tags are specified in the HTML standard, but are rarely used. I list them all in Table 4-1 for your information — you may want to experiment with them to see if they meet any of your specific formatting needs, but most likely you'll find that they're all synonymous with the ⟨TT⟩ monospace-type tag.

Table 4-1   **A Variety of Logical Text Tags**

HTML Tag	Close Tag	Meaning
`<CITE>`	`</CITE>`	Bibliographic citation
`<CODE>`	`</CODE>`	Code listing
`<DFN>`	`</DFN>`	Word definition
`<KBD>`	`</KBD>`	Keyboard text (similar to `<CODE>`)
`<SAMP>`	`</SAMP>`	Sample user input
`<VAR>`	`</VAR>`	Program or other variable

Putting It All Together

Following is an example of a complex HTML document viewed within a Web browser. The example includes material covered in Chapter 3, as well.

```
<HTML>
<HEAD>
<TITLE>Travels with Tintin</TITLE>
<BASEFONT SIZE=4>
</HEAD><BODY>
<H1><FONT COLOR=ORANGE>Travels with Tintin</FONT></H1>
Of the various reporters with whom I've traveled around
the world, including writers for <I>UPI</I>, <I>AP</I>,
and <I>Reuters</I>, the most fascinating has clearly been
<B>Tintin</B>, boy reporter from Belgium
(<TT>tintin@belgium.gov</TT>).
<P>
Probably the most enjoyable aspect of our travels was his
dog, <B>Snowy</B>, although I don't know that our hosts
would agree!
<P>
<FONT SIZE=6 COLOR=BLUE>The First Trip: Nepal</FONT>
<P>
After winning the Pulitzer for <I>Adventure with Red
Rackham's Treasure</I>, Tintin told me he wanted a
vacation. Remembering some of his earlier adventures, he
decided to visit Nepal. Early one Sunday, I was sipping
```

```
my tea and reading the <I>Times</I> when he rang me up,
asking whether I'd be able to take a break and come
along...
</BODY>
</HTML>
```

Can you guess how the preceding text will look from a browser? Check Figure 4-8 to find out.

The document in Figure 4-8 is quite attractive, albeit with some poor spacing around the italicized acronyms in the first sentence. Fortunately, some of the most recent Web browsers realize that an additional space is needed after the last italicized character, so this becomes even more readable. Also notice the spacing around the <H1> format compared to the two <P> tags I had to add by hand later in the document when I opted to use the <FONT SIZE=6> tag to create my own section head.

Table 4-2 provides a summary of the many character-formatting tags covered in this chapter.

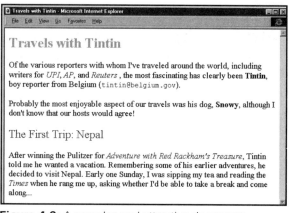

Figure 4-8: A complex and attractive document

Table 4-2	Summary of Tags in This Chapter	
HTML Tag	**Close Tag**	**Meaning**
`<B>`	`</B>`	Display text in bold
`<I>`	`</I>`	Display text in italic
`<U>`	`</U>`	Underline specified text
`<TT>`	`</TT>`	Monospace text
`<CITE>`	`</CITE>`	Bibliographic citation
`<CODE>`	`</CODE>`	Code listing
`<DFN>`	`</DFN>`	Word definition
`<EM>`	`</EM>`	Logical emphasis style
`<KBD>`	`</KBD>`	Keyboard text (similar to `<CODE>`)
`<SAMP>`	`</SAMP>`	Sample user input
`<STRONG>`	`</STRONG>`	Logical stronger emphasis
`<VAR>`	`</VAR>`	Program or other variable
`<BASEFONT`		Specify the default font size for the page
`SIZE=n>`		(range 1-7, 7 being largest. Default: 3)
`<FONT`	`</FONT>`	Specify attributes for the enclosed text
`SIZE=n`		size of text: range is 1-7, 7 being largest
`FACE="a,b"`		specify typeface to use: *a*, if available, or *b*
`COLOR=s`		color of text, either as color name or RGB value.

Summary

This chapter focused on formatting characters and words. Chapter 5 focuses on larger formatting issues, including how to add both numbered and bulleted lists to your HTML documents, and how to include glossaries or other definition lists.

Lists and Special Characters

In This Chapter

Definition lists

Ordered (numbered) and unordered (bulleted) lists

Special characters in HTML documents

Comments within HTML

This chapter introduces you to various types of lists for Web pages, including ordered (numbered) and unordered (bulleted) lists. It also explains how to add special and non-English characters and comments to your Web documents. You'll see lots of lists on the Web. After you read this chapter, you'll be able to use the different list styles to your advantage.

Definition Lists

One of the most common elements of multipage documents is a set of definitions, references, or cross-indexes. Glossaries are classic examples; words are listed alphabetically, followed by prose definitions. In HTML, the entire section of a glossary would be contained by a *definition list*, which is contained within a pair of *definition list tags*: `<DL>` and `</DL>`. Within the pair of listings, a definition has two parts:

➡ Definition term (`<DT>`)

➡ Definition description (`<DD>`).

Here's how a definition list can be used in HTML to define some genetics terms:

```
<HTML>
<HEAD></HEAD>
<BODY>
<H1>A Quick Glossary of Genetic Terms</H1>
<I>Adapted from Dawkins, The Extended Phenotype</I>
<DL>
<DT>allometry
<DD>A disproportionate relationship between size of a body
part and size of the whole body.
<DT>anaphase
<DD>Phase of the cell division during which the paired
chromosomes move apart.
<DT>antigens
<DD>Foreign bodies, usually protein molecules, which
provoke the
formation of antibodies.
<DT>autosome
<DD>A chromosome that is not one of the sex chromosomes.
<DT>codon
<DD>A triplet of units (nucleotides) in the genetic code,
specifying the synthesis of a single unit (amino acid) in
a protein chain.
<DT>genome
<DD>The entire collection of genes possessed by one
organism.
</DL>
</BODY>
</HTML>
```

Figure 5-1 shows how the preceding HTML code looks in a Web browser. Notice the automatic indentation and formatting.

If you're writing a book about herbal remedies, for example, you may want to have a cross-reference of herbs for specific problems. Certain key herbs could be italicized to highlight them. The following example shows how you might want such a listing to look:

Blood Pressure

Balm, Black Haw, *Garlic*, Hawthorn.

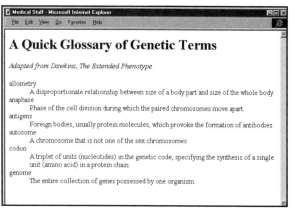

Figure 5-1: A glossary in HTML

Bronchitis

> Angelica, *Aniseed*, *Caraway*, Grindelia.

Burns

> Aloe, Chickweed, *Elder*.

Obtaining the preceding format within an HTML document would require the following tag placements:

```
<DL>
<DT><B>Blood Pressure</B>
<DD>Balm, Black Haw, <I>Garlic</I>, Hawthorn.
<DT><B>Bronchitis</B>
<DD>Angelica, <I>Aniseed, Caraway</I>, Grindelia.
<DT><B>Burns</B>
<DD>Aloe, Chickweed, <I>Elder</I>.
</DL>
```

Figure 5-2 shows the result, which is, if I do say so myself, quite attractive and similar to the original design. (By now, I hope that you can read the preceding HTML snippet and understand all the paired formatting tags. If not, you might want to skip back to Chapter 4 and study it a bit more to refresh your memory on text-style formatting.)

Figure 5-2 screenshot showing:

A Definition List - Microsoft Internet Explorer
File Edit View Go Favorites Help

Blood Pressure
 Balm, Black Haw, *Garlic*, Hawthorn.
Bronchitis
 Angelica, *Aniseed, Caraway*, Grindelia.
Burns
 Aloe, Chickweed, *Elder*.

Figure 5-2: *Medicinal herbs as a definition list*

The basic concept of a list is exhibited in the definition-list format: a pair of tags within which other tags have special meanings. Tags like <DT> and <DD> are context-sensitive tags: they only have any meaning if they appear within the <DL></DL> pair.

What happens if you use <DT> and <DD> without wrapping them in a <DL></DL> pair? Luckily, the result is identical to Figure 5-2: The default meanings of the <DT> and <DD> tags are consistent in the Web browser, whether they appear within a list or not. In a minute or two, you'll learn about a different context-sensitive tag that definitely will do the wrong thing if you don't ensure it's wrapped within its list-definition tags.

To avoid "lucky" defaults that aren't consistent across all browsers, always check your HTML formatting in multiple Web browsers before concluding that the formatting is correct. This can even trip up experienced Web page designers: my friend Linda has been developing some new pages for an existing Web site and she asked me to have a peek. I responded that it looked great, but was surprised she had left the default gray background (I'll show you how to change the page background color in Chapter 10). She was surprised by that: she'd forgotten that her particular Web browser used white, not gray, as the default background page color!

Unordered (Bulleted) Lists

Definition lists are handy, but the type of list that you see much more often on the World Wide Web is a bulleted list, also called an unordered list. Unordered lists start with `<UL>` and close with `</UL>`, and each list item is denoted by the list item (`<LI>`) tag. The format is similar to that of the definition list, as the following example shows:

```
Common Herbal remedies include:
<UL>
<LI>Blood Pressure— Balm, Black Haw, <I>Garlic</I>,
Hawthorn.
<LI>Bronchitis — Angelica, <I>Aniseed, Caraway</I>,
Grindelia.
<LI>Burns — Aloe, Chickweed, <I>Elder</I>.
</UL>
```

The result as viewed from a browser is attractive as Figure 5-3 shows.

Figure 5-3: A bulleted list

More useful is a combination of the two list types. The definition list looked very professional with the additions of boldface and indentation, but the bullets next to each item in the unordered list look slick, too. The solution is to nest lists within one another, as follows:

```
Common Herbal remedies include:
<DL>
<DT><B>Blood Pressure</B>
```

(continued)

```
(continued)
  <UL>
    <LI>Balm
    <LI>Black Haw
    <LI><I>Garlic</I>
    <LI>Hawthorn.
  </UL>
<DT><B>Bronchitis</B>
  <UL>
    <LI>Angelica
    <LI><I>Aniseed</I>
    <LI><I>Caraway</I>
    <LI>Grindelia.
  </UL>
<DT><B>Burns</B>
  <UL>
    <LI>Aloe
    <LI>Chickweed
    <LI><I>Elder</I>.
  </UL>
</DL>
```

Figure 5-4 shows the result of the preceding code, which is a very nice layout.

Figure 5-4: A nested list

Notice that I used some indentation on the HTML source in the previous listing to make it clearer which lists were subordinate to which. The indentation is ignored when the page is displayed in the browser, but it's a convenient organizational tool that I use frequently.

The output in Figure 5-4 is what you want. But is the HTML coding behind it the best possible approach? Think about it: You define terms with <DT>, but don't actually have any definition with <DD>. In this case, as it turns out, the nested list just adds to the confusion. You can achieve an identical output by skipping the definition list entirely, as the following, simpler example demonstrates:

```
Common herbal remedies include:
<P>
<B>Blood Pressure</B>
<UL>
   <LI>Balm
   <LI>Black Haw
   <LI><I>Garlic</I>
   <LI>Hawthorn.
</UL>
<B>Bronchitis</B>
<UL>
   <LI>Angelica
   <LI><I>Aniseed</I>
   <LI><I>Caraway</I>
   <LI>Grindelia.
</UL>
<B>Burns</B>
<UL>
   <LI>Aloe
   <LI>Chickweed
   <LI><I>Elder</I>.
</UL>
```

The preceding example illustrates the dangers and problems in description languages such as HTML. Because you can accomplish tasks in various ways, you have to wonder: Are the most obvious methods always the *best?*

Ordered (Numbered) Lists

What if you want to create a list, but with numbers instead of bullet points? The adage "simpler is better" suggests the formatting in the following example:

```
<HTML>
<HEAD>
<TITLE>Enchilada Recipe, v1</TITLE>
</HEAD>
<BODY>
<H2>Enchilada Sauce</H2>
1. Heat a large saucepan and saute the following
ingredients until soft:
<UL>
   <LI>Two tablespoons virgin olive oil
   <LI>Large onion, chopped
</UL>
2. Add a quart of water.<BR>
3. Sprinkle in a quarter-cup of flour.<BR>
4. Jazz it up by adding:
<UL>
   <LI>Two tablespoons chili powder
   <LI>Two teaspoons cumin
   <LI>One teaspoon garlic powder
</UL>
5. Finally, add a teaspoon of salt, if desired.
<BR>
Whisk as sauce thickens; then simmer for 20 minutes.
</BODY>
</HTML>
```

The result is quite attractive, as shown in Figure 5-5.

Before you carry this book into the kitchen, however, I need to tell you that I got confused while I typed this recipe. The water should be added at the end, *not* in Step 2.

Now what? You certainly don't want to have to renumber all the items in the numbered list. The situation calls for the cousin of the unordered list: The ordered list `<OL>`. The list ends with the close tag `</OL>`. Each item in the list has a list item tag `<LI>`.

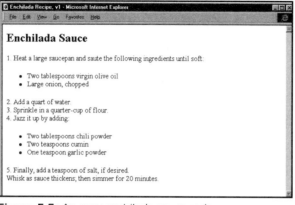

Figure 5-5: An easy enchilada sauce recipe

Now you can see what I was talking about earlier with context-sensitive tags: You specify the list items for an ordered list using exactly the same HTML tag as you do for an unordered, bullet list: <LI>. Without you specifying which type of list you want, how does the browser know what you mean? The meaning of the <LI> tag depends on what kind of list it lies within.

Following is how the recipe looks with my gaffe corrected and the HTML code rewritten to take advantage of the ordered list:

```
<HTML>
<HEAD>
<TITLE>Enchilada Recipe, v1</TITLE>
</HEAD>
<BODY>
<H2>Enchilada Sauce</H2>
<OL>
<LI>Heat a large saucepan, and saute the following
ingredients until soft:
<UL>
    <LI>Two tablespoons virgin olive oil
    <LI>Large onion, chopped
</UL>
<LI>Sprinkle in a quarter-cup of flour.
<LI>Jazz it up by adding:
<UL>
    <LI>Two tablespoons chili powder
    <LI>Two teaspoons cumin
```

(continued)

```
(continued)
        <LI>One teaspoon garlic powder
</UL>
<LI>Add a quart of water.
<LI>Finally, add a teaspoon of salt, if desired.
</OL>
Whisk as sauce thickens; then simmer for 20 minutes.
</BODY>
</HTML>
```

The output (see Figure 5-6) is not only correct, but is considerably more attractive because Web browsers automatically indent lists of this nature. As a result, the nested-list items are indented twice; once because they're part of the numbered list, and a second time because they're the list-within-the-list.

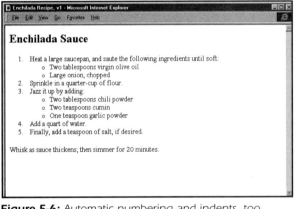

Figure 5-6: *Automatic numbering and indents, too.*

A final note on lists: There are a number of additional HTML tags from the early days of Web design that are supposed to offer further list-formatting capabilities, most notably `<DIR>` and `<MENU>`. Unfortunately, they were never widely implemented and are explicitly phased out in the HTML 4.0 specification. To produce multi-column text, by far the most common strategy turns out to be using zero-border tables, as we'll explore in depth in Chapter 9.

Special Characters in HTML Documents

If you're an alert reader, you may have noticed a typographical error in the recipe shown earlier. The recipe instructed the cook to *saute* the ingredients, yet the word should have an accent (*sauté*). Languages contain a variety of special characters that you may need to use, called diacriticals, particularly if you plan to present material in a language other than English. Not surprisingly, you can include special characters in HTML code by using special "tags," called *entities* or *entity references*.

Unlike the tags you've learned about so far, special character entities aren't neatly tucked into paired angle brackets (<>); instead, they always begin with an ampersand (&) and end with a semicolon (;). Most entities are somewhat mnemonic, as Table 5-1 shows.

Table 5-1	Special Characters in HTML	
Character	**HTML Code**	**Meaning**
&	&	ampersand
<	<	less than
>	>	greater than
á	á	lowercase *a* with acute accent
à	à	lowercase a with grave accent
â	â	lowercase *a* with circumflex
ä	ä	lowercase a with umlaut
å	å	lowercase *a* with ring
ç	ç	lowercase *c* with cedilla
ñ	ñ	lowercase *n* with tilde
ø	ø	lowercase *o* with slash
ß	ß	lowercase ess-zed symbol

Not all Web browsers can display all of these characters, particularly on Windows systems. Check them on a few browsers before you use them in your own Web page layout.

To create an uppercase version of one of the characters in Table 5-1, make the first letter of the formatting tag uppercase; `&Oslash;`, for example, produces an uppercase O with a slash through it, as in the word CØPENHAGEN (which you'd type as `C&Oslash;PENHAGEN`). To produce a different vowel with a diacritical mark, change the first letter of that tag. The word *desvàn,* for example, is correctly specified in an HTML document as `desv&agrave;n`.

The following example contains some foreign-language snippets so that you can see how these formatting tags work:

```
The following are formatted using &lt;b&gt; for
boldface and &lt;i&gt; for italics.
<P>
<B>Gibt es ein Caf&eacute; in der N&auml;he? </B><BR>
<I>Is there a caf&eacute; nearby?</I><P>
<B>Je voudrais un d&icirc;ner. </B><BR>
<I>I want to eat dinner.</I><P>
<B>Y una mesa por ma&ntilde;ana, por favor.</B><BR>
<I>And a table for tomorrow, please.</I><P>
<B>Oh! C'&egrave; una specialit&agrave; locale?</B><BR>
<I>Oh! Is there a local specialty?</I><P>
```

I don't actually speak French, German, Spanish, or Italian particularly well, but I guarantee the preceding set of questions will confuse just about any waiter in Europe! Figure 5-7 shows the result of the preceding formatting.

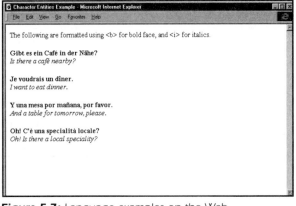

Figure 5-7: Language examples on the Web

Some problems occur with the international characters supported in the basic HTML code, not the least of these is that some elements are missing. This situation is improving; you no longer have to do without the upside-down question mark (¿), for example, if you want to write in Spanish. Use `&iquest;` to get this character in your documents. If you want to denote currency, you can code the pound sterling (£) and the cent sign (¢) as `&pound;` and `&cent;`, respectively. If you need to acknowledge copyrights, HTML now supports the copyright symbol (©) and the registered trademark symbol (®) with `&copy;` and `&reg;`, neither of which were supported in previous versions.

Nonbreaking spaces

A special character entity that people frequently use in Web page design is one that isn't even a character and doesn't even show up on the screen: the nonbreaking space. Included as ` `, it lets you force multiple spaces between items and ensures that items on either side of the space are always adjacent regardless of how the window may be sized.

Here's a typical scenario: you're working with a Web page where you want to have a word set off by a number of spaces on each side. Your first attempt would be:

```
words before           important           words after.
```

But that wouldn't work: the extra spaces would be ignored by the browser. The better way to specify that is:

```
words before     important     words
after.
```

which would accomplish exactly what you desire.

 I've made a copy of the entire entity reference list included in the HTML 4.0 specification. You can view it at *http://www.intuitive.com/coolweb/entities.html*.

Comments Within HTML Code

If you have spent any time working with complex markup languages such as HTML, you know that the ability to include tracking information and other comments can help you organize and remember your coding approach when you return to the pages later.

Fortunately, HTML supports a specific (if peculiar) notational format for comments within your documents. Any text surrounded by the elements <!-- and --> is considered to be a comment and is ignored by Web browsers, as you can see in the following example:

```
<HTML>
<!-- Last modified: 21 February 1995 -->
<TITLE>Enchilada Sauce</TITLE>
<!-- inspired by an old recipe I heard in Mexico,
but I must admit that it's going to be very
different, because even the flour is subtly different
in Juarez and elsewhere than in the States . . . -->
<H1>Enchilada Sauce</H1>
```

When I modify the Enchilada Sauce recipe by adding the comments shown above and feed the text to a Web browser, the browser does not display the comments, as you see in Figure 5-8 (which looks just like Figure 5-6).

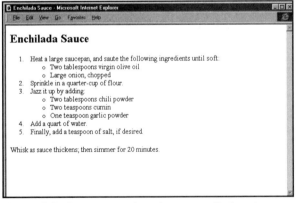

Figure 5-8: Comments galore, but none displayed

NOTE

You don't have to use comments, but if you're starting to build a complex Web space that offers many documents, just time-stamping each file could prove to be invaluable. Me? I sometimes put jokes in my Web pages as comments, just to see if people ever view the source!

Table 5-2 contains a summary of all commands you learned in this chapter:

Table 5-2	HTML Tags Covered in This Chapter	
Tag	**Close Tag**	**Meaning**
`<DD>`		Definition description
`<DL>`	`</DL>`	Definition list
`<DT>`		Definition term
`<LI>`		List item
`<OL>`	`</OL>`	Ordered (numbered) list
`TYPE=type`		Type of numbering. Possible values: A, a, I, i, 1
`START=x`		Starting number of ordered list
`<UL>`	`</UL>`	Unordered (bulleted) list
`TYPE=shape`		Shape of bullet to use. Possible values: circle, square, disc.
`<!--`	`-->`	Comments within HTML

Summary

Each chapter so far expands the depth and sophistication of your HTML skills. In this chapter, you learned about the various types of lists and how you can combine them — and many formatting tags — to produce attractive results. The next chapter is lots of fun. I show you the missing link — quite literally. Building on the explanation of URL formats in Chapter 2, the Chapter 6 talks about how to add links to other Web sites other places on the Internet.

Adding Pointers and Links

In This Chapter

Multiword HTML formatting tags

Pointers to other Web pages

Referencing non-Web information

Relative URLs

This chapter talks about actual HTML pointers to other Web and Internet resources, shows you how to include pointers to graphics and illustrations, and builds on the URL explanation found in Chapter 2.

At this point, you should feel comfortable with your HTML composition skills. You certainly know all the key facets of HTML, with three notable exceptions: adding links to other documents, adding internal links, and adding non-text information to your pages. This chapter shows you how to add links; Chapters 7 and 8 cover links to internal references and graphics.

Much of this information builds on the extensive discussion of *Uniform Resource Locators* (URLs) in Chapter 2. You may want to skim that chapter again to refresh your memory before you proceed.

Multiword HTML, Formatting Tags

So far, with one exception, every document formatting tag that you've seen has looked like a couple of letters surrounded by angle brackets. But, in fact, formatting tags can contain more information than just a few letters. All tags must begin with the open angle bracket, followed immediately by the *tag element;* no spaces are allowed. Inside the tag, however, you can specify other attributes in the format `attribute = value`. Want to include more than one word in the value area? Make sure you quote the value portion, as in `ALT="alternative information"`.

One of the tags you learned about earlier — `<PRE>`, for preformatted text — enables you to specify the set width that you'll be using, as shown in the following example:

```
It's a hot, hot day in the park and lots of people
are wandering around without clothes on! Here's a
text picture of what I'm talking about:
<PRE WIDTH=5>
   +----------------------
   |          CENSORED          |
   +----------------------
</PRE>
<I>Sorry, but until all the releases are signed,
I can't let you see this picture!</I>
```

In the preceding HTML example, I deliberately added an error: I specified that the preformatted text should be shown with the assumption that the maximum width of each line of text is five characters (`WIDTH=5`). The actual output makes it clear that the browser ignores this particular facet of formatting, as Figure 6-1 shows.

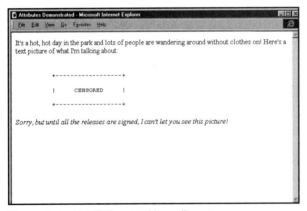

Figure 6-1: An HTML tag with attributes

The preceding proves to be a great example of one of the challenges facing Web page designers. The formatting information that you specify in your HTML code may not be interpreted as you think it will be (as shown in Figure 6-1) or at all.

Fortunately, most of the other HTML tags work if you specify the appropriate attributes. You can specify anything you want within an HTML formatting tag; the browser interprets only those attributes that make sense within the context of that tag. (You can have fun with this, too. How about a format tag of `<P aragraph=right-justified>`? This tag works identically to the format tag `<P>` by itself, because the attribute `aragraph` is — no big surprise — meaningless. On the other hand, it turns out that `<P ALIGN=right>` *does* work, but we'll talk more about this later in the book!)

 You can't have a space between the `<` and the tag name, but the elements are surrounded by spaces within the tag.

Pointers to Other Web Pages

The basic HTML formatting tag for external references is `<A>`, the *anchor* tag (its ending partner is `</A>`). It *must* contain attributes. Without any attributes, the `<A>` tag has no meaning and doesn't affect the formatting of information. The following, for example, would result in the display of text without formatting:

```
You can now visit <A>the White House</A> on-line!
```

To make this link *live,* meaning to make it cause a browser to do something, you need to specify the *hypertext reference* attribute: `HREF="value"`. The *value* can be empty if you don't know the actual information, but you must specify the attribute to make the link appear active to the viewer. You can rewrite the sentence as follows to make it a Web link:

```
You can now visit <A HREF="">the White House</A> on-line!
```

The preceding line of HTML code would be displayed in a Web browser with the portion between the `<A>` references (the anchor tags) appearing in blue with an underline or highlighted in some other fashion. The information that should be contained between the quotation marks is the URL for the Web page to which you want to link. The URL for the White House Web site, for example, is `http://www.whitehouse.gov/`.

 One classic problem that appears in HTML code is the use of curly, smart, or fancy quotes; Web servers just don't know what they mean. Double check to ensure that the quotes in your HTML documents are all straight: "like this" rather than "like this." The same applies to apostrophes and single quotes: make sure all the ones in your HTML documents are straight (') instead of curly (').

The following is the sentence with the correct, live hypertext link to the White House:

```
You can now visit <A HREF=http://www.whitehouse.gov/>the
White House</A> on-line!
```

The following is a more comprehensive example that combines various facets of HTML to build an interesting and attractive Web page:

```
<HTML>
<HEAD>
<TITLE>Visiting the White House and Other Government
Sites</TITLE>
</HEAD>
<BODY>
In cyberspace, you can virtually travel anywhere. Of the
various places that are fun to check out, however, few
are as interesting as the home page for the
<A HREF="http://www.whitehouse.gov/">White House</A>.
<H2>Government Sites on the Web</H2>
<UL>
<LI> <A HREF="http://www.fbi.gov/">Federal Bureau of
Investigation</A>
<LI> <A HREF="http://www.fedworld.gov/">FedWorld, a great
starting point for Government Research</A>
<LI> <A HREF="http://novel.nifl.gov/">National Institute
for Literacy
</A>
<LI> <A HREF="http://www.osmre.gov/">Office of Surface
Mining Reclamation and Enforcement</A>
<LI> <A HREF="http://www.sbaonline.sba.gov/">Small Business
Administration</A>
<LI> <A HREF="http://www.ssa.gov/">Social Security
Administration</A>
<LI> <A HREF="http://web.fie.com/fedix/aid.html">U.S.
Agency
for International Development (1)</A>
<LI> <A HREF="http://www.info.usaid.gov/">U.S. Agency for
International Development (2)</A>
</UL>
</BODY>
</HTML>
```

Figure 6-2 shows that the preceding HTML code is quite attractive when viewed in a browser. The ugliness and confusion of the URLs are neatly hidden; readers can simply click the name of an agency to connect directly to it.

Figure 6-2: Government sites on the Web

Notice in Figure 6-2 that the first link for the U.S. Agency for International Development is a complex URL with specified path and page. Also notice that the words White House in the prose at the beginning of the Web page now are highlighted and underlined, comprising a real Web link, too.

Understanding this section of this chapter is a terrific step forward in learning HTML. After you grasp how to build anchors, you'll be able to build Web tables of contents, starting points for exploration on the Internet, with the best of them.

But how do you point to information that isn't another Web document? The next section shows you how.

Referencing Non-Web Information

To point to material that isn't a Web document, you simply use the appropriate URL, as specified in Chapter 2. If you learn, for example, that the terrific FedWorld has an FTP site, you could build a URL for it, as follows:

```
ftp://ftp.fedworld.gov/
```

You could then drop the URL into your HTML code as a different value in an HREF attribute, as follows:

```
<A HREF=ftp://ftp.fedworld.gov/>The
FedWorld File Archive</A>
```

The following example shows how the HTML code I discussed in the preceding section looks with the addition of the FedWorld FTP site and the Consumer Product Safety Commission Gopher site:

```
<HTML>
<HEAD>
<TITLE>Visiting the White House and Other Government
Sites</TITLE>
</HEAD>
<BODY>
In cyberspace, you can virtually travel anywhere. Of the
various places that are fun to check out, however, few
are as interesting as the home page for the
<A HREF="http://www.whitehouse.gov/">White House</A>.
<H2>Government Sites on the Web</H2>
<UL>
<LI> <A HREF="http://www.fbi.gov/">Federal Bureau of
Investigation</A>
<LI> <A HREF="ftp://ftp.fedworld.gov/">The
FedWorld File Archive</A>
<LI> <A HREF="http://www.fedworld.gov/">FedWorld, a great
starting point for
government research</A>
<LI> <A HREF="http://novel.nifl.gov/">National Institute
for Literacy</A>
<LI> <A HREF="http://www.osmre.gov/">Office of Surface
Mining Reclamation and Enforcement</A>
<LI> <A HREF="http://www.sbaonline.sba.gov/">Small Business
Administration</A>
<LI> <A HREF="http://www.ssa.gov/">Social Security
Administration</A>
<LI> <A HREF="http://web.fie.com/web/fed/aid/">U.S. Agency
for International Development (1)</A>
<LI> <A HREF="http://www.info.usaid.gov/">U.S. Agency for
International Development (2)</A>
<LI> <A HREF="gopher://cpsc.gov/">U.S. Consumer Product
Safety Commission</A>
</UL>
</BODY>
</HTML>
```

In my Web browser, the preceding looks almost identical to the earlier version, except that it has two new items listed (see Figure 6-3). This example underscores one of the real strengths of the HTML language: *All anchors* (hypertext pointers), regardless of the kind of information they point to, look the same on a Web page. No funny little Gopher icons appear next to the Gopher items, no FTP icons appear next to FTP archives, and so on. The pages contain uniform sets of pointers to other spots on the Internet that contain interesting, valuable, or fun resources.

Figure 6-3: *Which sites are Gopher sites?*

In Chapter 1, Figure 1-7 showed how you can code various types of information in HTML format. I repeat that figure here as Figure 6-4.

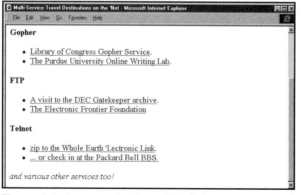

Figure 6-4: *An example of non-Web links*

Now you can appreciate the figure's surprising hidden complexity, as shown in the following HTML code:

```
<HTML>
<HEAD>
<TITLE>Multi-Service Travel Destinations on the
'Net</TITLE>
</HEAD><BODY>
<H1>Multi-Service Travel Destinations on the 'Net</H1>
<I>Did I miss one? <A
HREF="mailto:taylor@intuitive.com">Drop me a note!
</A></I>
<HR>
<B>Gopher</B>
<UL>
<LI><A HREF="gopher://gopher.loc.gov/">Library of Congress
Gopher Service.</A>
<LI><A HREF="gopher://owl.english.purdue.edu/">The Purdue
University Online Writing Lab.</A>
</UL>
<B>FTP</B>
<UL>
<LI><A HREF="ftp://gatekeeper.dec.com/">A visit to the DEC
Gatekeeper archive.</A>
<LI><A HREF="ftp://ftp.eff.org/">The Electronic Frontier
Foundation</A>
</UL>
<B>Telnet</B>
<UL>
<LI><A HREF="telnet://well.com/">zip to the Whole Earth
'Lectronic Link.
</A>
<LI><A HREF="telnet://bbs.packardbell.com/">...
or check in at the Packard Bell BBS.</A>
</UL>
<I>and various other services too!</I>
</BODY>
</HTML>
```

Of all the links demonstrated in this Web document, I think that the most notable is the `mailto:` link in the first line of text. Notice that the `mailto:` link is not presented as

```
<A HREF="mailto:taylor@intuitive.com">Click here</A> to
send me mail.
```

Instead, the link is smoothly and transparently integrated into the prose:

```
<A HREF="mailto:taylor@intuitive.com">Drop me a
note!</A></I>
```

 Try to avoid using *Click here* and similar labels for hypertext tags; cool Web pages come from creative, meaningful, and unobtrusive integration of links into the text.

Relative URLs

Being able to link to external information sources and sites on the Internet clearly is a huge boon to Web designers, but if you stopped at that and never learned any more, you'd be missing half the picture. The one piece that you still need to learn is how to reference other documents on your own server.

Although *personal* home pages often have a simple format similar to the examples in this chapter (that is, a few paragraphs about the person, perhaps a graphic or two, and then a list of favorite sites on the Web), more complex and sophisticated sites have a number of different Web documents available. These sites include the appropriate links to the other documents on the site so readers can easily jump between them.

There is an easy way and a hard way to reference internal documents (documents on your server). The hard way builds on the earlier examples: You figure out the full URL of each page and use those URLs as the hypertext reference tags. The easy way to reference another document on your server is to specify the document name only (or path and name) without any of the URL preface information. If you have a starting page called `home.html` and a second page called `resume.html` in the same folder or directory on the server, for example, you could create the following link:

```
You're welcome to <A HREF="resume.html">read my
resume</A>.
```

(Note: Purists would use the HTML code résumé instead of resume, of course.)

Relative URLs work by having the browser preface the hostname and path of the current page to each reference, so if your Web page is at `http://www.college.edu/joe/home.html` and there was a relative URL reference `A HREF=research.html`, then the actual reference built by the browser when it requested the page would be `http://www.college.edu/joe/research.html`.

You can change the default prefix for links on your page if you need to by using the `<BASE HREF=`*new-base-URL*`>` tag. For example: `<BASE HREF=http://alt-server.college.edu/joe/>` would cause all relative URLs to be resolved to the `alt-server` host rather than the `www` host.

Perhaps you want to make several files accessible on your Web server and you want some sensible way to organize them. A hierarchical directory structure can prove to be a big advantage.

Imagine you are building a Web site for a local delicatessen. In addition to the home page, you also want to have a variety of information about the sandwiches and soups available online. Planning for future growth, you might opt to organize the information as shown in Figure 6-5.

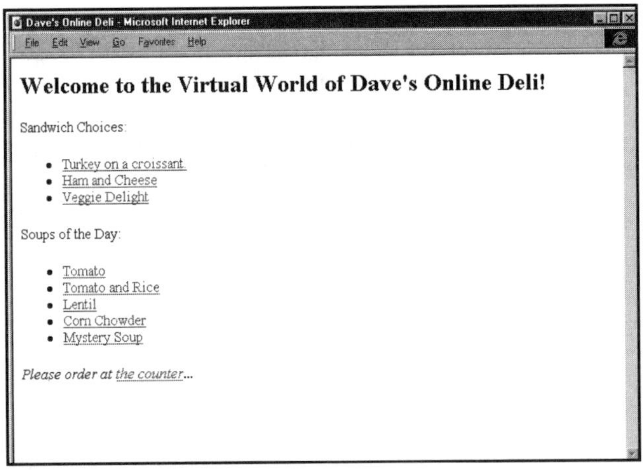

Dave's Online Deli - Microsoft Internet Explorer

File Edit View Go Favorites Help

Welcome to the Virtual World of Dave's Online Deli!

Sandwich Choices:

- Turkey on a croissant
- Ham and Cheese
- Veggie Delight

Soups of the Day:

- Tomato
- Tomato and Rice
- Lentil
- Corn Chowder
- Mystery Soup

Please order at the counter...

Figure 6-5: *Organizing the deli menu data*

Now, when people connect to the home page, the base URL (the address of the top-level menu itself), they will see the formatted results of the following HTML code:

```
<HTML>
<HEAD>
<TITLE>Dave's Online Deli</TITLE>
</HEAD><BODY>
<H2>Welcome to the Virtual World of Dave's Online
Deli!</H2>
Sandwich Choices:
<UL>
<LI><A HREF="sandwiches/turkey.html">Turkey on a
croissant.</A>
<LI><A HREF="sandwiches/ham.html">Ham and Cheese</A>
<LI><A HREF="sandwiches/veggie.html">Veggie Delight</A>
</UL>
Soups of the Day:
<UL>
<LI><A HREF="soups/tomato.html">Tomato</A>
<LI><A HREF="soups/tomato.html">Tomato and Rice</A>
<LI><A HREF="soups/lentil.html">Lentil</A>
<LI><A HREF="soups/corn-chowder.html">Corn Chowder</A>
<LI><A HREF="soups/mystery.html">Mystery Soup</A>
</UL>
<I>Please order at <A HREF="order-counter.html">the
counter</A> . . .
</I>
</BODY>
</HTML>
```

The new virtual deli *home page* (which Web folks call the *root*, or the first page that visitors see when reaching a site) would be formatted as previously shown in Figure 6-5.

You can't see it, but the HTML code contains an inadvertent error. To understand the problem — a relatively common one in complex documents like this — consider what happens if someone wants more information about the tomato and rice soup instead of the tomato soup. Both soup choices point to the same second page: <u>soups/tomato.html</u>, but this will only make sense to the user if that page has information on both soups. Odds are, it's just for the tomato soup, which could leave fans of tomato and rice (one of my favorites) a bit baffled.

If a Web user pops into the virtual deli and wants to find out more about the lentil soup, for example, he or she might click the hypertext link `Lentil`. The user would then see the page `soups/lentil.html`, offering information about the soup and perhaps even including a picture. But how could you add a link back to the deli home page? Consider the following listing, paying close attention to the last few lines:

```
<HTML>
<HEAD>
<TITLE>Lentil Soup: A Cornerstone of the Virtual
Deli</TITLE>
</HEAD>
<BODY>
<H1>Lentil Soup</H1>
It will come as no surprise to regular patrons of the
Virtual Deli that our lentil soup has quickly become one
of the most popular items. With its combination of six
different lentil beans, some succulent organic vegetables
and our carefully filtered fresh spring water, a hot bowl
of our lentil soup on a cold day is unquestionably one of
life's pleasures.
<P>
We'd love to tell you the recipe too, but we feel like you
really need come in and try it for yourself.
<P>
<B>We Also Recommend: <A HREF="../sandwiches/veggie.html">
a veggie sandwich to accompany.</A></B>
<HR>
<A HREF="../deli.html">Back up to the main menu.</A>
</BODY>
</HTML>
```

When visitors to the virtual deli arrive at the page created by the preceding HTML text, they have moved down a level in the server's hierarchical directory structure, but they don't know that. The URLs in the document, however, tell the story. The main menu is `../deli.html`. The recommended sandwich to accompany the soup is in another directory — hence its `../sandwiches/` folder specification. See Figure 6-6 to see what the page looks like from a browser (Explorer).

Figure 6-6: The lentil soup special

TIP

In the previous listings, you can see the use of relative filename addresses. For example, "../deli.html" pops up one level in the file system to find the deli.html page. This makes for easy HTML coding, but beware that problems can easily arise if you move any of the pages around without the rest of the files.

Having shorter URLs is a compelling reason to use relative URLs in your Web page design, but there's an even better reason: Your Web site (the collection of pages and graphics) is much more portable from system to system with relative addressing.

Imagine you've rented space from Best Internet Communications, say, and your home page address is http://www.best.com/~myacct/. Each absolute reference, therefore, has that address as the first portion, so the graphic myface.gif in the photos directory ends up with the URL http://www.best.com/~myacct/photos/myface.gif.

What if you end up registering your own domain a few weeks later and want to have all the references to the www.best.com domain vanish? With absolute URLs, you'd be stuck having to edit every single reference in every HTML file — a mondo drag. With relative URLs, on the other hand, where the photo would be referenced as photos/myface.gif, you'd simply move the entire set of files and graphics and it would work without a single modification!

Table 6-1 contains a summary of the HTML tags covered in this chapter.

Table 6-1	Summary of Tags in This Chapter	
HTML Tag	**Close Tag**	**Meaning**
<A>	</A>	Anchor tag
HREF=url		Pointer to hypertext reference

Summary

In this chapter, you learned how to include links to other sites on the World Wide Web and throughout the Internet. You also learned how to organize a set of Web documents in manageable folders and how to specify other documents on your own server with minimal fuss. Chapter 7 focuses on internal document references, which enable you to include a table of contents at the top of a large Web document. It also explains how to use internal document markers as hot links that enable people to jump to a specific spot in any Web document.

Internal Document References

In This Chapter

Defining Web document jump targets

Adding jump hot links to your Web pages

Jumping to organized lists

Linking to jump targets in external documents

This chapter shows you how to add a table of contents to a large Web document and use that table as a hot link to allow people to jump to a specific spot in that same or different document on your server.

In Chapter 6, you learned about the anchor tag <A>; you also learned how to use the HREF attribute to build links to other pages on the World Wide Web. Another, equally valuable use for the <A> tag is the internal document reference — the focus of this chapter. You will find that as documents become larger, the capability to zoom (jump) to a predefined spot in a document can be invaluable.

Defining Web Document Jump Targets

I commented in the last chapter that the anchor tag <A> is the first of the major HTML formatting tags in the book that enable you to specify attributes. Note that rather than a format like <URL="something"> </URL>, which would be more consistent with the other HTML tags you've seen so far, the format of the anchor tag is <A *something*></A>. This format is useful because some complex tags, particularly the instructions for including graphics, have dozens of variations. Imagine `<IMAGELEFTBOTTOM="imagefile">` or something similar. Instead, attributes were included in the design of HTML to allow a wide variety of different formats to be easily specified.

The greatest value of these attributes in formatting tags is that you can provide a wonderful sense of consistency in the interface and in the presentation of information. For example, you can have half your links lead to other pages on the Web, with three links moving the reader farther down in the document and the rest of the links leading to other pages on your own server. The links will all have the same appearance (blue and underlined, in most cases) and function (causing the browser to "jump" directly to the specified information).

Until now, the documents shown in this book have been short, with the majority of the information confined to the visible browser-window area. Such an approach to Web document design results in pages that are easy to navigate. Sometimes, however, it's impossible to keep a document from stretching over several screens.

If I wanted to write this chapter as an HTML document, I could make each section a different document. Even then, however, some of those sections would be sufficiently long that readers would be forced to scroll down to find the information they wanted. A better design is one in which the entire chapter is a single document, but the topic headers are actually links to the appropriate spots further down in the page. Clicking a table of contents entry, for example, would move you to that section of the document instantly.

One constant challenge for Web page designers is figuring out when a document works best as a single HTML file and when it works best as a set of files. My rule of thumb is to break pages at logical jump points and to minimize load time for readers. This chapter could be a single HTML document, but the book itself would clearly be a set of separate documents.

The targets of internal Web document jumps are known as *named anchors*. The HTML tag for an anchor point is an alternate value for the `<A>` tag: `<A name=value>`. The value can be any sequence of characters, numbers, and punctuation marks, but I recommend that you stick with a strategy of mnemonic anchor names, such as `section1` or `references`. Some browser software insists that all characters in the anchor be in lowercase, so you may want to experiment before you build a complex document or stick with lowercase to avoid any potential problems.

The following shows how a set of tags might look within a document on Web design guidelines. The anchors are built from the rule name and specific rule number, which can then be referenced as links in the rest of the document. Notice there are no spaces in anchor names:

```
<A NAME="guidelines">
<CENTER>
<H1>WEB DESIGN GUIDELINES</H1></A>
</CENTER>
<BLOCKQUOTE>
<DL>
<A NAME="rule1">
<DT><B>Rule #1:</A>
<DD>Understand the intended users and uses of your
Web site then focus the design and layout around their
needs
and interests.</B>
</DL>
<DL>
<A NAME="rule2">
<DT><B>Rule #2:</A>
<DD>Be sparing with graphical elements.</B>
</DL>
<DL>
<A NAME="rule3">
<DT><B>Rule #3:</A>
<DD>Pages should load within no more than
thirty seconds, including all graphical elements.</B>
</DL>
<DL>
<A NAME="rule4">
<DT><B>Rule #4:</A>
<DD>Minimize color palettes.</B>
</DL>
<DL>
<A NAME="rule5">
<DT><B>Rule #5:</A>
</DL>
</BLOCKQUOTE>
```

Viewed in a Web browser (see Figure 7-1), the preceding document looks like an attractive list of design rules. Because anchors are destinations on the current page rather than links to go elsewhere, the text between the <A NAME> and </A> is not highlighted in any way when displayed. However, because the definition of the destination point is a regular anchor tag — albeit with different attributes than an HREF — it does need to be closed like any other paired tag, so you need to ensure that you have a corresponding </A> for each named anchor. Because the text isn't high-lighted, you can have the </A> occur immediately after the spot is defined, as in <A NAME=rule4></A>. Early versions of HTML required something else to appear within any paired tag, however, so you'll see layouts similar to the above quite commonly on Web pages.

What I've done in this example is not only add links to each of the design guidelines, but also add a link to the very top of the document, which could then easily be used as a fast shortcut to the top of the page from anywhere in the document.

Note the introduction of the new tag <BLOCKQUOTE>. Text between <BLOCKQUOTE> and </BLOCKQUOTE> tags is block-indented; that is, indented a tab stop from both the left and right margins. I use <BLOCKQUOTE> quite a bit on my Web pages, and you'll find it's a general purpose indentation tag that will be a valuable addition to your Web design toolbox. The other new tag — <CENTER> — centers material horizontally on the page. I explore this tag a bit more in Chapter 10.

```
Intuitive Systems - Rules for Cool Web Pages - SUMMARY - Microsoft Internet Explorer   _ □ ×
 File  Edit  View  Go  Favorites  Help

                    WEB DESIGN GUIDELINES

   Rule #1:
         Understand the intended users and uses of your Web site then focus the
         design and layout around their needs and interests.

   Rule #2:
         Be sparing with graphical elements.

   Rule #3:
         Pages should load within no more than thirty seconds, including all
         graphical elements.

   Rule #4:
         Minimize color palettes.

   Rule #5:
         Design horizontally-oriented graphical elements where possible.
```

Figure 7-1: Helpful design guidelines

Adding Jump Links to Your Web Pages

The partner of an anchor in HTML documents is the formatting tag that defines the *jump*, or active link, within the document. It's a variant on the `<A>` tag that you already know; the necessary attribute turns out to be another `HREF` hypertext reference, this time with the URL replaced by the anchor name and prefaced by a number sign (#).

For example, if the *anchor* that you want to connect to is specified as `<A NAME="guidelines">`, as in the example above, you would specify the jump as `<A HREF="#guidelines">go to the guidelines</A>`.

In creating cool Web documents, the goal is to avoid phrases such as the following:

```
<A HREF="#guidelines">Click here</A> to see the
guidelines.
```

Instead, try to integrate the references more smoothly into the text, as follows:

```
<A HREF="#guidelines">Design Guidelines</A>.
```

One common way you might utilize the named anchors is to create a succinct summary line at the top of the document. Recall that `<FONT SIZE=2>` will create small type, so you should be able to see immediately what's going here:

```
<A NAME="guidelines">
<CENTER>
<H1>WEB DESIGN GUIDELINES</H1></A>
<font size=2>
<a href=#rule1>Rule 1</a> |
<a href=#rule2>Rule 2</a> |
<a href=#rule3>Rule 3</a> |
<a href=#rule4>Rule 4</a>
</font>
<p>
</CENTER>
<BLOCKQUOTE>
<DL>
```

(continued)

```
(continued)
<A NAME="rule1">
<DT><B>Rule #1:</A>
<DD>Understand the intended users and uses of your
Web site then focus the design and layout around their
needs
and interests.</B>
</DL>
<DL>
<A NAME="rule2">
<DT><B>Rule #2:</A>
<DD>Be sparing with graphical elements.</B>
</DL>
<DL>
<A NAME="rule3">
<DT><B>Rule #3:</A>
<DD>Pages should load within no more than
thirty seconds, including all graphical elements.</B>
</DL>
<DL>
<A NAME="rule4">
<DT><B>Rule #4:</A>
<DD>Minimize color palettes.</B>
</DL>
</BLOCKQUOTE>
```

This would extend the previous page to offer users a very simple way to jump to a specific guideline without having to scroll, as Figure 7-2 shows.

Figure 7-2: Guidelines, plus a quick jump list on top

For another way to use internal references, consider the following HTML that might replace the overly succinct introduction in the previous example. Notice how the links are much more informative and integrate more smoothly into the presentation:

```
<CENTER>
<A NAME="top">
<H1>WEB DESIGN GUIDELINES</H1></A>
</CENTER>
While the number of Web pages that are available online
increases every day, the quality of these pages seems to
be declining, with more and more people (and programs, to
be fair) violating basic design guidelines. There are
a variety of reasons involved, but one that's
common is a simple lack of experience with layout.
<P>
Some design rules might seem obscure, like
<A HREF="#rule4">minimizing the
color palette size</A>, which is
clearly specific to the World Wide Web, but
others, such as being
<A HREF="#rule2">sparing
with graphical elements</A> and
<A HREF="#rule1">focusing on the intended
user of the page</A>, are
basic rules of <I>any</I> design.
<P>
The most important idea is that <FONT COLOR=GREEN><B>
good web pages start with good content</B></FONT>
rather than with good form, layout or design. The
design should spring from the content and the
information therein.
```

In a browser, the Web design guidelines are quite pleasing to the eye and easy to navigate. All the hot links and anchor information are appropriately hidden from view or sufficiently subtle that the reader can focus on the material itself (see Figure 7-3).

What I'm showing in this example of rules is really an implementation of footnotes or citations in articles. Earlier in the book, I explained that hypertext is a logical extension of our existing writing style — with parenthetical remarks, word definitions in the margin, footnotes, and the like. Hypertext is more than just links from document to document, however, and HTML enables you to create all these reference items within the same page.

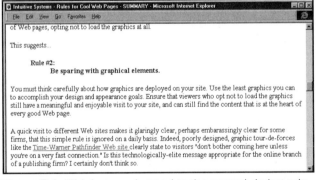

Figure 7-3: Design commentary with reference hot links

To go back a bit in time, when scholars first envisioned the need for citations in research to defend and explain where particular views and ideas originate, what they imagined is surprisingly close to what we can now produce with Web documents. If you are surprised by something in such an article, or if the article whetted your appetite for a more extensive treatment of the subject, you can click the relevant citation. You then instantly move to a references section, and the appropriate citation is shifted to the top of the screen so that you can learn where to get further information.

Figure 7-4 shows what would happen if you wanted more information on the second rule, referenced in the document with the `<A HREF="#rule2">` link.

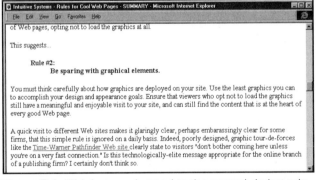

Figure 7-4: Web browser jumped to the second design rule

One thing to keep in mind when you specify your anchor points is that the *exact* spot of the reference becomes the top of the displayed document. A sequence such as the following shows the possible danger with this:

```
<H2>Bananas</H2>
<A NAME="bananas">The banana</A>
is one of the most exotic, yet most easily purchased,
fruits in the world.
```

The HTML source seems reasonable, but the resulting behavior will not be what you seek: Users who jump to the "bananas" tag will have "The banana is . . ." as the first line of their window; the <H2> header will be one line off screen.

A much better strategy is to flip the two items, as follows:

```
<A NAME="bananas">
<H2>Bananas</H2></A>
The banana is one of the most exotic, yet most easily
purchased, fruits in the world.
```

Always test your Web documents before unleashing them on the world. I can't overemphasize this. Subtle problems, such as where anchor tags are placed, are classic mistakes found in, otherwise, spiffy Web pages.

Jumping into Organized Lists

Anchors and jump points also are commonly used to help readers navigate large lists of alphabetically sorted information. Consider the following simple phone book layout:

```
<TITLE>Jazz Institute Internal Phone Book</TITLE>
<H1>Jazz Institute Internal Phone Book</H1>
<P>
Section Shortcut:
<A HREF="#a-c">[A-C]</A>
<A HREF="#d-h">[D-H]</A>
<A HREF="#i-l">[I-L]</A>
<A HREF="#m-n">[M-N]</A>
<A HREF="#o-s">[O-S]</A>
<A HREF="#t-z">[T-Z]</A><BR>
<H2><A NAME="a-c">A-C</A></H2>
Benson, George (x5531)<BR>
```

(continued)

```
(continued)
Coleman, Ornette (x5143)<BR>
Coltrane, John (x5544)
<H2><A NAME="d-h">D-H</A></H2>
Dorsey, Tom (x9412)<BR>
Ellington, Duke (x3133)<BR>
Getz, Stan (x1222)<BR>
<H2><A NAME="i-l">I-L</A></H2>
Jackson, Milt (x0434)<BR>
Laffite, Guy (x5358)<BR>
<H2><A NAME="m-n">M-N</A></H2>
Monk, Thelonious (x3333)<BR>
Noone, Jimmie (x5123)<BR>
<H2><A NAME="o-s">O-S</A></H2>
Parker, Charlie (x4141)<BR>
Peterson, Oscar (x8983)<BR>
Reinhardt, Django (x5351)<BR>
<H2><A NAME="t-z">T-Z</A></H2>
Taylor, Billy (x3311)<BR>
Tyner, McCoy (x4131)<BR>
Waller, Fats (x1321)<BR>
```

Although the HTML in the preceding example is complex, Figure 7-5 shows that the result not only looks attractive, but is also quite a useful way to present the information.

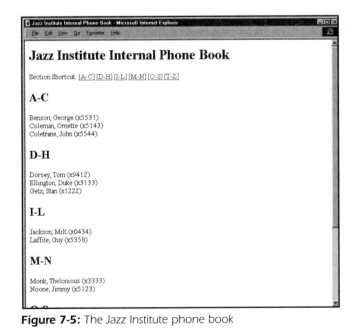

Figure 7-5: The Jazz Institute phone book

You can start to get a feeling of how complex HTML text can become if you imagine that each entry in the phone list actually is a link to that person's home page or other material somewhere else on the Web. Every line of information displayed in the browser could easily be the result of four or more lines of HTML.

Linking to Jump Targets in External Documents

Now that you're familiar with the concept of jumping around within a single document, you'll be glad to hear that you can also add the *#anchor* notation to the end of any Web URL to make that link move directly to the specific anchor point in the document.

Suppose, for example, the Web design guidelines page resided on a system called `www.intuitive.com` and that its full URL was `http://www.intuitive.com/articles/design-guide.html`. (It is, actually. Try it!)

A visit to the page reveals that a variety of anchor tags are embedded in the HTML, including the `#highlights` reference at the beginning of the document, enabling you to jump directly to the executive summary. You could link directly to that spot from another Web page, as in the following example:

```
<CENTER>
<FONT SIZE=6><B>What Makes a Good Web Page?</B></FONT><BR>
<A HREF="#highlights">read the highlights</A>
</CENTER><P>
There's no consensus on what makes for good Web design
and various companies offer their own set of guidelines
for open-minded Web developers. One of the most succinct
and easily understood is
<A HREF="http://www.intuitive.com/articles/design-
guide.html">the
Intuitive Systems Web design guidelines</A>. If you're
impatient like I am, however, you'll be glad
to know that you can skip the opening prose and
<A HREF="http://www.intuitive.com/articles/design-
guide.html#rules">read the
guidelines thereon</A>.
```

(continued)

```
(continued)
<P>
<A NAME="highlights">
<B>Here are the highlights</B></A><BR>
<UL>
<LI><A HREF="http://www.intuitive.com/articles/design-
guide.html#rule1">Design for your intended users</A>
<LI><A HREF="http://www.intuitive.com/articles/design-
guide.html#rule2">Be sparing with graphical elements</A>
<LI><A HREF="http://www.intuitive.com/articles/design-
guide.html#rule3">Pages should
load in less than 30 seconds</A>
<LI><A HREF="http://www.intuitive.com/articles/design-
guide.html#rule4">Minimize color palettes</A>
<LI><A HREF="http://www.intuitive.com/articles/design-
guide.html#rule5">Prefer horizontally oriented graphics</A>
<LI><A HREF="http://www.intuitive.com/articles/design-
guide.html#rule6">Web sites should always
be content-centric</A>
<LI><A HREF="http://www.intuitive.com/articles/design-
guide.html#rule7">One qualified visitor is
worth a dozen anonymous browsers</A>
<LI><A HREF="http://www.intuitive.com/articles/design-
guide.html#rule8">Pages should
constantly be new and up to date.</A>
</UL>
```

The prose is displayed in a Web browser, as you would expect. Figure 7-6 shows that the external reference links are displayed identically to the internal HREF; they're all underlined and in blue.

Pointing to external anchors can be useful for linking to large Web documents, which contain a great deal of information that may otherwise confuse your reader. Be careful: If anyone but you maintains the anchors, the names may change, the documents may be reorganized, or other changes may suddenly invalidate your links *without you even knowing about it.* There's always a chance that a whole document will vanish from the Web, of course, but the chance that a link *within* a document will change is considerably higher.

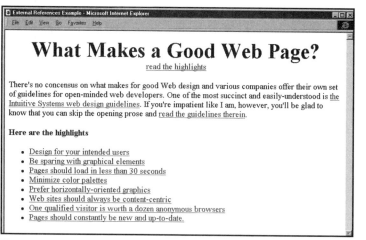

Figure 7-6: Most of these link to external anchors

Table 7-1 contains a summary of the HTML-tag information covered in this chapter.

Table 7-1	Summary of Tags in This Chapter	
HTML Tag	**Close Tag**	**Meaning**
<A	</A>	Anchor tag
HREF=#name		Reference to internal anchor name
NAME=name		Defining an internal anchor

Summary

This chapter introduced two useful devices for organizing and navigating large Web documents: internal anchors and links to those anchors. The same links can be accessed as part of a general Web URL, but beware: Anchor names may change or move without your knowledge, thereby invalidating your connection. Chapter 8 shows you how to make your Web pages even more visually appealing by adding graphics.

Adding Graphics to Jazz Up Your Pages

In This Chapter

Different image formats

Including images in Web documents

Text alternatives for text-based browsers

Image alignment options

Where to find images

Transparent colors

Audio, video, and other media

This chapter shows you how to jazz up your Web pages with multimedia elements and includes discussion of how to create and edit graphic images, audio, and even video clips. This is the only chapter in the book that contains platform-specific information. Here you will learn about graphical editors and GIF translators for Macintosh and PC/Windows.

You have learned enough HTML by this point to make you dangerous: You should be able to create complex webs of information with sophisticated text formatting. But that isn't all there is to Web design; the missing ingredient in this soup is graphics. The capability to place large and small images — and even to make them hypertext references — is a crucial element of good Web page design — not to mention that it's great fun to have Web pages with pictures, audio, and even video clips!

In this chapter, I diverge slightly from the platform-independent approach that I have taken in this book so far and delve into some specifics of creating graphics and images for Windows PCs and Macintoshes. Most of the examples in this chapter were created with programs that are available for both Macintosh and Windows machines.

Different Image Formats

Before we go further with the HTML tag itself, it's important for us to spend some time talking about the acceptable graphic formats, because there are hundreds of different formats and only two are really widely understood by Web browser software. The two formats supported by HTML are:

➡ GIF: CompuServe's *Graphics Interchange Format*

➡ JPEG: *Joint Photographic Expert Group* format

If you have graphics in another format — for example, TIFF, BMP, PCX, or PICT — a user at the other end of the Web wire may be able to display those graphics, but only in a separate application, which may or may not be automatically launched by their Web browser.

There is a new graphics format called *Portable Network Graphic*, or PNG (pronounce it "ping" to sound like an expert), that's being promoted by the big software companies. PNG offers many of the best capabilities of both GIF and JPEG. Stay tuned to the PNG home page — `http://www.wco.com/~png/` — because once it's widely supported in graphics programs and Web browsers, it'll be a real winner!

Some older Web browsers support only the GIF format, which is the de facto standard for graphics on the Web. GIF is a great thing, and the addition of support for graphics clearly has been a boon to the Web, but many of the most powerful graphics programs haven't supported the GIF format until quite recently. Why? Typical graphics programs support PICT (for the Mac), BMP, and PCX (for Windows), and various proprietary formats, but supporting GIF requires software developers to license the encoding technologies separately, which most of those companies are loath to do.

The trade-off between GIF and JPEG formats is in the subtleties. GIF images can only use a maximum of 256 colors, whereas JPEG supports millions of unique colors in a graphic (though whether they'll show up correctly depends on the particular display system the user has in his or her computer). Both graphic formats attempt to compress images to shrink down the file size, but because they compress in different ways, some images will prove considerably smaller in one format versus the other.

The main reason that the GIF image format is so attractive to Web design-ers, however, isn't that it has a small color palette, but that you can trim down the palette to the bare minimum you need for a particular graphic and, thereby, shrink down its file size dramatically.

Graphic images are built out of pixels: individual dots of information in the graphic. With a GIF image, each pixel can have one of up to 256 different colors, but what if, in fact, the image only uses two colors instead of 256? Perhaps it's a company logo or something similar. In that case, you can chop the size of the GIF image down quite a bit: each pixel requires one bit of information (there are 8 bits in a byte), versus 8 bits of information for the full 256-color option. In other words, you've just chopped your file down to one eighth its original size.

With any good graphics editor, you can easily trim your color palette to minimize your file sizes; officially, GIF supports 1-bit (2 color), 2-bit (4 color), 4-bit (64 color) and 8-bit (256 color) formats. I should point out that with 1-bit, it's *any* two colors you can work with, so a blueprint that's white on light blue is still only a 1-bit image.

While GIF supports up to 256 colors, not all of these colors are the same on both the Mac and PC, which can be a nightmare. A picture that looks great on your PC looks awful on a Mac, and vice versa. To avoid this, you will want to explore the so-called Netscape-safe Color Palette, a set of 216 colors that are identical on both computers.

 You can see all 216 safe colors on the same Web page by looking on the CD-ROM for the file "safe-colors.html" in the "Examples" folder, or look online at http://www.intuitive.com/safe-colors.html

Other useful characteristics of GIF images are that you can designate any one color as a transparent color — we'll look at that more closely later in this chapter — and you can create graphics that are interlaced. If you've been to a Web page and watched the images come in line by line, going from out of focus into their final crisp rendition, that's what you've been seeing, and while it adds about 5–10 percent to the size of the file, if your images are large, interlacing is a nice way to let the user get a rough idea of what they're downloading.

In general, then, GIF format is used for the majority of images on the Web, particularly buttons, banners, and similar, due to their smaller file size. JPEG is necessary when you want to be able to most closely duplicate the exact colors of the original image. For example, a friend of mine has a Web site where he highlights some of his many excellent nature photographs, and for photographic reproduction, it's imperative that he use JPEG format for all his images. Otherwise, the nuances of color would be lost.

See the photographs I'm talking about at:

```
http://www.sagarmatha.com/calendar/
```

For your Web pages, you will mostly want your images to be in GIF format. Fortunately, a variety of freeware and shareware programs — all available on the Net — can translate common graphics formats into GIF format. For the Mac, I recommend GraphicConverter; for Windows systems, you can use Paint Shop Pro or Lview Pro. If you have the latest version of your graphics editor or image-manipulation program, it probably has the ability to save directly into GIF format, too. Check with the vendor or your local computer store to make sure. A great starting point for finding graphics software packages on the Net is Yahoo! Specifically, go to: `http://www.yahoo.com/Computers/Software/Graphics/` and have a look at what they offer.

If you want to find the specific shareware packages mentioned above, here are their official Web site addresses:

➡ GraphicConverter: `http://www.lemkesoft.de/`
➡ Paint Shop Pro: `http://www.jasc.com/psp.html`
➡ Lview Pro: `http://www.lview.com/`

Including Images in Web Pages

Including images in a Web document is easy — you use the `<IMG>` (*image*) format tag. Just like the `<A>` anchor tag, the IMG tag has a single critical attribute, `SRC=graphicname`, and like the `<HR>` horizontal rule, there's no paired close tag. To include the graphic banner.gif, the HTML would be:

```
<IMG SRC=banner.gif>
```

When you have a GIF file, the `<IMG>` tag is used to place that file in the text. Suppose that I have a file called black-box.gif that I want to use as the opening graphic in my Web page. The following example shows how this file might appear in an HTML document:

Animated GIF Images

Special note should be made of something called *animated GIFs*. These are based on a very simple premise that's remarkably like the flip-books of yore: a sequence of graphic images with subtle changes between them can be cycled in such a way as to appear to be animated. Frankly, that's how film works, too. If you've ever looked at an individual cel of a motion picture reel, you know that it's a still image. Watch the *still* images at a sufficiently fast speed and you'll have the illusion of motion and life.

Animated GIF images are available through a variety of sources, particularly the clip-image archive packages and Web sites listed below, but you can also create your own with some shareware animation packages. For the Macintosh, I recommend GIFBuilder, and for Windows 95, I suggest you explore GIF Construction Set. Here are their homes on the Web:

- GIFBuilder:
  `http://iawww.epfl.ch/Staff/Yves.Piguet/clip2gif-home/GifBuilder.html`

- GIF Construction Set:
  `http://www.mindworkshop.com/alchemy/gifcon.html`

```
<HTML>
<HEAD>
<TITLE>The Dark Box</TITLE>
</HEAD><BODY>
<IMG SRC="black-box.gff">
<H1>Welcome to the Dark Box</H1>
There are boxes you've encountered that aren't very well
lit, there are boxes that might even be
sealed, but I guarantee that you've never seen
anything quite as terrifying as
<I>The Dark Box</I>.
<P>
Dare you continue? <A HREF="blackbox2.html">yes</A> no.
</BODY>
</HTML>
```

As you can see, `<IMG>` is a formatting tag that enables you to specify different attributes. The one attribute that must appear in the `<IMG>` tag is a specification of the image source file itself, in the format `SRC=filename`. Figure 8-1 shows how the preceding HTML snippet appears when viewed in a browser.

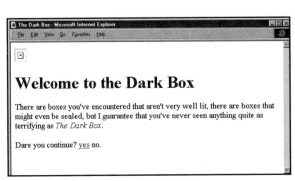

Figure 8-1: Graphics specified, but not loaded

The small box in Figure 8-1 that contains the red box (well, gray box in the illustration) with the *x* within is not the graphic that I wanted to include, but an indication from Internet Explorer that an inline graphic was specified with the `<IMG>` tag, but not loaded. In this case, the graphic was not loaded because I mistyped the name of the graphics file, specifying blackbox.gff rather than blackbox.gif. (Did you notice?) A mistake like that is another good reason to test your Web pages extensively before letting other users visit it.

To correct the problem, I fixed the spelling. Figure 8-2 shows what the resulting Web page looks like with all the information properly loaded (more attractive than with the unloaded graphic, eh?).

Figure 8-2: The Dark Box Web page

You may have a fast connection to the Internet, but remember that many people are trapped with very slow dial-up connections at 28,800 baud or — horrors! — slower. Prodigy, America Online, and CompuServe users can access Web pages, but performance can be quite slow. Bigger graphics have more data to transfer to the user and, therefore, take longer on slower network connections. Also bear in mind that, to speed up access, many users simply skip loading the graphics unless required to understand a page.

A rule of thumb is each 1K of graphics size translates to one second of download time for dial-up users. So, when you create graphics, it's a good idea to look at the file sizes and ask yourself whether the specific graphic is worth the wait. Sometimes it is, but often it isn't, which just creates a frustrating, slow-loading page.

A popular use of graphics is for buttons, which is done by wrapping the IMG tag with an anchor. If I had two button graphics — yes.gif and no.gif — here's how I could spiff up the Dark Box page:

```
<HTML>
<HEAD>
<TITLE>The Dark Box</TITLE>
</HEAD><BODY>
<IMG SRC="black-box.gif">
<H1>Welcome to the Dark Box</H1>
There are boxes you've encountered that aren't very well
lit, there are boxes that might even be
sealed, but I guarantee that you've never seen
anything quite as terrifying as
<I>The Dark Box</I>.
<P>
Dare you continue? <A HREF="blackbox2.html">
<IMG SRC="yes.gif"></A>
<A HREF="not-ready.html"><IMG SRC="no.gif"></A>
</BODY>
</HTML>
```

The graphics that are included in this page (that is, yes.gif and no.gif) are separate files in the same directory as the Web page. Figure 8-3 shows the new, cooler Web page with all graphics included.

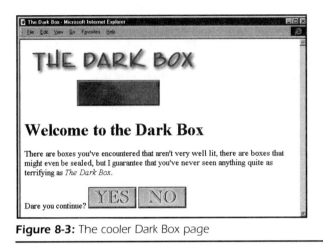

Figure 8-3: The cooler Dark Box page

A page in which graphics are a vital part of the design, however, can end up looking peculiar to some Web users because a percentage of people on the Web either cannot or opt not to download graphics when viewing Web pages. This creates a design dilemma: Should pages be designed to omit the graphics, to include them as critical, or just to add them as an afterthought?

Some Web pundits tell you to just go wild with the graphics because "within a few months" everyone will have a fast, powerful computer and a high-speed connection. I don't agree with that advice. Because the various graphic formats, already compressed, still produce large files, you should ensure that people who omit the images still see a meaningful page.

It breaks down like this: Some designers insist that you should be able to design for a specific browser and platform. Those sites, say stuff like "Enhanced for Internet Explorer 4.0 and Windows 95." I think they're missing the boat. Another group believes that specific browsers shouldn't be required, but that no-graphics viewers are irrelevant to their online experience. They eschew ALT attributes (as you'll see shortly) or any text alternatives for the graphical buttons and pictures. For some sites that's cool, but for many, it's just a sign of poor implementation. Finally, there are people who think that every graphic should have a text alternate and that the pages should work wonderfully for all users. That's the safest bet, but if you want to advertise your T-shirt designs online, then clearly, text descriptions aren't very useful! Which road you take definitely depends on the goal of your site and your vision of the target audience.

You can eliminate the blue border around a graphic image that's serving as a hyperlink by adding another attribute to the IMG tag: BORDER=0. If the preceding example had <IMG SRC=yes.gif BORDER=0>, the blue border would vanish. I'll show you more about this later, so stay tuned.

Text Alternatives for Text-Based Web Browsers

Although the most popular browsers — Navigator and Internet Explorer — offer support for a variety of graphic formats, there is also an important Web browser called Lynx that is designed for text-only display; Lynx is found most commonly on UNIX systems where users have dial-up accounts. Even at a very slow connect speed, Lynx enables many users to navigate the Web and have fun.

With Lynx, however, graphics can't be shown. So, an additional attribute is allowed in the <IMG> format tag for just that situation. ALT=alternative-text is the magic sequence. Whatever replaces alternative-text is displayed if the user can't view graphics or chooses to skip loading graphics to speed up surfing the Web (which about 10 percent of Web users currently do, according to most estimates I've seen).

To understand why the ALT= element is necessary, see Figure 8-4, which shows how the Dark Box page shown in Figure 8-3 would appear in Lynx.

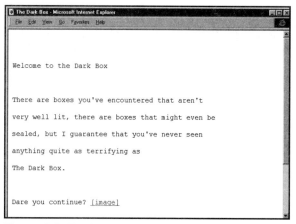

Figure 8-4: The Dark Box in Lynx's text-only display

The user faces a problem, obviously: How do you answer the question posed? That's why you should always include some meaningful information in the ALT attribute. The following example shows how a slight rewrite of the HTML code makes the page clear to a text-only user:

```
<HTML>
<HEAD>
<TITLE>The Dark Box</TITLE>
</HEAD><BODY>
<IMG SRC="black-box.gif" ALT="[wicked cool graphic]">
<H1>Welcome to the Dark Box</H1>
There are boxes you've encountered that aren't very well
lit,
there are boxes that might even be
sealed, but I guarantee that you've never seen
anything quite as terrifying as
<I>The Dark Box</I>.
<P>
Dare you continue? <A HREF="blackbox2.html">
<IMG SRC="yes.gif" ALT="<yes>"></A>
<A HREF="not-ready.html"><IMG SRC="no.gif"
ALT="<no>"></A>
</BODY>
</HTML>
```

When displayed within Lynx, the preceding offers meaningful and helpful information that enables users to work with the page and explore the Dark Box, even when they're missing the graphic image (see Figure 8-5).

Even better is that both Explorer and Navigator show this ALT text immediately upon loading a page, then gradually replace each placeholder with the actual graphic. Carefully planned ALT text can enhance the user experience and can even be fun. For example, the text alternative for my photograph on one page I designed is "weird picture of some random guy or other" rather than "my photo."

You don't have to place brackets, parentheses, or anything else around the text in the ALT= section of the <IMG SRC> tag, but in my experience, brackets or parentheses help users figure out the page (and look better, as well). Experimentation is the key for learning how to make this work best for your own page design.

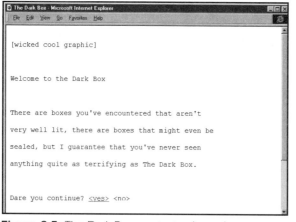

Figure 8-5: The Dark Box — text-only version

Image Alignment Options

Go to the first section of this chapter and refer to Figure 8-3. Look carefully at the relative alignment of the text `Dare you continue?` with the YES and NO icons. The text is aligned with the bottoms of the icons, which looks good.

But what if you want a different alignment? Or what if you use different alignments for multiple graphics? You can specify a third attribute in the `<IMG>` formatting tag, `ALIGN`, which gives you precise control over alignment.

Standard alignment

The three standard alignments are `ALIGN=top`, `ALIGN=middle`, and `ALIGN=bottom`. By default, images and adjacent material are aligned with the bottom of the image, as you can see in Figure 8-3. The following HTML snippet demonstrates these three alignment options:

```
<H1>IMG Alignment Options</H1>
<H2>Align=top</H2>
Dare you continue? <A HREF="blackbox2.html">
<IMG SRC="big-yes.gif" ALIGN=top BORDER=0></A>
Be careful! This takes courage! (ALIGN=top)
```

(continued)

```
(continued)
<H2>Align=middle</H2>
Dare you continue? <A HREF="blackbox2.html">
<IMG SRC="big-yes.gif" ALIGN=middle BORDER=0></A>
Be careful! This takes courage! (ALIGN=middle)
<H2>Align=bottom</H2>
Dare you continue? <A HREF="blackbox2.html">
<IMG SRC="big-yes.gif" ALIGN=bottom BORDER=0></A>
Be careful! This takes courage! (ALIGN=bottom)
```

Figure 8-6 shows this example in a Web browser.

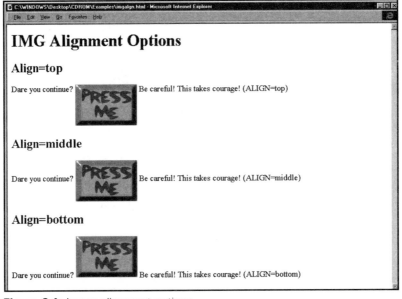

Figure 8-6: Image alignment options

The preceding example demonstrates the options for a graphic surrounded by text. However, you may want to align the YES and NO buttons at the bottom and align the preceding text with the centers of the two icons. The following example shows a simple way to accomplish this task:

```
Dare you continue? <A HREF="blackbox2.html">
<IMG SRC="yes.gif" ALIGN=middle BORDER=0></A>
<A HREF="not-ready.html">
<IMG SRC="no.gif" ALIGN=bottom BORDER=0></A>
(be careful! This takes courage!)
```

Upon looking at this seemingly reasonable HTML snippet in a Web browser, I realize that the code doesn't do what I want it to do. Figure 8-7 shows the rather cheery and festive, albeit incorrect, result.

Figure 8-7: *So much for aligning the icons.*

The truth is that centering text on bottom-aligned graphics is beyond the capability of HTML-using this approach. At best, you could make all your buttons part of a single graphic element and then use an image map — an <ISMAP> tag — to tell your server which area corresponds to which option. (See Chapter 11 for information on image mapped graphics.) The correct solution in this situation would be to not specify the alignment at all. Try it — this correct formatting is on the CD-ROM.

When you lay out your graphics, remember that different browsers have different screen widths and that browsers are enabled to move elements around to fit the screen. A classic mistake in an, otherwise, great-looking Web page is previewing it with a relatively narrow window and thinking that it looks fine. A user with a huge screen would see all the graphics and text bubble up toward the top — an arrangement that ruins the overall appearance of the page.

A simple rule of thumb for images: If you don't want any material to appear to the right of the graphic, add a <BR> tag to the end of the HTML sequence that specifies the graphic.

The three basic image-alignment options refer to the alignment of information that appears subsequent to the image itself. There is an additional set of image-alignment options that has shown up more recently in the life of the HTML language that refers to the alignment of the image relative to the window, rather than the adjacent material relative to the graphic.

More sophisticated alignment

The three basic image-alignment options shown previously offer considerable control of graphics and text interleaving, but the problem is you can't wrap text around a graphic, either left or right, on the screen. To remedy this, some additional image-alignment options offer much more control, but beware: They also make formatting more confusing because of the difference between alignment of the image and alignment of the adjacent material. I'll try to make sense of all the options for you by using lots of examples, because the new alignment choices *are* terrific.

These options are better demonstrated than discussed. The following example uses both options:

```
<B>Generic File Icon</B><BR>
<IMG SRC="generic-file.gif" ALIGN=left>
This is a generic file — that is, one that doesn't have
any
application ownership information stored in the Mac file
system or
its own resource fork. Opening these files typically
results in the use of the
<B>TeachText</B> or <B>SimpleText</B> application, if
possible, although you can fine-tune that with the new
<B>Easy Launch</B> control panel.
<P>
<B>Generic Folder Icon</B><BR>
<IMG SRC="generic-folder.gif" ALIGN=right>
This is a standard folder icon on the Macintosh. Folders
can
contain just about anything, including files,
applications,
and other folders. Opening a folder results in the display
of the contents of that folder in a separate window on
the Macintosh.
```

Figure 8-8 shows how the preceding text is formatted within Internet Explorer — quite a step up from the primitive placement options shown earlier.

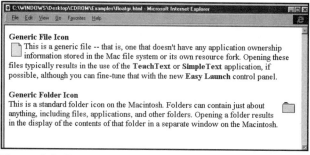

Figure 8-8: Floating graphics in Explorer

Further options have been added to the now complex `<IMG>` formatting tag. One new option enables you to specify the `WIDTH` and `HEIGHT` of the graphic before the graphic is loaded, which enables the document to be rendered on the screen faster, even before the graphic is received. Values are specified in pixels, as follows:

```
<IMG SRC="windows.gif" WIDTH=200 HEIGHT=350>
```

The preceding example would reserve a 200×350-pixel box on the screen for the graphic, which would enable the page to be displayed, including all text, even before the graphic is received from the Web server. This enables the reader to begin reading the text portion of the Web page immediately. Be careful with these attributes, however, because if you actually had a 100×200 graphic, Navigator and Explorer would both stretch it to fit the 200×350 space, making it look pretty weird.

Another attribute that I mentioned earlier in this chapter is `BORDER`, which can be used to great effect: it enables you to specify the exact width of the border around a linked image. The following shows an example:

```
<!-- Tic-Tac-Toe -->
<CENTER>
<FONT SIZE=+3><B>Tic-Tac-Toe</B></FONT>
<FONT SIZE=+1><BR>
It's X's Turn... (<FONT COLOR=blue>This color</FONT>
indicates a recommended move)</FONT>
<P>
<A HREF="topleft"><IMG SRC="box+x.gif" BORDER=0></A>
<A HREF="topcntr"><IMG SRC="box.gif" BORDER=0></A>
```

(continued)

```
(continued)
<A HREF="topright"><IMG SRC="box.gif" BORDER=0></A>
<BR>
<A HREF="left"><IMG SRC="box+o.gif" BORDER=0></A>
<A HREF="center"><IMG SRC="box+o.gif" BORDER=0></A>
<A HREF="right"><IMG SRC="box.gif" BORDER=2></A>
<BR>
<A HREF="btmleft"><IMG SRC="box+x.gif" BORDER=0></A>
<A HREF="btmcenter"><IMG SRC="box.gif" BORDER=0></A>
<A HREF="btmright"><IMG SRC="box.gif" BORDER=0></A>
</CENTER>
```

The resulting graphic is displayed in Figure 8-9. Notice the BORDER specification enables me to indicate the recommended next move by simply placing a blue (or gray, for our figures in this book) border around the box. This same attribute is how I turned *off* the blue border on the yes and no buttons earlier in this chapter.

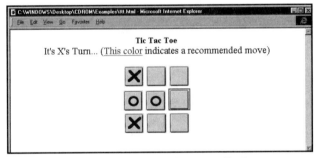

Figure 8-9: Tic-tac-toe in Microsoft Internet Explorer

Two more attributes that I think are also useful for image alignment are VSPACE and HSPACE, which control the vertical and horizontal space around each graphic. Consider an example of left and right alignment. When displayed, the text started at a different distance from the left margin, based on the width of the graphic. With HSPACE, I can fix this problem by specifying a different number of pixels as a horizontal spacing between the graphics and the adjacent text, as follows:

```
<B>Generic File Icon</b><br>
<IMG SRC="generic-file.gif" ALIGN=left HSPACE=12>
This is a generic file, that is, one that doesn't have
any application ownership information stored in the
Mac file system or its own resource fork. Opening
these files typically results in the <b>TeachText</b>
```

```
or <b>SimpleText</b> application being used, if possible,
though you can fine tune that with the new
<b>Easy Launch</b> control panel.
<p>

<B>Generic Folder Icon</b><br>
<IMG SRC="generic-folder.gif" ALIGN=left HSPACE=10>
This is a standard folder icon on the Macintosh.
Folders can contain just about anything, including
files, applications and other folders. Opening a folder
results in the contents of that folder being displayed
in a separate window on the Macintosh.
```

Figure 8-10 demonstrates the result of the preceding text.

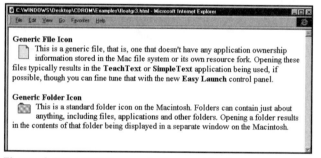

Figure 8-10: HSPACE corrects the graphic alignment.

A subtle thing to note in Figure 8-10 is that HSPACE adds the specified number of blank pixels on both sides of the graphic. VSPACE does the same thing with vertical space. If you specify ten pixels of empty space above a graphic, you end up with ten pixels of space below it, too. An alternative — if you really only want space on one side of the image, not both — is to add the empty space as part of the graphic itself.

At this point, you're learning to have some real control over the display of the document and can begin to design some cool Web pages. But I need to mention one more formatting addition before you go wild with the various options for the <IMG> tag.

If you experiment, you'll find that if you're wrapping text around a large graphic, it's difficult to move any material below the graphic.
 and <P> simply move to the next line in the wrapped area. That effect is not always what you want. To break the line and move back to the margin, past the graphics, you need to add a special attribute to the useful `<BR>` tag: `CLEAR=`. For example, use `<BR CLEAR=left>` to move down as needed to get to the left margin, `<BR CLEAR=right>` to move down to a clear right margin, or `<BR CLEAR=all>` to move down until both margins are clear of the image. Most commonly, you'll see `<BR CLEAR=all>`.

Tossing all the additions into the mix, here's a Macintosh icon tutorial:

```
<HTML>
<HEAD>
<TITLE>An Introduction to Mac Icons</TITLE>
<BASEFONT SIZE=+2>
</HEAD><BODY>
<CENTER>
<FONT SIZE=+2><B>Intro to Macintosh Icons</B></FONT><BR>
<FONT SIZE=-1><I>Some of these are System 7.x
only...</I></FONT>
</CENTER>
<P>
<B>Generic File Icon</B><BR>
<IMG SRC="generic-file.gif" ALIGN=left HSPACE=18 VSPACE=8>
This is a generic file, that is, one that doesn't have
any application ownership information stored in the Mac
file system or its own resource fork. Opening
these files typically results in the use of the
<B>TeachText</B>
or <B>SimpleText</B> application, being used, if
possible, though you can fine tune that with the new
<B>Easy Launch</B> control panel.
<P>
<B>Generic Folder Icon</B><BR>
<IMG SRC="generic-folder.gif" ALIGN=left HSPACE=15
VSPACE=6>
This is a standard folder icon on the Macintosh. Folders
can contain just about anything, including files,
applications and other folders. Opening a folder results
in the contents of that folder being displayed in a
separate window on the Macintosh.
<P>
<B>System Folder Icon</B><BR>
<IMG SRC="system-folder.gif" ALIGN=left HSPACE=15
VSPACE=11>
A special folder at the top-most level of each hard disk
on the Macintosh is the <I>System Folder</I>. It
contains all the files, applications, and information
```

```
needed to run and maintain the Macintosh operating
system and all the goodies therein. The tiny Mac
icon inside the folder indicates that this
particular <I>System Folder</I> is <I>live</I> and that
the information inside was used to actually start up
the current Macintosh.
<P>
Many files are located in the
<B>System Folder</B>, including the following:
<P>
<B>Apple Menu Icon</B><BR>
<IMG SRC="apple-menu.gif" ALIGN=left HSPACE=15 VSPACE=8>
Ever wondered where all the information that shows up on
the Apple menu (the menu you get when you click
the <IMG SRC="apple-icon.gif"> in the top
left corner of the menu bar)? They're all just
files, folders, applications and aliases tucked into
the Apple folder itself. Open this folder some time
and compare the contents with the results of clicking
on the Apple icon itself.
</BODY>
</HTML>
```

Figure 8-11 shows the result.

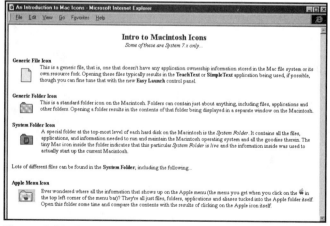

Figure 8-11: The Macintosh icon tutorial

A Few Real-World Examples

This section examines some interesting graphics and layout options that I've used for different designs on the Web. All of them are also online if you'd like to examine them yourselves, but here you can get a guided tour.

Trivial Net

Our first stop is the home page of Trivial Net, a computer trivia site that my pal Kevin Savetz and I designed for fun. My goal with this particular site is to have the interface be straightforward, but attractive and quite quick to load. You'll notice in the listing that I make heavy use of the `<BLOCKQUOTE>` tag, as discussed earlier: Here you can see how helpful it is for pulling text off the edges of the page.

 Visit the page and try the game for yourself by popping over to:

`http://www.trivial.net/`

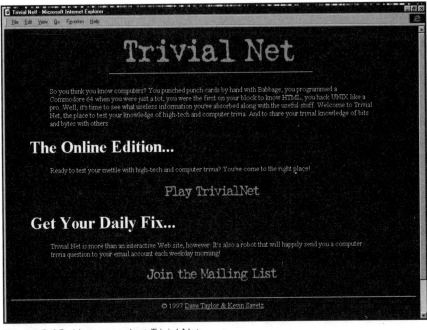

Figure 8-12: Have a peek at Trivial Net.

You can see the page itself in Figure 8-12, and following is the actual source to the page:

```
<HTML><HEAD>
<TITLE>Trivial Net!</TITLE>
</HEAD>
<BODY BGCOLOR=#000000 TEXT=#FFFFFF LINK=#FFFFFF
VLINK=#FFFFFF>
<BASEFONT SIZE=4>
<CENTER>
<IMG SRC=animated-banner.gif ALT="Trivial Net!">
</CENTER>
<HR WIDTH=50%>
<BLOCKQUOTE>
<BLOCKQUOTE>
So you think you know computers? You punched punch cards
by hand with Babbage, you programmed a Commodore 64 when
you were just a tot, you were the first on your block to
know HTML, you hack UNIX like a pro. Well, it's time to
see what useless information you've absorbed along with
the useful stuff. Welcome to Trivial Net, the place to
test your knowledge of high-tech and computer trivia. And
to share your trivial knowledge of bits and bytes with
others.
</BLOCKQUOTE>
<P>
<font size=+3><B>The Online Edition...</B></font>
<P>
<BLOCKQUOTE>
Ready to test your mettle with high-tech and computer
trivia?
You've come to the right place!
<P>
<CENTER>
<a href=playgame.cgi>
<img src=play-the-game.gif ALT="Play TrivialNet!"
border=0></a>
</CENTER>
</BLOCKQUOTE>
<P>
<font size=+3><B>Get Your Daily Fix...</B></font>
<P>
<BLOCKQUOTE>
```

(continued)

```
(continued)
Trivial Net is more than an interactive Web site, however.
 It's
also a robot that will happily send you a computer trivia
question
to your e-mail account each weekday morning!
<P>
<CENTER>
<a href=signup.html>
<img src=signup-now.gif ALT="Click Here to Signup!"
BORDER=0></a>
</CENTER>
</BLOCKQUOTE>

</BLOCKQUOTE>
<P>
<HR>
<CENTER>
&copy; 1997 <a href=mailto:nerds@trivial.net>Dave Taylor
&amp; Kevin Savetz</a>
<P>
<font size=-1>Learn more about
<a href=http://www.intuitive.com/taylor>Dave Taylor</a> and
<a href=http://www.savetz.com/>Kevin Savetz</a></font>
<P>
<A HREF=kudos/index.html><IMG Src=kudos.gif border=0
ALT="Some of our fans..."></A>
</CENTER>
</BODY>
</HTML>
```

We'll discuss it further in Chapter 10, but I'll briefly note that the attribute BGCOLOR in the <BODY> tag specifies the background color, and #000000 is black, so <BODY BGCOLOR=#000000> gives us a black background for the entire page. Adding TEXT=#FFFFFF gives us white text (otherwise, black text on a black background is a sure way to guarantee confidentiality — no-one could read it!).

Notice that I use a 50 percent-width horizontal rule to break the logical pieces of the page up right after the initial graphic, and another, 100 per-cent-width, at the bottom of the page just before the copyright and other "small print" information on the page. Also, note the use of the character entity © to produce a real copyright symbol.

Other than that, the ton of blockquotes on this page are to have the main text all moved in one blockquote level (one tab stop), and then each paragraph of information indented a second level. Simple tags, but a very attractive result.

"Silencing Critical Voices"

When a psychologist friend of mine asked me for some assistance in designing an online magazine focused on the critical voices that impede people becoming who they want to be, I realized that the key element for this design was simplicity. Just as importantly, the site needed to be clean and attractive, and I latched onto the visual metaphor of a notebook with scribbled notes.

 Visit this Web page for yourself:

http://www.intuitive.com/voices/

In this case, being able to specify typefaces by name was a tremendous boon. As you can see in the listing, the entire page uses specific typefaces to achieve the informal appearance desired:

```
<HTML>
<TITLE>Silencing Critical Voices</TITLE>
<BODY BGCOLOR=#FFFFFF BACKGROUND=blue-bg.jpg
      TEXT=#000000 LINK=#000000 VLINK=#000000
ALINK=#0000FF>
<basefont size=+1>
<font face="Tekton,Arial">        <!-- for the remainder of
this page -->
<CENTER>
<IMG SRC=banner.gif HEIGHT=59 WIDTH=428
      ALT="SILENCING CRITICAL VOICES">
</CENTER>
<HR WIDTH=80%>
<blockquote><blockquote>
<P ALIGN=right>
<B>
An Internet journal published by<br>
Marie-Nathalie Beaudoin, Ph.D.<br>
Bay Area Family Therapy & Training Associates
</B>
</P>
```

(continued)

(continued)

```
<P>
<font size=+1>
Welcome to <b>Silencing Critical Voices</b>.  The
purpose of this journal is to honor the successes of
people of all ages that I work with through Bay Area
Family Therapy & Training Associates and to hopefully
assist some of you who may struggle with similar issues.
Each edition of this journal will  be a homage to
different groups such as women, mothers, men, people of
color, therapists etc. with whom I have had the privilege
to work with.
</font>
</blockquote>
<a href=issue1.html><font face=Tekton,Arial><b>The First
Issue</b></font></a> is a tribute to kids and teenagers
who have successfully reclaimed their lives from problems
created by Critical Voices.  In this edition, you have
the privilege of reading the stories of a 10 year old
boy who successfully fought shyness, a 12 year old girl
who reclaimed her life from depression and a 15 year old
teenager who defeated self-doubt and a beginning of
anorexia.  All these problems were intrinsically created
and supported by Critical Voices.
</blockquote>
<HR WIDTH=80% noshade>
<CENTER>
<a href=index.shtml><img src=home.gif alt="HOME"
border=0></a>
 
<a href=intro.html><img src=welcome.gif alt="WELCOME"
border=0></a>
 
<a href=issue1.html><img src=issue1.gif alt="ISSUE #1"
border=0></a>
 
<a href=who.html><img src=who-we-are.gif alt="WHO WE ARE"
border=0></a>
<HR WIDTH=80% noshade>
<P>
<font size=3>&copy; 1997 by Marie-Nathalie Beaudoin,
Ph.D.</font>
<P><HR><P>
<font size=2>Silencing Critical Voices is realized online
by
```

```
<a href=http://www.intuitive.com/>Intuitive
Systems</a></font>
</font>
</CENTER>
</BODY>
</HTML>
```

Again, there are no particularly complex tags or tricks I'm playing with the HTML here to achieve the effect shown in Figure 8-13. The background graphic was created with another attribute of the `<BODY>` tag: `BACKGROUND=graphicname` (and it can be any GIF or JPEG graphic file) which gives the rough-paper appearance shown.

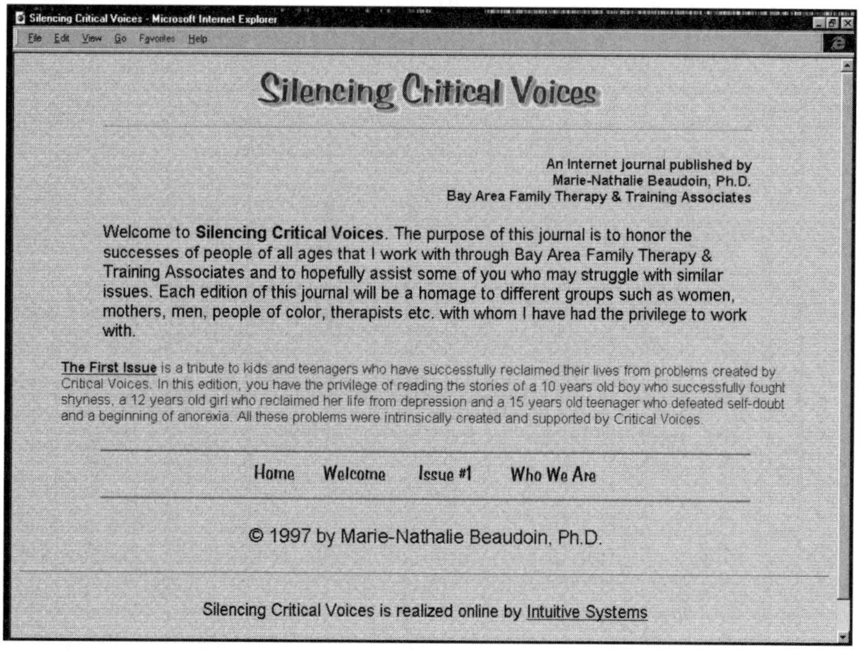

Figure 8-13: Silencing Critical Voices Online

It's a bit confusing: background colors are set with the BGCOLOR attribute, but background graphics are specified with BACKGROUND. I'll explain and demonstrate both in greater detail in Chapter 10.

Notice the use of the non-breaking space character entity —   — to space out the graphical buttons at the bottom of the page. Without this, I could have used HSPACE within each IMG tag as an alternative way to accomplish this goal. Because it's all centered (using the <CENTER> and </CENTER> tag pair), the additional space on the left and right edges of the line of graphics wouldn't have made any difference.

Another HTML tag that you might not have seen before is the close-paragraph tag, </P>. According to the HTML 4.0 specification, a closing tag is not necessary for any paragraph tag, but if you are going to specify the alignment of the paragraph (you can use <P ALIGN=right> to right-align text, ALIGN=left, which is the default, or ALIGN=center for cen-tered material) you will usually use the close paragraph tag, too, to clearly specify where the alignment option ends.

One more thing to highlight: Did you see the line

```
<a href=issue1.html><font face="Tekton,Arial"><b>The First
Issue</b></font></a>
```

in the listing? This was an attempt to bypass a bug in the Web browsers where whatever typeface was being used to display the paragraph of text, as soon as a hypertext reference was encountered, the subsequent text was displayed in the default typeface — not what I wanted, so I am forcing the text back to Tekton or Arial before I actually list the linked phrase "The First Issue."

One thing that I've found during the process of creating a wide variety of different kinds of browsers is that whatever the specifications suggest, as a designer, you're really at the mercy of the people who actually program the specific Web browsers, and sometimes that can be frustrating. I have spent hours fiddling with simple HTML to achieve just the effect desired, and I'm not alone. That's one reason why simple things like the nonbreaking space get used quite a bit. Another trick people use: blank 1-bit graphics that are exactly the size of an empty area you want, so you can space things exact-ly as desired.

History of the Internet Mall

The Internet Mall, the largest shopping site on the Internet, is a site that I created a number of years ago and have continued to work on through a number of redesigns. While parts of the site are quite complex, other areas, like the discussion of the history of the Internet Mall, are an example of how simple HTML can produce an attractive Web page. Figure 8-14 shows you the page and you can visit it live on the Net by going to `http://www.internetmall.com/about/history.html`.

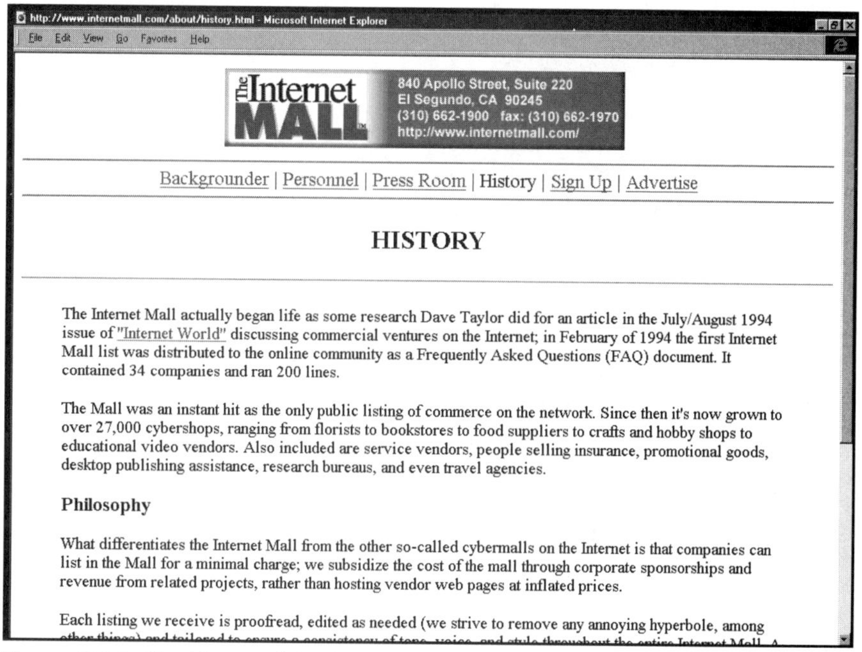

Figure 8-14: The History of the Internet Mall

Here's the source to that page:

```
<HTML>
<BODY BGCOLOR=#FFFFFF>
<CENTER>
<a href="http://www.internetmall.com/">
<IMG SRC=imlogo.gif border=0 VSPACE=5></A><br>
<HR NOSHADE>
<font size=+1>
```

(continued)

```
(continued)
<A HREF=background.html>Backgrounder</a> |
<A HREF=people.html>Personnel</a> |
<A HREF=press>Press Room</a> |
History |
<A HREF=http://www.internetmall.com/howto.html>Sign Up</a>
|
<A HREF=http://www.internetmall.com/info>Advertise</a>
</font>
<HR NOSHADE>

<h2>HISTORY</h2>
<P><HR>
</CENTER>
<BLOCKQUOTE>
The Internet Mall actually began life as some research
Dave Taylor did for an article in the July/August 1994
issue of <a href=http://www.internetworld.com/>"Internet
World"</a> discussing commercial ventures on the
Internet; in February of 1994 the first Internet Mall
list was distributed to the online community as a
Frequently Asked Questions (FAQ) document. It contained
34 companies and ran 200 lines.
<P>
The Mall was an instant hit as the only public listing of
commerce on the network. Since then it's now grown to
over 27,000 cybershops, ranging from florists to
bookstores to food suppliers to crafts and hobby shops to
educational video vendors. Also included are service
vendors, people selling insurance, promotional goods,
desktop publishing assistance, research bureaus, and even
travel agencies.
<H3>Philosophy</H3>
What differentiates the Internet Mall from the other so-
called cybermalls on the Internet is that companies can
list in the Mall for a minimal charge; we subsidize the
cost of the mall through corporate sponsorships and
revenue from related projects, rather than hosting vendor
web pages at inflated prices.
<P>
Each listing we receive is proofread, edited as needed
(we strive to remove any annoying hyperbole, among other
things) and tailored to ensure a consistency of tone,
voice, and style throughout the entire Internet Mall. A
typical entry is five lines of text, specifying what
```

```
company, what's for sale, and how to contact them for
more information. As we are trying to promote
<i>Internet-based commerce</I>, we don't list postal
addresses, phone numbers, FAX numbers, or any other non-
electronic contact information.
<P>
Plenty of books and magazines purport to list companies
on the Internet, and try to offer a shoppers guide
(notably the various Internet Yellow Pages books
available) but none are anywhere near as comprehensive,
up-to-date and readable as the Internet Mall.
<P>
<a href="/howto.html">Sign your company up right now!</a>
</BLOCKQUOTE>
<P>
<CENTER>
<HR NOSHADE>
<font size=+1>
<A HREF=background.html>Backgrounder</a> |
<A HREF=people.html>Personnel</a> |
<A HREF=press>Press Room</a> |
History |
<A HREF=http://www.internetmall.com/howto.html>Sign Up</a>
|
<A HREF=http://www.internetmall.com/info>Advertise</a>
</font>
<HR><P>
&copy; 1997 The Internet Mall, Inc.
</CENTER>
</BODY>
</HTML>
```

You can see a very common approach to letting people jump between a number of different pages: a line of HREFs where the word (or button) for the current section isn't an active link. In this case, I repeat the sequence at both the top and bottom of the page for ease of navigation. Also, notice the use of the "|" character between each entry, to have the dividers split the words attractively rather than having them all be immediately adjacent.

In that same few lines, another thing to catch is that some of the HREFs link to other pages on the same site, while others point to a different Web site entirely. As you learned a few chapters back, the links are all displayed identically to the user.

At the top, some poor HTML-coding style: The logo is included, but there's no ALT text specified. If someone came to the site with a text-only browser, with the graphics turned off, or with a device to make it possible for people with visual handicaps to explore the Web, they'd have an unlabeled image. Another mistake with this page: no TITLE!

It's almost impossible to have every page of a Web site be perfect, unfortunately, however much you — like me — may be a perfectionist. To give you an idea of the scope of some of these sites, the Internet Mall site is comprised of over a thousand different Web pages!

Where Can You Find Images?

Considering that all graphics are specified with the same basic HTML tag, it's remarkable how much variation exists among different sites on the Web. Web designers create varied appearances for their pages through the types of graphics they use and their unique combination of graphics, text, and background images.

Where do these graphics come from? Here are the most common sources:

➡ New images they've created themselves

➡ Clip art or other canned image libraries

➡ Text-manipulation programs

➡ Scanned photographs

➡ Grabbing images off the Net

New images they've created themselves

If you're artistically inclined or want to use straightforward graphics, buttons, or icons, the easiest way to produce graphics for your Web pages is to create them yourself. A wide variety of graphics applications is available for Windows and Mac users, at prices ranging from free to fifty dollars to thousands of dollars for real top-notch stuff.

To give you an example, I created the opening graphic for the Dark Box (shown in Figure 8-2) from scratch in about 15 minutes. I used the powerful Adobe Photoshop application, a rather expensive commercial package available for both Mac and PC platforms. Photoshop has the capability to save directly to GIF format (and JPEG format, for that matter), so it was easy to get just the effect I sought.

Having said that, I will admit that Photoshop is not for the faint of heart! It's a highly sophisticated program that takes quite a bit of training before you can be really productive. If you're looking for something that you'll be productive with the same afternoon, it's not the best choice. On the other hand, once you do master it, you'll be among the ranks of some of the best digital artists on the Net.

If you'd prefer something more simple, GraphicConverter for the Mac and Paint Shop Pro and Lview Pro for the PC are both quite useful programs that offer you the ability to create graphics and save them in either GIF or JPEG format. Earlier in this chapter, I indicated the official Web sites for each of these. I'll list them here again for your convenience:

➡ GraphicConverter: `http://www.lemkesoft.de/`

➡ Paint Shop Pro: `http://www.jasc.com/psp.html`

➡ Lview Pro: `http://www.lview.com/`

The overall number of graphics programs is staggering, however, and regardless of how fast or capable your machine, there are unquestionably some terrific software solutions available. Some of the best are shareware — such as the three listed — but there is also a plethora of commercial packages available. Here are some of the more popular commercial graphics packages for each platform:

➡ Windows: Among the many applications for developing graphics in Microsoft Windows are Adobe Illustrator, Aldus FreeHand, MetaCreations Painter, Dabbler, Canvas, Ray Dream Designer, SmartSketch, CorelDRAW!, MacroModel, AutoSketch, Kai's Power Tools, 3D Sketch, and Elastic Reality.

➡ Macintosh: Because it remains the premier platform for graphics, you'll find that most graphics applications are available for the Mac. In addition to the "big three" — Adobe Photoshop, Aldus FreeHand, and Adobe Illustrator — you'll find Macintosh graphics programs such as Drawing Table, Color It, Specular Collage, KPT Bryce, Paint Alchemy, TextureScape, Painter, Kai's Power Tools, and Alias Sketch.

➡ UNIX: Fewer graphics programs are available for UNIX systems, but the programs that are available are quite powerful. Look for IslandDraw and IslandPaint, Adobe Photoshop, FusionArt, GINOGRAPH, Adobe Illustrator, Image Alchemy, Magic Inkwell, and Visual Reality.

> **NOTE** One request: If you do opt to use a shareware program, please remember to pay for it and register it with the shareware author. That's the only way we'll be able to continue relying on the generosity of these programmers writing such excellent software and then making it available to us directly.

Clip art or canned image libraries?

One result of the explosion of interest in the Web and Web page design is the wide variety of CD-ROM and floppy-based clip art and canned image libraries now available. From thousands of drawings on multi-CD-ROM libraries (I have one image library that sprawls across thirteen different CD-ROMs!) to hand-rendered three-dimensional images on floppy — or available for a fee directly on the Net — there are lots of license-free image sources. At the same time, most of the CD-ROMs I've seen that are supposedly for Web designers are pretty mediocre — tossed-together collections of clip art that would look okay on your page if you could just figure out where it is on the disk and how to get it into your own program.

The clip-art library that I'm most enamored of is the Adobe Image Club series. The products in this series are expensive — almost $100 for a set of floppy disks typically holding 35 or fewer images — but the quality is excellent and the results are flawless every time.

If you opt to explore the clip-art route, I strongly recommend you be a skeptical consumer and make sure that the interface and ease of finding specific images in a particular product meet your needs. I have a CD-ROM of clip art for Web pages, for example, that's packaged in a very cool-looking box and includes some undeniably spiffo images, but finding the exact one I want and saving it as a separate image is surprisingly difficult.

There are also some clip-art Web sites, and one that I'll highlight as being particularly interesting is Art Today. It's a membership site that costs — as of this writing — under $20 for the year, and they have over 600,000 different royalty-free clip-art images available online, 50,000 stock photographs, and over 1,500 different typefaces, all ready for you to download as needed.

They're online at:

```
http://www.arttoday.com/
```

Text-manipulation programs

I really like funky or interesting text effects in Web pages — not just simple things such as text in boxes, but shadows, textured letters, and twisted or wavy baselines. Look at the lettering in the Dark Box image shown earlier, in Figure 8-3, to see what I think looks cool.

I manipulated the text in the Dark Box page the hard way, from within a general-purpose graphics editor. A better method would have been to use one of the many type-manipulation programs that are available. I have two favorites: Pixar Typestry (available for both Macs and PCs) and Brøderbund TypeStyler (Mac only).

Typestry is quite powerful, offering a staggering variety of options. Figure 8-15 shows a simple graphic produced in the program (it looks much better in color).

Figure 8-15: Text graphics in Typestry

TypeStyler is easier to use and offers a more general-purpose graphics environment, but lacks the sophistication of Typestry. As Figure 8-16 shows, the program enables you to produce attractive text for Web pages.

Figure 8-16: Text graphics in TypeStyler

If you can afford the package and have the willingness to learn the weird interface, Adobe Photoshop is an amazingly powerful image and graphics editor. With the addition of some third-party plug-ins, such as the excellent Eye Candy filter package from Alien Skin Software, you can produce stunning text graphics with just a few mouse clicks.

Another valuable set of filters is from the Auto F/X company, whose Photo/Edges suite let you create a wide variety of unusual and interesting edges to your photographs and other graphics. And don't forget: Adobe includes a large set of filters called the Gallery Effects suite, letting you turn graphics into paintings, watercolors, etchings, and many other styles of artwork.

Figure 8-17 shows an example of what can be done with Photoshop. Many of the graphics included with the HTML documents on the CD-ROM were done in Photoshop.

Figure 8-17: Text graphics in Photoshop

Scanned photographs

Another way to produce graphics for your Web site is to use a scanner and work with existing art. If you're a photography buff, you probably have hundreds of original photographs from which you can glean cool additions for your site.

A few years ago, I was traveling in Paris and took what turned out to be a great photograph of the beautiful Sacré Coeur. A few minutes of work with a scanner made the photo instant artwork to include in my Web page, as shown in Figure 8-18.

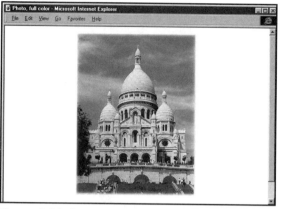

Figure 8-18: Scanned image of Sacré Coeur

Scanners offer further options for producing fun and interesting graphics. I also scanned the image shown in Figure 8-18 as black-and-white line art, producing the interesting abstract graphic in Figure 8-19.

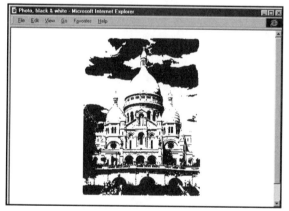

Figure 8-19: Sacré Coeur as line art

If I were designing a Web site that I expected to attract users with slow connections, I could use small black-and-white representations of art to save people time waiting for data that they may not want. Each small image, or thumbnail image, would serve as a button that produces the full color image when clicked. The HTML would look like the following:

```
<A HREF="big-image.gif"><IMG SRC="little-image.gif"
BORDER=0></A>
```

Thumbnail versions of large graphic images are common (and appreciated by just about everyone), so if you create a page that contains many pictures, think about minimizing the data transfer with smaller versions that refer to larger images.

Another difference between the images in Figures 8-18 and 8-19 is file size. Figure 8-18 is a JPEG image, to ensure that all the colors in the original photograph are viewable in the Web artwork. It's 99KB in size. Figure 8-19, however, is a 1-bit GIF image, and even though it's exactly the same image-size as the JPEG color photo, the file is only 17KB, less than 25 percent of the size of the color image.

Another way to work with scanners is to scan scrawls, doodles, or pictures you create with pencils, pens, color markers, paint, pastels, or what have you, and then incorporate those objects into your Web page. Or get even more creative: Scan in aluminum foil, crumpled tissues, your cat (note that this would be a "cat scan"), wood, a piece of clothing, or just about anything else.

Copyright laws are serious business, and I strongly discourage you from scanning in images from any published work that is not in the public domain. The cover of Sports Illustrated might be terrific this week, but if you scan it in and display it in your Web page, you're asking for some very serious legal trouble.

If you're working with scanners, you already know about some of the best software tools available. I'll just note that I always use Photoshop when I'm working with color or gray-scale scans. One important scanner trick if your output is for the Web: Scan the images at between 100 dots per inch (dpi) and 75dpi because the additional information you get from, say, a 2400dpi scan is wasted, slows down the editing process, and produces fantastically large graphics files anyway. (I've scanned in images that produced 17MB files!)

There's a slick scanning FAQ online, too. Check it out at:

http://www.infomedia.net/scan/

Grabbing images off the Net

There's another way to get images that doesn't involve being artistic or using a scanner: You can find interesting, attractive graphics online. Think of Net graphics as being virtual clip art (you can use real clip art, too), though don't forget that many of the images may be copyrighted. Just because MCI has a Web site (at `http://www.mci.com/`) doesn't mean that you can pop over and borrow its logo without permission!

The good news is that there are a number of different sites that are archives of publicly available graphics, clipart, background graphics, and more. Here are a few of the best:

The Shock Zone

Chris Stephens offers a terrific set of icons that loads quickly and can quickly add pizazz to your Web site. His site also includes a range of animated graphics, and much more. Connect to `http://www.TheShockZone.com/,` and you'll see much more than the small portion shown in Figure 8-20.

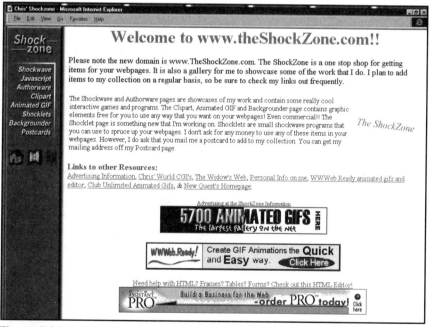

Figure 8-20: Some of the images at The Shock Zone

Realm Graphics

Another useful site is Realm Graphics, which you can find online at `http://www.ender-design.com/rg/`. It features a very attractive design, over 380 different kinds of bullets (who thought there could be so many choices?), 150 different buttons, and 330 different textures. Well worth visiting.

But Wait! There's More . . .

After a while, the different graphic repositories start to look alike. Call me a curmudgeon, but there are only so many different ways you can create a 50x50-pixel bullet graphic, right? Well, anyway, if the previous two don't have what you seek, here are a couple more that are fairly decent:

- Graphics Station:

  `http://www.geocities.com/SiliconValley/6603/`

- Webular Wasteland:

  `http://www.aceent.com/w2/`

- The Design Shoppe:

  `http://www.thedesignshoppe.com/`

Of course, you can just travel the Net and when you see something you like, grab it with a screen-capture program or download it directly. Different Web browsers offer different tools to accomplish just this task. With Explorer, for example, right-click a graphic and hold the mouse button down, and suddenly there's a pop-up menu with the option of saving that graphic to the disk. If you take this route, however, be doubly sensitive to possible copyright infringement. It would be quite easy to create a site using existing graphics just to find out later that there are legal complications.

Another thing to be aware of: If you're creating a Web site for someone else, don't be surprised if part of your agreement letter specifies that you certify that all images used on the site are legally theirs. I've seen contracts that even include a clause stating that if there were any questions about the legality of material on the site, that it was my problem and that I'd have to pay any and all damages for any legal action that might ensue.

Transparent Colors

One subtle thing that I did with some of the graphics in this chapter was replace the background around the edges of the image with a transparent color — one that enables the background color of the window to bleed through. You could see that most dramatically with the lettering on the Trivial Net site. Transparent colors (available only with GIF-format images today) almost instantly make pages look cooler. Of course, in this book, we're printing without any colors, but you've been pretending pretty well up to now, haven't you?

Figure 8-21 shows two versions of the same type of icon. The graphic on the top hasn't had its background set to transparent; the one on the bottom has. Some difference, eh?

All of the major graphics and type-manipulation packages support transparent GIFs.

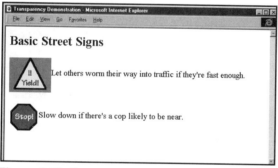

Figure 8-21: Transparent graphics

For Windows users, if your current graphics programs don't support transparent GIF colors, then the shareware program of choice is GIFTRANS. You can obtain this program from the University of North Carolina at Chapel Hill archive; the URL is:

```
ftp://sunsite.unc.edu/pub/packages/infosystems/
WWW/tools/giftrans
```

 Documentation for GIFTRANS can also be found on my Web site. Look in the FAQ area at:

```
http://www.intuitive.com/coolweb/
```

On the Macintosh, the program Transparency is rough and primitive, but does the job admirably. You can get a copy of this program off the Net at:

```
ftp://ftp.the.net/mirrors/ftp.utexas.edu/
graphics/transparency-10-fat.hqx
```

or:

```
ftp://ftp.med.cornell.edu/pub/aarong/transparency/
```

GraphicConverter also works with Transparency.

For a comprehensive list of utilities and all sorts of goodies, zip over to Yahoo! (`http://www.yahoo.com/`) and look in `Computers/World Wide Web/Programming`.

Audio, Video, and Other Media

Graphics definitely add pizzazz to a Web site, but there are more media that you can use to develop your cool Web pages, including audio and video. Some significant limitations plague these add-on media, however, not the least of which is that they're large and take quite a while to download.

Audio fragments are probably the most fun — it's great to hear voices or music coming from your computer and they're quite easy to add to your own pages. The audio recordings are usually in what's called a micro-law (or you'll see this written as μ-law) format, and can be included as a button or hot spot just like any other URL. Here's an example:

```
You're invited to listen to <A HREF="audio.au">a sample of
my latest album</A>
```

Users who clicked the phrase *a sample of my latest album* would next download an audio file (typically 75K or larger); then an audio player program would be launched to actually play the audio clip. A simple audio clip is also included on the CD-ROM in the back of this book — Enjoy!

There are two other common audio formats in use on the Web today. WAV files started their life on Windows machines, but can be played on Macs and UNIX systems, too, with the latest browsers. MIDI files are another way to squeeze a lot of audio into a remarkably small file, because they're actually written in a musical instrument language rather than simply being compressed recordings.

Another way to add audio is to use either the `EMBED` or `BGSOUND` HTML extensions. I'll talk about these further in Chapter 10.

In the meantime, if you're dying to explore some online audio files, I strongly encourage you to check out the dynamite MIDIfarm site. It has an incredible archive of over 4,000 different audio files in MIDI format, including the theme to Mission Impossible, Star Wars, and just about any other song or music you can imagine! It's online at:

```
http://www.midifarm.com/
```

My only caution is the usual one about copyright and legal restrictions. If you're going to use these MIDI files on a commercial page, make sure you have permission from the original music copyright holder.

Be careful when you're adding audio to your site; these files can grow incredibly large. A ten-second audio clip can grow to over 150K, which could represent quite a long download period for people accessing the Web via slow dial-up connections.

Multimedia PCs and AV Macintosh have a variety of built-in audio capabilities, including the capability to record audio directly from an attached microphone. Save the file that's produced and ensure it has a WAV or AU filename suffix. My personal favorite for recording and editing audio is a great shareware program called Wham. You can learn more about this, and many other audio tools, by visiting the audio tools on the Web area on Yahoo!.

Movies all night

Movies are found in two formats: QuickTime and MPEG (Motion Picture Experts Group). MPEG is the format of choice for the Web, however, because it's the most universal, with MPEG players available for Mac, PC, and UNIX systems.

If you think audio files can expand rapidly to take up lots of space, you haven't seen anything till you try video on the Web!

The format for including an MPEG sequence is simple:

```
The latest <A HREF="video.mpg">Music Video</A> is finally
here!
```

The Web browsers see the filename suffix MPG and know to download the file specified and launch a video player program.

The other popular movie format is Apple's QuickTime, which has players available for the Mac and Windows machines. QuickTime movies use the MOV filename extension.

You can learn a lot more about working with MPEG and other video formats, and sneak a peek at some public domain video and animation archive sites, by popping over to Yahoo!. Do so, and check out:

```
http://www.yahoo.com/Computers/Multimedia/Video
```

Streaming audio and video

Another technology that's come up in the last year or so are the so-called streaming media technologies. The concept is quite logical: instead of forcing the user to wait for the entire audio or video sequence to download, why not get enough to ensure you're downloading a few seconds ahead and start playing the audio or video sequence?

The biggest proponent of this technology is RealAudio Corporation, which you can visit online at:

```
http://www.realaudio.com/
```

There are a bunch of different sites using the RealAudio audio technology, including National Public Radio (`http://www.npr.org`) and C-SPAN (`http://www.c-span.org`). You can also listen to 2FM live from Ireland at `http://www.2fm.ie//`, and check out some obscure music groups from Artist Underground Music, at `http://www.aumusic.com/`.

RealAudio also has a streaming video technology, ingeniously called RealVideo. I think it's a relatively primitive technology, but there are a number of different sites you can visit so you can draw your own conclusions. Start with Polygram Records (`http://www.polygram.com/`), then peek in at United Airlines Zurich (`http://www.united-airlines.ch/`) and wrap up your exploration of streaming video with Comedy Central, online at `http://www.comedycentral.com/`.

I think the streaming technologies are cool, but the biggest problem is that they assume transfers on the net happen at a steady speed, and that's rarely true. So instead, you get a few seconds of audio then it stops, or a very low quality audio signal, and the videos either jump or are used as fancy slide-shows rather than a simulated live video feed. If you have a slow net connection, you will find the situation even more frustrating; I have very fast connections and still tend to avoid these most of the time.

Having said that, my expectation is that things will continue to improve and that streaming audio and video technologies will eventually become the ideal way for you to offer access to audio and video on your site. For today, however, the server software costs a fair bit and isn't something I can explain to you in a paragraph or two. Stay tuned (so to speak). There'll be more from this corner of the Web soon.

In Closing

I could say lots more about the fun and frustration of working with graphics and other media in Web pages, and I will over the next few chapters. One thing's for sure: However people accomplish the task, you'll see a million slick graphics, icons, buttons, separator bars, and other gizmos all over the Web. Keep a skeptical eye on your own work, though, to make sure that your neat doodads don't overtake the theme and message — the content — of your site. *Good Web sites are built around content, not appearance.*

Table 8-1 contains a summary of the HTML tags covered in this chapter.

Table 8-1	Summary of Tags in This Chapter	
HTML Tag	**Close Tag**	**Meaning**
`<IMG`		Image inclusion tag
`SRC=url`		Source to the graphic file
`ALT=text`		Text alternative to display, if needed
`ALIGN=alignment`		Image alignment on page / alignment of material surrounding the image. Possible values: top, middle, bottom, left, right.
`HEIGHT=x`		Height of graphic (in pixels)
`WIDTH=x`		Width of graphic (in pixels)
`BORDER=x`		Border around graphic when used as hyperlink
`HSPACE=x`		Additional horizontal space around graphic (in pixels)
`VSPACE=x`		Additional vertical space around graphic (in pixels)
`<BR`		Line break
`CLEAR=opt`		Force break to specified margin. Possible values: left, right, all.

Summary

In my view, at least, cool Web pages are those that intelligently incorporate their graphics into the overall design and that don't fall apart or become unusable (or otherwise frustrating) when users don't or can't load everything. In Chapter 9, you learn about two very important design options, tables and frames, that offer much finer control over your page layout.

Tables and Frames

In This Chapter

Organizing information in tables

Advanced table formatting

Tricks with tables

Pages within pages: frames

Sophisticated frame layouts

If you've been diligently reading each chapter, I have good news! You've reached the point where most of the Web page design consultants were considering themselves experts as recently as a year ago. From this point, we'll be looking at a wide variety of different advanced formatting features starting in this chapter with two essentials for modern site design: tables and frames.

What's most interesting about this point in the book is that it has primarily covered the HTML 1, HTML 1.1, and HTML 2.0 formatting language, though I've delved a tiny bit into some further advances that showed up in HTML 3.2. Can you keep all these numbers straight? I can't. Remember, the sequence was 1, 1.1, 2.0, 3.2, and now 4.0. For some cryptic reason, there was never a 3.0 release of the standard. Along the way, the two formatting capabilities covered in this chapter — tables and frames — brought about some of the most dramatic improvements in Web site design. As you read this chapter and see all the examples, you'll begin to see why.

Organizing Information in Tables

Tables are an important addition to HTML that originated in the development labs at Netscape Communications Corporation. Unlike the tables in your favorite word processor, however, these can be quite compelling, and you might find yourself naturally boxing up groups of like icons, taking a list of bullet items and making a table out of them, or who knows what else! If you want to have material adjacent on a page, perhaps multiple columns of text, tables are unquestionably your best bet.

Basic table formatting

While tables offer a lot of cool capabilities, there's a downside to them: Tables are pretty hard to build. You have to specify the parameters for the table; then the parameters for each row, and then each cell element must be surrounded by <TD></TD> — table data — tags. Here's a simple example of a table:

```
<B>Common Cable TV Channels</B>
<TABLE BORDER=1>
<TR>
<TD>MTV</TD>
<TD>ESPN</TD>
<TD>Headline News</TD>
<TD>WTBS Atlanta</TD>
</TR>
</TABLE>
```

This formats with all data on the same line (that is, in the same row, denoted by <TR> and </TR>), as shown in Figure 9-1.

Figure 9-1: The simplest table possible

If you want to have all the same information, but one item per row (that is, line), it instantly gets more complex by leaps and bounds:

```
<B>Common Cable TV Channels</B>
<TABLE BORDER=1>
<TR>
<TD>MTV</TD>
</TR>
<TR>
<TD>ESPN</TD>
</TR>
<TR>
<TD>Headline News</TD>
</TR>
<TR>
<TD>WTBS Atlanta</TD>
</TR>
</TABLE>
```

You can see the difference in format by viewing Figure 9-2.

Figure 9-2: A simple table, with each element on its own line.

Needless to say, this stuff can get quite complex, because you can include graphics, text, and just about anything else (including other tables) within any element of a table. Each row can have a specific alignment specified with ALIGN= as part of the tag, and the TABLE tag itself has a plethora of options, including all those shown in Table 9-1.

Table 9-1	TABLE Attributes
TABLE Tag	**Meaning**
BORDER=n	Width of shaded area surrounding table. If BORDER=0, this also eliminates the grid lines within the table itself.
CELLSPACING=n	Spacing between individual cells
CELLPADDING=n	Space between border and contents of cell
WIDTH=n	Desired width, overrides automatic width calculations (value or percentage)

One useful thing to consider is how to stretch out the table so that things aren't so jammed together. There are two basic strategies for accomplishing this: WIDTH and CELLPADDING.

The WIDTH attribute enables you to specify the exact width of the table, regardless of contents, on the screen. You can specify it either as a specific number of pixels or as a percentage of the overall width of the current viewer window. I always use the latter form, which makes for a slight modification to the preceding table:

```
<B>Common Cable TV Channels</B>
<TABLE BORDER=1 WIDTH="75%">
<TR><TD>MTV</TD></TR>
<TR><TD>ESPN</TD></TR>
<TR><TD>Headline News</TD></TR>
<TR><TD>WTBS Atlanta</TD></TR>
</TABLE>
```

Notice here that I've also shrunk the HTML a bit. As you'll recall from the discussion in the earlier chapters, your entire Web page can be on one long line, if you'd like; so certainly in a case like this, there's no reason not to put the row and data specs on the same line. As you can see in Figure 9-3, the output is considerably more open than the previous table.

The other way to open up the design of your table is to specify a CELLPADDING factor. There are two attributes that initially seem similar, but serve important, and different, functions in the layout of the table. CELLPADDING indicates the amount of space — in pixels — between the inner edge of the table cell border and the material within, whereas CELLSPACING refers to the width of the grid lines between the data cells.

Figure 9-3: Adding width improves the table

Here's an example of two tables, each setting one of these parameters:

```
<B>Common Cable TV Channels</B>
<TABLE BORDER=1 CELLPADDING=10>
<TR><TD>MTV</TD></TR>
<TR><TD>ESPN</TD></TR>
<TR><TD>Headline News</TD></TR>
<TR><TD>WTBS Atlanta</TD></TR>
</TABLE>

<HR>

<TABLE BORDER=1 CELLSPACING=10>
<TR><TD>MTV</TD></TR>
<TR><TD>ESPN</TD></TR>
<TR><TD>Headline News</TD></TR>
<TR><TD>WTBS Atlanta</TD></TR>
</TABLE>
```

Consider the differences between these in the output shown as Figure 9-4. Slightly upping the CELLPADDING is a nice way to improve the look of your tables.

Within a table, not only can you specify the rows with TR and individual data elements with TD, but you can also specify column headings with TH (which replaces the TD tag in the row). TH is mostly identical to TD, with two important changes: text in a TH tag is in bold and is horizontally centered in the cell.

Figure 9-4: PADDING versus SPACING

You can also specify the horizontal alignment of data cells within their space with the ALIGN option. The options are ALIGN=left (the default), ALIGN=center, and ALIGN=right, as demonstrated in the following HTML snippet. VALIGN lets you specify the vertical alignment, too — VALIGN= top, for example, ensures that all cells on a row have their information at the top rather than the default of vertically centered. The VALIGN options are top, middle, and bottom.

```
<CENTER>
<TABLE BORDER=5 WIDTH=50%>
<TR>
<TH>Show</TH><TH>Day On A&E</TH>
</TR>
<TR ALIGN=CENTER>
<TD>Sherlock Holmes</TD><TD>Monday</TD>
</TR><TR ALIGN=CENTER>
<TD>Lovejoy</TD><TD>Monday</TD>
</TR>
</TABLE>
</CENTER>
```

Look at Figure 9-5 to see how the TH tag changes the layout of the information on the page. You can also see what happens when a larger BORDER is specified.

Also, notice the use of the <CENTER> tag to center the table on the page rather than having it against the left side. We'll revisit the CENTER tag in the next chapter.

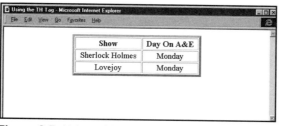

Figure 9-5: Using table headers

Rows and columns can span more than one table unit if needed, so we could add a nice header to the previous table by specifying `COLSPAN=2` to a new data cell:

```
<CENTER>
<TABLE BORDER=5 WIDTH=50%>
<TR>
<TD COLSPAN=2 ALIGN=center><FONT SIZE=5>Arts &
Entertainment</FONT></TD>
</TR>
<TH>Show</TH><TH>Day On A&E</TH>
</TR>
<TR ALIGN=CENTER>
<TD>Sherlock Holmes</TD><TD>Monday</TD>
</TR><TR ALIGN=CENTER>
<TD>Lovejoy</TD><TD>Monday</TD>
</TR>
</TABLE>
</CENTER>
```

This simple change offers considerable control over the layout of the individual cells within the table, as shown in Figure 9-6.

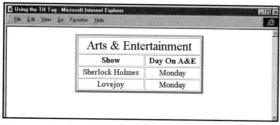

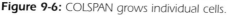

Figure 9-6: COLSPAN grows individual cells.

Advanced table formatting

There are a number of additional table formatting options that help you learn how to really exploit this powerful set of features embodied in the table tag set. One of the most important is to control the colors involved with the table: the color of the cell background.

Colors within a specific data cell show up within the <TD> tag in a way that won't surprise you:

```
<TD BGCOLOR=yellow>text on yellow background</TD>
```

This would have the single cell yellow with default black text. Have a look at how adding colors perks up the previous table:

```
<CENTER>
<TABLE BORDER=5 WIDTH=50%>
<TR>
<TD COLSPAN=2 ALIGN=center BGCOLOR=yellow>
<FONT SIZE=5>Arts & Entertainment</FONT></TD>
</TR>
<TH BGCOLOR=red>Show</TH><TH BGCOLOR=red>Day On A&E</TH>
</TR>
<TR ALIGN=CENTER>
<TD>Sherlock Holmes</TD><TD>Monday</TD>
</TR><TR ALIGN=CENTER>
<TD>Lovejoy</TD><TD>Monday</TD>
</TR>
</TABLE>
</CENTER>
```

The result of this formatting is quite attractive, as shown in Figure 9-7.

Figure 9-7: Colored table cells

COLSPAN is pretty easy to understand, I think; but the real conceptual challenge is trying to figure out how to use ROWSPAN, which lets you have a data cell across multiple lines of the table.

The next example demonstrates ROWSPAN; in this case, I include a graphic image in the multi-row data cell. The graphic, stuff2watch.gif, is some text that's been rotated 90 degrees counterclockwise. Here's the source:

```
<TABLE BORDER=1 CELLPADDING=5>
<TR><TD BGCOLOR=blue ROWSPAN=5><IMG
SRC=Graphics/stuff2watch.gif></TD><TD>MTV</TD></TR>
<TR><TD>ESPN</TD></TR>
<TR><TD>Headline News</TD></TR>
<TR><TD>WTBS</TD></TR>
<TR><TD>Sci-Fi</TD></TR>
</TABLE>
```

And the results, a very sophisticated table, are shown in Figure 9-8.

Figure 9-8: ROWSPAN demonstrated.

Internet Explorer table capabilities

While all of the table attributes shown so far work across the major Web browsers — notably Netscape Navigator/Communicator and Microsoft Internet Explorer — it turns out that Microsoft expanded the definition of tables a bit further than even the HTML 4.0 specification details.

The most recent HTML specification details how to set background colors for specific cells using BGCOLOR, but Internet Explorer adds to it: The BACKGROUND tag allows background graphics in table cells, and the BORDERCOLOR tag allows detailed control over the border color. If the latter's not exact enough, Internet Explorer also offers the capability to set the two colors used in the border with `BORDERCOLORLIGHT` and `BORDERCOLORDARK`. Further, Internet Explorer is the only Web browser that enables you to specify background graphics within individual data cells by using `BACKGROUND=graphic-file` rather than the `BGCOLOR` solid colors.

All of these new attributes are demonstrated in the following example:

```
<TABLE BORDERCOLOR=blue BORDER=5 CELLPADDING=20>
<TR>
<TD BACKGROUND=Graphics/backgnd.gif>
<FONT SIZE=5 COLOR=teal>What a Long,
Strange Road It's Been</FONT></TD>
</TR>
</TABLE>
<HR>
<TABLE BORDERCOLORLIGHT=yellow BORDERCOLORDARK=red
CELLPADDING=10 BORDER=10>
<TR><TD>
<FONT SIZE=4>Classic Rock From Guys In BMWs</FONT>
</TD></TR>
</TABLE>
```

This example looks good here in the book, as you can see in Figure 9-9; but to really see this rainbow of colors at its best, you'll want to view the file on your own computer!

Figure 9-9: Edge colors specified: IE only.

Modifying edges and grid lines

Two table attributes are new to the HTML 4.0 specification, introduced by the group at Microsoft working on Internet Explorer. Both offer even finer granularity of control over the borders around the table and between the individual data cells. They're FRAME and RULES, and the values are defined as shown in Tables 9-2 and 9-3:

Table 9-2	The Many Values for <TABLE FRAME=
Values of	**Attribute <TABLE FRAME=**
VOID	Removes all outside table borders.
ABOVE	Displays a border on the top side of the table frame.
BELOW	Displays a border on the bottom side of the table frame.
HSIDES	Displays a border on the top and bottom sides of the table frame.
LHS	Displays a border on the left-hand side of the table frame.
RHS	Displays a border on the right-hand side of the table frame.
VSIDES	Displays a border on the left and right sides of the table frame.
BOX	Displays a border on all sides of the table frame.
BORDER	Displays a border on all sides of the table frame.

Table 9-3	Specifying RULES in a Table
Values of	**Attribute <TABLE RULES=**
NONE	Removes all interior table borders.
GROUPS	Displays horizontal borders between all table groups. Groups are specified by THEAD, TBODY, TFOOT, and COLGROUP elements.
ROWS	Displays horizontal borders between all table rows.
COLS	Displays vertical borders between all table columns.
ALL	Displays a border on all rows and columns.

These two combine to produce a remarkable amount of control over the borders and edges in a Web table, but they're pretty complex, too. I'll offer you one example and encourage you to tweak the source yourself to see how they work in different combinations:

```
<TABLE BORDER=7 FRAME=vsides CELLSPACING=0
RULES=ROWS WIDTH=50%>
<TR ALIGN=center>
<TD>January</TD>
<TD>$25,404,384.08</TD>
</TR><TR ALIGN=center><TD>February</TD>
<TD>$28,498,294.38</TD>
</TR><TR ALIGN=center>
<TD>March</TD>
<TD>$31,978,193.55</TD>
</TR><TR ALIGN=center>
<TD>April</TD>
<TD>$18,559,205.00</TD>
</TR>
</TABLE>
```

Read through that code example closely (and remember that all the important work is being done in the `<TABLE>` tag itself) and compare it to Figure 9-10 to see if this makes sense to you. Try opening the same example in Netscape Navigator — which doesn't yet support these HTML 4.0 additions in its 4.01 release — and consider how differently the table is displayed.

Figure 9-10: A sample table with FRAME and RULES

One tip: Try taking out the "CELLSPACING=0" in the previous example and you'll notice the rule lines are broken with a very small invisible grid line or 3D bar (depends on which browser you're using). Specify that there should be no spacing, and the problem goes away. This is also true for when you work with background colors in your data cells.

Tricks with Tables

Before we leave tables, I'd like to show you two more examples of how you can use tables to dramatically change the appearance of material on your Web page.

The first example is to have a table within a table. This is a real-life example: the merchant login screen from the OrderEasy commerce service I helped design. Here's the source:

```
<HTML>
<HEAD>
<TITLE>Order Easy Merchant Entrance</TITLE>
</HEAD>
<BODY BGCOLOR=white>
<CENTER>
<IMG SRC=Graphics/oe-logo.gif>
<P><font size=7><b>Merchant Entrance</b></font><P>
<FORM ACTION="validate.cgi" METHOD=post>
<TABLE BORDER=0 WIDTH=75% BGCOLOR=#DDDDDD
CELLPADDING=15>
<TR><TD>
<font size=+1>
<B>For security reasons, merchants need to identify
themselves with their merchant ID number, as assigned by
your Order Easy administrator. It's probably something
like "m0203". You will also need your account password to
access your merchant account:</B>
</font>
<P>
  <CENTER>
  <TABLE BORDER=1 CELLPADDING=10 BGCOLOR=white>
  <TR>
    <TD>Merchant Account Identification:</TD>
    <TD><input type=text name=merchantid size=30></TD>
  </TR><TR>
    <TD>Account Password:</TD>
    <TD><input type=password name=password size=30></TD>
  </TD></TR>
  </TABLE>
    <P>
    <input type=submit value="access my account">
  </CENTER>
```

(continued)

```
(continued)
</TD>
</TR>
</TABLE>
</FORM>
<HR>
<h5>OrderEasy is a trademark of The Internet Mall,
Inc.</h5>
</CENTER>
</BODY>
</HTML>
```

Figure 9-11: The OrderEasy merchant entrance screen, showing a table within a table.

There's one big part of this listing that you haven't seen yet: forms. The INPUT tags and the FORM and /FORM tags are all part of the HTML needed to have a Web page send data back to the server for processing. The other bit that might be new is that instead of specifying a color by name, the outer gray box is specified as BGCOLOR=#DDDDDD, which is the hexadecimal specification for the exact color I seek. I'll talk about hex colors in more detail in Chapter 10.

The second table trick I want to demonstrate is using a table as a tool for developing the layout of an entire page rather than an element within the page. For this, I'll go to another live example: the home page for the home site of Retail Ventures International, at `www.retailventures.com`.

This design also has a table-within-a-table. See if you can spot it:

```
<TABLE BORDER=0 WIDTH=640 CELLSPACING=0>
<TR><TD width=115 align=center valign=top bgcolor=yellow>
<font size=+1 face="Arial">Retail Ventures International,
Inc.</font>
<P>
<table border=1 cellspacing=10 cellpadding=10
bgcolor=#DDDDDD>
<tr><td align=center>
<a href=http://www.retailventures.com/mission.html><font
size=+1 face=Arial>Mission</font></a>
</td></tr>
<tr><td align=center>
<a href=http://www.retailventures.com/approach.html>
<font size=+1 face=Arial>Approach</a>
</td></tr>
<tr><td align=center>
<a href=http://www.retailventures.com/staff.html> <font
size=+1 face=Arial>Staff</a>
</td></tr>
<tr><td align=center>
<a href=http://www.retailventures.com/links.html> <font
size=+1 face=Arial>Links</a>
</td></tr>
<tr><td align=center>
<a href=http://www.retailventures.com/rvi.html> <font
size=+1 face=Arial color=green>Home</a>
</td></tr>
</table>
</td><td width=525>
<blockquote>
<center><img src=Graphics/rvi-logo.gif></center>
<p>
Retail Ventures International, Inc. ("RVI") is a strategy
consulting and new venture development firm serving the
global retail industry. The firm was founded in 1996 to
assist US-based retail enterprises in realizing their
```

(continued)

```
(continued)
international growth objectives and to capitalize on
emerging retail trends through the creation and financing
of promising new ventures.
<center>
<img src=Graphics/rvi-image1.gif vspace=3><br>
A strategic focus: Japan.
</center>
</blockquote>
</td></tr>
</table>
```

By now every line of this example should make sense to you. There's nothing being used here that you haven't seen explained earlier in the book. However, a quick glance at 9-12 and you can immediately see that this is how people create multiple column designs, like that used on the Microsoft home page (http://www.microsoft.com/), for example.

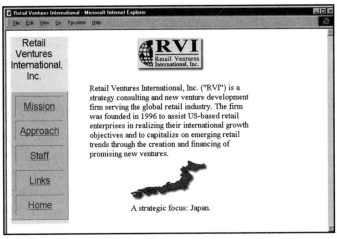

Figure 9-12: Nifty table-based page layout

The hidden problem with this design, however, is that it's explicitly designed for a standard VGA monitor resolution: 640 pixels wide. You can see that in the TABLE WIDTH specification:

```
<TABLE BORDER=0 WIDTH=640 CELLSPACING=0>
```

If the user has a screen that's considerably wider (800, 1024, or more pixels), then there's going to be a lot of unused blank space on the right side of the screen, and there's little you can do about it.

One thing you can try that you might experiment with and have good results is to use relative widths on the table, something like:

```
<TABLE BORDER=0 WIDTH=100% CELLSPACING=0>
```

at the top of the table, then specify the exact size of the column you are working with:

```
<TD WIDTH=150>
```

and let the browser calculate the width of any other columns of data you might specify. This works reasonably well, but you'll find that there's a hidden "gotcha" if you have a screen that's too small, and it's a problem that is present on the Retail Ventures page, too: When you specify relative widths on a narrow screen, the browser sometimes calculates the width of a column to be narrower than the items within.

The neat table of possible areas to explore on the RVI page can end up being resized and having its edge actually overlapping the main column of data, a quite unacceptable result.

 If your table is looking bizarre when you view it and you're using a mix of specific pixel widths and percentage widths, try switching to exclusively pixel widths or percentage widths. It's not always a problem, but I've definitely seen some weird table layouts suddenly fix themselves when I change from mixed specifications to a single type.

A solution to try, and avoid this, is to create a blank graphic that's the specific width of the widest element in the column plus a dozen pixels or so, then include that as a hidden spacer element. Here's a snippet of HTML that demonstrates what I mean from my own Web site; you can see the results online (and try to resize the page) at http://www.intuitive. com/taylor/websites/.

```
<TABLE BORDER=0 WIDTH=100% CELLPADDING=5 CELLSPACING=0>
<TR><TD WIDTH=160 ALIGN=left valign=top>
<IMG SRC =../Graphics/project-nav.gif
     ALT="Project 11-15-XM/7"
     WIDTH=130 HEIGHT=72>
<p>
< IMG SRC =../Graphics/small-bar.gif ALT="------"
     WIDTH=98 HEIGHT=23>
<br>
<IMG SRC=../Graphics/tiny-spacer-bar.gif WIDTH=154
HEIGHT=3>
<P>
<A HREF=../areas/><IMG
    SRC=../Graphics/cool-nav.gif BORDER=0
    ALT="Cool Areas" WIDTH=119 HEIGHT=37></a>
<br>
                etc, etc. for quite a few lines
```

The invisible graphic that's wider than any other information in this column is called "tiny-spacer-bar.gif" and by forcing it to be 154 pixels wide, I can force the Web browser to give me at least that much width regardless of how small the actual window is. Notice that the first column is only specified at 160 pixels in width (in the second line).

Pages Within Pages: Frames

Okay, I think you're ready. Take a deep breath. It's time for us to explore something that makes tables look easy: frames. Frames answer the question: What if each data cell in your table was its own Web page?

When frames were first introduced by Netscape, prior to the release of HTML 3.2, lots of people didn't like them. Enough sites, however, started to develop around a frame design, splitting a single Web page into separate panes, that they gradually became popular in spite of complaints.

Meanwhile, many sites that had introduced frames versions of their home pages had to also offer a no-frame version for people who didn't like frames, and today the first frame site I ever saw, the Netscape home page, defaults to a no-frame version and offers a frames-version choice hidden on the very bottom of the page. If you want to be an HTML expert, you must know how to work with frames.

The basics of frames

Unlike many of the tags you've seen so far, frames are an all-or-nothing proposition: individual frames are specified with the <FRAME> tag, which is itself wrapped in a <FRAMESET> specifier that indicates the amount of space to allocate to each "pane" of information. Here's a very basic frame page that breaks the screen into two sections, the first 75 pixels high, and the second the remainder of the screen:

```
<HTML>
<FRAMESET ROWS="75,*">
    <FRAME SRC="Frames/top.html">
    <FRAME SRC="Frames/bottom.html">
</FRAMESET>
</HTML>
```

Figure 9-13 shows what happens in the browser: You have the single page split into two rows as specified in the <FRAMESET> tag, the first 75 pixels high with a white background and the second, with its black background, consuming the remaining space (specified by *).

What you can't see here is that there are actually three Web pages involved in getting this to format correctly: the 'root' page shown above and two additional pages: top.html and bottom.html. The former contains:

```
<BODY BGCOLOR=white>
<CENTER><h2>This is the top pane on the page!</h2>
</CENTER>
</BODY>
```

The file bottom.html looks like this:

```
<BODY BGCOLOR=black TEXT=white>
<TABLE WIDTH=100% HEIGHT=100%>
<TR><TD ALIGN=center VALIGN=center>
<h2>This is the bottom section of the page!</h2>
</TD></TR>
</TABLE>
</BODY>
```

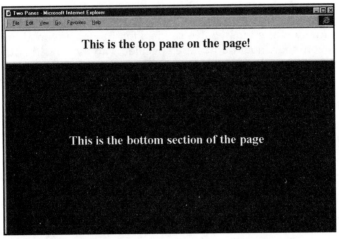

Figure 9-13: A two-pane frame page

That's the basic trick of frame documents: Instead of a single page defining all the information displayed to the visitor, the information is split into multiple pages, each given its own small piece of the data.

Notice a cool table trick I'm demonstrating in the bottom.html page: If you specify a table that's 100 percent the height and 100 percent the width of the screen, then specify that the information therein should be horizontally and vertically centered (ALIGN and VALIGN); you can automatically have material appear exactly centered onscreen, regardless of how big the screen might be.

Specifying frame panes and sizes

Now that you're an expert with tables, it will come as no surprise to you that there are lots of options for frames, too, most of which are vitally important to understand.

The most important tag to understand is <FRAMESET>. The <FRAMESET> tag creates a frameset: a set of frames into which the Web page will be split. In addition to being able to specify ROWS to split the Web page into horizontal panes, you can use COLS to specify vertical panes. There are three different values you can use for these two attributes: A simple number specifies the desired size in screen pixels. You've already seen the asterisk as a way to specify the rest of the space remaining, and you can also specify a percentage of width with the n% notation. So here's a test for you, if you think you got all that: What's <FRAMESET COLS=30%,19,*> mean?*

The sequence COLS=30%,19, will be interpreted as the first column being allocated 30 percent of the width of the window, the next column a slim 19 pixels, and the third column the remainder of the space on the window.

You can create complex multipane Web pages, where each pane has autonomous behavior, by combining them in creative ways:

```
<HTML>
<FRAMESET COLS="80%,*">
    <FRAMESET ROWS="30%,70%">
        <FRAME SRC="Frames/top.html">
        <FRAME SRC="Frames/bottom.html">
    </FRAMESET>
    <FRAMESET ROWS="33%,33%,*">
        <FRAME SRC=Frames/advert1.html>
        <FRAME SRC=Frames/advert2.html>
        <FRAME SRC=Frames/advert3.html>
    </FRAMESET>
</FRAMESET>
</HTML>
```

In this case, what I've done is specify that there are two columns of information, one 80 percent of the width of the screen, the latter the remaining width. That's specified with the following line:

```
<FRAMESET COLS="80%,*">
```

The first frame of these is the second frameset: two rows, the first (top.html) 30 percent of the available height, and the second (bottom.html) the remaining 70 percent:

```
<FRAMESET ROWS="30%,70%">
        <FRAME SRC="Frames/top.html">
        <FRAME SRC="Frames/bottom.html">
    </FRAMESET>
```

The second column of information (the "*" width in the first frameset specification) contains three advertisements evenly spaced, each 33 percent of the vertical space:

```
<FRAMESET ROWS="33%,33%,*">
        <FRAME SRC=Frames/advert1.html>
        <FRAME SRC=Frames/advert2.html>
        <FRAME SRC=Frames/advert3.html>
    </FRAMESET>
```

The results are shown in Figure 9-14.

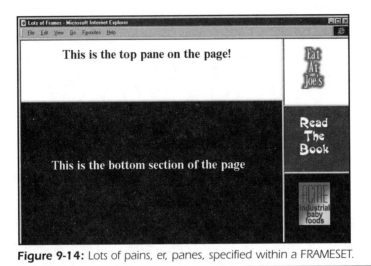

Figure 9-14: Lots of pains, er, panes, specified within a FRAMESET.

There are a couple of different attributes that you can specify for frames, the most important of which is the NAME= attribute. Each specific frame can be given a unique name (similar to <A NAME=>) that can then be used as a way to control which window is affected by specific actions. What's the point of this? Imagine you could have a table of contents of your site in a small pane that's always present and have any user click the table to actually change the information shown in the main pane, not the small table of contents pane. That's the idea of this, and there's a partner attribute that appears in the anchor tag for any hypertext reference (<A HREF). Here's an example of this at work. First, a simple frames page:

```
<HTML>
<FRAMESET cols="20%,*">
   <FRAME SRC="Frames/toc.html">
   <FRAME SRC="Frames/default.html" NAME=main>
</FRAMESET>
</HTML>
```

Here are the contents of the default.html page:

```
<BODY BGCOLOR=white>
<img src=animal-image.gif>
</BODY>
```

And here's the all-important toc.html page with the HREF extensions:

```
<BODY BGCOLOR=yellow>
<CENTER>
<FONT SIZE=6 COLOR=blue>
<B>Pick An Animal</B>
</FONT>
<P>
<FONT SIZE=5>
<A HREF=dog.html target=main>DOG</A>
<P>
<A HREF=cat.html target=main>CAT</A>
<P>
<A HREF=bird.html target=main>BIRD</A>
<P>
<A HREF=default.html>[home]</A>
</FONT>
</CENTER>
</BODY>
```

Figure 9-15 shows how it looks. You'll definitely want to try this out on the example CD-ROM to see how it works. In particular, notice what happens when you click the [home] button (the one that doesn't have a target attribute) and what happens when you use the Back button on your browser.

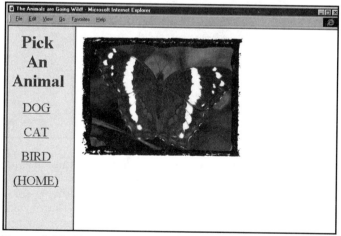

Figure 9-15: Navigational pane works!

The <FRAME> tag itself also has two attributes worth highlighting here before you escape this chapter. The first enables you to specify the width of a frame border: frameborder (makes sense, eh?), with an attribute in pixels. The second, scrolling, enables you to force a scroll bar or prohibit a scroll bar, even if the pane is too small for the information therein. A small sample of these:

```
<HTML>
<FRAMESET cols="20%,*">
  <FRAME SRC="Frames/toc.html" frameborder=5
scrolling=yes>
  <FRAME SRC="Frames/default.html" NAME=main>
</FRAMESET>
</HTML>
```

Compare the results (see Figure 9-16) with the earlier example above.

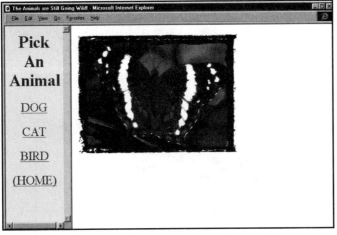

Figure 9-16: Navigational panes with an added scroll bar

Another important aspect to working with frames is to realize and compensate for the visitors who might not be able to see your frames-based design. The most recent versions of the major Web browsers, Navigator and Explorer, support frames quite well, but if you have visitors with older software — or the WebTV unit — then their browser doesn't support the entire frames tagset.

Remembering that any HTML tags that aren't understood are ignored, what do you think would be the result of having a non-frames browser receive something like the listing immediately prior for Figure 9-16? If you guessed that it'd be a blank page, you're right on the mark!

As a result, the standard way that people circumvent this problem is to have a section in their frames root page that's wrapped with the NOFRAMES option. If the browser understands frames, it ignores what's in that passage, and if it doesn't, the material in the NOFRAMES area is all that it's going to understand and display.

Here's how I might modify the previous listing to include some NOFRAMES information:

```
<HTML>
<FRAMESET cols="20%,*">
  <FRAME SRC="Frames/toc.html" frameborder=5
scrolling=yes>
  <FRAME SRC="Frames/default.html" NAME=main>
</FRAMESET>
<NOFRAMES>
<BODY>
<CENTER>
<H2>Sorry, but our site is designed for a frames-compliant
browser</h2>
To visit us you'll need to upgrade your Web software.
</CENTER>
</BODY>
</NOFRAMES>
</HTML>
```

Displaying the above source with your regular Web browser, if it's at least Internet Explorer 3.0 or Netscape Navigator 2.0, will show you the multiple-frame design as expected. Otherwise, you'll see the page that would be rendered as if you'd been sent the following HTML sequence:

```
<HTML>
<BODY>
<CENTER>
<H2>Sorry, but our site is designed for a frames-compliant
browser</h2>
To visit us you'll need to upgrade your Web software.
</CENTER>
</BODY>
</HTML>
```

If you're interested in learning more about the nuances of frames, there are two terrific spots on the Web to explore. Microsoft offers lots of information at:

```
http://www.microsoft.com/workshop/author/newhtml/
```

If you're interested in the Netscape tutorial on frames, it's terrific, and you can find it at:

```
http://home.netscape.com/assist/net_sites/frames.html
```

Creating a multipane frame site isn't too difficult. What's tricky is to do a really good job of it: to produce a site that makes sense and actually helps people find what they want when they explore your site. There are a number of really good examples online, fortunately, that you can study and learn from, including these:

Rockweb Interactive	`http://www.rockweb.com/`
Carly Simon Online	`http://www.ziva.com/carly/`
The Microsoft Site	`http://www.microsoft.com/`
Knowledge TV UK	`http://www.knowledgeTV.co.uk/`

Another thing you can do, of course, is to explore the on-disk examples, because they're all frame-based design. In Chapter 15, we'll return to both tables and frames and look at a number of advanced features and capabilities that you can exploit to create some pretty nifty Web sites.

Table 9-4 summarizes the many HTML tags presented in this chapter.

Table 9-4	Summary of Tags in This Chapter	
HTML Tag	**Close Tag**	**Meaning**
`<TABLE`	`</TABLE>`	Web-based table
`BORDER=x`		Border around table (pixels or percentage)
`CELLPADDING=x`		Additional space within table cells (in pixels)
`CELLSPACING=x`		Additional space between table cells (in pixels)

HTML Tag	Close Tag	Meaning
WIDTH=*x*		Forced table width (in pixels or percentage)
FRAME=*val*		Fine tuning the frames within the table (see Table 9-2)
RULES=*val*		Fine tuning the rules of the table (see Table 9-3)
BORDERCOLOR=*color*		Specifies color of table border (RGB or color name)
BORDERCOLORLIGHT =*color*		Lighter of the two colors specified (RGB or color name).
BORDERCOLORDARK =*color*		Darker of the two colors specified (RGB or color name)
<TR	</TR>	Table row
BGCOLOR=*color*		Specify the background color for the entire row (RGB or color name)
ALIGN=*align*		Alignment of cells in this row (left, center, right)
<TD	</TD>	Table data cell
BGCOLOR=*color*		Background color for data cell (RGB or color name)
COLSPAN=*x*		Number of columns for this data cell to span
ROWSPAN=*x*		Number of rows for this data cell to span
ALIGN=*align*		Alignment of material within the data cell. Possible values: left, center, right.
VALIGN=*align*		Vertical alignment of material within the data cell. Possible values: top, middle, bottom.
BACKGROUND=*url*		Specify the background picture for the cell

(continued)

Table 9-4 *(continued)*

HTML Tag	Close Tag	Meaning
`<FRAMESET`	`</FRAMESET>`	Frame-based page layout defined
`COLS=x`		Number of, and relative sizes of, column frames
`ROWS=x`		Number of, and relative sizes of, column rows
`<FRAME`		Definition of a specific frame
`SRC=url`		Source URL for the frame
`NAME=name`		Name of the pane (used with `TARGET=name` as a part of the `<A>` anchor tag)
`SCROLLING=scrl`		Set scrollbar options. Possible values: on, off, auto.
`FRAMEBORDER=x`		Size of border around the frame
`<NOFRAMES>`	`</NOFRAMES>`	Section of page displayed for users who can't see a frames-based design

Summary

This chapter gave you a whirlwind tour of the remarkable formatting capabilities offered by the table and frame tag sets. There are some tricky formatting tag sets herein, so make sure you've had a chance to digest these before you proceed. Chapter 10 introduces a bunch of advanced design features, including changing backgrounds, Explorer marquees, and lots more!

Advanced Design: Backgrounds, Marquees, and More!

One of the hidden dark sides in the world of the World Wide Web, and particularly the hypertext markup language, is that while there are a lot of different standards agreed upon by all the major players (including the new HTML 4.0 standard), the harsh reality is that every Web browser developer has its own set of "proprietary" tags that only its browser understands. Try to avoid these, but, in fact, some of them are quite cool and can offer you remarkable control over aspects of your page design.

The HTML discussed in this chapter all started out as proprietary tags available in either Navigator or Explorer, not both. The good news is that each of the two big companies learn from the other, and while in the first edition this chapter was called "Browser-specific HTML," now almost all of these are widely supported. However, having said that, there are some formatting additions herein that are not standardized and that might not be supported widely across the Web visitors to your site.

The original vision of Web browsers was that they'd all support the same language and differ in support for the specific operating system, how they managed your list of favorite sites, and other incidentals. Netscape Navigator changed all that when the company released a browser late in 1994 that had its own set of extensions to the HTML language. Since then, it's continued as a free-for-all, with each Web browser trying to outdo all the others by adding unique and interesting extensions.

Text Alignment and Horizontal Rules

Of the many additions to the original HTML, the one that I like most is `<CENTER>`, with its partner tag `</CENTER>`. Any information between the two tags is centered on the screen of the browser. This extension is particularly useful for opening graphics, but as you begin to design more complex pages, you will probably find other places where it can be a great help.

One situation in which using `<CENTER>` is a big win is centering the headline or title of a text HTML page. Remember the enchilada sauce recipe from Chapter 5? The following example shows how the recipe could be enhanced with the simple addition of a graphic and the `<CENTER>` tag:

```
<HTML>
<HEAD>
<TITLE>Dave's Enchilada Sauce</TITLE>
</HEAD><BODY>
<CENTER>
<IMG SRC=jalapeno.gif ALT="Dave's Enchilada Sauce"><BR>
<I>guaranteed to enhance any enchilada!</I>
</CENTER>
<OL>
<LI>Heat a large sauce pan and saut&egrave; until soft:
<UL>
<LI>Two tablespoons virgin olive oil
<LI>A large onion, chopped
</UL>
<LI>Sprinkle in a quarter cup of flour.<BR>
<LI>Jazz it up by adding:
<UL>
<LI>Two tablespoons of chili powder
<LI>Two teaspoons of cumin
<LI>One teaspoon of garlic powder
```

```
</UL>
<LI>Mix in a quart of water.
<LI>Finally, add a teaspoon of salt if desired.
</OL>
Whisk as sauce thickens then simmer for 20 minutes.
</BODY>
</HTML>
```

Figure 10-1 shows how the preceding recipe looks. The new title makes the recipe considerably more visually interesting!

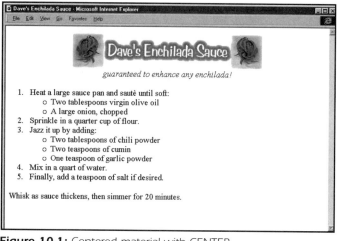

Figure 10-1: Centered material with CENTER

Before we leave the topic of centering material, it's important to highlight another way to do this, a way that's a bit more confusing, but that fits better into the future plans for HTML: the ALIGN attribute for the paragraph tag. To center material, use <P ALIGN=center> and finish the centered material with </P>. What's nice is that you can also use <P ALIGN=right> to have material right-aligned and, as of HTML 4.0, you can specify ALIGN=justify and have both the left and right margins neatly aligned (though the results look much better in a printout than on screen due to the higher level of resolution on the printed page).

I find it a bit confusing, because 99 percent of the time you can use the <P> tag without worrying about closing it; indeed, it's not usually considered a paired open/close tag set. If you want to use the alignment options of the paragraph itself, however, you'll need to remember to close any specially aligned paragraph you open.

Here's how this might be used to great advantage:

```
<CENTER>
<FONT COLOR=green>this text is centered the old way</FONT>
</CENTER>
<P ALIGN=left>
this is on the left margin...
</P>
<P ALIGN=center>
<FONT COLOR=blue>this is centered the new, fancy
way...</FONT>
</P><P ALIGN=right>
and this material is tucked rightmost<BR>
so what do you think?
</P>
<P ALIGN=justify>
At the beginning of time there was data. Lots of data. And
then, gradually out of the data swamp began to coalesce
information, first tentatively and then a rushing wave of
information, gems, nuggets of value. A short eon or two
later and the world was awash in layers of information,
leading to...
</P>
```

Figure 10-2 shows how this formats. It's colorful and quite cheery, don't you think?

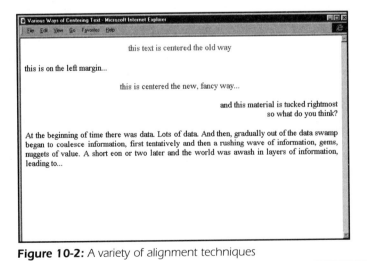

Figure 10-2: A variety of alignment techniques

Presently, neither Internet Explorer 4.0 nor Netscape Communicator 4.0 supports the ALIGN=justify attribute.

Rules on the horizon

Horizontal rules — the product of the <HR> tag — are helpful, but let's be honest: A uniform line across the screen can get boring. The Web developer community thought so, too, so they extended the <HR> command with a bunch of additional attributes: SIZE, WIDTH, ALIGN, and NOSHADE. The first three of these options take values, the last toggles the presentation style of the rule itself.

The SIZE attribute enables you to specify the height of the horizontal line, in pixels. Want the slimmest line possible? Try using <HR SIZE=1> in your document. Want something fat? Try SIZE=10.

A pixel is a single dot on a computer screen. A horizontal line that is 1 pixel high, therefore, is the tiniest line possible. SIZE=1 specifies a single pixel-high line.

The WIDTH attribute can be specified either in absolute pixels (a typical screen is 600 to 800 pixels wide) or in a percentage of the screen width. If you want a horizontal rule that is exactly 75 percent of the width of the current viewing window, you could use <HR WIDTH=75%>.

Because you can have lines that don't extend over the entire width of the browser, you can also specify where you want the line snippet to be placed. Just as you can with the ALIGN options for the <P> tag, you can specify that horizontal lines be placed LEFT, CENTER, or RIGHT. To have a line that's half the width of the browser window and against the left side, you would use <HR WIDTH=50% ALIGN=left>.

Rule shades and colors

Finally, close examination of these fancy horizontal lines shows that the lines are shaded to offer a quasi-three-dimensional appearance. If you really want a solid bar, use the NOSHADE option, which avoids the 3D look.

You can combine these options in fun and interesting ways, as in the following example:

```
<HR WIDTH=50% NOSHADE ALIGN=left>
<CENTER>
<FONT SIZE=+2><B>A Visit to the Pyramids!</B></FONT>
</CENTER>
<HR WIDTH=50% NOSHADE ALIGN=right>
<HR SIZE=3 WIDTH=5%>
<HR SIZE=3 WIDTH=10%>
<HR SIZE=3 WIDTH=20%>
<HR SIZE=3 WIDTH=30%>
<HR SIZE=3 WIDTH=40%>
<HR SIZE=3 WIDTH=50%>
<HR SIZE=3 WIDTH=60%>
<HR SIZE=3 WIDTH=100% NOSHADE>
```

This kind of detail can get complex, but the result can be pretty visually interesting, as shown in Figure 10-3.

Figure 10-3: A pyramid — one line at a time

Were you surprised by the results?

There's a danger in this type of design, as illustrated in 10-4. How does your page look in an older browser? You may design a wickedly cool Web page with the latest extensions, but seen from other browsers, your page looks like you used the Paste command too many times (or worse).

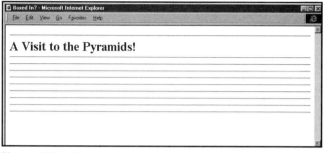

Figure 10-4: Not much of a pyramid in an old browser

Even more slick, you can actually specify the color of a specific horizontal rule in Internet Explorer: Add the attribute `COLOR=colorname`, with color names (or RGB values) as explained later in this chapter. For example, `<HR COLOR=green>`. This does not work with Navigator.

Fiddling with Lists

There are three types of lists in Web pages, and the two simplest, ordered lists and unordered (bullet) lists, have some helpful additional attributes worth exploring.

Standard ordered-list HTML tags specify that you have an ordered list, and the list items are displayed with incremental numeric values: 1, 2, 3, and so on. If you're creating a multilevel outline or other multilevel list, however, or just want to have an alternative to numbering, the ability to specify different forms of notation for the different levels can be quite useful. You might want *A* to *Z* for the highest level, numbers for the second level, and *a* to *z* for the lowest level. That format is, of course, the typical outline format, taught in English class, and an example of it looks like the following:

A. Introduction

    1. Title

        a. Author

        b. Institution

        c. Working title (20 words or fewer)

    2. Justification for research

        a. What? Why?

3. Findings

4. Conclusions

B. Body of Paper

1. Previous research

2. Research methods used

3. Results and findings

C. Conclusion

1. Implications

2. Directions for future research

D. References

If you were to try to reproduce the preceding example on a Web page, the best you could do would be to have three levels of numbered-list items, many bullet points, or no indentation at all. None of those options is what you want, naturally, and that's where the enhanced ordered-list extensions come in handy.

Ordered lists have two extensions: TYPE, which specifies the numeric counter style to use; and START, which begins the count at the value you specify, rather than 1.

You can use any of five different types of counting values:

➡ TYPE=A is uppercase alphabetic (A, B, C, D).

➡ TYPE=a is lowercase alphabetic (a, b, c, d).

➡ TYPE=I is uppercase Roman numerals (I, II, III, IV).

➡ TYPE=i is lowercase Roman numerals (i, ii, iii, iv).

➡ TYPE=1 (the default) is Arabic numerals (1, 2, 3, 4).

To have an ordered list count with Roman numerals, in uppercase, and start with item 4, you would use <OL TYPE=I START=4>. The default for a list is <OL TYPE=1 START=1>.

Here's how I'd produce the previous outline as a Web page:

```
<OL TYPE=A>
<LI>Introduction
   <OL>
   <LI>Title
       <OL TYPE=a>
           <LI>Author
           <LI>Institution
           <LI>Working title (20 words or fewer)
       </OL>
   <LI>Justification for research
       <OL TYPE=a>
           <LI>What? Why?
       </OL>
   <LI>Findings
   <LI>Conclusions
    </OL>
<LI>Body of Paper
   <OL>
   <LI>Previous research
   <LI>Research methods used
   <LI>Results and findings
   </OL>
<LI>Conclusion
   <OL>
   <LI>Implications
   <LI>Directions for future research
   </OL>
<LI>References
</OL>
```

This outline is displayed exactly as I'd hope when viewed in a Web browser, as you can see for yourself in Figure 10-5.

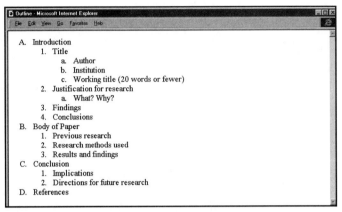

Figure 10-5: *An outline using special OL attributes*

If you've been experimenting as you've been reading this book — and I hope you are — you may already have found that different levels of unordered lists produce differently shaped bullets. In fact, Web browsers support three types of bullets — a solid disc, a circle, and a square — and you can specify which should be used for your unordered list with TYPE. For example, do you want a list in which every item is tagged with a square? <UL TYPE=square> does the trick.

Within the <LI> tag, you can specify TYPE=shape (if you're in the middle of an unordered list) or START=value (to change the current count for an ordered list). The following example shows how some of these features can be used in a Web document:

```
<B>Geometric Ramblings</B>
<OL TYPE=i>
<LI>Facets of a Square:
<UL TYPE=square>
<LI>four sides of equal length
</UL>
<LI>Interesting Facts about Circles:
<UL TYPE=disc>
<LI>maximum enclosed area, shortest line
</UL>
</OL>
<CENTER>Weird, unrelated information.</CENTER>
<OL TYPE=i>
<LI VALUE=3>and much, much more!
</OL>
```

Figure 10-6 shows how the preceding HTML text would be presented to the user. Note particularly that the numbered list seems to flow without any interruption, something that would be impossible to accomplish without these additions to the ordered list.

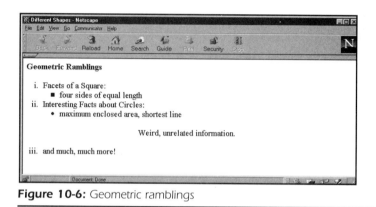

Figure 10-6: Geometric ramblings

Background Colors and Graphics

One aspect of Web page design that I really enjoy fiddling with, an area that can dramatically change the character of your Web site, is to specify a different background color for your page. If that's not enough, you can also load any graphic as the background to the entire page: a graphic that's either subtle (such as a marbled texture), or way over the top (such as a picture of your cat).

To do either of these, you need to add an attribute to the <BODY> tag that should already be an integral part of your existing Web pages. Once you start modifying the <BODY> tag, it becomes absolutely crucial that you place it in the correct spot on your pages. Remember, all Web pages should start with <HTML>, then have <HEAD> and a <TITLE>. </HEAD> ends the header section and then immediately you should have the <BODY> tag. If you have it in the wrong place — particularly if you have it subsequent to any specification of information to appear on the Web page itself (like a <H1> or even a <CENTER> tag) — then the background changes will be ignored by the browser.

Background colors are added with BGCOLOR=colorname or BGCOLOR=#rgb-value, and you specify a background graphic with BACKGROUND=filename.

It's fairly straightforward to work with background graphics, but the color specification for a background color, unfortunately, isn't quite so simple. If you want to have complete control, your colors will need to be specified as a trio of red-green-blue numeric values, two letters for each, in hexadecimal.

"Hexa-what?" I can hear you asking.

Hexadecimal is a numbering system that's base-16 rather than our regular numbering scheme of base-10 (decimal, as it's called). The number 10, for example, is $1 \times 10 + 0$, but in hexadecimal, it'd have the base-10 equivalent of $1 \times 16 + 0$, or 16.

Hexadecimal numbers range from 0 to 9 and also use A, B, C, D, E, and F to represent larger numbers. Instead of base 10, our regular numbering system, hex uses a base-16 numbering system, so in hex A = 10 decimal, B = 11 decimal, C = 12 decimal, D = 13 decimal, E = 14 decimal, and F = 15 decimal. 1B hex is $1 \times 16 + 11 = 27$ decimal. FF, therefore, is $F \times 16 + F$, or $15 \times 16 + 15 = 255$ decimal.

Don't worry too much if this doesn't make much sense to you. It's just important to know what some typical color values are, and they're shown in Table 10-1.

Table 10-1	Common Colors as Hex RGB Values
Hex Color Value	**Common Color Name**
00 00 00	Black
FF FF FF	White
FF 00 00	Red
00 FF 00	Green
00 00 FF	Blue
FF FF 00	Yellow
FF 00 FF	Purple
00 FF FF	Aqua

You should experiment with different colors to see how they look on your system. If you're working with basic colors, however, you can use their names (thankfully). A list of some of the most common are shown in Table 10-2.

Table 10-2	Popular Colors Available by Name		
AQUA	BLACK	BLUE	FUCHSIA
GRAY	GREEN	LIME	MAROON
NAVY	OLIVE	PURPLE	RED
SILVER	TEAL	WHITE	YELLOW

A word of warning: If you specify a color that can't be displayed on your system, the browser will try to produce a similar color by dithering, or creating a textured background with elements of each of the two closest colors. Sounds nice, but it isn't; you end up with a pebbly background that can make your text completely unreadable. The trick is to use the so-called Internet-safe color choices, if you're specifying color with a hex value. The good news is that it's pretty easy: just remember that each of the three basic colors (red, green, blue) should be chosen from 00 33 66 99 CC FF and you'll be fine. For example, CCCCCC is a light gray, and CCCCFF is an attractive light blue. I've included a file on the CD-ROM that enables you to see all 216 safe colors at once, called "safe-colors.html."

Have a look at a page that specifies a yellow background with BGCOLOR=yellow:

```
<HTML>
<BODY BGCOLOR=yellow>
One of the nice things about background colors is that you
can produce interesting and unusual effects with
relatively little work.
<P>
Want to have something look exactly like a piece of paper?
Use &lt;BGCOLOR=#FFFFFF&gt; or its equivalent
&lt;BGCOLOR=white&gt;.
<P>
Is green your favorite color? Try either
&lt;BGCOLOR=green&gt; or &lt;BGCOLOR=#00FF00&gt;.
</HTML>
```

Viewing this in your browser, as shown in Figure 10-7, affirms that the result indeed gives us a bright, cheery, and attractive yellow background.

Here you can see another HTML trick: to have ⟨ or ⟩ show up on a Web page, you have to do something special — specify the character as either the lt or gt (less than or greater than) symbol, wrapped in an ampersand and semicolon. Hence, < and >. I talked about these character entities in Chapter 5.

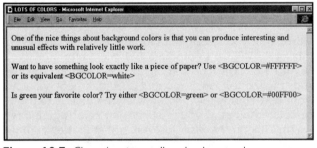

Figure 10-7: *Changing to a yellow background*

Graphical backgrounds are also easy to work with, albeit a bit more dangerous; even the most simple graphic can potentially obscure the text that you have on a particular page. Here's a simple example using a gridline graphic as the repeating background graphic:

```
<HTML>
<BODY BACKGROUND="gridline.gif">
<FONT SIZE=6>
<B>One of the nice things about background colors is that
you can produce interesting and unusual effects with
relatively little work. Background graphics, however, are
much more dangerous. How easy is this to read against the
grid background? You'll see even more wild examples as
you surf around on the Web, believe me!</B></FONT>
</BODY>
```

If you look closely at this HTML snippet, you'll see that I have not only made all the text larger with the ⟨FONT SIZE=6⟩ command, but I've also enclosed the entire passage within a bold formatting tag. Nonetheless, a glance at Figure 10-8 shows that it's still difficult to read.

Notice one other thing in Figure 10-8, however. The graphic "gridline.gif" is actually a small graphic – 100x300 – and instead of just having it show up once, the Web browser has tiled the graphic, repeating it over and over again to cover the entire page background.

The moral of this story: By all means, use these fun options, but be sensitive to the potential problems and nuances you might force onto your viewers because of their own hardware or preferences.

```
A Poor Background Graphic Choice - Microsoft Internet Explorer
File  Edit  View  Go  Favorites  Help

One of the nice things about background colors is
that you can produce interesting and unusual effects
with relatively little work. Background graphics,
however, are much more dangerous. How easy is this
to read against the grid background? You'll see even
more wild examples as you surf around on the Web,
believe me!
```

Figure 10-8: Background graphics can make pages unreadable.

Changing Text and Link Colors

Once you have the ability to change the color of the background on your Web page, the very next thing you need to learn is how to change the color of text and links on your site. All of these are controlled with additional attributes in the BODY tag:

Attribute	Meaning
TEXT	Color of the text on the page
LINK	Color of hypertext references
VLINK	Color of links you've visited
ALINK	Color of link while mouse button is down

These are almost always used together. For example, if you recall the Trivial Net screen shot from Chapter 8, you know that it had white text displayed on a black background. That was done with the following line of code:

```
<BODY BGCOLOR=#000000 TEXT=#FFFFFF>
```

If I wanted to have the links in yellow and the visited links in red, with the color of the hypertext text displayed in green while the user actually had their mouse button held down, I could use:

```
<BODY BGCOLOR=#000000 TEXT=#FFFFFF LINK=yellow VLINK=red
ALINK=green>
```

You can also see that you can mix and match color names and hexadecimal color values.

Scrolling Text in Explorer Marquees

Here's a fun tag that I think adds some appreciated pizzazz to a Web page, and with remarkably little work. The <MARQUEE> tag defines text that is displayed to the user in an animated region within a Web page. With a little tweak, you can take what's currently a phrase or two that's sitting passively on your page and transform it into a cheery animated area.

 This particular tag, however, is one that I won't be able to demonstrate here in the book because we don't yet have animated book pages! As you read this, therefore, please try the examples included on the CD-ROM.

The most basic use of the <MARQUEE> tag is:

```
<MARQUEE>text to animate</MARQUEE>
```

Because we already know that unknown HTML tags are just ignored by browsers that don't understand them, the text to animate will be displayed passively within Navigator or any other browser that doesn't include this feature. Note that MARQUEE is not a part of the HTML 4.0 specification, so it remains an oddball.

The <MARQUEE> tag has many possible attributes, the key one being BEHAVIOR, which can be specified as scroll, slide, or alternate. Scroll causes text to appear one letter at a time, scroll all the way across, vanish, and then start again (the default). Slide causes text to slide onto the screen and stop once the text touches the other margin. Alternate causes text to bounce back and forth within the marquee. You can specify the direction from which text scrolls with DIRECTION and a value of either left or right.

The size of a MARQUEE space is defined by the WIDTH and HEIGHT of the box, in either pixels or a percentage of screen size. Just like a graphics image, you can also specify the space around the marquee box with HSPACE and VSPACE, too.

Here's a relatively simple example:

```
<MARQUEE WIDTH=75%>Welcome to DeliveryTrac Online</MARQUEE>
```

This is included on the CD-ROM — try it and see what you think. If you're in Internet Explorer, you'll see the text scroll from the right onto the screen, slide to the left, and vanish, just to appear on the right again. Think of it as a tiny Times Square marquee hidden in your computer!

BGCOLOR enables you to specify the color of the marquee region. You can't have the background match a background image or pattern, alas, nor can you in any way modify the size or color of the text in the marquee. A refinement of the above, therefore, is:

```
<MARQUEE WIDTH=75% BGCOLOR=yellow>Welcome to DeliveryTrac
Online</MARQUEE>
```

Two more useful attributes for fine tuning your results: SCROLLAMOUNT lets you specify the exact number of pixels between each successive draw of the marquee text (which is most important when you have a small text region and lots of text), and SCROLLDELAY specifies the number of milliseconds — thousandths of a second — between each redraw of the marquee text.

Here's an example that combines a number of different possibilities:

```
<MARQUEE WIDTH=40% BGCOLOR=yellow BEHAVIOR=slide
    SCROLLDELAY=350>Slowly I creep onto your
screen...</MARQUEE><HR>
<MARQUEE BGCOLOR=#DDDDFF BEHAVIOR=alternate HEIGHT=10%>A
strange light
blue box size within which to spend my
days...</MARQUEE><HR>
```

Figure 10-9 shows the marquees at work a few seconds after loading the page in Internet Explorer, and Figure 10-10 shows the very same page within Netscape Navigator, which doesn't understand the <MARQUEE> tag.

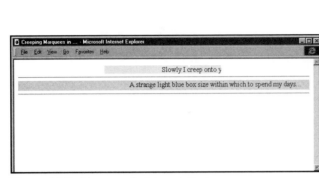

Figure 10-9: Marquees in Internet Explorer

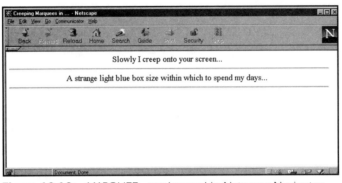

Figure 10-10: <MARQUEE> tag ignored in Netscape Navigator

I'm quite a fan of the <MARQUEE> tag when used judiciously. It frustrates me that <MARQUEE> didn't make it into the HTML 4.0 specification, because it's such a fun and easy way to add some life to your pages and assemble information in front of your visitors' eyes. Ah, well — maybe the 5.0 specification will include it.

Embedded Audio

Here's a scenario: You're working on a Web page for a pal and they turn around and ask if it's possible to add some background music to the page, something that helps "set the mood." You should answer: You bet!

There are two ways to include background audio, one of which works only with Internet Explorer and the other which works with the last few releases of Navigator and the most recent release of Internet Explorer.

Adding background audio

There are a small number of HTML tags that are free-form extensions, the most notable of which are the <META> tag (which we'll talk about in Chapter 18) and the <EMBED> tag. <EMBED> is being replaced by the more general <OBJECT> tag as per the HTML 4.0 specification, but it will continue to work just fine and, more importantly, will be understood by older browsers, too. The <EMBED> tag is similar to the <IMG> tag: you specify the SRC for the embedded element, an optional height and width, and any other attributes desired.

What makes this interesting to work with is that within Navigator, you can have a small audio control panel pop up on your screen if you don't specify a height and width of 0, but that exact same page displays no controls in Internet Explorer.

Here's how you might create a small control panel that'll play a WAV audio file as soon as someone loads the page in their browser:

```
<embed SRC="storm.wav" width=145 height=60>
```

If you want to have the audio control panel show up, but the audio not start until the user presses the "play" button, add AUTOSTART=false to the list of attributes. There's a HIDDEN=true attribute you can specify with the <EMBED> tag. Try it!

There are a couple of other attributes of interest: CONTROLS can be set to console or smallconsole to change the appearance of the player; VOLUME can be set from 1 to 255, with 255 being incredibly loud and 1 being quite soft. There's also a LOOP attribute, with its value set to either true or false. LOOP=true will play the audio forever, and LOOP=false (the default) causes the audio file to be played just once.

There are three common audio formats with this tag: WAV or AU audio samples, or a MIDI file, typically with the suffix MID.

If you're interested in MIDI files, I highly recommend a visit to MIDIFarm at http://www.midifarm.com/.

Explorer background audio

Explorer can understand the EMBED form of including a background audio file, but it also supports a different tag that you might consider if you're writing your page just for Explorer users. This variant is the <BGSOUND> tag and it has two possible attributes: SRC enables you to specify the actual audio file, and LOOP enables you to either play the audio track once or loop it for hours on end, eliciting cries of frustration and protest from otherwise calm and relaxed users.

An example follows:

```
<BGSOUND SRC=storm.wav LOOP=5>
```

would play the sound of a storm rumbling overhead — once loaded from the server — five times and go silent. This example is on disk, so you can try it for yourself if you like!

Explorer's Watermark Backgrounds

Earlier you learned how to add the BACKGROUND attribute to a Web page so you could specify a background graphic of some sort. Internet Explorer offers an interesting, if subtle, modification to this with the attribute BGPROPERTIES, which has only one possible value: fixed. Further, if you'd like to have your material appear slightly offset from the left edge of the page, you can use LEFTMARGIN=n to specify the width of your indent (in pixels). TOPMARGIN does the same thing for the very top of a page, too.

An example showing all of these:

```
<HTML>
<HEAD>
<TITLE>Sample of Watermark Backgrounds</TITLE>
</HEAD>
```

```
<BODY BACKGROUND=logo.gif BGPROPERTIES=fixed
LEFTMARGIN=20 TOPMARGIN=5>
One nifty new tag that's expected to show up in the
HTML 9.1 specification is the HOLO tag with the
all-important DIMENSIONS attribute that will let you
explore n-dimensional space on your own site.<br>
To see how this is a watermarked page, you'll want to
shrink the browser
window sufficiently small so that this information doesn't
all fit and
you have a scroll bar pop up on the right side.
<P>
Then you should  scroll the material and watch what
happens to the
background graphic.
<P>
Pretty cool!
</BODY>
</HTML>
```

The results are shown in Figure 10-11. Notice, in particular, the location of the text on the page.

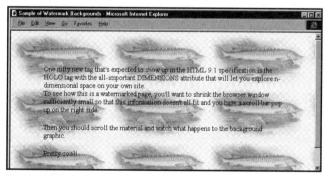

Figure 10-11: Custom body attributes in Explorer

Table 10-3 summarizes the HTML tags covered in this busy chapter.

Table 10-3 **HTML Tags Covered in This Chapter**

Tag	Close Tag	Meaning
`<CENTER>`	`</CENTER>`	Center material on the page
`<HR`		Horizontal rule
`SIZE=x`		Height of rule (in pixels)
`WIDTH=x`		Width of rule (in pixels or percentage)
`NOSHADE`		Turn off shading in horizontal rule.
`ALIGN=align`		Alignment of horizontal rule on page. (left, center, right)
`COLOR=color`		Color of horizontal rule (RGB or name) (IE only)
`<OL`		Ordered list
`TYPE=type`		Type of numbering. Possible values: A, a, I, i, 1.
`START=x`		Starting number of ordered list
`<UL`		Unordered list
`TYPE=shape`		Shape of bullet to use. Possible values: circle, square, disc
`<BODY`		Body of the document
`BGCOLOR=color`		Background color for page (RGB or color name)
`TEXT=color`		Color of text on page (RGB or color name)
`LINK=color`		Color of unvisited links on page (RGB or color name)
`VLINK=color`		Color of visited links on page (RGB or color name)
`ALINK=color`		Color of links during user click (RGB or color name)
`BACKGROUND=url`		Background graphic for page
`<MARQUEE`		Scrolling marquee (IE only)
`BEHAVIOR=opt`		Behavior of the marquee

Tag	Close Tag	Meaning
DIRECTION=*opt*		Direction from which the marquee scrolls (left, right)
HEIGHT=*x*		Height of marquee
WIDTH=*x*		Width of marquee
HSPACE=*x*		Additional horizontal space around marquee
VSPACE=*x*		Additional vertical space around marquee
BGCOLOR=*color*		Background color of marquee (RGB or color name)
SCROLLAMOUNT=*x*		Amount of material to add per unit time (in pixels)
SCROLLDELAY=*x*		Delay between refreshes in marquee (in milliseconds)
<EMBED		Embed audio on a Web page
SRC=*url*		Source of the audio file
WIDTH=*x*		Width of the displayed control, if any
HEIGHT=*x*		Height of the displayed control, if any
HIDDEN=*value*		If "true," then control is hidden from view
CONTROLS=*opt*		Type of display: "console" or "smallconsole"
VOLUME=*x*		Specify volume of the playback (0-255)
LOOP=*x*		Number of times to loop the audio
<BGSOUND		Background sound (IE only)
SRC=*url*		Source of the audio file
LOOP=*opt*		Number of times to loop the audio

This chapter gave you an overview of a number of advanced HTML tags offering the ability to include neat, simple additions to your page. Some of them only worked with a particular browser, which is something you need to consider carefully before you use them extensively in your design. Chapter 11 continues the exploration of advanced Web page elements with image maps, JavaScript, and more.

Image Maps, JavaScript, and Plug-Ins

In the early days of the Web, life was fairly simple for the inveterate Web page designer. There were perhaps 30 or so tags that needed to be understood to create powerful and visually exciting sites that offered compelling content. The vision of the original creators was enough impetus for things to get rolling, but in the last year or two, the Web has taken on a life of its own, not entirely unlike the ungainly monster of Mary Shelley's book. In this chapter, I'll explore some of these interesting new areas, most notably focusing on image maps, a tremendously powerful aspect of page design, JavaScript, the Java language itself, and we'll explore the plug-in architecture.

These extensions offer the potential to make your Web pages really state-of-the-art (and art is an important facet of Web page design, in case that hasn't become obvious as you've traveled through the chapters in this book).

Now that you've spent a fair amount of your time getting to understand the innards of HTML, you probably understand that it's extensible, and that people who write browsers can pretty much add whatever they want. In some sense that's true, but at its most fundamental, HTML is based on a page and document layout description language called *Standard Generalized Markup Language* (SGML). It offers some remarkable capabilities, but there are definite rough edges, areas where it just doesn't work. Designers have, therefore, rushed in with new scripting and programming languages to further expand the capabilities of the Web. Any of these additions is worthy of its own book — and many are covered in detail in other books in the Creating Cool Web Pages series from IDG Books Worldwide, Inc. — but it's useful to have a look at them here.

Before I take you to this brave new world, however, there are a few topics that haven't been discussed yet, but that you'll want to know before hanging your "Web Page Designer" shingle on your door, and that's how I'll start this chapter.

Image-Mapped Graphics

As you've explored the Web on your own, you've doubtless encountered sites on the Web that eschew mundane bulleted lists in favor of sexy, all-encompassing graphics. When you click a particular spot on the graphic, the system somehow knows where you clicked and moves you to the appropriate next page. This impressive trick is performed through the use of image maps, graphics that have specific regions associated with different URLs.

There are two ways to create an image map, the first and older being what are called server-side image maps. With a server-side image map, the HTML code that includes the mapped graphic is wrapped by an HREF pointing to a MAP file and the <IMG> tag is expanded to include the all-important ISMAP attribute. The MAP file, contained on the Web server, specifies all the known regions in the picture and associates them with specific URLs. ISMAP indicates that the image you're including is a mapped image; clicking different spots on the image produces different results.

A very simple example consists of three parts: the graphic, a few lines of HTML to specify the image map, and the region-to-URL MAP document. For example, an Arizona tourist site could allow visitors to click a map and find out more about the popular tourist destinations.

Following is the HTML. Notice the ISMAP addition to the arizona.gif image instruction:

```
<CENTER>
<IMG SRC="arizona-head.gif"><BR>
<A HREF="http://www.mysite.com/arizona.map">
<IMG ISMAP SRC="arizona.gif" BORDER=0></A><BR>
<B>Pick a City to Visit!</B>
</CENTER>
```

When displayed, the preceding snippet produces the graphic shown in Figure 11-1. Notice the map is displayed as a typical GIF image, without any special border or other indication that it is, in fact, an image map or anything other than a regular included graphic. Having an entire image as a single button, however, results in the standard colored border, which I turned off using the BORDER=0 attribute.

Figure 11-1: A clickable image map

The next step in creating our Arizona travel overview map is to identify the areas on the graphic that are the center of the desired hot spots — specific points on the image that are to have specific actions. I loaded the map into a simple graphics editor and, by moving the mouse pointer to the regions immediately surrounding Tucson and Phoenix, I ascertained that the surrounding rectangles are x,y coordinates 121,208 and 207,242 for Tucson, and 76,148 and 185,193 for Phoenix. (The coordinate 0,0 is the upper left-hand corner of the image.) The regions are shown in Figure 11-2.

I've already decided what geometric figure I want to use to define the limits of the hot spot. I opted for the rectangles shown in Figure 11-2 because they enable me to define a region easily around each of the two cities identified. Other choices could have been squares, circles, or others, as shown in Table 11-1.

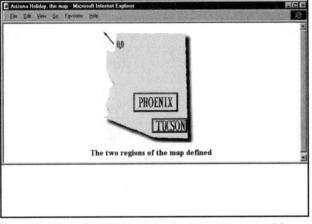

The two regions of the map defined

Figure 11-2: Defined regions on the image map graphic

Table 11-1	Shapes Available for ISMAP Files
Name	**Coordinates Needed in MAP File on Server**
circle	Center-point radius or, for NCSA image maps, center, edge point
poly	List of vertices, maximum 100
rect	Upper-left, lower-right
point	x,y

Here's where things get a bit puzzling if you're planning on experimenting with this yourself: The specific format of the map file, and even testing server-side image maps, is dependent on the type of server you're running. Some servers let you simply point to a "map" file anywhere on the system, others want them in a special shared mapfile directory, and yet others might not support image maps at all. That's okay, because in a moment, you'll learn about a superior alternative: client-side image maps. For now, however, let's continue with the server-side form.

There are two choices of Web servers from which everything else has sprung: CERN or NCSA. *CERN* is the Swiss organization that invented the World Wide Web, and NCSA is the group that developed the popular Mosaic Web browser that really started the Web growing at its current phenomenal rate. NCSA is the National Center for Supercomputer Applications at the University of Illinois, Urbana-Champaign. Most of the Web servers you'll find today that support server-side image maps use the NCSA-format maps.

NCSA servers use the format `Region/URL/Points`. CERN-style MAP files use the general layout `method/coordinates/URL`, with points surrounded by parentheses. All of this is shown in the actual image map file shown here:

```
rect tucson.html 121,208 207,242
rect phoenix.html 76,148 185,193
default countryside.html
```

The two regions defined will let users click near the cities of Phoenix or Tucson and learn more about those specific places. That's the first two lines above. The Phoenix entry is exemplary: The region defined for this action within the graphic image (arizona.gif) is a rectangle defined by the two points 76,148 and 185,193, and any clicks within it result in the user being transferred to the URL phoenix.html. Because users might well click outside of the two spots I've defined, I also added a default action with the default specification: users who click any area that is not covered by the two rectangles will be connected to the countryside.html page.

By contrast, if I were using a CERN server, my MAP file would look somewhat different, because CERN changes the order of fields to `method/ coordinates/URL` and adds parentheses around map points. Consider the changes to the specification:

```
default countryside.html
rect (76,148) (185,193) phoenix.html
rect (121,208) (207,242) tucson.html
```

Although defining and calculating all the points in complex ISMAP graphics may be tedious, the result can be tremendously effective, as you've seen in the attractive opening graphics of many of the sites you see online every day.

Seeing the complexity of the MAP file, you can understand why specific tools that help you create ISMAP data files are wonderful things that save Web page developers lots of time. Even better, you can obtain a variety of different image map assistants for free on the Internet, whether you're on a Macintosh, a UNIX workstation, or a PC running Windows. The two programs I use for creating image maps are:

LiveImage for Windows95	`http://www.mediatec.com/`
Mapper for Macintosh	`http://www.calles.pp.se/nisseb/`

You will unquestionably want to have one of these programs; I do all my image maps in Mapper. Without this type of software, you'll go crazy trying to get things right, but with them, it's quite fun!

Client-Side Image Mapping

Image maps are very useful for complex Web site design, but there's one small problem: You need to be constantly interacting with the server. There's another, better way you can have active regions on an image: client-side image maps.

Until client-side image mapping was widespread in the popular Web browsers (mid-'97), all the definition of regions, calculation of which area you typed, and what should happen took place on the server, but only if the server allowed that particular page to include image maps. By moving the processing to the client side, it means you're freeing up server resources, speeding up the user experience and gaining greater control over the map itself. In my opinion, it's a great improvement.

To build a client-side image map, I first define a set of regions on the desired graphic, in this case a map of the Virgin Islands, that I want to have as active spots on the graphic. Figure 11-3 shows this as a series of rectangular regions.

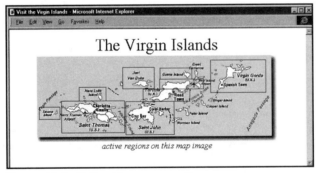

Figure 11-3: Defined hot spots on the map

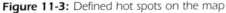

Armed with that, and with a little help from one of the many image map editors available as shareware on the Net, I produce a MAP data file in CERN format.

 Both the programs I talk about above can produce client-side image maps directly. I'll show you the typical automated output in a few paragraphs, but I think it's useful to see how image maps evolved.

```
default default.html
rect (9,120) (56,149) savanna.html
rect (67,106) (220,168) stthomas.html
rect (109,76) (173,107) hans.html
rect (208,28) (287,81) vandyke.html
rect (431,7) (561,89) gorda.html
rect (299,32) (378,57) guana.html
rect (222,112) (329,181) stjohn.html
rect (235,82) (417,111) tortola.html
rect (290,57) (426,84) tortola.html
```

It turns out this isn't quite what is needed for a client-side map, because this format, besides being a bit ugly, is also a format for a server-side image map. Neither of the possible formats is quite right for client-side maps, but CERN is probably a smidgen closer.

To define client-side image regions, each of the lines above is re-spun so that each field is an attribute within the new <AREA> HTML tag.

Here's how the region data appears in an HTML file to create a client-side map:

```
<HTML>
<TITLE>Visit the Virgin Islands</TITLE>
<CENTER>
<FONT SIZE=6>The Virgin Islands</FONT><BR>
<IMG SRC="virgin.gif" USEMAP="#map1" BORDER=0><BR>
<B>Where would you like to go?</B>
</CENTER>
<MAP NAME="map1">
<AREA SHAPE="rect" COORDS="9,120,56,149"
HREF="savanna.html">
<AREA SHAPE="rect" COORDS="67,106,220,168"
HREF="stthomas.html">
<AREA SHAPE="rect" COORDS="109,76,173,107"
HREF="hans.html">
<AREA SHAPE="rect" COORDS="208,28,287,81"
HREF="vandyke.html">
<AREA SHAPE="rect" COORDS="431,7,561,89"
HREF="gorda.html">
<AREA SHAPE="rect" COORDS="299,32,378,57"
HREF="guana.html">
<AREA SHAPE="rect" COORDS="222,112,329,181"
HREF="stjohns.html">
```

(continued)

```
(continued)
<AREA SHAPE="rect" COORDS="235,82,417,111"
HREF="tortola.html">
<AREA SHAPE="rect" COORDS="290,57,426,84"
HREF="tortola.html">
<AREA SHAPE="rect" COORDS="0,0,600,200"
HREF="default.html">
</MAP>
</HTML>
```

There's a lot to see here, so let's take it in order. First, notice the new option to the <IMG> formatting tag: USEMAP=*internal-reference-name*. Like the internal document anchors you learned about earlier, the reference to the map data must have a # as the first character, and the actual target omits that symbol. Here, I'm leaving the option of having multiple maps on this page by naming this map1.

Below this is the fun stuff: the tag that defines the region of a defined map (<MAP>) and the specific regions defined for each spot within the image (<AREA>). Still with me?

Here's how a specific rectangular region translated from CERN to AREA format. The region for Guana Island started out defined as:

```
rect (299,32) (378,57) guana.html
```

but because HTML wants name=value parameters, I had to change that format to one where the shape of the region is defined, then the coordinates for that region, then the URL connected with the specified region. That is:

```
<AREA SHAPE="rect" COORDS="299,32,378,57"
HREF="guana.html">
```

Outside of this simple mapping of fields to values, the biggest change you can see in the changes for a client-side image map is that there's no default area anymore. Instead, I simply defined a region that was the size of the image (0,0 to 600,200 in pixels from the top left of the image) and specified that its action should be to go to the URL default.html. By definition, the list of map coordinates is only perused until the spot you click is found, so having two identical regions specified in the <MAP> tag means that you'd never get to the second choice.

On server-side image maps, you can choose from a wide palette of different geometric shapes. Client-side maps are no different, as shown in Table 11-2.

Table 11-2	Shapes and Required Parameters for Client-Side Maps	
SHAPENAME	**Meaning**	**Parameters Required**
rect	Rectangle	Takes four coordinates: x_1, y_1, x_2, and y_2
rectangle	Rectangle	Takes four coordinates: x_1, y_1, x_2, and y_2
circ	Circle	Takes three coordinates: center$x$, center$y$, and radius
circle	Circle	Takes three coordinates: center$x$, center$y$, and radius
poly	Polygon	Takes three or more pairs of coordinates denoting a polygonal region
polygon	Polygon	Takes three or more pairs of coordinates denoting a polygonal region

As promised, the latest breed of Web graphic mapping tools can output a client-side image map directly. Thank goodness; this saves all the twiddling shown above and makes life quite a bit better.

Let's look at another example to see how it works. Figure 11-4 shows a photograph that I'd like to turn into a client-side image map so that if you click the woman, you get information about her, and clicking the man shows information about him.

Figure 11-4: Cameo photo, ready for image map creation

Both LiveMap and Mapper can directly output a client-side image map; here's a typical output:

```
<MAP NAME="cameo">
<AREA SHAPE="polygon"
COORDS=    "94,28,188,244,46,216,36,103,94,28"
HREF="her.html"><AREA SHAPE="polygon" COORDS=
    "96,29,188,245,255,162,201,37,96,29"
HREF="him.html">
</MAP>
```

Obviously, it doesn't produce the entire Web page, but this client image map — one that consists of multi-point polygons — would have been just about impossible to create by hand.

 The Microsoft Web site has some excellent further documentation on client-side maps and their other extensions to HTML. Check it out at: http://www.microsoft.com/workshop/author/default.asp.

Animated GIFs

Let's continue looking at some fun additions that you probably see daily on your Web visits without knowing exactly how they work. The first capability that has taken the Web by storm is animated GIF graphics.

GIF format, as you'll recall, is the basic graphics format used by most pages on the Web. It allows the designer to create a single graphic, large or small, which is displayed on the page. But what if, just like an old-time movie, you could have a sequence of graphics and instead of just a single picture, the browser would continually cycle through the sequenced images?

That's exactly what animated GIFs are all about, and their use can range from a whirring disk or star to bouncing letters, even to the Microsoft Internet Explorer logo itself. You have learned a bit about animated GIF, the format, but this time I'd like to explore how to create an animation.

To create an animated GIF you need one thing — patience. I created the dancing "jazz" GIF included on the CD-ROM by creating a single graphic, and then duplicating it four times, each time moving the letters around a bit. Then I used an animated GIF program (GIFBuilder on the Mac, actually, but GIF Construction Set is also terrific) to bring in each of the images as an individual frame of the resulting animation. Check out the results (shown in Figure 11-5) and see what you think!

Note that you can specify the delay time between images. With a longer delay time, you can have completely different graphics on individual images and use the set of images as a sort of slide show.

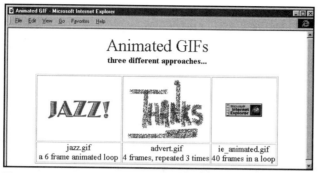

Figure 11-5: An example of animated GIF images

 There's another approach to animation that's worth mentioning here — progressive JPEGs. The idea is that they combine animation with the greater color quality of the JPEG format, but the reality is that it's extremely rare to see animation that isn't an animated GIF. If you'd like more information, Netscape has some information on progressive JPEGs on its site.

Multiple-Resolution Graphics

A neat trick that Netscape Navigator lets you do — but Internet Explorer ignores — is having two versions of a graphic sent to the user: a low-resolution, smaller image that loads quickly, and a higher-resolution, full-color image that replaces the coarse or low-color image when received. The idea is that you can have a rough version of your graphics that downloads quickly, letting users immediately start working with your page and having a rough idea of the included images. If they remain on the page, the higher-quality version of the images gradually replaces the low-resolution version, and the final page is very attractive and highly functional.

To accomplish this, Navigator understands a new attribute in the <IMG> tag: LOWSRC. If seen, the LOWSRC graphic will be loaded into the page first, and then the default higher resolution image will replace it. Here's an example:

```
<IMG SRC="photo-hires.jpg" LOWSRC="photo-lores.gif"
HEIGHT=300 WIDTH=150>
```

In this case, I have two versions of my graphic: a black-and-white GIF image that's about 15K, and a full-color JPEG version that's just under 60K in size. This example is explored on the CD-ROM.

A second way to work with low-res/high-res graphics is to take advantage of the auto-scaling feature of Navigator. I warned you earlier that specifying a `HEIGHT` and `WIDTH` different from the actual size of the image causes the browser to automatically blow up the image to fit, regardless of how attractive it looks. Now you can use it to your advantage: The `LOWSRC` image could be a thumbnail version of the larger image, but if you specify the exact size of the larger image, the browser will show a very fuzzy version and then replace it with the clean version. Figures 11-6 and 11-7 show how this might look as a two-step process.

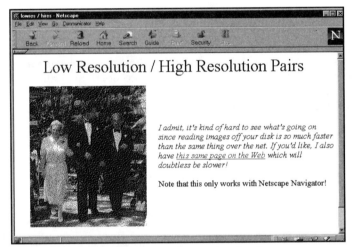

Figure 11-6: Low-resolution image, sized to fit a larger area.

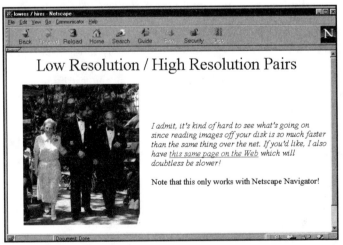

Figure 11-7: High-resolution image replaces the low-resolution image.

JavaScript

Here's a common point of confusion for not only people who use the Net, but even people who write about it. JavaScript is a simple programming language, a scripting language, for defining the behavior of elements on a Web page. It's not the same as the much more complex Java programming language, which offers a robust and sophisticated environment for creating lots of applications.

JavaScript is not dissimilar to BAT batch files, which you might be familiar with from DOS, or UNIX shell scripts. Typically just a few lines long, JavaScript can specify responses to actions or events like the page being opened, the mouse moving to a specific spot, or a field in a form being cleared. The structure of the language itself is a bit weird, alas, so let's just jump in and have a look.

The simplest JavaScript application is one that pops up a message:

```
<HTML>
<HEAD>
<SCRIPT LANGUAGE="JavaScript">
<!-- sample JavaScript
alert('When you're ready to see this page...')
// end of script -->
</SCRIPT>
</HEAD>
<BODY BGCOLOR=white>
Clicking on "OK" got you here!
</BODY>
</HTML>
```

Notice here that the script is wrapped in `<SCRIPT>` and `</SCRIPT>` and that it's all buried in a comment so that browsers that don't understand JavaScript won't get confused by the script itself. Figure 11-8 shows what happens when you first visit this page.

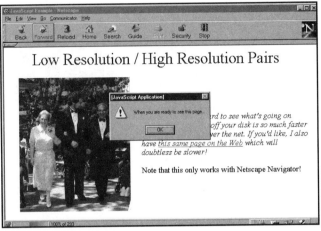

Figure 11.8: JavaScript pop-up dialog box

Here's another example, this time one that changes what's displayed on the status line of your browser based on where you move your mouse:

```
<HTML>
<BODY BGCOLOR=white>
<BASEFONT SIZE=4>
<CENTER>
<FONT SIZE=6>Embedded Javascript events:
<B>onMouseOver</B></FONT><BR>
<I>move your mouse onto the two lines below<BR>
and watch the status window on the very bottom of your
browser</I>
</CENTER>
<P>
<A HREF="javaspt2.html"
    onMouseOver="self.status='you have no status, but you
DO have bananas!';return true">
drag your mouse over me</A>
<P>
<A HREF="javaspt2.html"
    onMouseOver="self.status='no, you got no bananas
either!';return true">
or better yet, drag your mouse over me!</A>
</BODY>
</HTML>
```

Lots of different events can be scripted with JavaScript. In the example above, things happen when you move your mouse over either of the two hyperlinks, as shown in Figure 11-9.

Figure 11-9: Notice the status bar message.

It turns out that there are a number of scriptable events in JavaScript, as shown in Table 11-3.

JavaScript is a simple language to use, but it will still take some time to master. There are some terrific online tutorials that can help you out, fortunately, including the JavaScript Guide at Netscape: `http://developer. netscape.com/library/documentation/communicator/jsguide4/ index.htm`. You also can find a wealth of information and example scripts by exploring the links shown on the CD-ROM.

Table 11-3	Scriptable Events in JavaScript	
Event	**Occurs When**	**Event Handler**
blur	User removes input focus from form element	onBlur
click	User clicks form element or link	onClick
change	User changes value of text, text area, or select element	onChange
focus	User gives form element input focus	onFocus
load	User loads the page in the browser	onLoad
mouseover	User moves mouse pointer over a link or anchor	onMouseOver
select	User selects form element's input field	onSelect
submit	User submits a form	onSubmit
unload	User exits the page	onUnload

Before we leave JavaScript, let's look at two more, considerably more sophisticated, examples. In this first case, we want to actually change the graphic itself when the cursor is placed over it — exactly as you see with the CD-ROM examples.

The key to this is that there are two versions of each graphic: the "on" graphic and the "off" graphic. For this example, I'm going to have a company logo that animates when the cursor is placed over it; then goes back to a static graphic otherwise.

Here's the listing:

```
<SCRIPT LANGUAGE="JavaScript">
<!--
// We want to have the logo animated when the cursor is
over it.
logo_on  = new Image();          //  allocate space for the
on image
logo_off = new Image();          //  and the off image too
logo_on.src  = 'logo-on.gif';    //  next set the actual
graphics
logo_off.src = 'logo-off.gif';

function activate(image) {        //  switch the image from
'off' to 'on'
     imagesrc = eval(image + '_on.src');
     document[image].src = imagesrc;
}

function deactivate(image) {    //  switch back to 'off' from
'on'
     imagesrc = eval(image + "_off.src");
     document[image].src = imagesrc;
}
// end of script               -->
</SCRIPT>

<CENTER>
<a href=logo.html
   OnMouseOver="activate('logo');return true;"
   OnMouseOut="deactivate('logo');return true;" >
<img src=logo-off.gif alt="[company logo]" border=0
name='logo'></a>
</CENTER>
```

Now, before you panic, let's go through this step by step: First, to accomplish any dynamic change of graphic on the page, we need to name the actual graphic. Notice that the <IMG> tag includes the new name='logo' attribute. The JavaScript line

```
document[image].src = imagesrc;
```

uses the image name (in this case 'logo') to figure out which of the graphics on the page to change to the specified image source.

The real key to having this work, of course, is to tie the activate and deactivate events to specific Web events: OnMouseOver and OnMouseOut. The first invokes the activate JavaScript procedure when the mouse is put over the graphic, and the second switches it back when out. Figures 11-10 and 11-11 show you the page with the cursor off the graphic and on the graphic.

Figure 11-10: JavaScript-enabled logo: MouseOut

Figure 11-11: JavaScript-enabled logo: MouseOver

Both procedures have an identical line: `imagesrc=eval(image+'_on.src')`. This calculates the specific image name needed: the result of the call to activate (`'logo'`), for example, produces an `imagesrc` of `logo_on.src`.

Whether you fully understand what's happening, I encourage you to not only experiment with the existing sample on the CD-ROM, but to try creating new graphics of your own. Create "on" and "off" graphics, and simply copy and paste the JavaScript shown above. You'll need to call the `Image()` routine for each graphic, then set the file with `name.src` as shown above.

Of course, another way to see how this works is to view the source to some pages that are using JavaScript in interesting ways. One example is on the CD-ROM, but I'll also invite you to visit my home page and pay particular attention to the home page and how things are working underneath.

One final note: Some earlier browsers support JavaScript but don't necessarily interpret it all correctly. You can wrap your JavaScript with some statements that force the script to only run on the more recent software. It'd look like this:

```
if (parseInt(navigator.appVersion.substring(0,1)) >= 3)   {
```

Scrolling messages

A second capability that JavaScript offers is a scrolling message on the bottom of the page, on the status line. You already saw how to set the status value based on a specific event by changing the `window.status` value, but the following script demonstrates how to take this idea considerably further:

```
<SCRIPT LANGUAGE="JavaScript">
<!--

function StartScroll() {
  msg="---      The latest results from the New York Stock
Exchange: " +
      "Microsoft: up 1.5, Netscape: up 1.5, Sun Micro:
down 3.4      ";
  ScrollMessage();  // now let's get the scrolling started!
}
```

```
function ScrollMessage() {
  window.status = msg;          // set the message to the
current substring...
  msg=msg.substring(1,msg.length) + msg.substring(0,1);
// produce a new subset
  timer=setTimeout("ScrollMessage()", 100);  // in specified
1000ths of a sec do it again.
}

StartScroll();     // start the scrolling sequence going.

// done with script listing   -->

</SCRIPT>

<BODY BGCOLOR=white>
<CENTER>
<FONT SIZE=+2>
The scrolling ticker below is courtesy of JavaScript.
<P>
You might well want to "view source" to see what you
think.
</CENTER>
</BODY>
```

Figure 11-12 shows a snapshot of how this would display, though you really need to bring this example up on your screen to see what's really going on.

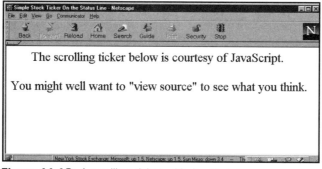

Figure 11-12: A scrolling ticker with JavaScript

The script starts running as soon as the browser sees the line:

```
StartScroll();     // start the scrolling sequence going.
```

which then initializes the message string — in this case, it's a mock stock ticker — and calls the `ScrollMessage()` procedure. `ScrollMessage` changes the status window, chops a new slice of the message string, then uses the `setTimer` routine to call itself again the specified number of thousandths of a second later (in this case, it's 100 thousandths, or **1/10** of a second).

Digging more deeply

This has only scratched the surface. If you really want to learn about all the capabilities of JavaScript, you'll want to get an additional book just on the subject. Or check out some of the cool online sites offering information about JavaScript:

JavaScript Made Easy `http://www.calpoly.edu/~dpopeney/javascript.html`

JavaScript `http://javascript.developer.com/`

JavaScript Planet `http://www.geocities.com/SiliconValley/7116/`

Visual Basic Script

JavaScript is powerful, but unlike any language that most programmers and users have ever learned. Visual Basic, on the other hand, is a language based on the one most everyone learned when they were first starting out with computers. Microsoft offers Visual Basic Script for Internet Explorer — VBScript — as an alternative to JavaScript.

Here's how a simple VBScript program might look:

```
<HTML>
<BODY BGCOLOR=white>
<SCRIPT LANGUAGE="VBScript" EVENT="OnClick" FOR="Button1">
<!--
    MsgBox "You clicked on the button and up popped me!"
-->
</SCRIPT>
<CENTER>
<FORM>
<INPUT NAME="Button1" TYPE="BUTTON"
       VALUE="Roses are red, beloved by the bee..."><BR>
<I>click the button</I>
</FORM>
</CENTER>
</HTML>
```

The script appears very similar to JavaScript in the HTML document, but the language itself is easier to work with, in my opinion. Unfortunately, you can do the math: VBScript is only supported in Internet Explorer, but JavaScript is supported in both Navigator and Internet Explorer. As a result, JavaScript, is unquestionably, the scripting language of choice.

One group that could have gone a long way to minimize this confusion is the World Wide Web Consortium, W3, the group that defined and standardized the HTML specifications, including HTML 4.0. Unfortunately, they decided not to take a stance on anything and simply note how to include a scripting language on a Web page, rather than which language they recommended.

If you're not dissuaded, try this particular example in your own Internet Explorer program. When you click the button, you should see a dialog box pop up identical to Figure 11-13.

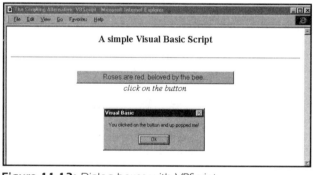

Figure 11-13: Dialog boxes with VBScript

You can learn a lot more about Visual Basic Script by visiting the terrific http://www.vbscripts.com; or you can check out the information Microsoft has at http://www.microsoft.com/VBASIC/.

Java

In terms of sheer enthusiasm in the press and incessant commentary from pundits everywhere, no new technology introduced on the Net has been as widely heralded as Java, from Sun Microsystems. Your favorite computer magazine probably told you that Java would save the world, cure world hunger, and, did I mention, lower the prime lending rate or wash your car?

The reality is somewhat different. Java is a complex, object-oriented programming language based on a powerful language called C++, which itself was a modified version of the C programming language so beloved by UNIX folks. C was originally developed to write UNIX device drivers, so it shares many characteristics with the most primitive of languages: assembler. Add a layer of object-oriented capabilities and you've got C++. Tweak it further for the Net and you have Java.

The good news is that there is a wide variety of different Java-development environments available for Windows and Macintosh systems, and they make things quite a bit easier. Even better, you can use Java applets, as they're called, without even having much of a clue about Java itself.

Let's start, nonetheless, by having a look at a simple Java program:

```
class HelloWorld {

  public static void main (String args[]) {

    System.out.println("Hello World!");

  }
}
```

That is what's involved in getting the program to say "Hello World!" within a Web page. You can't send this script directly in your HTML page, though. You need to actually translate it into a Java applet binary by compiling it; to work with Java, you must have some sort of development environment.

Referencing Java applets

If you can't include the Java source or compiled binary in your HTML code, you might wonder just how you actually include Java applets on your page. The answer used to be the <APPLET> tag, but HTML 4.0 replaces that with the OBJECT tag instead. OBJECT has a variety of parameters, the most important of which is the classid parameter, which specifies the exact name of the applet desired. At its simplest:

```
<OBJECT codetype="application/octet-stream"
  classid="java:DrawStringApplet.class"
  width=100 height=100></OBJECT>
```

The codetype specified is actually what's called a MIME type. Originally, the MIME standard was intended for e-mail attachments — indeed, it's the Multimedia Internet Mail Extensions — but it's now used as a general purpose media attachment standard. In this case, you're informing the Web browser that the Java applet is a stream of program data.

 If you're used to the APPLET tag, the previous example would have been written as: `<APPLET code="DrawStringApplet.class" width=100 height=100></APPLET>`. You should start to use OBJECT, however, because APPLET is being phased out of the HTML language.

The above HTML snippet defines a 100 × 100 box that shows the results of the DrawStringApplet when loaded and run.

To send information to an applet prior to it running, you need to use the `<PARAM>` tag, which actually hasn't changed, even though the `<APPLET>` tag has transmogrified into `<OBJECT>`. Here's how you'd use it:

```
<P>
<OBJECT codetype="application/octet-stream"
    classid="DrawStringApplet.class" width=200 height=200>
<PARAM name="String" value="Hi there!">
Text to display if OBJECT isn't loaded
</OBJECT>
</BODY>
</HTML>
```

Online Java applets

You can add all sorts of Java applets to your own Web pages by simply adding the appropriate reference to your pages. There are dozens upon dozens of nifty applets online, many of which live at Sun's Java division Web site, Javasoft (go to `http://www.javasoft.com/applets/js-applets.html` or `http://java.sun.com/applets/js-applets.html`) and many more that live at Gamelan's online Java library at `http://www.gamelan.com/`. There's also an online magazine just about Java that is not only very good, but run by a bunch of friends of mine: It's called JavaWorld, and you can visit it at `http://www.javaworld.com`. I encourage you to explore some of these resources online!

 There's a fabulous Java programming tutorial written by Elliotte Rusty Harold at `http://sunsite.unc.edu/javafaq/javatutorial.html`.

ActiveX

If Java is going to save the world, then ActiveX is going to save us from Java — or something like that. ActiveX is Microsoft's contribution to the programming-languages-on-the-Net debate and offers many of the same capabilities and complexities. The big difference: Java works with both Navigator and Explorer, but ActiveX is only for the Microsoft browser at this point.

 Not necessarily: NCompass Labs has a plug-in called Ncompass for Netscape Navigator that enables it to use ActiveX Controls. Find out more at http://www.ncompasslabs.com.

If you haven't been keeping track, ActiveX evolved from Microsoft's OLE technology by way of the OCX implementation. If that's Greek to you, don't worry; it's Greek to me, too!

ActiveX functions as a wrapper called an ActiveX control. The code being included interacts with the wrapper (ActiveX), and the wrapper interacts with the browser directly. Using this technique, just about any code can run within the browser space, from word processors and spreadsheets to simple games and animation.

Each ActiveX control has a unique class ID and is included as an <OBJECT> tag, with parameters specified in the <PARAM> tag, remarkably similar to JavaScript:

```
<OBJECT ID="ClientLayout"
    CLASSID="CLSID:812AE312-8B8E-11CF-93C8-00AA00C08FDF">
    <PARAM NAME="ALXPATH" REF VALUE="Client.alx">
</OBJECT>
```

There are a couple of sites to learn more about ActiveX, thank goodness, because it's easy to include, but difficult to understand. Microsoft is an obvious one: Go to http://www.microsoft.com/sitebuilder/. ZDNet also has a nice resource on-line at http://www.zdnet.com/products/activexuser.html, and CMP has one at http://www.activextra.com.

VRML

So far, everything we've done with Web pages has happened in two dimensions: Things either move horizontally or vertically. Indeed, because a computer screen is only two-dimensional, that probably makes sense. But you need merely glance at Myst or Doom to realize that simulating a three-dimensional world on a computer screen isn't too hard, and so, if it can be done, it can be done on the Web!

That's where the *Virtual Reality Modeling Language* (VRML) comes into the picture. VRML is a simple language that lets you create complex and sophisticated three-dimensional worlds that users can navigate through using any of a variety of VRML viewer applications or plug-ins.

The current version of VRML is quite simple and looks somewhat like Java. Here's a snippet that defines a single green globe in space:

```
Material {
    diffusedColor 0.2 1 0.2   # red, green and blue values}
Sphere {
    radius 10
}
```

Once you start using a VRML development environment you can really create some amazing worlds, and there are people on the Net who have done some fabulous work. Figure 11-14 shows one such example, a snapshot of the VRML version of San Diego by ultimately cool Planet 9 multimedia (`http://www.planet9.com`).

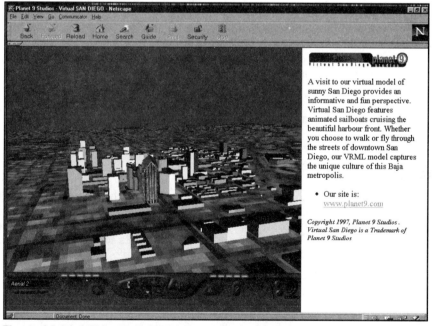

Figure 11-14: VRML virtual San Diego, a space through which to fly.

Netscape Navigator includes a nice viewer application called Live3D that enables you to work with VRML worlds while within the browser: It's included in the full version of Navigator 3.0 and 4.0. There are also a variety of other companies offering VRML utilities, including Virtus (http://www.virtus.com), Microsoft (http://www.microsoft.com), and more.

 Check out *VRMLSite* magazine online for lots of fun stuff: http://www.vrmlsite.com.

Plug-Ins: Shockwave and RealAudio

Some of what's been covered in this chapter are specific elements of a general software architecture shared by both Navigator and Explorer called "plug-ins," small helper applications that manage a region of a Web page you're viewing. There are more than a hundred different plug-ins available from a wide variety of sources, and they range from a MIDI player from Yamaha (the musical keyboard people) to a 3D world exploration plug-in from Sony — from the RealAudio audio player to Macromedia's Shockwave. The best place to find out about plug-ins is to visit the Netscape plug-in information page by clicking About Plug-ins from the Navigator Help menu.

Having said that, I have to admit that, in general, I don't really like plug-ins. The problem is, if they aren't already incorporated into the Web browser itself, it's quite a stumbling block for people coming to your site. Imagine: to fully enjoy a particular page, you have to actually stop, download some new software (if you can find it), install it, relaunch your browser, and hope to remember the page you were on in the first place.

Two plug-ins, though, are worth special mention before I wrap up this chapter: RealAudio and Shockwave.

RealAudio

If you experimented with the audio clips I included to demonstrate the background audio capabilities in Chapter 10, you already know that it works like this: You request the audio, wait for the entire audio file to load, and then start to hear the music. That works fine for small music samples of 10KB to 50KB, but if you have more audio, the size of the file could produce a delay of five minutes or more before any audio is played. That's unacceptable.

The solution is RealAudio, a streaming audio player. Once RealAudio receives a few seconds' worth of music, it actually plays the audio simultaneously to receiving further information. This is a great idea, and one that makes audio on the Web a reality. Even better, both Netscape and Microsoft have licensed and included the RealAudio plug-in with their latest browsers, so you can simply click a RealAudio stream and tune in to a cyberspace radio program. Most excellent.

On the CD-ROM in this book, there's a short list of some fun RealAudio servers; if you have a Net connection, I encourage you to visit a few and see what you think.

Visit the RealAudio home page at `http://www.realaudio.com` for lots of samples, and don't miss National Public Radio on the Web while you're there.

Shockwave

The other slick, must-have plug-in is Shockwave. It evolved from a terrific multimedia authoring program called Director from Macromedia. If you've ever seen a demo program running on a computer at a trade show or computer store, or even explored an interactive CD-ROM catalog, you've probably been using a Director presentation. With its capability to simultaneously work with audio, animation, video, text and user input, it's a powerful package. When the Web craze hit, the folks at Macromedia started thinking about extending Director so that its data files could be used directly on the Net, and that's Shockwave in a nutshell.

Most sites that use Shockwave today create fancy animation with synchronized sound (which is harder to do than you'd think), but in the future, I think there are going to be some amazing Shockwave files floating around on the Net.

You can learn more about Shockwave, get the Shockwave plug-in, and view lots of examples and demonstrations of the technology on the Macromedia Web site at `http://www.macromedia.com`.

Table 11-4 shows you the new HTML tags presented in this chapter.

Table 11-4	HTML Tags Covered in This Chapter	
Tag	Close Tag	Meaning
`<IMG`		Image inclusion tag
`ISMAP`		Specifies that it's a server-side image map
`USEMAP=mapname`		Use the specified client-side image map
`LOWSRC=url`		Lower-resolution image to load first (Navigator only)
`<MAP`	`</MAP>`	Specifies regions of a client-side image map

(continued)

Tag	Close Tag	Meaning
NAME=#mapname		Name of image map (corresponds to USEMAP in <IMG> tag)
<AREA		Defines a specific region in an image map
SHAPE=shape		Shape of region. Possible values: rect, circ, point, poly.
COORDS=coords		Coordinates on image. Value varies by region shape.
HREF=url		URL associated with the specified region.
<SCRIPT	</SCRIPT>	Include a script, usually JavaScript, in Web page
LANGUAGE=lang		Language used for script
EVENT=event		Event that triggers specified script.
FOR=objectname		Name of object on page upon which script acts
<OBJECT>	</OBJECT>	Include an arbitrary object on the page
CODETYPE=opt		MIME type of object (ex: application/octet-stream)
CLASSID=url		Identifies the object or class of object (Java only)
WIDTH=x		Width of space needed for object on page
HEIGHT=x		Height of object on page
<PARAM		Parameters to send to <OBJECT>
NAME=name		Name of parameter
VALUE=str		Value of named parameter

Table 11-4 *(continued)*

Summary

This chapter gave you an overview of the many extensions to HTML and scripting capabilities offered through plug-ins and additions to the top Web browsers. Chapter 12 explores how to create interactive Web pages and obtain information from the viewer through HTML forms.

Forms and User Input

In This Chapter

An introduction to HTML forms

Extending your forms with fancy formatting

Easy searching from your page

More form tricks

This chapter provides an introduction to forms. Just like the ubiquitous paper with the dozens of fill-in boxes from the government and just about any bureaucratic institute with which you're involved, Web pages can not only model paper forms, but have some very interesting and valuable capabilities of their own. Chapter 13 is a close companion, covering how to receive the information from the forms you'll learn how to construct herein.

I'm going to be honest with you right up front: I've broken this topic into two separate chapters to highlight that working with forms, requesting information from the user, and sending it to a designated program, is a separate task from the more challenging programming work needed on the server to receive the data. The communication path between the browser and server is called the *common gateway interface* (CGI) and that's the topic of Chapter 13.

For now, let's explore the wide range of <FORM> tags and how to use them to spice up your site with easy access to search engines, login sections, and more.

An Introduction to HTML Forms

Forms enable you to build Web pages that let users actually enter information and send it back to the server. The forms can range from a single text box for entering a search string — common to all the search engines on the Web — to a complex multipart worksheet that offers powerful submission capabilities.

All forms are the same on the Web, but there are two ways that information might be transmitted from the Web browser software back to the server on the other end. If you submit information from a form and the URL that it produces includes the information you entered, that's what's called a METHOD=GET, or "get" form. The alternative is when you submit the information and the URL of the next site looks perfectly normal, with no cryptic stuff stuck on the end. If that's the case, then you have a METHOD=POST or "post" form.

We'll explore the differences between these two in depth in the next chapter, but for now, it's helpful to be aware that there are these two ways that information on forms can be sent. For now, let's look at the design and specification of forms themselves.

HTML forms are surrounded by the <FORM> tag, which is specified as <FORM ACTION=url METHOD=method> and </FORM> tags. The url points to the remote file or application used for digesting the information, and the method is specified as either GET or POST.

Inside the <FORM> tag, your Web page can contain any standard HTML formatting information, graphics, links to other pages, and a bunch of new tags specific to forms. For the most part, all input fields within a form are specified with the <INPUT> tag and different attributes thereof. The various new tags let you define the many different elements of your form, as shown in Table 12-1.

Table 12-1	FORM Tags
Tag	**Meaning**
<INPUT	Text or other data-input field
TYPE=opt	Type of <INPUT> entry field
NAME=name	Symbolic name of field value
VALUE=value	Default content of text field
CHECKED=opt	Button/box checked by default
SIZE=x	Number of characters in displayed text box
MAXLENGTH=x	Maximum characters accepted
<SELECT>	Pop-up menu
<TEXTAREA>	Multiline text-entry field

The sheer number of different attributes within the <INPUT> tag can be confusing, but the way to understand the overloaded <INPUT> tag is to realize that the original design for forms had all possible input specified as variants to this tag. It didn't quite work out, however, because two types of information, pop-up menus and textarea boxes, ended up spilling out as their own tags: SELECT and TEXTAREA.

Current Web browsers support nine different <INPUT> types, each of which produces a different type of output. The user input types are:

➡ TEXT is the default, with SIZE used to specify the default size of the box that is created.

➡ PASSWORD is a text field with the user input displayed as asterisks or bullets for security. MAXLENGTH can be used to specify the maximum number of characters entered in the password.

➡ CHECKBOX offers a single (ungrouped) checkbox; CHECKED enables you to specify whether or not the box should be checked by default. VALUE specifies the text associated with the checkbox.

➡ HIDDEN enables you to send information to the program processing the user input without the user actually seeing it on the display. Particularly useful if the page with the HTML form is automatically generated by a CGI script.

➡ FILE gives you a way to let users actually submit files to the server. Users can either type in the filename or click the Browse button to select it from the PC.

➡ RADIO displays a toggle button; different radio buttons with the same NAME= value are grouped automatically, so that only one button in the group can be selected.

 Note that TYPE=FILE is still experimental, difficult to program on the server end, and only supported by Navigator. You can find out more about this funky tag by popping over to ftp://ds.internic.net/ rfc/rfc1867.txt and reading the official specification.

The most important <INPUT> types, however, are:

➡ SUBMIT, which produces a push button in the form that, when clicked, submits the entire form content to the remote server.

➡ IMAGE, which is identical to SUBMIT, but instead of a button, enables you to specify a graphical image for the submission or enter button.

➡ RESET, which enables users to clear the contents of all fields in the form.

<SELECT> is a pop-up menu of choices, with a </SELECT> partner tag and <OPTION> denoting each of the items therein. You must specify a NAME that uniquely identifies the overall selection within the <SELECT> tag itself. In fact, all form tags must have their NAME specified and all names must be unique within the individual form. You'll see why when we consider how information is sent to the server in the next chapter.

You can also specify a SIZE with the <SELECT> tag, indicating how many items should be displayed at once, and MULTIPLE, indicating that it's okay for users to select more than one option. If a default value exists, add SELECTED to the <OPTION> tag (as in <OPTION SELECTED>) to indicate that value.

The <TEXTAREA> tag enables you to produce a multiline input box. Like <SELECT>, <TEXTAREA> requires a unique name, specified with NAME=. The <TEXTAREA> tag enables you to specify the size of the text input box with ROWS and COLS attributes, specifying the number of lines in the box and the width of the lines, respectively. <TEXTAREA> has a closing tag: </TEXTAREA>.

Produce feedback on your site

Always wanted to have some mechanism for letting visitors come to your site and send you e-mail if they have comments? Of course, you could use <a href=mailto:youraddress>, but that's rather dull. Instead, a Web page that prompts users for some simple information and then automatically sends what they specify would be much more fun. Figure 12-1 shows a form that prompts for the user's name and e-mail address and then offers a text box for the user to enter their comments.

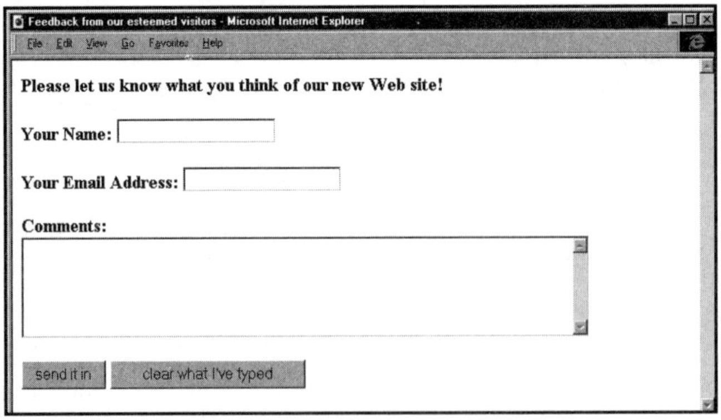

Figure 12-1 A simple input form

The source to this form shows that the forms tags aren't too difficult to use:

```
<FORM ACTION=http://www.intuitive.com/coolweb/apps/
query.cgi
  METHOD=get>
<B>Please let us know what you think of our new Web
site!</b>
<P>
<B>Your Name:</B>
<INPUT TYPE=text NAME=yourname>
<P>
<B>Your E-mail Address:</B>
<INPUT TYPE=text NAME=e-mail>
<P>
<B>Comments:</B><br>
<TEXTAREA NAME=feedback ROWS=5 COLS=60>
</TEXTAREA>
<P>
<INPUT TYPE=SUBMIT VALUE="send it in">
<INPUT TYPE=RESET VALUE="clear what I've typed">
</FORM>
```

Perhaps the most complex line of this form is the very first, the <FORM> tag. It specifies two things: the METHOD by which the information from the form is to be sent to the server program, and the ACTION, the actual URL of the program that receives the information from the form.

Other than that, the name and e-mail address are both one-line text boxes, so INPUT TYPE=text is the needed specifier, with each being assigned a unique name by the designer — in this case, yourname and e-mail. The multiline input box is specified with TEXTAREA, the name of the box is specified with NAME=feedback, and we want it to be 60 characters wide by 5 lines tall.

The submit button (TYPE=SUBMIT) is crucial to any form: It's the button that, when pressed, actually packages up and transmits the information to the program specified with the ACTION attribute in the <FORM> tag. All forms must have a submit button; though, if you want to have your own graphic as the button rather than a text button, you can use INPUT TYPE=image and specify it therein. Because I've opted for a simple text button, I can specify the text on the button being displayed as the VALUE of the button.

Finally, there's also a reset button that, if clicked, sets all the fields on the form back to their default value. Most forms tend not to include the reset button, but the more complex the form, the more the reset button could prove helpful for people.

Adding pop-up menus

The next example form includes some more complex form elements, most notably a family of radio buttons and a pop-up menu by using the <SELECT> tags. Figure 12-2 shows how the form looks on the screen.

Figure 12-2: A more complex form

Notice that the pop-up menu only shows you a single value: clicking the value brings up all the possible choices; then moving the cursor enables the visitor to select the specific value that's best.

Here's the source to this more complex form:

```
<FORM ACTION=http://www.intuitive.com/coolweb/apps/
query.cgi
   METHOD=get>
<B>Please let us know what you think of our new Web
site!</b>
<P>
<B>Your Name:</B>
<INPUT TYPE=text NAME=yourname>
<P>
<B>Your E-mail Address:</B>
<INPUT TYPE=text NAME=e-mail>
<P>
<B>You Found Our Site From:</B>
<SELECT NAME=foundus>
<OPTION SELECTED>(choose one)
<OPTION>Yahoo
<OPTION>Excite
<OPTION>HotBot
```

```
<OPTION>BigBook
<OPTION>PC Magazine
<OPTION>USA Today
<OPTION>CNN Online
<OPTION>Other...
</SELECT>
<P>
<B>You Are:</B>
<INPUT TYPE=radio NAME=age VALUE="kid"> Under 18
<INPUT TYPE=radio NAME=age VALUE="genx">18-30
<INPUT TYPE=radio NAME=age VALUE="30something">30-40
<INPUT TYPE=radio NAME=age VALUE="old">Over 40
<P>
<B>Comments:</B><br>
<TEXTAREA NAME=feedback ROWS=5 COLS=60>
</TEXTAREA>
<P>
<INPUT TYPE=SUBMIT VALUE="send it in">
<INPUT TYPE=RESET VALUE="clear what I've typed">
</FORM>
```

You can see that there are only two new areas added. The `<SELECT>` tag builds the pop-up menu, and the set of four radio buttons are specified with the INPUT TYPE=radio. The first pop-up menu item is the default, which is indicated with the addition of the SELECTED attribute:

```
<OPTION SELECTED>(choose one)
```

Pay careful attention to the radio button set, too. Notice they all share the same NAME value. That's how they become a "family" of radio buttons, ensuring that only one of them can be selected out of the set. If they had different names, you could easily select both the Under 18 and Over 40 categories, for example, which would be confusing.

You can also see a secret with the radio buttons: the actual value they send back to the server if checked is specified with the VALUE attribute. The actual text displayed next to a radio button is irrelevant to the program on the server: the only thing it'll know about what's selected is that the specified family (by NAME) had a radio button selected with the specified VALUE. If you choose 18-30, then the value that would be sent back to the server would be age=genx.

Which brings up a valuable observation: You recall that I said each input type in a form requires a name? Now you can see the reason for that: Each form element is packaged up and sent back to the server as a name=value pair. The pop-up menu, for example, might be foundus=HotBot, and the user name, when typed, could be sent back to the server as `yourname=Janine`. If you neglected to name an input, it's often not even displayed in the browser because there's no way for the specified information to be sent back to the server.

A pop-up menu of Web pages

Here's a useful trick that's used all over the Web, from the Microsoft home page to some pages I've developed for clients: a pop-up menu of page titles as a shortcut to navigating the site. There are two parts to this: the HTML source that's included on the page with the shortcuts, and the CGI script on the server that receives the request and turns it into a request for a specific Web page.

For this chapter, let's focus on the passage included on the Web page:

```
<BODY BGCOLOR=black TEXT=white>
<CENTER>
<h2>Some Of My Favorite Sites</h2>
</CENTER>
<form method="GET" action="http://www.intuitive.com/apps/
relayto.cgi">
<select name="url">
<option value=http://www.intuitive.com/>Intuitive Systems
<option value=http://www.internetmall.com/>The Internet
Mall
<option value=http://www.cnn.com/>CNN Online
<option value=http://www.altavista.digital.com>Alta Vista
<option value=http://www.cnet.com/>C|Net
</select>
<input type=submit value="Go!">
</FORM>
</BODY>
```

This formats to a simple pop-up box, as shown in Figure 12-3.

Figure 12-3: A pop-up menu with my favorite Web sites listed.

Notice that I've specified a VALUE for each <OPTION> tag. This enables me to specify exactly what I want to be sent regardless of what's displayed to the user. It's identical to what I showed earlier with the radio buttons, where the text displayed to the user was unrelated to the actual text value sent back to the server. With this example, if you choose CNET from the list of options, what would actually be sent back to the server would be URL=http://www.cnet.com.

The other half of this particular example, of course, is the CGI script on the server end, which we'll explore in the next chapter.

Let's experiment a bit with this form before we go, to illustrate some spiffy things you can do with forms. The first change is that I'd like to have more than one menu item displayed: rather than having it be a pop-up menu, I'd like it to be a scrolling selection box. To change this is remarkably easy. Simply change the <SELECT> tag by adding the attribute SIZE. With this I can specify how many choices should be visible at the same time.

If I add SIZE=4 to the SELECT tag above, Figure 12-4 shows that the output is dramatically different.

Figure 12-4: Select the site from a selection box.

It wouldn't make sense for this example, but if you wanted to let the visitor to your site possibly choose multiple values from the selection box, you could add a second attribute: MULTIPLE. A list such as the following:

```
<SELECT SIZE=3 MULTIPLE NAME=favorites>
<OPTION>Blue   <OPTION>Green   <OPTION>Red
<OPTION>Yellow   <OPTION>Orange   <OPTION>Gold
<OPTION>White   <OPTION>Black   <OPTION>Brown
</SELECT>
```

would display a three-line-high select box with nine different values therein. You could select any number of these colors as your favorites, or, if you didn't select any, and because there isn't a default specified, the default value for favorites would be none.

More form options

The other unusual tag you can include in a form is `<TEXTAREA>`, which enables you to create large spaces for users to type in their information. It has several options, starting with the mandatory `NAME` tag that denotes the symbolic name of the field. You can can specify `ROWS` and `COLS` to indicate the size of the resulting text field with units in characters. `WRAP` means that the text the user enters should automatically wrap when the user reaches the right margin. `<TEXTAREA>` also is a paired tag, partnered by `</TEXTAREA>`. Any text between the two tags is displayed as the default information in the text box.

You saw this demonstrated with the e-mail feedback form earlier, but let's create a more complex form to see how things can work together.

Consider the following HTML text and the way it's displayed. This form could be used as the beginning of a Web order-counter form for Dave's Virtual Deli:

```
<FORM ACTION="http://www.intuitive.com/coolweb/apps/
process-form.cgi"
   METHOD=GET>
<CENTER>
<IMG SRC=deli-logo.gif ALT="Dave's Virtual Deli -- The
Order Menu">
</CENTER>
 <HR>
Your name? <INPUT TYPE=text NAME="name" SIZE=30>
<BR>
Secret Code: <INPUT TYPE=password NAME="password">
<HR>
<B>What kind of Sandwich? </B>
<SELECT NAME="Sandwich">
<OPTION>(none)
<OPTION>Turkey on a croissant
<OPTION>Ham and cheese on wheat
<OPTION>Veggie on nine-grain
</SELECT>
<BR>
<B>Any Soup? </B>
<SELECT NAME="Soup">
<OPTION>(none)
<OPTION>Tomato and rice
<OPTION>Cream of asparagus
<OPTION>Lentil Madness
```

```
</SELECT>
<P>
How you'll pay:
<INPUT TYPE=radio NAME="payment" VALUE="visa">VISA
<INPUT TYPE=radio NAME="payment"
VALUE="mc">MasterCard
<INPUT TYPE=radio NAME="payment" VALUE="account"
CHECKED>Account
<INPUT TYPE=radio NAME="payment" VALUE="dishes">Wash dishes
<HR>
<INPUT TYPE=checkbox NAME="firstorder" VALUE="yes">
First time ordering from the Virtual Deli
<P>
<CENTER>
<INPUT TYPE=image SRC="submit.gif" ALT="Submit Order"
BORDER=0>
</CENTER>

</FORM>
```

Figure 12-5 shows the preceding form with some of the information filled out by a hungry user. The secret code value is displayed as a series of bullets, even though the user entered an actual password. The user could opt to pay by washing dishes, having seen that the default option was to put the bill on her account (as specified by the CHECKED option in the HTML).

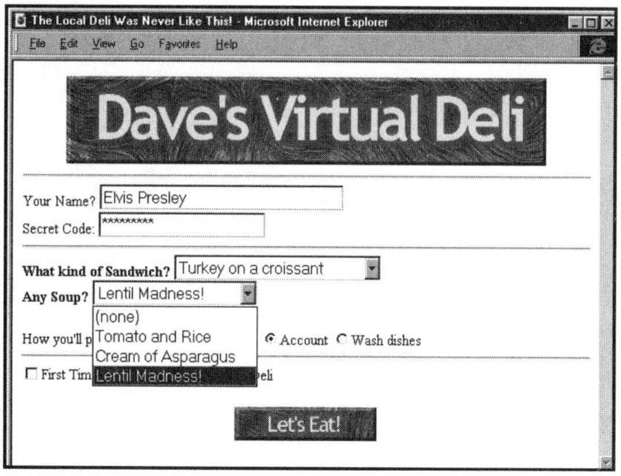

Figure 12-5: The Virtual Deli order form

It's worth looking more closely at the variant of the SUBMIT button that's included in this example:

```
<INPUT TYPE=image SRC="submit.gif" ALT="Submit Order" BORDER=0>
```

Here you can see the TYPE=image and that you need to also then specify the graphic with a SRC=attribute. Like a graphic surrounded by an anchor, the default for a submit button is to wrap it in a blue border. Instead, I opt to avoid that with the BORDER=0 specified. Finally, in case they don't have their graphics displayed, an ALT option lets me include some text to display, just in case.

Extending Your Forms With Fancy Formatting

These forms shown so far are reasonably attractive, but when you start combining this with other formatting tags that you've already learned, you can start producing really beautiful pages requesting user input. Let's look at a couple of examples.

Probably the most common strategy for creating attractive forms is to drop the various fields into a table. This enables you to line up all the prompts and input boxes quite easily. To spruce up the Virtual Deli form, let's do that as appropriate and also add a background graphic appropriate to the style of the page. I also took all the text prompts and made them bold to ensure that they stand out against the busy swirling background I've added:

```
<BODY BACKGROUND=Graphics/swirl.gif>
<FORM ACTION="http://www.intuitive.com/coolweb/apps/
process-form.cgi"
  METHOD=GET>
<CENTER>
<IMG SRC=Graphics/deli-logo.gif
ALT="Dave's Virtual Deli -- The Order Menu">
<HR>
<TABLE BORDER=1 WIDTH=75%>
<TR><TD COLSPAN=2 ALIGN=center>
<B>Who Are You?</B>
</TD></TR>
<TR><TD ALIGN=right>
<B>Your Name?</B>
</TD><TD ALIGN=left>
<INPUT TYPE=text NAME="name" SIZE=30>
```

```
</TD></TR>
<TR><TD ALIGN=right>
<B>Secret Code:</B>
</TD><TD ALIGN=left>
<INPUT TYPE=password NAME="password">
</TD></TR>
</TABLE>
<HR>
<TABLE BORDER=1 WIDTH=75%>
<TR><TD COLSPAN=2 ALIGN=center>
<B>Whaddya Want Today?</B>
</TD></TR>
<TR><TD ALIGN=right>
<B>What kind of Sandwich? </B>
</TD><TD ALIGN=left>
<SELECT NAME="Sandwich">
<OPTION>(none)
<OPTION>Turkey on a croissant
<OPTION>Ham and cheese on wheat
<OPTION>Veggie on nine-grain
</SELECT>
</TD></TR>
<TR><TD ALIGN=right>
<B>Any Soup? </B>
</TD><TD ALIGN=left>
<SELECT NAME="Soup">
<OPTION>(none)
<OPTION>Tomato and Rice
<OPTION>Cream of Asparagus
<OPTION>Lentil Madness!
</SELECT>
</TD></TR>
</TABLE>
<P>
<TABLE BORDER=1 WIDTH=75%>
<TR><TD ALIGN=center>
<B>How You Gunna Pay For Dis?</B>
</TD></TR>
<TR><TD ALIGN=center>
<INPUT TYPE=radio NAME="payment" VALUE="visa"><B>VISA</B>
<INPUT TYPE=radio NAME="payment" VALUE="mc"><B>
MasterCard</B>
<INPUT TYPE=radio NAME="payment" VALUE="account"
CHECKED><B>Account</B>
<INPUT TYPE=radio NAME="payment" VALUE="dishes"><B>Wash
dishes</B>
</TD></TR>
</TABLE>
```

(continued)

```
(continued)
<HR>
<INPUT TYPE=checkbox NAME="firstorder"
VALUE="yes"><B>First Time Ordering from the Virtual
Deli</B>
<P>
<INPUT TYPE=image SRC="Graphics/submit.gif"
 ALT="Submit Order" BORDER=0>
</CENTER>
</FORM>
</BODY>
```

This is a pretty long example, but if you compare it to Figure 12-6, you'll see that it's a great improvement over the earlier form we had.

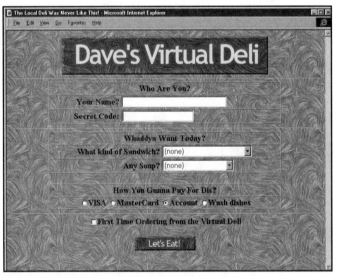

Figure 12-6: The Virtual Deli enhanced order form

A second example plays on the same theme, but is considerably more succinct. In fact, you've already seen it in a previous chapter — it's the OrderEasy merchant login screen. Let's revisit it now that you know how forms work so you can understand more fully what's going on with the formatting itself:

```
<CENTER>
<IMG SRC=Graphics/oe-logo.gif>
<P>
<font size=7><b>Merchant Entrance</b></font>
<P>
```

```
<FORM ACTION="none" METHOD=post>
<TABLE BORDER=0 WIDTH=75% BGCOLOR=#DDDDDD
CELLPADDING=15>
<TR><TD>
<font size=+1>
<B>
For security reasons, merchants need to identify
themselves with their merchant ID number, as assigned by
your Order Easy administrator. It's probably something
like "m0203". You will also need your account password to
access your merchant account:
</B>
</font>
<P>
  <CENTER>
  <TABLE BORDER=1 CELLPADDING=10 BGCOLOR=white>
  <TR>
    <TD>Merchant Account Identification:</TD>
    <TD><input type=text name=merchantid size=30></TD>
  </TR><TR>
    <TD>Account Password:</TD>
    <TD><input type=password name=password size=30></TD>
  </TD></TR>
  </TABLE>
    <P>
    <input type=submit value="access my account">
  </CENTER>
</TD>
</TR>
</TABLE>
</FORM>
<HR>
<h5>OrderEasy is a trademark of The Internet Mall,
Inc.</h5>
</CENTER>
```

The page is displayed for you as Figure 12-7: simple, elegant and another
good example of how tables and forms can work very well together.

Notice I've disabled the form for the book: ACTION=none definitely will not
work as desired.

Figure 12-7: The OrderEasy merchant login screen

Easy Searching from Your Page

Now that you're becoming an absolute forms genius, let's look at how you can exploit forms on other sites to actually duplicate their input on your own page. As an example, perhaps you'd like to have a Yahoo! search area on your own page to let people who visit your site easily flip over to Yahoo! to find something.

Popping over to the Yahoo! home page, you can do a view source and see, in their veritable thicket of HTML, a rather convoluted sequence of lines that define their simple search form. Bubbling it down to just the entries needed for the search itself, you end up with the following snippet:

```
<form action="http://search.yahoo.com/search" method=get>
<input size=30 name=p>
<input type=submit value=Search>
<font size=-1>
<a href="http://search.yahoo.com/search/options">options
</a>
</font>
</form>
```

This is the actual search box shown on the top of their home page. Because we've pulled the code out, however, it's just as easy to include this sequence of commands on our own Web page, as you can see in Figure 12-8.

Figure 12-8: My personal Yahoo! search

You can dig out the same sort of code from any site that has an input box for searching. Here is the HTML source for some other popular sites that you could drop right into your own pages:

```
<TITLE>Search Central</TITLE>
<BODY BGCOLOR=white>
<CENTER>
<font size=+2><B>Looking for something online?</B></font>
</CENTER>
<BLOCKQUOTE>
There are lots of places you might go online to find web
sites related to a specific topic. Please enter a key
word or two in each of the following to see which has the
best matches for you.
</BLOCKQUOTE>
<CENTER>
<TABLE BORDER=0 CELLSPACING=5>
<TR><TD BGCOLOR=#CCCCCC ALIGN=center>
<B>YAHOO</B>
</TD><TD VALIGN=center ALIGN=center>
<!-- YAHOO -->
<form action="http://search.yahoo.com/search" method=get>
<input type=text size=35 name=p>
<input type=submit value="Search">
</form>
</TD>
</TR>
<TR><TD BGCOLOR=#CCCCCC ALIGN=center>
```

(continued)

```
(continued)
<B>Excite</B>
</TD><TD VALIGN=center ALIGN=center>
<!-- Excite -->
<form action=http://www.excite.com/search.gw method=get>
<input type=hidden name=trace value=a>
<input type=text name=search  size=35>
<input type=submit value="Search">
</form>
</TD>
</TR>
<TR><TD BGCOLOR=#CCCCCC ALIGN=center>
<B>InfoSeek</B>
</TD><TD VALIGN=center ALIGN=center>
<!-- InfoSeek -->
<FORM METHOD="get" action="http://www.infoseek.com/Titles">
<INPUT type="text" NAME="qt"  size=35 VALUE=""
MAXLENGTH=511>
<INPUT TYPE=hidden NAME="col" VALUE="WW">
<INPUT TYPE=submit VALUE="Search">
</FORM>
</TD>
</TR>
<TR><TD BGCOLOR=#CCCCCC ALIGN=center>
<B>AltaVista</B>
</TD><TD VALIGN=center ALIGN=center>
<!-- Alta Vista -->
<FORM method=GET action="http://www.altavista.digital.com/
cgi-bin/query">
<INPUT TYPE=hidden NAME=pg VALUE=q>
<INPUT TYPE=hidden NAME=what VALUE=web>
<INPUT TYPE=hidden NAME=kl VALUE=en>
<INPUT TYPE=text    NAME=q size=35 maxlength=800 wrap=
virtual>
<INPUT TYPE=submit VALUE="Search">
</FORM>
<!-- The Internet Mall -->
</TD>
</TR>
<TR><TD BGCOLOR=#CCCCCC ALIGN=center>
<B>The Internet Mall</B>
</TD><TD VALIGN=center ALIGN=center>
<FORM ACTION=http://search.internetmall.com/apps/
searchfor.cgi METHOD=get>
<input type=text name=match  size=35>
<input type=submit value="Search">
</FORM>
</TD></TR>
</TABLE>
</CENTER>
</BODY>
```

If you look closely at the different search options on this page — as shown in Figure 12-9 — you'll notice that many of them have hidden additional information that is being sent along. For example, in the Excite search box, there's the line:

```
<input type=hidden name=trace value=a>
```

Figure 12-9: Search the Net!

For the program on Excite that receives and processes the search, having the trace variable sent as `trace=a` (check out the "value" specified) means that the search from my page is indistinguishable from their own home page. Hidden variables are most helpful as you start to produce more sophisticated forms, and viewing the source of forms you fill out online will show you that other folk think so, too!

More Form Tricks

Before we leave the topic of forms, I want to show you one more trick that you might find interesting. It again revolves around being able to see the source to an existing form and duplicating it on your own page, but either preloading the inputs with the values you want, or changing input variables to hidden variables and hiding them entirely.

For this example, I'm going to pop over to LinkExchange, a great cooperative ad network that I'll talk about at length in Chapter 18. For now, the important thing is that, when you join the LinkExchange network, you are assigned an account and password pair. The account name is the letter 'X' followed by six or seven digits.

On their site — at `http://www.linkexchange.com/` — the member login area has a snippet of code that boils down to:

```
<form method="POST"
    action="http://member.linkexchange.com/cgi-bin/
SMTMlogin">
    <input type="text" name="account" value="X" size=12>
Account
    <input type="password" name="pwd" value="" size=12>
Password
    <input type="submit" value="Log in"><br>
</form>
```

Three input tags; nothing at all complex about this form. Notice that the *X* for the account name is preloaded into the text box by having the text field VALUE set to "X".

Now I can start slicing and dicing this to work differently.

First off, if my account with LinkExchange were X123456, then I could modify the input value on my personal LinkExchange login page so that I don't ever have to remember the number:

```
<input type="text" name="account" value="X123456" size=12>
Account
```

Doing it this way means that the account number will already be in the box, but that I'll still have to type in my password to log in.

Perhaps I'm less concerned about security and just want to have a button on my page that logs directly into my account on LinkExchange. I could add a VALUE attribute to the password prompt (which would be a little weird), but better to make them both hidden variables and have them vanish from the page completely.

Here's how that'd look if my password was "!secret!":

```
<form method="POST"
    action="http://member.linkexchange.com/cgi-bin/
SMTMlogin">
    <input type="hidden" name="account" value="X123456"
size=12>
    <input type="hidden" name="pwd" value="!secret!"
size=12>
    <input type="submit" value="Log in to LinkExchange">
<br>
</form>
```

What makes this work is that the variables are sent to the server identically: `name=value` pairs. If they're `type=hidden`, then everything happens behind the scenes.

Figure 12-10 shows how I could exploit this to have a LinkExchange button on my page let me quickly and directly log in to their system to check the status of my advertisements on their network.

Figure 12-10: Log in to LinkExchange.

The HTML source for this should be no surprise to you:

```
<HTML>
<BODY BGCOLOR=white>

<CENTER>
<form method="POST"
     action="http://member.linkexchange.com/cgi-bin/
SMTMlogin">
     <input type="hidden" name="account" value="X123456">
     <input type="hidden" name="pwd" value="!secret!">
     <input type="image" src=linkexch.gif border=0>
</form>
</CENTER>

</BODY>
</HTML>
```

Table 12-2	HTML Tags Covered in This Chapter	
Tag	**Close Tag**	**Meaning**
`<FORM`	`</FORM>`	Interactive HTML form
`ACTION=url`		CGI program on server that receives data
`METHOD=method`		How data is transmitted to server (`GET` or `POST`)

(continued)

Table 12-2 *(continued)*

Tag	Close Tag	Meaning
`<INPUT`		Text or other data-input field
`TYPE=opt`		Type of `<INPUT>` entry field. Possible values: text, password, checkbox, hidden, file, radio, submit, reset, image.
`NAME=name`		Symbolic name of field value
`VALUE=value`		Default content of text field
`CHECKED=opt`		Button/box checked by default
`SIZE=x`		Number of characters in text field
`MAXLENGTH=x`		Maximum characters accepted
`<SELECT`	`</SELECT>`	Grouped check boxes
`NAME=name`		Symbolic name of field value
`SIZE=x`		Number of items to show at once (default = 1)
`MULTIPLE`		Allow multiple items to be selected
`<OPTION`		Specific choice within a `<SELECT>` range
`VALUE=value`		Resultant value of this menu choice
`<TEXTAREA`	`</TEXTAREA>`	Multiline text-entry field
`NAME=name`		Symbolic name of field value
`ROWS=x`		Number of rows in textarea box
`COLS=x`		Number of columns (characters) on a line within the box

Summary

This chapter gave you a wealth of ideas about how to create interactive Web forms and how to add your own front-end to existing sites on the Net by duplicating — and customizing — their forms on your own pages. Chapter 13 will look at the other side of the equation, the *common gateway interface* (CGI) and how to work with it on your server.

The Common Gateway Interface

This chapter provides an introduction to the process of programming your Web pages and making smart sites, whether you're using a PC, a Mac, or renting space on a UNIX server. This is accomplished by understanding and exploiting the Web programming environment: the Common Gateway Interface, or CGI. Programs can be written in any of a wide variety of different languages, but if they interact with a Web server, they're all generally called "CGI programs" or "CGI scripts."

I'm going to be honest with you right up front: Getting back-end CGI scripts to work on your Web server is the most difficult part of sophisticated Web site design. It's programming, and it's typically programming in a weird language that's much more difficult to learn than HTML. For this book, I'll show the simple examples as UNIX shell scripts (because odds are very good that the server upon which all your pages will reside will be running UNIX, and because it's also a very clear way to show what's going on) and the more complex examples in Perl, a popular multiplatform language. You can, however, write your scripts in just about any language, and, in fact, most of my longer, more sophisticated CGI programs are written in the C programming language. The long and short of it — take a deep breath and let's go!

The CGI Inside Your Web Server

By now, you've seen that you can have fun creating slick-looking Web pages and complex sites, adding animation, frames, and lots of other sophisticated markup. What's missing from this picture, so far, is any sort of interaction between the user and the Web server. Whether it's showing the current time, asking for feedback, presenting a different page to users of different systems, or even presenting the latest news or stock ticker values dynamically, those are all done from the server end rather than from within the HTML document itself.

To understand how this works, let's take a brief step back to the most basic of Web concepts. All Web browsers talk with Web servers using a language (well, protocol, to be exact) called HTTP, the *HyperText Transfer Protocol*. At its simplest, HTTP defines the interaction between the browser and server, which can be boiled down to "I want" from the browser and "here is" or "don't have" from the server. It looks like Figure 13-1.

Figure 13-1: The handshake between the browser and server

Forget all the fancy stuff from the last twelve chapters. The simple dialog shown in Figure 13-1 is what the Web and, indeed, the Internet are really all about: Your PC asking a server somewhere on the Net for a particular file, picture, resource, or what-have-you and the Net responding either "Here it is!" or "I don't have it!" In fact, when you have an HTML document that includes graphics, each graphic is requested from the server through its own dialog of a similar nature. That's why you see the source to some pages before you get all the graphics, because it ends up looking like:

```
I want "test.html"
here is "test.html"
oh, now I want "opening.gif"
here is "opening.gif"
and I want "photo.jpeg"
here is "photo.jpeg"
and I want "logo.gif"
here is "logo.gif"
and finally I want "lastpict.gif"
I don't have "lastpict.gif" Error 440: file not found
```

Although this may seem tremendously tedious — and it is — it's also a
great design because it's so easily extended into other areas. In particular,
what happens if instead of the "I want" request, the browser asked, "Please
run the following program and send me the output."?

That capability is what programming Web servers is built around, and the
environment on the server within which you communicate with the browser
is the Common Gateway Interface. By working within the CGI environment,
in the programming language of your choice, you can replace any Web
page or graphic with a program that performs calculations, looks up information in a database, checks the weather, reads a remote sensor, or whatever you'd like, and then returns the results of that action to the user as
Web data.

On many servers you can tell what's a CGI script by the .cgi filename suffix
that would occur within the URL of the referenced page, but any file or
graphic can actually be a program, the output of which is sent to the user.
The best news is that the use of CGI scripts can be invisible to the Web
visitor. Visitors just wander through your site and see page after page, and
if some of the pages are the result of running scripts, the visitors might well
never know.

The World's Simplest CGI Example

Let's dive right in and have a look at a CGI script that might replace a static Web page with something more dynamic: hello.cgi, written as a UNIX
shell script, which is very similar to a Windows batch file:

```
echo "Content-type: text/html"
echo ""
echo "<HTML><BODY>"
echo "<H1>Hi Mystery Web Visitor</H1>"
echo "</BODY></HTML>"
```

The echo command outputs whatever you specify to standard output, which, in this case, because it's being run as a CGI script, will be sent to the remote Web browser. As you can see, the program hello.cgi is required to return an actual HTML document. This is so everything remains transparent to the user: The user requests a Web document and it comes back all neatly formatted and ready to be displayed by the browser.

That's a crucial point: The #1 responsibility of any CGI program is to return a valid HTML document to the browser. Any additional capabilities must be built on top of that basic requirement, and if you forget, you'll get various scary error messages when you try to test things yourself.

There's an important thing to notice on the very first line of this example script: The first output line of any CGI script must identify the particular type of information being sent back to the browser. In this case, it's HTML text, and the formal description for that is Content-type: text/html. That line must be followed in the output by a blank line and then, finally, the actual HTML code can appear. This first section is called the preamble, and I like to think of it as the envelope within which the Web page is sent.

Functionally, this program output is identical to a "static" Web page that contains:

```
<HTML>
<BODY>
<H1>Hi Mystery Web Visitor </H1>
</BODY></HTML>
```

So why go through the bother? Because these scripts can output virtually *anything* your heart desires. Let's look at a slightly more sophisticated example. This one uses the date command on the UNIX server, a command that returns the current date and time when run:

```
echo "Content-type: text/html"
echo ""
echo "<HTML><BODY>"
echo "<H1>Oh Mystery Web Visitor, the time is...</H1>"
date
echo "</BODY></HTML>"
```

Figure 13-2 shows how that script would look to a user visiting my Web site and requesting date.cgi.

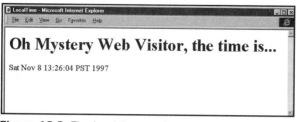

Figure 13-2: The local time on the server

There's a lot you can do with programs that output content based on the environment at the moment the page is requested. For example, the date command has some options you can specify that let you get just the day of the week, the month name, or similar. You could get the hour of the day and have a page that displays differently during daylight and nighttime hours. Or here's another example from my own Web site

```
today="date +%y%m%d"
echo -n "Location: http://www.historychannel.com/
echo "historychannel/thisday/today/${today}.html"
echo ""
```

In this case, I wanted to have a link on my site pointing to the History Channel's "today in history" page, but instead of it having a single URL such as today-in-hist.html, it opted to have its site designed so that each date has its own page, in the format YYMMDD. If it were November 15, 1997, for example, the file would be called 971115.html. Kind of ugly, but because I didn't have control over their site implementation (and over-all, I have to say that I really like how they've designed the site!), I needed to figure out a way to have a step between my clicking a "today in history" button and the page being requested from the server.

Fortunately, the date command came through! By specifying "date +%y%m%d" I can get exactly the weird YYMMDD format that's needed. Then a second trick gets this all to work. In addition to the usual Content-type: text/html in the preamble, another extremely valuable addition to the pre-amble you can include is the Location: line, which immediately switches users to the specified URL instead of the CGI script they're invoking.

Add the two up and that's what the previous four-line script does for me. It first figures out the MMDDYY value for the current day, saves that value in a variable called today, then outputs a Location: URL that points to the http://www.historychannel.com site, specifying the exact page for today. The program wraps up with the blank line that's always required to indicate the end of the preamble, and it's done — nice and succinct. Figure 13-3 shows what was up early in November 1997, when I was writing this chapter on my computer!

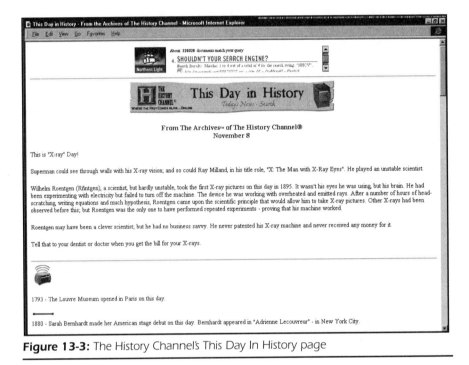

Figure 13-3: The History Channel's This Day In History page

You can try the CGI program by pointing to it on my server:

```
http://www.intuitive.com/taylor/websites/histbounce.cgi
```

While these little scripts are useful, CGI offers a considerably richer environment for developing sophisticated sites than just this type of approach. It's an environment where you can make decisions about what kind of HTML to output based on the browser that's in use, where the user's located, and much more.

Smart Web Pages Using CGI Scripts

Every HTTP transaction (the "I want"/"here is" pair) actually includes a set of environment characteristics that is sent along and accessible from the CGI script. I like to think of it as a special briefcase chock full of information on the user, and what might surprise you is that all of the information is sent on *every interaction between the browser and server*, even if it's just a request for a graphic or static Web page.

To see all the environment variables, I've created a CGI script that uses the UNIX command `printenv` to list the environment given to the script:

```
echo "Content-type: text/html"
echo ""
echo "<HTML><BODY>"
echo "<H1>Your environment is:</H1>"
echo "<PRE>"
printenv
echo "</PRE>"
echo "</BODY></HTML>"
```

The results when this is run from within Internet Explorer are as shown in Figure 13-4.

Your environment is:

```
GATEWAY_INTERFACE=CGI/1.1
REMOTE_HOST=ws4.hostname.com
REMOTE_ADDR=205.158.215.133
QUERY_STRING=
HTTP_USER_AGENT=Mozilla/4.0 (compatible; MSIE 4.0; Windows 95)
HTTP_ACCEPT=*/*
HTTP_HOST=www.intuitive.com
SERVER_SOFTWARE=BESTWWWD/1.0
HTTP_CONNECTION=Keep-Alive
PATH=/sbin:/bin:/usr/sbin:/usr/bin:/usr/local/sbin
HTTP_ACCEPT_LANGUAGE=en-us
SERVER_PROTOCOL=HTTP/1.0
HTTP_ACCEPT_ENCODING=gzip, deflate
REQUEST_METHOD=GET
SERVER_PORT=80
SCRIPT_NAME=coolweb/apps/env.cgi
SERVER_NAME=www.intuitive.com
```

Figure 13-4: My CGI environment for writing scripts

Notice particularly the two variables REMOTE_HOST and

HTTP_USER_AGENT. The former identifies the host name of the browser —
here you can see that my computer is called ws4.hostname.com — and
the latter identifies the specific browser in use. In this case, you can also
see a bit of a trick that Microsoft's Internet Explorer performs: It identifies
itself as Netscape 3.0, but then correctly identifies itself in the parentheses
as Internet Explorer 4.0.

The code name for Navigator is *Mozilla*.

If I request the very same Web CGI script from Navigator, the output is very
different, as shown in Figure 13-5.

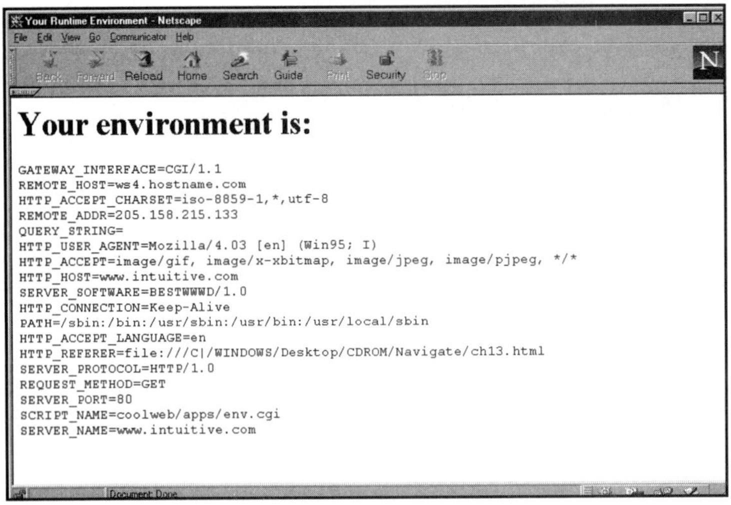

Figure 13-5: My CGI environment in Navigator

The differences are interesting, but note that the variable REMOTE_HOST is
identical, while the HTTP_USER_AGENT is quite different. Table 13-1 shows
some common values for the user agent.

Table 13-1	HTTP_USER_AGENT Values
Lynx/2-4-2 libwww/2.14	
Lynx/2.7.1f libwww-FM/2.14	
Mozilla/0.96 Beta (Windows)	
Mozilla/2.0 (compatible; MSIE 3.0; Windows 95)	
Mozilla/2.0 (compatible; MSIE 2.1; Mac_PowerPC)	
Mozilla/3.0 (compatible; MSIE 4.0p1; Mac_PowerPC) Mozilla/3.0b7Gold (Win95; I)	
Mozilla/3.0 (Macintosh; I; PPC)	
Mozilla/4.01 (Macintosh; I; PPC)	
NCSA Mosaic for the X Window System/2.4 libwww/2.12 modified	
NetCruiser/V2.00	
PRODIGY-WB/1.3e	
Spyglass Mosaic/1.0 libwww/2.15_Spyglass	

Let's have a closer look at one of these variables and how we might use it: REMOTE_HOST. You can see that it is the host and domain name of the Web browser. A CGI program that outputs a different page based on the domain of the person visiting could be created by extracting the top-level domain name and using it as the basis of an if-then statement.

Here's how I'd accomplish it using the UNIX command cut, which in this case is going to extract the third word of the REMOTE_HOST, with words assumed separated by dots. That is, for the REMOTE_HOST of "ws4.hostname.com", the cut command would extract "com".

A script that shows how this could be used is:

```
echo "Content-type: text/html"
echo ""
echo "<HTML>"
echo "<BODY BGCOLOR=white>"
topdomain="`echo $REMOTE_HOST | cut -d. -f3`"
echo "<CENTER>"
echo "<h2>"
echo "You're visiting from <TT><B>.$topdomain</B></TT>"
echo "</h2>"
echo "</CENTER>"
```

This displays the specific top-level domain as extracted from the
REMOTE_HOST variable, as you can see in Figure 13-6.

What's Your Domain? - Microsoft Internet Explorer
File Edit View Go Favorites Help
You're visiting from .com

Figure 13-6: What's my top-level domain?

To use it in a conditional is slightly more complex, but here's how we could
display either the com-home.html or generic-home.html page based on
the users domain:

```
echo "Content-type: text/html"
echo ""
topdomain="`echo $REMOTE_HOST | cut -d. -f3`"
if [ $topdomain = "com" ] ; then
  cat com-home.html
else
  cat generic-home.html
fi
```

Of course, the Location: preamble would be a much better — and more
succinct — way to do this, ultimately:

```
topdomain="`echo $REMOTE_HOST | cut -d. -f3`"

if [ $topdomain = "com" ] ; then
  echo Location: com-home.html
else
  echo Location: generic-home.html
fi
echo ""
```

About as short as you can imagine!

Another fun one: You can now write a simple script that outputs different
HTML based on what kind of computer a visitor is using. In this case, I offer
different messages based on whether my visitor is using a Mac or PC. To do
this, I need to look for the sequence Mac in the user agent string, which is
done in UNIX with the oddly named grep command. Here's the script:

```
echo "Content-type: text/html"
echo ""

x="`echo $HTTP_USER_AGENT | grep Mac `"

echo "<center>"
echo "Welcome to my Web site"
echo "<P>"

if [ "$x" = "" ] ; then
   echo This page enhanced for Macintosh
else
   echo This page enhanced for Windows
fi

echo "</center>"
```

The idea here is that I'm asking UNIX to peek at the user agent value for the sequence "Mac": If there's a match, then the variable x will contain the Mac-user agent value, otherwise it'll be blank and will match the "" in the conditional. Figure 13-7 shows what this program outputs when I run it from my Windows PC.

Welcome to my Web site

This page enhanced for the Macintosh

Figure 13-7: A page enhanced for the OTHER platform!

TIP Try this online: http://www.intuitive.com/coolweb/apps/ platform.cgi.

If you're paying attention here — and I hope you have been able to follow this explanation — then you have caught that the script above is a dirty Web trick: It'll always say that the site was enhanced for the system other than the one you're using. Visit from a Mac, and it'll say it's enhanced for Windows; visit from a PC and it'll say it's a Mac site!

Sending and Reading Data

There's another variable in the environment set that's very important for interactive pages; something that to this point in the book hasn't had any value. That variable is QUERY_STRING.

If you've gotten this far, I think it's safe for me to assume that you've spent some time traveling around the Web. I also bet you've been to a site where you were asked for some data and then given a page of information based on what you specified. The search engines highlighted in the previous chapter examples are demonstrations of just this type of interaction.

As touched on briefly in Chapter 12, there are two ways to accomplish the transfer of information from the browser to the server, based on the setting of the METHOD parameter in the <FORM>. You'll recall that there are two possible values: GET and POST. If the form specifies a METHOD=GET, that means that the information entered by the user, in *name=value* pairs, will be available to the CGI program as the environment variable value QUERY_STRING.

Go to Yahoo! and enter a word or phrase for it to seek. When you get the search results, you'll see a page of matches as you'd expect. Most importantly, however, you'll also see a slightly weird URL. If I search for "disneyworld," the URL shown in the Address box of the browser is:

```
http://search.yahoo.com/bin/search?p=disneyworld
```

This is consistent with what I explained about URLs way back in Chapter 2, but there's a new twist; the ? indicates that there's information to send to the remote system, and the p=disneyworld is the value sent to the server *from the client.* For the CGI program on the server specified in the ACTION attribute of the <FORM> tag, the QUERY_STRING variable contains the exact information specified after the question mark.

Now, let's try another script, one that actually assumes that you're going to enter a special URL (for now) that includes some information following the ? symbol:

```
echo "Content-type: text/html"
echo ""
echo "<BODY BGCOLOR=white>"
echo "You sent me $QUERY_STRING"
echo "</BODY>"
```

This script is available on the Web as query.cgi, so if I invoke it as `http://www.intuitive.com/coolweb/apps/query.cgi`, but append `?SleepyPuppy`, the results will be as shown in Figure 13-8. Note particularly the Address box in the screen shot.

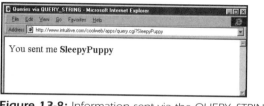

Figure 13-8: Information sent via the QUERY_STRING value

There are some neat things you can do now that you know about this `QUERY_STRING` URL format. Perhaps you're working on a Web site that's all about the films of Alfred Hitchcock. Now you can add a link to your Web page that would automatically search Yahoo! for sites related to the director without the user entering anything:

```
<a href=http://search.yahoo.com/search?p=alfred+hitchcock
>Information on Alfred Hitchcock</a>
```

Overall, however, it'd be a lot easier if you could actually ask users for information and then process it once they tell you something or other. That's the exact purpose of HTML forms, as you learned in the last chapter.

Notice that the search I really wanted to do was "alfred hitchcock," but because you already know that spaces aren't allowed in URLs, you can see the secret encoding: spaces are sent as "+" and decoded at the server.

A pop-up menu of Web pages

In Chapter 12, I showed how a pop-up menu of Web URLs could be easily added to your site, including the HTML form code, duplicated here. This time, let's look at the CGI script on the other end that's going to receive the requested URL and take the user to the requested site.

Here's how to produce the Web page:

```
<FORM METHOD="GET"
ACTION="http://www.intuitive.com/coolweb/apps/relayto.cgi">
<b>Some of My Favorite Sites:</b>
<SELECT NAME="url">
<OPTION VALUE="http://www.intuitive.com/">Intuitive Systems
<OPTION VALUE="http://www.internetmall.com/">The Internet
Mall
<OPTION VALUE="http://www.yahoo.com/">Yahoo!
<OPTION VALUE="http://www.altavista.digital.com">Alta Vista
<OPTION VALUE="http://www.cnet.com/">C|Net
</SELECT>
<INPUT TYPE=submit VALUE="Go!">
</FORM>
```

This formats to a simple pop-up box, as shown in Figure 13-9.

Figure 13-9: A pop-up menu with my favorite Web sites listed.

The other half of this is the CGI script on the server end. It again takes advantage of the `Location:` preamble information. Before we get to the final script, however, here's an intermediate version to show you something rather remarkable that happens:

```
echo "Content-type: text/html"
echo ""

if [ "$QUERY_STRING" = "" ] ; then
echo "Relayto needs a valid URL"
else
  echo "QUERY_STRING = $QUERY_STRING"
echo ""
fi
```

If you try the first of the options in the pop-up menu, you'll see that the actual information sent as the QUERY_STRING is encoded and rather cryptic:

```
QUERY STRING = url=http%3A%2F%2Fwww.intuitive.com%2F
```

You saw earlier that the spaces needed to become "+"s so that they'd transmit safely. A variety of other characters are also encoded specially so that they can be transmitted safely, as detailed in Table 13-2.

Table 13-2	Common Character Encodings
Code	**Real Meaning**
%21	!
%22	"
%23	#
%24	$
%25	%
%26	&
%27	'
%28	(
%29	)
%2B	+
%2F	/
%3A	:
%3D	=
%3F	?
%5C	\

Armed with this, the first step the real script will have to do is to decode the given URL. I'll accomplish this within UNIX by using the sed program, telling it to replace all %3A sequences with a colon, and all %2F sequences with a slash.

Now, the final relayto.cgi script, having also added an additional snippet to the `sed` invocation to remove the `URL=` sequence, too (which is necessary, otherwise, we'd try to move to URL `url=http://...`):

```
if [ "$QUERY_STRING" = "" ] ; then
    echo "Content-type: text/html"
    echo ""
    echo "Relayto needs a valid URL"
else
    url="`echo $QUERY_STRING | sed \
    's/%3A/:/g;s/%2F/\//g; s/URL=//;s/url=//'`"
    echo Location: $url
    echo ""
fi
```

It's remarkably simple, given the slick functionality it lets you add to your Web site.

You can experiment with the `Location:` line in other ways, too; you might have a script called testme.cgi on your server that has two lines:

```
echo "Location: http://www.idgbooks.com/"
echo ""
```

Any time someone visits `testme.cgi`, they'd immediately pop over to the IDG Books Worldwide site.

Receiving Information from Forms

Forms are standard HTML. Whether your server is a Windows NT box, a UNIX system, or a Macintosh, the tags needed to define an input form are identical. When the time comes to consider how to process the information that users are submitting, however, you get into some sticky, system-dependent questions. With server-side image maps, you saw that the format of the MAP file depends on the type of server you're running.

The CGI behind forms is even more complex, because the very environment you work with when processing the form depends heavily on the operating system used on the server. Scripting a gateway (hence, the common gateway interface, or CGI, moniker for these scripts) is dramatically different on a UNIX system than it is on a Windows machine or a Macintosh — not to mention Windows NT, Amiga ;-), and other types of servers.

The biggest difference involves what programming languages and tools are available. On a UNIX system, it's quite simple to create a shell script, Perl script, or even a C program or two to process and act on input. Shell scripts aren't a possibility on a Mac, however, so AppleScript or MacPerl are used instead. Windows machines rely on either a DOS command template or what's known informally as a jacket script. Fortunately, the Perl-interpreted programming language is also available on PCs, and that's what I recommend you use if you have a PC server, though there are a number of Windows-based CGI scripts written in C and Visual Basic.

Perl is an interpreted programming language designed for working with text and text files. The language, created by Larry Wall, is intended to be practical rather than beautiful, which is its major shortcoming: It can be quite cryptic if you're not used to reading C-like programs.

Find out more about Perl: The Perl home page is at `http://www.perl.com`, and there's also a terrific Perl FAQ at `ftp://ftp.cis.ufl.edu/pub/perl/faq/FAQ`. You can also get a free Perl interpreter for Windows; go to `http://www.ActiveState.com/` and get a copy of Perl 5 for Win32.

The `FORM` method has two options: `GET` and `POST`. Now I can explain the difference between these two. When a `GET` method is used, the information is appended to the URL and handed, as such, to the script. All information shows up encoded and stored in the `QUERY_STRING` environment variable. By contrast, `POST` causes the information to be sent to the server as a data stream rather than a single environment variable. Because of this, `POST` is much better when significant amounts of information are to be transmitted.

To keep the scope of this explanation manageable, however, I'll stick with the `GET` method to illustrate how the forms shown in previous chapters would be sent to the CGI server script. First, the simple e-mail form, filled in, would be sent as:

```
yourname=Lawrence+Olivier&e-
mail=olivier@moviestars.com&feedback=Marvelous+site%2C+very
+nice.+Keep+up+the+good+work.
```

Go to Figure 12-1 on the CD-ROM and enter some information, then press the Submit button. That'll send the data to the server and you can see how everything is encoded, as shown above.

The + encodes spaces to keep the URL legal, and each `field=value` pair is separated by an ampersand. (Remember, spaces and carriage returns aren't allowed in any URL.) It would be up to the server script to unravel this tangle of information and process it.

Another example — the order form from the Virtual Deli. In this example, I'm going to enter an order then see how everything is packaged up to send to the server.

You can, too: Go to Figure 12-6 on the CD-ROM and enter a lunch order for yourself.

I place an order and here's how it's sent:

```
name=Ashley+Taylor&password=hi+mom&Sandwich=Veggie+on+nine-
grain&Soup=Tomato+and+Rice&payment=dishes
```

An important thing to see here is that while the password was shielded from prying eyes when the user entered the information, when it was sent to the server, it wasn't encrypted or, otherwise, hidden. In fact, you can see that Ashley used "hi mom" as her password.

Because the output of any CGI must also include some valid HTML, the basic algorithm you'll use is something like the following:

```
replace all '+' with ' '
replace all '&' with a return
send request to kitchen
return the following to the user:
<HTML>
<HEAD>
<TITLE>It's Cookin'!</TITLE>
</HEAD><BODY>
Thank you for your order. We're now busy preparing
the meal that you selected. We invite
you to stop by the <B>Virtual Deli</B> in about
15 minutes to pick up your food.
<HR>
<A HREF="deli.html">Back to the Deli</A>
</BODY>
</HTML>
```

Of course, processing the information is more complex. Following is a portable Perl CGI script that processes the virtual deli form information and echoes back a few of the key items to confirm the order:

```perl
print "Content-type: text/html\n\n";

print "<HTML>\n";
print "<BODY BGCOLOR=white>\n";

$buffer = $ENV{'QUERY_STRING'};    # grab info


# Split the name-value pairs into an array
@info = split(/&/, $buffer);

foreach $pair (@info) {
  ($name, $value) = split(/=/, $pair);
  # fix the '+' and '%' encodings
  $value =~ tr/+/ /;
  $value =~ s/%([a-fA-F0-9][a-fA-F0-9])/pack("C",
hex($1))/eg;
$DATA{$name} = $value;
}


# now we can echo back their order to confirm

print "<h2>$DATA{'name'}</h2>";
print "You ordered: ";
print "<b>$DATA{'Soup'}</b> and
<b>$DATA{'Sandwich'}</b>.<P>\n";
print "You'll be paying for your order with
$DATA{'payment'}";
print "<P>\n";
print "<HR><A HREF=\"home.html\">let's go home</A>\n";
print "</BODY></HTML>\n"
```

The variables I'm using for the output have names that are identical to those in the original HTML form. That is, the payment information field was identified as NAME=payment and the variable was referenced in the Perl script as $DATA{'payment'} once it was unpacked and stored in the Perl DATA space. HTML formatting tags can also be embedded in print statements, as you can see. Figure 13-10 shows the result of sending a filled-in form to this data processing CGI script.

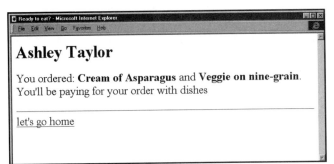

Ashley Taylor

You ordered: **Cream of Asparagus** and **Veggie on nine-grain**.
You'll be paying for your order with dishes

let's go home

Figure 13-10: Thanks for your order!

You could change the script and get the data from a METHOD=POST form by replacing the line $buffer = $ENV{'QUERY_STRING'} with the Perl instruction to read from the input stream: read(STDIN, $buffer, $ENV{'CONTENT_LENGTH'});

Hop over to http://www.yahoo.com/Computers/World_Wide_Web/ Programming to see all the different options for CGI processing tools. Quite a few helper programs are available, too, thank goodness, but don't be worried if this seems complex. It is. The good news is that many of the larger Web page hosting companies, or Internet Service Providers in the lingo, offer a set of useful CGI scripts that you can use without having to do any custom programming.

I also have a number of additional CGI tutorials online that you will find greatly useful if you'd like to travel further along this path. Go to http://www.intuitive.com/CGI/.

Summary
This chapter gave you a wealth of ideas about how to create interactive Web pages and obtain information from the viewer through forms and *Common Gateway Interface* (CGI) programming. Chapter 14 looks at what is the greatest change to Web page design with the HTML 4.0 specification: style sheets.

Style Sheets

If there's one thing that's constant with the Web, it's change. The HTML language itself is no different, as you have learned, but the one change that's formalized in the 4.0 specification of the hypertext markup language that has the potential to totally change the Web is style sheets. Known more formally as *Cascading Style Sheets* (CSS), it's a way for us Web designers to redefine the meaning of any HTML tag within a document or throughout a site.

That's the good news. The bad news is that the way you work with style sheet information is awkward and a bit cryptic because it's been retrofitted into the existing HTML language. Nonetheless, if I have to point to one change in HTML 4.0 that's most significant, it's unquestionably the addition of cascading style sheets.

It's interesting to note that the different releases of the major Web browsers on the Mac and PC have varying levels of support for the attributes you can set within style sheets. In particular, while Netscape Navigator 4.0 for Windows 95 has a considerable amount of support for style sheets, the same release for the Macintosh only supports a small subset of style sheets. Microsoft's Internet Explorer has supported the additional style sheet capabilities since its 3.0 release. Even with the support in the latest versions, there are still elements in the style specification that aren't supported at all yet.

And that brings up the biggest dilemma for designers who want to leap headlong into using style sheets: If it's not even fully supported in the very latest version of the most popular browser on the Net, what percentage of people who come to your CSS-dependent Web site will be able to see what you've designed? In the marketing biz, people often refer to a bell-shaped curve of technology adopters, talking about the "early adopters" as those who jump onto a bandwagon because it's new and different. But these early adopters are always a small subset of the overall market (how many of your friends have a DVD player or digital cellular phone today?). That's exactly the same problem with style sheets as I write this chapter: Are my Web pages targeted to a small subset of the online community, or am I seeking to appeal to the majority of online people within a specific interest group?

For your projects, it's a question only you can answer. Some sites you design might be ultimately for yourself as a learning experience, and so using the best, coolest, state-of-the-art formatting tags and style sheet information is perfect. Other sites that you're developing for a paying client whose mom has a WebTV unit, well, you'll want to be more careful about relying on the style sheet information on the page to get the effect you seek.

There is a middle ground. As we'll see in a bit, you can definitely add style sheet information to your page, but have the page gracefully degrade and still be attractive in earlier browsers. Indeed, this concept of "graceful degradation" is critical to successful Web page design. It's okay in my book (which this is!) to use the newest tags if the page still looks acceptable with older browsers or less high-tech equipment.

Okay, enough warnings. Let's jump in headfirst and look at the style sheet specifics and how to use them to have a far greater level of control over the appearance of your pages and overall site.

Introduction to Style Sheets

Even with all the comments above, I really want to emphasize here that of the changes that the 4.0 spec have brought to the Web developer community, none will be more pervasive and important, eventually, than style sheets. It's a big step away from the original paradigm of the Web, where you have "suggestions" for formatting like <STRONG> and <H1>, and the browser (as configured by the user) would decide exactly how it should appear on the screen. Instead, style sheets will let you, the Web page designer, define the exact size of typeface to use, the color, the typeface itself, and lots more for any given HTML tag.

Read the entire CSS specification for yourself, if you're so inclined, by popping over to `http://www.w3.org/TR/REC-CSS1-961217.html`. Even better, *WebReview* has a terrific online table that shows you what specific style attributes are supported by which versions of the major browsers. You can see it for yourself at `http://style.webreview.com/mastergrid.html`.

All of this magic is buried in HTML comments that are, themselves, buried in the `<STYLE>` tag. Why buried in comments? So browsers that don't understand styles won't get confused — just like how JavaScript and VBScript are included in Web documents.

Let's start by looking at a simple Web page using existing HTML tags to accomplish some indentation and typeface changes:

```
Here's a regular paragraph of information.
<P>
<FONT FACE=courier>
This is some code to show, it should be in 'courier' and
it should have lots of space between the lines of text,
more than would normally be the case with a medium-size
typeface.
</FONT>
<BLOCKQUOTE>
<FONT SIZE=+1 FACE="helvetica" COLOR=red>
And don't forget this important - indented - note too!
</FONT>
</BLOCKQUOTE>
```

This page is shown in Figure 14-1.

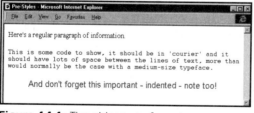

Figure 14-1: The old way to format a page

This is basic HTML layout that you learned quite a few chapters ago and is not very exciting. Let's stretch things now. It turns out that the second paragraph needs to be double-spaced and the third paragraph should only have an indent on the left side, not both the left and right, as is the wont of the `<BLOCKQUOTE>` tag. How can you do this?

Inline Style Sheets

The need by designers for this high level of control over the presentation of information is exactly why style sheets are so exciting. With style sheets, we can change the spacing between lines, affect one margin but not others, and much more. Here's the same page as shown earlier, rewritten to include the characteristics desired with style sheets:

```
Here's a regular paragraph of information.
<P TYPE="text/css" STYLE="font: 12pt/20pt Courier">
This is some code to show, it should be in 'courier' and
it should have lots of space between the lines of text,
more than would normally be the case with a 12 point
typeface.
<P TYPE="text/css"
    STYLE=" font: 14pt/11pt helvetica; margin-left: 1in;
color: red">
And don't forget this important - indented - note too!
But look, it's only indented on one side, not both the
left and right. Finally a way to accomplish this!
```

The changes are actually added as attributes to the specific HTML tags. In this case, these changes are specified in the `<P>` tag. You can see that there are two new attributes. The first should always be specified with inline style information: `TYPE=text/css`. The CSS, as you know, means *cascading style sheets* (I always envision a beautiful waterfall of information cascading down a virtual hillside when I hear the name, I must admit) and the "text" specifies that the style information is specified in text form, which is the only choice, actually.

The second attribute is the actual style specification. In the second line in the above example, the style specifies 12-point Courier with a 20-point leading. The later style specification is a bit more complex: 14-point type with 11-point leading (which means that the lines will just about overlap), bold, with a left margin one inch from the edge. The type should also be in red. Figure 14-2 shows the results.

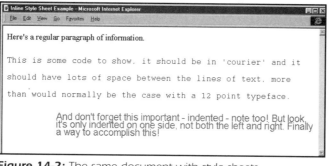

Figure 14-2: *The same document with style sheets*

There are things I'm doing on this page with style sheets that can't be done with any HTML, however much you might try. You could get the left indent, for example, by having a 100-percent width zero-border table, and then specify the first column is blank, for spacing, but there's no way to affect the leading of a paragraph of text short of making the text a graphic, which defeats the purpose of the Web.

A point is a unit of measurement for type size: 10-point type measures 10 points from the very top of a full-height letter, such as *h* or a capital, to the bottom of a descending letter such as *g, y,* or *p*. Historically, a point was actually the unit of measurement for the metal slug that held the letters on an old-fashioned printing press, if you want to be completely accurate. Nonetheless, it's a very common gauge of type size, and there are 72 points in an inch.

You can control a remarkable range of different page presentation attributes with a style specification, including all of those shown in Table 14-1.

Table 14-1	**Style Sheet Attributes**		
Attribute	**Description**	**Values**	**Example**
background	Sets background images or colors	URL, color-name, RGB value (hex)	{background: white}
color	Sets color of text	color-name, RGB value (hex)	{color: blue}

(continued)

Table 14-1 *(continued)*

Attribute	Description	Values	Example
font-family	Sets typeface	typeface name, font family name	{font-family: courier}
font-size	Sets size of text	points (pt), inches (in), centimeters (cm), pixels (px)	{font-size: 12pt}
font-style	Italicizes text	normal, italic	{font-style: italic}
font-weight	Sets thickness of type	extra-light, light, demi-light, medium, demi-bold, bold, extra-bold	{font-weight: bold}
line-height	Sets the distance between baselines	points (pt), inches (in), centimeters (cm), pixels (px), per-centage (%)	{line-height: 24pt}
margin-left	Sets distance from left edge of page	points (pt), inches (in), centimeters (cm), pixels (px)	{margin-left: 1in}
margin-right	Sets distance from right edge of page	points (pt), inches (in), centimeters (cm), pixels (px)	{margin-right: 1in}
margin-top	Sets distance from top edge of page	points (pt), inches (in), centimeters (cm), pixels (px)	{margin-top: 20px}

Attribute	Description	Values	Example
text-align	Sets justification	left, center, right	{text-align: right}
text-decoration	Underlines or otherwise highlights text	none, underline, italic, line-through	{text-decoration: underline}
text-indent	Sets distance from left margin	points (pt), inches (in), centimeters (cm), pixels (px)	{text- indent: 0.5in}

One more snippet to make sense of this table. There are six different units of measurement you can use with style sheets: "px" is pixels, "in" is inches, "cm" is centimeters, "mm" is millimeters, "pt" is points and "pc" is percentage. Further, text-based measures can also be specified in em spaces with the "em" unit.

 An *em space* is traditionally the widest possible character space in a font: it's the width of the capital letter "M". Typographers also pay attention to "N" space (*en space*) and "I" space.

Now, armed with this table of options, let's try some further tweaking to some Web pages to see what kind of hoops we can make the browser jump through!

When you look at the table above, you might be a bit puzzled by the previous example: most of these specific elements don't appear in the style information shown. That's because you can use a shorthand notation for style sheet information to save lots of typing.

Here's an example:

```
<H1 TYPE="text/css" STYLE="font-weight: bold;
    font-size: 12pt;
    line-height: 14pt;
    font-family: helvetica">Important Header</H1>
```

is exactly equivalent to:

```
<H1 TYPE="text/css" STYLE="font: bold 12/14
helvetica">Important Header</H1>
```

Notice here that we're not specifying a typeface, but rather a font family. There are a small number of font families defined as part of the CSS specification that allow you to avoid worrying about the specifics of exact typeface names on each machine and instead pick the kind of typeface you desire. The families are defined in Table 14-2:

Table 14-2:	Generic Font Families
Family Name	**Example**
`'serif'`	(Times)
`'sans-serif'`	(Helvetica)
`'cursive'`	(Zapf Chancery)
`'fantasy'`	(Western)
`'monospace'`	(Courier)

Let's look at another example of inline style modifications:

```
<H1 TYPE=text/css STYLE="text-align: center; font: 0.5in
helvetica;
color: blue;  border-width: 0.15in; border-color: red;
border-style: groove">
Corporate Information Center</H1>
versus
<H1 TYPE=text/css STYLE="text-align: center; font: 0.5in
serif;
color: blue;  background-color: yellow; border-width:
0.15in; border-color: red;
border-style: ridge">
Corporate Information Center</H1>
```

This takes advantage of some elements that are not widely supported in style sheets. The border of an element can be displayed by specifying its size and some attributes. In this case, I've specified that it should be 0.15 inches in size, red, and that the visual appearance of the border should be a "groove" or cutout. Other values include "none," "dotted,""dashed," "solid," "double," "ridge," "inset," and "outset."

Figure 14-3 shows you the wonderful results of this fancy style specification. Notice the difference between the "ridge" and "groove" style of border, and how changing the typeface family from Helvetica (a sans-serif, or no serif, typeface family) to the "serif" family has dramatically changed the feel of the second header. Of course, the yellow background helps differentiate the two onscreen, too.

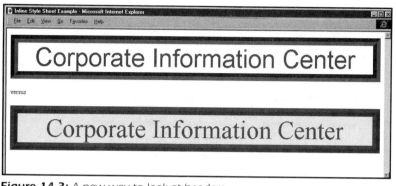

Figure 14-3: A new way to look at headers

You're starting to see the amount of control you have with style sheet information. It's really remarkable if you're willing to spend the time to figure it out. Here's another example of how I might combine all of these style sheets:

```
<H1 TYPE=text/css STYLE="text-align: center; font: 0.5in
helvetica;
color: blue;  border-width: 0.1in; border-color: #999999;
border-style: inset">
The Winter's Grove</H1>
<P TYPE=text/css STYLE="text-align: justify; font:
14pt/17pt;
border-width: 0.15in; border-color: #CCCCCC; border-style:
double;">
It was a cool evening and I was sitting on the stoop,
wondering whether to finish the shed roof or enjoy the
companionship of the dogs, sprawled at my feet. All at
once a bright light shone at the eastern edge of the
forest followed almost immediately by a loud crack, as if
the heavens themselves had suddenly been split asunder.
I jumped up following my dogs, who had already begun
barking and running towards the strange phenomenon.
</P>
So begins the first chapter of ...
```

I have to admit that working on these examples has proven highly frustrating because not only do the different browsers support different pieces of style sheets, but with Navigator, if you have anything that diverges even slightly from the standard it understands, it'll ignore everything in your style specification. Explorer is much friendlier, ignoring what it doesn't understand and showing you the results of everything else.

You can see the difference between the two in Figures 14-4, 14-5, 14-6, and 14-7, which show exactly the same page displayed in Internet Explorer on Windows 95, Netscape Navigator on Windows 95, Internet Explorer on the Macintosh, and Netscape Navigator on the Macintosh.

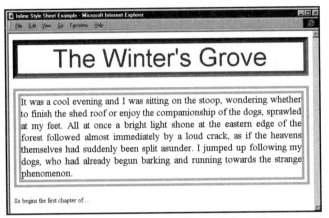

Figure 14-4: Styles rendered in Navigator 4.0 on Windows 95

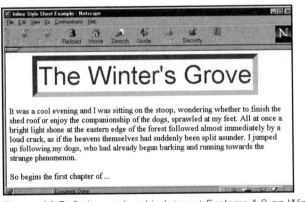

Figure 14-5: Styles rendered in Internet Explorer 4.0 on Windows 95

Style sheet specifications clearly offer considerable power — even if the results are quite different on the different possible browsers — but having to add all these tags on every single HTML tag would make this quite a hassle. The good news is there are two important alternatives. Having the style information within a specific HTML tag is known, as I said, as "inline" style information, but, in fact, there are three different ways to specify styles in your documents: inline, within the document header, and with an external style sheet.

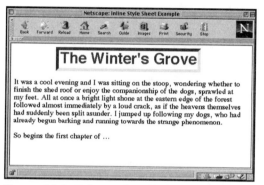

Figure 14-6: Styles rendered in Navigator 4.0 on the Macintosh

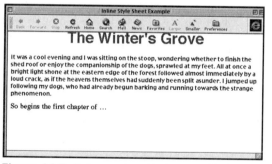

Figure 14-7: Styles rendered in Internet Explorer 4.0 on the Macintosh

Header Styles

You've already seen how to specify style specifics within an HTML tag, but the good news is you can actually redefine HTML tags at the top of your document and then have the changes apply to all uses of that tag within the page.

For example, say you want to have all header-level-one tags in 28-point Arial, green, and center-aligned. Here's the style tag:

```
<STYLE TYPE="text/css">
<!--
   H1 { font: 28 pt "Arial Black"; color: green; text-
align: center }
-->
</STYLE>
```

Once you've created this definition, every use of the <H1> tag in your document will produce the style specified in the header.

Worth noting is that the <STYLE> tag wraps all style definitions, but older browsers might try to actually display the style definition itself, so, like scripting inclusions, style definitions should be wrapped in HTML comments.

There's even a shorthand way for specifying some of these style characteristics. If you want to specify a variety of font details, you can pour them all into one tag:

```
H1 {font: 15pt/17pt "Arial Black" }
```

You can also create your own types of HTML tags by using classes within style sheets. Let's say that I want to have two paragraph styles: one that includes code listings (just like this book!) and another that includes handy notes shown in red. I could do this with style sheets as:

```
<STYLE TYPE="text/css" >
   P.code { font: 12pt/20pt "Courier" }
   P.notes { font: 14pt/16pt; margin-left: 0.5in; color:
red }

</STYLE>
```

Now you can use this within your own documents, as shown with yet another rewrite of the first example page:

```
<STYLE TYPE="text/css" >
   P.code { font: 12pt/20pt "Courier" }
   P.notes { font: 14pt/16pt; margin-left: 0.5in; color:
red }
</STYLE>
<P>
Here's a regular paragraph of information.
<P CLASS=code>
This is some code to show, it should be in 'courier' and
it should have lots of space between the lines of text,
more than would normally be the case with a 12 point
typeface.
<P CLASS=notes>
And don't forget this important - indented - note too!
```

You can see how this could let you have attractive and very consistent Web pages across various sites. See Figure 14-8 for an example of how this formats.

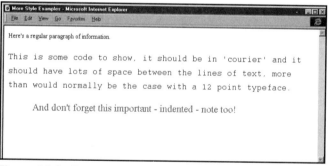

Figure 14-8: Classes of HTML tags with style sheets

Now you can see what's cool about this: With a slight modification to the top of the document, all the material in the Web page is automatically changed. No tedious item-by-item modifications.

For example, I'll change the top STYLE definition to the following:

```
<STYLE TYPE="text/css">
   P.code  { font: 16pt/20pt cursive; margin-left: 1in;
background=#cccccc }
   P.notes { font: 18pt/20pt; color: red }
</STYLE>
```

Consider how differently the Web page now displays on the screen, as shown in Figure 14-9.

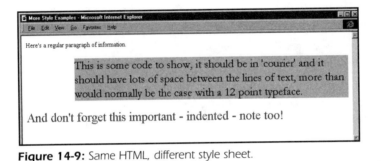

Figure 14-9: *Same HTML, different style sheet.*

External Style Sheets

Having all your styles specified at the top of the page can be a real time-saver and ensure a high level of consistency throughout the document, but if you have a multipage Web site, you'll be delighted to know that you can actually have a single style sheet for an entire site. The style sheet is saved as a ".css" document and is referenced within the header of each page that needs it:

```
<HEAD>
<TITLE>Nine Reasons to Stay In Durango, Colorado</TITLE>
<LINK REL=STYLESHEET
      HREF="http://www.intuitive.com/stylesheet.css"
      TYPE="text/css">
</HEAD>
```

Here, the style sheet is saved as the document
`http://www.intuitive.com/stylesheet.css` on my server.

Cool Style Sheet Tricks

There's a lot more to style sheets that's worth exploring, but we're still a bit ahead of the game — it's hard to find a Web browser that even implements the majority of the possibilities as defined in the CSS specification, let alone all of them.

Nonetheless, there are some fun things you can try in your Web pages using the various style sheet attributes.

Links change size

Have you always wanted to have links shrink when visited? You can do that using some style specifications:

```
<STYLE TYPE="text/css">
    A:link     { font-weight: bold; font: 18pt "Arial
Black";  color: blue; }
    A:visited { font-weight: lighter; font: 14pt "Times
Roman"; color: black; }
</STYLE>
```

You don't have to look too closely at Figure 14-10 to see the difference between the link you've seen and the one you haven't.

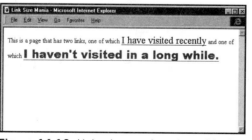

Figure 14-10: Links change size when visited.

Text superimposed

Another part of the CSS specification that I haven't talked about too much herein is the ability to gain fine control over the placement of items, even to superimpose or overlap material:

```
<STYLE TYPE="text/css">

#background {
   color: #9999CC;
   font: 100px Impact, sans-serif;
}
#foreground {
   color: #000000;
   font: italic 30px Georgia, serif;
}

</STYLE>
<BODY BGCOLOR=white>

<P ALIGN=center>
<SPAN ID=background>Meet the Gang</SPAN>

<P TYPE="text/css" STYLE="margin-top: -48px;text-align:
center;">
<SPAN ID=foreground>Dave, Linda, Ashley, Jasmine &amp;
Karma</SPAN>

<P STYLE="text-align: center; font: bold 20pt serif"
TYPE="text/css">
Overlapping text without any graphics. Very nice.
```

Before I talk about what I'm doing in this particular example, have a peek at Figure 14-11 to see the excellent output of this particular use of style sheets.

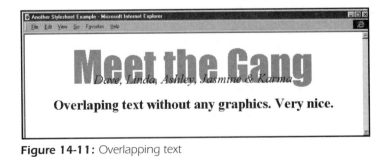

Figure 14-11: Overlapping text

Nice, eh? The most important style sheet attribute I'm using here is the specification "margin-top: -48px" which indicates that the top of the subsequent information should be 48 pixels *higher* than normal. Since the background words are 100 pixels high ("font 100px"), that means we're almost exactly over the lower half of the background letters.

I'm also taking advantage of another way you can use style sheets: Using the ID attribute, I've created another kind of style sheet specification to use, almost a macro, if you're familiar with programming MS Word or similar programs. Exactly the opposite of internal anchors, IDs are defined by prefacing the definition with '#' within the <STYLE> tag, then used with "id=name" later in the HTML.

Finally, a tag that really has no value other than in this kind of context: The <SPAN> tag by itself doesn't change the presentation of information on your page, but lets you specify attributes for any text within. In this case, I'm using this to utilize the style IDs already defined.

Table 14-3	HTML Tags Covered in This Chapter	
Tag	**Close Tag**	**Meaning**
<STYLE	</STYLE>	Style sheet information specified
TYPE=*val*		Type of style sheet. Usually "text/css."
<SPAN>	</SPAN>	Generic HTML range tag, for styles only

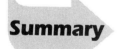

Summary

This chapter gave you a good idea of the future of much of HTML: Style sheets give you a remarkable amount of control over the layout and appearance of your content. It was also clear as you went along, however, that style sheets are still part of the future, because even the most recent browsers don't agree on the CSS format and on which styles they can interpret correctly. Chapter 15 continues the exploration of the HTML 4.0 specification by looking at how they've improved tables and frames for designers.

Improvements in Tables and Frames

Advanced Tables

New HTML 4.0 Table Elements

Advanced Frames

Inline Frames

Imagine, for a moment, that there are two main companies and dozens of individuals trying to modify and enhance HTML capabilities so they can produce exactly the pages they desire. As much as possible, the companies try to collaborate so their improvements are compatible (which is, of course, the purpose of the standards organizations) but there are no guarantees: Each company feels that its individual contribution is worth more than 100 percent compatibility.

You would be very close to the state of HTML with the release of the Cougar (HTML 4.0) specification. What's fun is that you can actually trace the history of just about any HTML tag. For example, tables weren't part of the original HTML specification; tables were introduced by Netscape with the 2.0 browser release. NCSA Mosaic, an early competitor, didn't support tables, nor did the very first release of Navigator or Internet Explorer. Zoom forward in time and not only are tables incredibly complex and sophisticated, but Cougar adds new capabilities, too.

This chapter covers a variety of extensions to tables and frames, some of which are new with the 4.0 specification, but most of which have crept into the markup language over the past year or two of its evolution. Unfortunately, you will find that some of the examples won't work on your particular browser, either because the browser isn't yet fully compliant with HTML 4.0, or because the development team has deliberately chosen its own, incompatible solution.

The frustrating part is that these additional capabilities are invaluable if you want to really get the most out of your Web site designs — it's a matter of balancing capabilities against possible incompatibilities. The moral is: Test your site designs on as many possible hardware and browser platforms as you can.

Advanced Tables

There are a number of additional capabilities of tables that I skipped over in Chapter 9 — not because I didn't think they were important, but because Chapter 9 was focused on getting you up to speed, able to produce attractive and functional table-based designs.

In this chapter, I'm going to dig much deeper into the capabilities hidden in HTML tables, starting with the following example:

```
The history of mankind has been interwoven with the
history of money, and the various attempts of bright
people to identify a useful mechanism for what is
essentially an abstract form of barter.
<TABLE BORDER=1 WIDTH=75% ALIGN=left HSPACE=10 VSPACE=10>
<TR BGCOLOR=#cccccc>
<TH>Currency</TH><TH>President on Bill</TH></TR>
<TR ALIGN=center>
<TD>$1</TD><TD>George Washington</TD>
</TR><TR ALIGN=center>
<TD>$5</TD><TD>Abraham Lincoln</TD>
</TR><TR ALIGN=center>
<TD>$10</TD><TD>Alexander Hamilton</TD>
</TR><TR ALIGN=center>
<TD>$20</TD><TD>Andrew Jackson</TR>
</TR>
<CAPTION>Who Are Those People On Our Currency?</CAPTION>
</TABLE>
Of course, the colorful history of the U.S.A. has also
been a part of this grand tapestry, and, as is obvious
from the faces on our currency, the design of money is
both a social and political process. Indeed, it's no
coincidence that the most famous of Presidents are not
those that adorn our bills.
```

There are many parts to this table that you've never seen before, starting with the *table header* tag, <TH>, standing in for the <TD> table data cell. As you can see in Figure 15-1, the table header tag within a table automatically centers the text in the box and also shows it in bold. I can, of course, accomplish the same thing with <TD ALIGN=center><B>, but <TH> is a convenient shortcut. To get the top to have a gray background, I use BGCOLOR=#cccccc within the <IR> tag. That sets the color of each data cell (or table header, in this case) to the same background.

Figure 15-1: A more sophisticated use of tables

Once you glance at the figure, the most dramatic change is that the text on the page is actually flowing around the table, rather than displaying it as a standalone table with text above and below only. That's done with the ALIGN=left attribute to the <TABLE> tag itself. ALIGN=right would move the table to the right margin and have the text flow around on the left, and if you're guessing that ALIGN=center will have the text flow on both sides, I'm sorry to disappoint you. ALIGN=center centers the table horizontally, but doesn't let the text flow around the table on either side.

The HSPACE and VSPACE attributes enable you to specify additional pixels of border to expand the space between the table and the surrounding text, both left and right (horizontal or HSPACE), and above and below (vertical, or VSPACE). These are used exactly like you have already learned with <IMG> tags and included graphics.

The final addition to this table is the <CAPTION> tag, which enables you to specify a floating caption associated with the table. In this case, I want the caption immediately below the table, so I specify ALIGN=bottom. There are four different alignment options for the caption: top, bottom, left, and right. If you want to have the caption to the side of the table itself, you can use ALIGN=left or ALIGN=right and watch how it does interesting things to your tables!

There are two more attributes you can use with HTML tables that are worth exploring before we delve into the nether reaches of the restructured HTML 4.0 table specification: NOWRAP and VALIGN=baseline. Here's an attractive table that demonstrates both:

```
<TABLE BORDER=1 CELLSPACING=0 CELLPADDING=3
ALIGN=center HEIGHT=300>
<TR><TD COLSPAN=3 BGCOLOR=#999999 ALIGN=center>
<font size=+2><B>Places to Eat In Our House</TD></TR>
<TR BGCOLOR=#cccccc><TH>Location</TH>
<TD ROWSPAN=6 WIDTH=1 BGCOLOR=black> </TD>
<TH>Comments</TH></TR>
<TR><TD>Dining <br>Room</TD>
<TD VALIGN=top>How mundane...</TD></TR>
<TR><TD>Living <br>Room</TD>
<TD VALIGN=baseline>Casual, but hard to clean up</TD></TR>
<TR><TD>Exercise <br>Room</TD>
<TD>Well, if you don't mind sweating into your
food!</TD></TR>
<TR><TD>Kitchen</TD>
<TD>Excellent for meals on the run</TD></TR>
<TR><TD>Office</TD><TD NOWRAP>Alright, this is a very
90's sort of thing, being so busy that you end up having
to eat a meal while in your office.</TD></TR>
</TABLE>
```

As you see in Figure 15-2, the ROWSPAN element can be used in interesting ways to accomplish vertical bars within tables. In this case, however, because I've set the CELLPADDING to 3, it means the minimum size of the vertical bar is twice that (padding on each side) plus the 1 pixel for the specified width itself (in the <TD> attributes), or 7 pixels. One final note on this: Because I don't have any information for this data cell, I use the   nonbreaking space character so the cell has some contents. Without it, a data cell without any contents is not rendered in the table and leaves a "hole." (Try it, you'll see what I mean.)

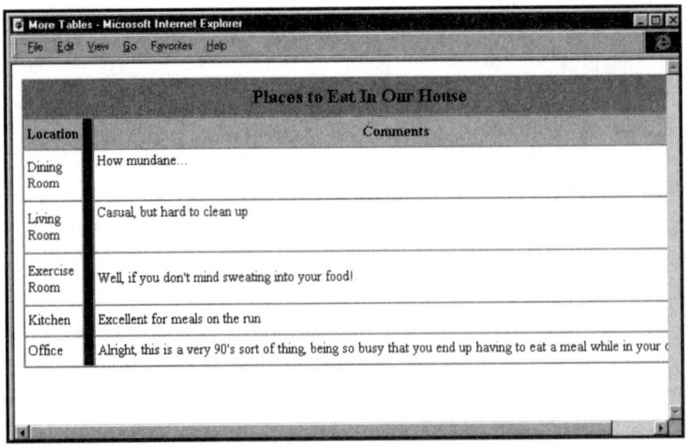

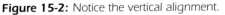

Figure 15-2: Notice the vertical alignment.

Pay close attention to the vertical alignment of the descriptions associated with the dining room, living room, and exercise room: the first has the description vertically aligned TOP with the first data cell in the row; the second has BASELINE alignment; and the third is the default, CENTER alignment. The BASELINE alignment, as is clear, ensures that the first line of text in the cell is on the same "line" as the bottom of the first line of text in the previous cell.

The NOWRAP attribute makes the table wider than the window in which it's being viewed (see in Figure 15-2). This attribute forces the data cell to be rendered with the line breaks explicitly included in the HTML itself. A <BR> would help immensely, but NOWRAP forces the browser to not otherwise split the text for convenience. As with many examples, NOWRAP is very awkward here and breaks an otherwise reasonably attractive table of information.

Be warned: In the HTML 4.0 specification, the NOWRAP attribute has been "deprecated," which means it's on the way out. Eventually, it'll be replaced by forcing designers to use the text wrap parts of style sheets to accomplish this same effect.

New HTML 4.0 Table Elements

The new HTML 4.0 specification — known as "Cougar" — includes a number of new features for tables. In fact, I think tables have changed and improved more than any other area of the new specification. Having said that, however, I will admit that while some of the changes are very valuable, many of the additions seem a bit daft to me.

The change you should care most about is that you can now specify the number and exact size of each row of a table with a combination of the <COLGROUP> and <COL> tags within a <TABLE> tag. There is a COLS attribute to the <TABLE> tag, but if you want to start including hints about your table size in your page, then <COLGROUP> is a much better, more flexible strategy.

Why bother indicating the number of columns? Because if you have ever worked with complex tables, you already know that the browser can't start rendering the first line of the table until it's received every snippet of information. To understand why you should indicate the number of columns, consider this example. What happens when the following table is displayed onscreen?

```
<TABLE BORDER=1>
<TR><TD>The</TD><TD>Rain</TD><TD>In</TD><TD>Spain</TD>
</TR><TR>
<TD>Falls</TD><TD>Mainly</TD><TD>On</TD><TD>The</TD><TD>
Plain</TD>
</TR><TR>
<TD>and where is that plain?</TD><TD>in Spain! In
Spain!</TD>
</TR>
</TABLE>
```

Figure 15-3 shows the result: pay close attention to the spacing of cells and the number of cells in the first row of the table.

Figure 15-3: How big is this table?

If the table is as small as the previous example, a delay of a second or two on rendering the page isn't a big deal; but when you get into large tables — and I've created tables with over 200 lines — the delay in transmitting information can be substantial.

The solution is to use the <COLGROUP> and <COLS> tags to give the browser an idea of what's coming next. Here's how the above table would be rewritten to use these new tags:

```
<TABLE BORDER=1>
<COLGROUP>
   <COL WIDTH=3"*">
   <COL WIDTH=3"*">
   <COL><COL WIDTH=15%><COL WIDTH=150>
</COLGROUP>
<TR><TD>The</TD><TD>Rain</TD><TD>In</TD><TD>Spain</TD>
</TR><TR>
<TD>Falls</TD><TD>Mainly</TD><TD>On</TD><TD>The</TD><TD>
Plain</TD>
</TR><TR>
```

```
<TD>and where is that plain?</TD><TD>in Spain! In
Spain!</TD>
</TR>
</TABLE>
```

This looks a bit confusing, but the sizing parameters are similar to those you already saw when I talked about specifying frame sizes with the `<FRAMESET>` tag. In a nutshell, you can specify sizes by percentage of width of the window (`WIDTH=15%`), specific number of pixels (`WIDTH=150`), have it compute the smallest possible width for the cells in the row (`<COL>`), and, the fourth possibility, specify how much of the available space should be allocated to the different rows.

In the previous example, `3*` appears twice and `<COL>` appears once without a specification, which is identical to `COL WIDTH=*` or `COL WIDTH=1*`. Add these specs up and you get 7 portions. Subtract the space for the 15 percent width and 150-pixel-width columns and the remaining space on the window will be allocated for the remainder of the table, broken into $3/7$, $3/7$ and $1/7$. If the entire width of the screen was 1000 pixels, then 15 percent would be 150 pixels and the width consumed by the last two columns would be 300 pixels (15 percent + 150). The remainder would be 700 pixels, which would be divided up into seven equal portions and then allocated. The result: Column 1 would be 300 pixels wide, column 2 would be 300 pixels wide, column 3 would be 100 pixels wide, and the last two you already know.

Neither Internet Explorer 4.0 nor Navigator 4.0 have yet implemented the extensions to TABLES in their browsers (which is frustrating), so I can't include any illustrations in this section.

Not only is `<COL>` therefore useful for specifying the number of columns, it's also quite useful for specifying the width of a given column. Even better, you can also specify other attributes for a given column, as demonstrated in the following example:

```
<TABLE BORDER=1>
<COLGROUP>
<COL ALIGN=right><COL ALIGN=char CHAR=":">
<THEAD>
<TR><TH>What I'm Doing<TH>Time Of Day
<TBODY>
<TR><TD>Waking Up<TD>8:30 am
<TR><TD>Driving to Work <TD>9:00 am
<TR><TD>Eating Lunch<TD>12:00 noon
<TR><TD>Driving Home <TD>6:00 pm
</TABLE>
```

You'll first notice that I have omitted all the closing tags in this example. Much to my surprise, the Cougar specification states directly that you should be able to skip all the closing tags in an HTML table. As you can see, it certainly makes life easier! To help organize complex tables, <THEAD> and <TBODY> have been added: they're not mandatory and it's too soon to tell if people will actually start using them.

The other interesting thing about this example is that I'm specifying that I want to have the second column of information aligned by the colon character. ALIGN=char specifies a character alignment and CHAR is where you specify the character to use for alignment. If you don't specify a CHAR value the default is '.', which will cause numeric values to line up along the decimal point.

There's another possible ALIGN option (and, like the ALIGN=char option, it can appear anywhere you can specify an alignment) that you might well have been waiting for since the first release of HTML: justified text. ALIGN=justify should eliminate the ragged right margin of text, even while keeping the left margin also aligned.

Of course, Internet Explorer 4.0 is a bit confused about that: ALIGN= justify is identical in result to ALIGN=right. On the other hand, Navigator 4.0 doesn't recognize it as a known alignment option and ignores it.

I wish that I was able to show you spiffy examples of how these format and look gorgeous in a Web browser, but the reality is that I don't have a browser that understands enough about the HTML 4.0 specification to interpret these add-ons. Clearly, it's far too soon to make any of these a vital part of the design of your site, but we hope that sometime before the end of 1998 the browsers will begin to understand more and more of Cougar.

Advanced Frames

As with tables, there are aspects to a frames-based design that I didn't cover in Chapter 14. The previous information is plenty to get your frameset up and running, but there are some nuances that can really improve the appearance of your Web site and, more importantly, improve the user experience itself.

First and foremost is getting rid of an unwanted annoyance: The border around each of the panes in a frame-based design. You'll recall that the basic approach for creating a frames-based site is:

```
<HTML>
<TITLE>Weird things to do to your Browser!</TITLE>
<FRAMESET COLS="40%,60%">
    <FRAME SRC=leftside.html>
    <FRAME SRC=rightside.html NAME=right>
</FRAMESET>
</BODY>
</HTML>
```

This example produces a very simple frames-based site where the left side of the window is the Web page leftside.html, and the right side of the page is rightside.html. The problem is that the dividing line between the two pages is quite obvious because it's about 5 pixels wide.

To eliminate this, the first step — the only one necessary in Navigator — is to add the BORDER=0 attribute to the <FRAMESET> tag. Internet Explorer, however, needs a bit more convincing, so adding FRAMEBORDER=0 and FRAMESPACING=0 to the <FRAMESET> tag (and remember, there's nothing wrong with specifying redundant attributes; the browser will only pay attention to the attribute it understands) makes the border vanish for both browsers.

Navigator, by the way, is the one that's compliant with the HTML 4.0 specification this time. The official specification is that BORDER=0 should turn off the borders between panes unless otherwise specified within the <FRAME> tag itself.

Here's the rewritten page:

```
<HTML>
<TITLE>Weird things to do to your Browser!</TITLE>
<FRAMESET COLS="40%,60%" BORDER=0 FRAMEBORDER=0
FRAMESPACING=0>
    <FRAME SRC=leftside.html>
    <FRAME SRC=rightside.html NAME=right>
</FRAMESET>
</BODY>
</HTML>
```

As you can see in Figure 15-4, the different panes seamlessly merge, creating a page with a blue box on the left and green on the right. (Or, in this book, one shade of gray on the left and another for the rest of the page.)

Figure 15-4: A frames-based page without any seams

It's worth experimenting with specifying just FRAMEBORDER=0 or FRAMESPACING=0 if you're working with Internet Explorer, because they have rather interesting results.

The next tweak you might want to make to your frames-based design, whether you want to have visible borders or not, is to move the contents of the page off the very edge of the pane. You can do this with a combination of MARGINHEIGHT and MARGINWIDTH, which specify, in pixels or percentage, how far from the top and left side of the margin the contents should be shown. Even better, it works exactly the same for both browsers.

An example of how it might work will contrast two panes with the very same content, one with the margins specified in the <FRAMESET> tag, and the other without it:

```
<FRAMESET COLS="40%,60%">
      <FRAME SRC=contents2.html>
      <FRAME SRC=contents2.html MARGINHEIGHT=50
MARGINWIDTH=100>
</FRAMESET>
```

Figure 15-5 tells the story here. The two panes should look exactly identical except that the right side has a 50-pixel margin from the top and bottom, and a 100-pixel margin from the edge of the left and right side of the pane. Notice that the frame border is back because I omitted the BORDER=0 (and so on, and so on) that was part of the previous example.

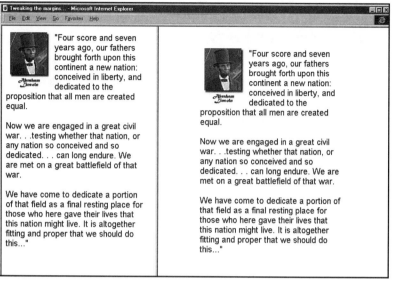

Figure 15-5: *Increasing the margins on frames*

Another tweak you might find valuable is to specify NORESIZE on a frame design where you don't want to let people drag and move around the frame borders to resize things the way they think is best. Combined with SCROLLING=no, you can chop off a piece of your graphic or page and leave the user no alternative way to see the entire thing, so do be careful with this. Both of these attributes would appear in the <FRAME> tag, not <FRAMESET>.

Special TARGET values

In Chapter 9 you learned about how you can "aim" events at a specific pane of a frames design by using NAME= to specify the name of the pane within the <FRAME> tag, then, on the navigational pages, using TARGET= as part of the HREF to have them affect the specified pane rather than the one that you're working within. It turns out, however, that you can specify other values within the TARGET attribute, values that let you gain a bit more control over what's going on. Table 15-1 summarizes the four key targets with which you should experiment:

Table 15-1   TARGET values for greater frame control

Name	Meaning
_blank	Load the document in a new, unnamed window.
_self	Load the document into the current window (the default).
_parent	Load the document into the parent window (only relevant when you have more than one window on the screen).
_top	Load the document into the very topmost window, thus canceling all other frames that might be on the screen.

When you see a Web site that has a frames-based design and a button that says "no frames," the code underneath that is doubtless similar to:

```
<A HREF=noframes.html TARGET=_top>no frames</a>
```

and if you explore the examples on the CD-ROM included with this book, you've already encountered a variation of the above TARGET values. The fifth possible value is that if you use the TARGET attribute to point to a named window that doesn't exist, a new window with that name will be created. In my case, I used the name "demo" throughout, so a typical entry in the examples page would be:

```
<a href=frames2.html TARGET=demo>Increasing the margins on frames</a>
```

Judicious use of the special TARGET values can considerably improve your frames-based design and offer, for example, a navigational window that sticks even while the user wanders around other areas of the site.

Oh! If you don't want to type in the TARGET value for each of your links, and they're all pointing to the same place, it turns out that there's a short-cut in HTML that will save you oodles of typing:

```
<BASE target=value>
```

For example, all my examples are written more simply, as exemplified by:

```
<a href=frames2.html>Increasing the margins on frames</a>
```

because at the top of the page, it specifies:

```
<BASE TARGET=demo>
```

If specific links are supposed to aim elsewhere, you are still free to override things with a TARGET attribute within an individual <A HREF tag.

Inline Frames

One of the coolest things that Microsoft introduced into the HTML language with its popular Internet Explorer browser is the concept of inline frames — frame windows that are completely enclosed by their surrounding window. Not supported yet in any version of Netscape Navigator I've seen, they are now an official part of the HTML 4.0 specification.

An inline frame is specified with the <IFRAME> tag in a manner quite similar to how you specify the <FRAME> tag, as shown by the following simple example:

```
<IFRAME SRC=inset-info.hml height=40% width=50%>
```

In this case, I'm specifying that I want an inline frame window that's 40 percent of the height and 50 percent of the width of the current page, and that the HTML within should be the page inset-info.html. To use this in a more complex example:

```
<BODY BGCOLOR=#99cc99>          <!-- a medium, kinda dark
green -->
<font size=+1>
<BLOCKQUOTE>
The Gettysburg Address, as delivered by President Abraham
Lincoln to the soldiers and general assembly at the
Gettysburg battlefield during the American Civil War,
November 19, 1863.
</BLOCKQUOTE>
<P>
<CENTER>
<IFRAME SRC=contents2.html HEIGHT=50% WIDTH=75%>
   <TABLE BORDER=1 CELLPADDING=20><TR><TD ALIGN=center>You
   can't see the information here, which should be in a
   separate inline frame.
   <p>
   <a href=contents2.html>read the Gettysburg Address</a>
   </TD></TR></TABLE>
</IFRAME>
<P>
More information about Lincoln can be found at
<a href=http://www.netins.net/showcase/creative/
lincoln.html>Lincoln Online</a>
</CENTER>
</BODY>
```

The results in Internet Explorer, as shown in Figure 15-6, are quite attractive. Netscape Navigator, because it doesn't (yet) understand the `<IFRAME>` tag, ignores both parts of the `<IFRAME> </IFRAME>` pair and instead interprets the HTML between the two tags. Figure 15-7 shows the table that is displayed instead: still all right, but not as functional.

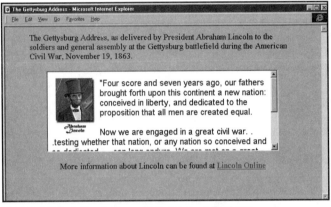

Figure 15-6: Inline frame within Internet Explorer

Figure 15-7: Same page source within Netscape Navigator

Again, I highlight that `<IFRAME>` is included within the HTML 4.0 specifications, so we should see this included in future versions of the Netscape browser, too.

There are a number of options to `<IFRAME>` worth highlighting, particularly `FRAMEBORDER`, which can have a value of 0 or 1, depending on whether you'd like a border. `MARGINWIDTH` and `MARGINHEIGHT` offer finer control over the spacing between the margin of the inline frame and the contents and SCROLLING can be yes, no, or auto, exactly as the <FRAME> tag lets you specify.

One final mechanism you can explore as you further exploit inline frames on your site: You can name the inline frame with the NAME attribute and you can point references to the inline frame with TARGET, just as you would for a regular frames layout.

Table 15-2 has a summary of tags covered in this chapter.

Table 15-2	HTML Tags Covered in This Chapter	
Tag	**Close Tag**	**Meaning**
<TABLE		
ALIGN=left		Aligns table on the left side of the page, with text flowing around the right.
ALIGN=right		Aligns table on the right side of the page, with text flowing to left.
HSPACE=x		Additional horizontal space around table (pixels).
VSPACE=x		Additional vertical space around table (pixels).
COLS=x		Specify the number of columns in the table.
<TD		
NOWRAP		Prevent word wrap within a data cell (be careful with this tag).
ALIGN=baseline		Align data cell with the baseline of adjacent text.
ALIGN=char		Align a column on a specific character (default '.').
ALIGN=justify		Line up both the left and right margin for the text..
<COLGROUP>	</COLGROUP>	Define a set of column definitions with COL tags.
<COL		A specific column width defined.

(continued)

Table 15-2 *(continued)*

Tag	Close Tag	Meaning
WIDTH=*x*		Width of the column, in pixels, percentage or '*' notation.
<THEAD>	</THEAD>	Organization for tables: this denotes table head material.
<TBODY>	</TBODY>	Denotes the body of the table.
<FRAMESET		
BORDER=*x*		Specify border on or off for the frameset (0 or 1).
FRAMEBORDER=*x*		Specify size of frame border.
FRAMESPACING=*x*		Amount of spacing between frame panes.
<FRAME		
MARGINHEIGHT=*x*		Additional spacing above and below specific pane.
MARGINWIDTH=*x*		Additional spacing to the left and right of the pane.
<IFRAME		Inline frame.
SRC=*url*		Source for the frame.
NAME=*s*		Name of the window (for TARGET usage).
HEIGHT=*x*		Height of the embedded frame (pixels or percentage).
WIDTH=*x*		Width of the embedded frame (pixels or percentage).

Summary

This chapter expanded your knowledge of additional table and frame capabilities, including detailing the now standardized <IFRAME> inline frame tag. Chapter 16 continues the theme with an exploration of the many new additions to forms introduced in the Cougar specification.

Advanced Forms and HTML 4 Additions

The BUTTON input type

Using labels to organize user focus

Dividing forms into fieldsets

Keyboard control

Disabled and read-only elements

When you were young, if you were like most kids, you judged the value of a book by the number of pictures inside. Lots of pictures meant it wouldn't be too boring, and absolutely no pictures meant that it was likely to drag. This book should be judged by a similar criterion, I think, because the only way to really understand HTML is to see lots and lots of examples of what it is and how it works. That's why I've ensured throughout that there are a lot of screen shots, to let you easily see the relationship between the HTML source and the results on a computer screen.

Unfortunately, with this chapter, that's all going to come to an end. As you learned in Chapter 15, while the HTML 4.0 specification is available now (the very beginning of 1998), the features within haven't been widely implemented yet. When it comes to all the useful additions to the forms area, none of them are implemented. So, while I would really like to include pictures that demonstrate the new capabilities, I can't; because none of the browsers I use can correctly read the HTML. By the time you read this book, however, I expect that the HTML 4.0 additions will have started their migration into the popular Web browsers (indeed, Microsoft promised full Cougar support in Internet Explorer 4.0 preview 2, but my results varied considerably).

As a reflection of this state of affairs, I am including on the CD-ROM the source to every example discussed in this chapter, but there are no screen shots herein once we get past the brief discussion of the `<INPUT TYPE=BUTTON>` addition to forms.

The BUTTON Input Type

In Chapter 12 you learned about the overloaded `<INPUT>` tag and its many possible `TYPE` values, including text, checkbox, radio, password, submit, and reset. Another value that I didn't talk about in that chapter is `TYPE=BUTTON`. The `BUTTON` type is intended to be a general-purpose button on a Web page, perhaps not even associated with a specific script, whereas the `click` event must be defined by a local script.

Let's have a look at a pretty slick example:

```
<INPUT TYPE=button VALUE="Open window"
    onClick="miniWindow=window.open('','mini','resizable=no,
width=200,height=200')">
 
<A HREF="navigate.html" TARGET="mini">LOAD FILE</A>
 
<INPUT TYPE="button" VALUE="Close window"
onClick="miniWindow.close()">
```

Figure 16-1 shows what appears when this snippet is first loaded into the browser: two buttons and a small hypertext reference between them.

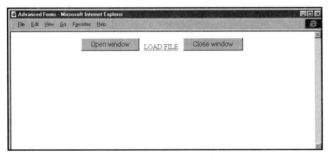

Figure 16-1: Buttons and a hypertext reference

Click the button labeled "Open window" and a new window pops up on the screen, 200 pixels by 200 pixels, called "mini." The window object is saved in the JavaScript environment with the name "miniWindow." That's all defined in the `onClick` event on the second line. A click on the hypertext reference "LOAD FILE," and the contents of the file navigate.html is loaded into the new navigational window (that's what the `TARGET="mini"` does for me). Figure 16-2 shows how that looks on the screen.

Figure 16-2: Pop-up navigational controls

Click the second button, "Close window," and the separate window is closed, vanishing entirely from the screen. This is done with a request for the browser to run the close() function for the miniWindow object.

These input buttons don't need to be part of a form, even though the `<INPUT>` tag is defined to only have meaning within the context of the `<FORM>` `</FORM>` pair. Navigator is picky, and even if you have blank `<FORM>` tags, it will require them. Let me state that more directly: If you have the code listed above, but don't have `<FORM>` before it and `</FORM>` afterwards, it won't work. Internet Explorer doesn't care, and the above code snippet, typed in exactly as written, will work fine.

There's also a new `<BUTTON>` tag (that is, `<BUTTON onClick=...`) that offers many of the same capabilities as `INPUT TYPE=BUTTON` but isn't yet widely supported.

While this might seem like a simple use of an input button, this can, in fact, be quite a powerful mechanism for helping people explore a very complex Web site, or popping up a window that contains a cycling sequence of advertisements, or even as part of a game.

Actually, if you've ever heard about "interstitial" advertisements on the Web, you now know how it's done: an interstitial is an advert that pops up and plays for ten or fifteen seconds when you request to move to another page. Once the advert is done playing, the small window vanishes and the next page is displayed.

One more neat trick with this:

```
<INPUT TYPE="button" VALUE="CloseMe" onClick="window.close()">
```

If a user clicks the CloseMe button, the window vanishes. You can imagine how you might have a new window pop up for user feedback and if they cancel their message, the `window.close()` JavaScript snippet closes the window and enables them to focus on the main Web page.

Using Labels to Organize User Focus

While Web-based forms are quite powerful, there are some areas that need improvements. A small, but annoying, area that's finally been improved is the capability to have the text associated with an input element actually associated with the element itself. The value of having the text associated with the element is most commonly seen within specific computer programs. If you click the description adjacent to an element, that element will be modified.

On a Web page, however, the text adjacent to an input element is dead, useless text. For example:

```
❑Call for a Taxi
```

If this were part of the configuration options page for your favorite program, moving the mouse over "Taxi" and clicking would select the option.

This association of text with a specific form element is exactly what the new `LABEL` element accomplishes.

There are two ways to work with labels in your HTML form. Either you can "aim" labels at specific form elements by using the `ID` attribute within a form element, or you can wrap a form element within a `<LABEL></LABEL>` pair.

Here's how the first might look:

```
<FORM METHOD=POST ACTION=someURL>
    <INPUT TYPE=radio NAME=gender VALUE=male ID=radio1>
    <LABEL FOR="radio1">Male</LABEL>

    <INPUT TYPE=radio NAME=gender VALUE=female ID=radio2>
    <LABEL FOR="radio2">Female</LABEL>
<INPUT TYPE=submit VALUE=submit>
</FORM>
```

Based on the HTML 4.0 specification, the above should enable you to click the word Male or Female to select the associated radio button. Of course, you could still click the radio button itself to change the values.

The second way you could use the <LABEL> tag is as a wrapper:

```
<FORM METHOD=POST ACTION=someURL>
   <LABEL>
      <INPUT TYPE=radio NAME=gender VALUE=male>
      Male
</LABEL>
<LABEL>
      <INPUT TYPE=radio NAME=gender VALUE=female>
      Female
</LABEL>
<INPUT TYPE=submit VALUE=submit>
</FORM>
```

One of the most frustrating aspects of the Web has been for people who have disabilities. There are <ALT> tags for graphics, but for the vast majority of sites, just about everything is quite difficult to work with, particularly forms. That's where the <LABEL> tag will prove quite valuable — special browsers for visually handicapped people might have the specified labels conveyed differently.

The two examples are available on the CD-ROM for you to experiment with within your own modern browser.

Dividing Forms into Fieldsets

In very much the same spirit as the <LABEL>, the combination of the <FIELDSET> and <LEGEND> elements enable you to create a document that is much more accessible for people with disabilities. The intent of the tags is to allow grouping of thematically related controls within a form.

Like the table head and table group elements discussed earlier, neither <FIELDSET> nor <LEGEND> will change the appearance of the page (except for in older, incompatible browsers, but I'll get back to that issue). They are interwoven into existing forms.

First off, here's a fancy but straightforward form that is actually organized into multiple logical areas:

```
<FORM METHOD=POST ACTION=someURL>
<TABLE CELLPADDING=2 WIDTH=100%>
<TR><TD BGCOLOR=#003333 ALIGN=center><FONT COLOR=white
SIZE=+2>
Software Defect Report</FONT>
</TABLE>
<TABLE CELLPADDING=2 WIDTH=75%>
<TR><TD BGCOLOR=#003333 ALIGN=center><FONT COLOR=white>
User Profile Information</FONT>
</TABLE>
<TABLE BORDER=0>
<TR><TD>
Name:<TD><INPUT TYPE=text NAME=name SIZE=50>
<TR><TD>Company:<TD><INPUT TYPE=text NAME=company SIZE=50>
</TABLE>
<P>
<TABLE CELLPADDING=2 WIDTH=75%>
<TR><TD BGCOLOR=#003333 ALIGN=center><FONT COLOR=white>
Software Version Information</FONT>
</TABLE>
<TABLE BORDER=0>
<TR><TD>
Software Product: <TD>
<SELECT NAME=product>
<OPTION>SpiffyPhoto
<OPTION>PerfectEditor
</SELECT>
<TR><TD>
Version:
<TD><INPUT TYPE=text NAME=version size=50>
</TABLE>
<P>
<TABLE CELLPADDING=2 WIDTH=75%>
<TR><TD BGCOLOR=#003333 ALIGN=center><FONT COLOR=white>
What seems to be the problem?</FONT>
</TABLE>
<TEXTAREA NAME=problem ROWS=4 COLS=60></TEXTAREA>
<P>
<CENTER>
<INPUT TYPE=submit VALUE=submit>
</CENTER>
</FORM>
```

As is obvious from your first glance of the source, or the form itself, as
shown in Figure 16-3, the layout is attractive, but quite complex. If you
were reading this page through a braille-reader system, the form would end
up being confusing.

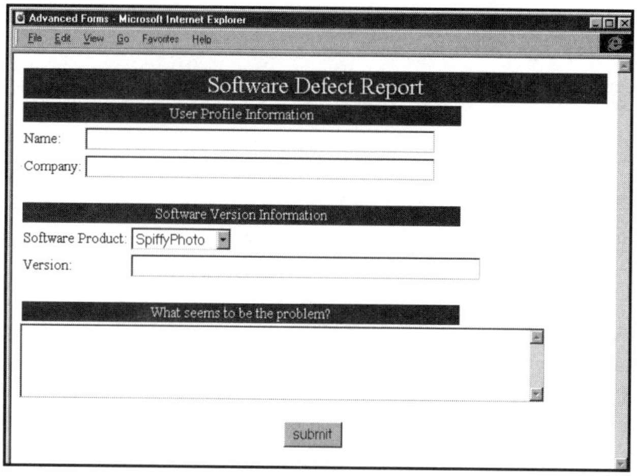

Figure 16-3: An attractive forms layout

This is where the `<FIELDSET>` and `<LEGEND>` tags become important.
`<FIELDSET>` is a paired tag that enables you to organize your form into
logical sections, and the `<LEGEND>` enables you to assign a caption to a
specific `<FIELDSET>` area. The form in Figure 16-3 could be rewritten as:

```
<FORM METHOD=POST ACTION=someURL>
<TABLE CELLPADDING=2 WIDTH=100%>
<TR><TD BGCOLOR=#003333 ALIGN=center><FONT COLOR=white
SIZE=+2>
Software Defect Report</FONT>
</TABLE>
<FIELDSET>
<LEGEND ALIGN=bottom>User Information</LEGEND>
<TABLE CELLPADDING=2 WIDTH=75%>
<TR><TD BGCOLOR=#003333 ALIGN=center><FONT COLOR=white>
User Profile Information</FONT>
</TABLE>
<TABLE BORDER=0>
<TR><TD>
Name:<TD><INPUT TYPE=text NAME=name SIZE=50>
<TR><TD>Company:<TD><INPUT TYPE=text NAME=company SIZE=50>
</TABLE>
</FIELDSET>
<P>
<FIELDSET>
<LEGEND ALIGN=bottom>Software Information</LEGEND>
<TABLE CELLPADDING=2 WIDTH=75%>
<TR><TD BGCOLOR=#003333 ALIGN=center><FONT COLOR=white>
Software Version Information</FONT>
```

(continued)

```
(continued)
</TABLE>
<TABLE BORDER=0>
<TR><TD>
Software Product: <TD>
<SELECT NAME=product>
<OPTION>SpiffyPhoto
<OPTION>PerfectEditor
</SELECT>
<TR><TD>
Version:
<TD><INPUT TYPE=text NAME=version size=50>
</TABLE>
</FIELDSET>
<P>
<FIELDSET>
<LEGEND ALIGN=bottom>Problem Report</LEGEND>
<TABLE CELLPADDING=2 WIDTH=75%>
<TR><TD BGCOLOR=#003333 ALIGN=center><FONT COLOR=white>
What seems to be the problem?</FONT>
</TABLE>
<TEXTAREA NAME=problem ROWS=4 COLS=60></TEXTAREA>
</FIELDSET>
<P>
<CENTER>
<INPUT TYPE=submit VALUE=submit>
</CENTER>
</FORM>
```

There are no options or attributes for the `<FIELDSET>` tag. The `<LEGEND>` tag has four possible values for the `ALIGN` attribute: top, bottom, left, and right. The default location is top.

Look closely and you'll see the mistake that the HTML standards group made with this extension in my view: The `<LEGEND>` value isn't hidden on browsers that don't yet know the tag. What would have been considerably more flexible and compatible would have been to have the actual legend value as an attribute, something like:

```
<LEGEND ALIGN=bottom VALUE="User Profile">
```

With the design as it is, Figure 16-4 shows the problem I'm talking about; the legend is displayed, as is the colored bar that also labels the area. It's another demonstration of the challenge of using cool new tags in a manner that looks good in both new and older browsers.

Figure 16-4: The legends creep into view.

It will be interesting to see how things change as people begin to implement the FIELDSET tags in their tables.

Tab Key Control on Input

If you've filled out any forms online, you already know that it can be a huge pain to move the cursor to each input field, click to move the focus of the browser, and then type in the specific value. It turns out that you can use the Tab key on regular Web input forms to step from the top left to the bottom right. Unfortunately, only a subset of elements can be selected with this "tabbing": if you're in a TEXTAREA, for example, the tab is assumed to be part of the information you're entering.

That's where the TABINDEX attribute comes into play. HTML 4.0 adds the capability for you to define the exact tabbing sequence on your form. If you want to move people down the entries on the left side, then the right side, instead of left-right, left-right, you can do so by specifying the appropriate ascending TABINDEX values.

Table 16-1 shows which HTML tags can have a TABINDEX specified.

Table 16-1	TABINDEX Enabled HTML TAGS
Tag Name	**Meaning**
A	Anchor tag.
AREA	Client-side image map.
OBJECT	Object inclusion (see Chapter 19).
INPUT	Text, radio button, checkbox input field.
SELECT	Pop-up or multiple selection menu.
TEXTAREA	Multiline text input box.
BUTTON	Analogous to INPUT TYPE=button.

As you can see, the TABINDEX can help you make your Web page much more accessible to people who want to stick with a keyboard rather than fiddling with a mouse.

Here's an example of a form that uses the TABINDEX attributes to ensure that users can step through the entries with the Tab key in the order the designer wants:

```
<HTML>
<TITLE>Tab-enabled FORM</TITLE>
<BODY BGCOLOR=white>
<CENTER>
<A HREF=index.html TABINDEX=10><IMG SRC=logo.gif
     BORDER=0 ALT="logo"></A>
<FORM METHOD=POST ACTION="">
<TABLE BORDER=1 CELLPADDING=15 WIDTH=90%>
<TR><TD>
Name: <INPUT TYPE=text NAME=name TABINDEX=2>
<P>
Addr: <INPUT TYPE=text NAME=addr TABINDEX=3>
<P>
Phone: <INPUT TYPE=text NAME=phone TABINDEX=4>
<P>
Email: <INPUT TYPE=text NAME=email TABINDEX=1>
</TD><TD>
Closest Ocean: <SELECT NAME=ocean TABINDEX=5>
<OPTION>Atlantic
<OPTION>Pacific
</SELECT>
<P>
```

```
You Prefer:
<blockquote>
<input type=radio name=prefer value=beach
TABINDEX=6> The Beach<br>
<input type=radio name=prefer value=lake
TABINDEX=7> The Lake<br>
<input type=radio name=prefer value=outdoors
TABINDEX=8> The Outdoors
</blockquote>
<P>
</TD></TR>
</TABLE>
<INPUT TYPE=submit VALUE="Join The Acme Mailing List"
TABINDEX=9>
</FORM>
</CENTER>
</BODY>
</HTML>
```

If you follow the numbering, you'll see that the first entry in the tab sequence is the e-mail address, followed by the name, address, and telephone number. Then the visitor could tab to the `<SELECT`; then step through the three possible radio button values for the preferred spot. Finally, the Submit button itself is in the `TABINDEX` sequence and the anchor wrapping around the company logo, which returns to the home page of the site, is the last (10th) entry in the `TABINDEX`.

ACCESSKEY Attributes

There's an additional attribute you can use to offer even easier navigation of your web pages via keyboard: You can assign keyboard shortcuts to let people quickly get to a specific spot on a form or a specific anchor. This is done with the `ACCESSKEY=key` sequence, though don't be fooled — on a PC, you'll need to use Alt and the key specified, and on the Macintosh you'll need the Command key, too.

On the Mac, you might be more familiar with the Command key if I call it the Apple or "cloverleaf" key. It's usually to either side of your spacebar.

Here's a small example of how this might be used:

```
<A HREF=http://www.yahoo.com/ACCESSKEY="y">Yahoo</a>
```

Of course, if you're going to have a keyboard shortcut, it might well be valuable to show the user what key to use. The Windows system has a nice standard for this: the letter in question is underlined. You can do this with the otherwise marginally useful ⟨U⟩ underline tag:

```
<A HREF=http://www.yahoo.com/ACCESSKEY="y"><U>Y</U>ahoo</a>
```

As this becomes widely implemented in Web browsers, it will undoubtedly prove a great addition to your design toolkit.

Disabled and Read-Only Elements

The TABINDEX and ACCESSKEY attributes will both prove to be quite valuable in future Web site design, but two more attributes that have been added to HTML forms leave me a bit more unsure about their ultimate utility.

The DISABLED attribute will enable you to display form elements that cannot be changed by the user, and are intended to be displayed in a "greyed out" or other fashion that makes the disabled status obvious. The READONLY attribute is very similar, but shouldn't be visually different from the other fields, just unchangeable.

Here's how you might use these two in your own form:

```
<FORM METHOD=post ACTION=someURL>
Name: <input type=text name=yourname><br>
Login: <input type=text name=login><br>
Host: <input type=text name=host
        value="hostname.com" READONLY><br>
Date: <input type=text value="1 Jan, '98" DISABLED>
<P>
<INPUT TYPE=submit>
</FORM>
```

In this example I'm going to fill in the value of "host" for the visitor (probably based on their REMOTE_HOST CGI environment variable; see Chapter 13 for more details), and show the date, but have it be a disabled field so that it's clearly not something that can be changed.

A subtle nuance here: Notice that I didn't specify a NAME attribute for the Date: input tag. This is a simple way to avoid having the information sent back to the server when the form is submitted — only those fields that have names specified are included in the return data stream.

Table 16-2 shows the HTML tags covered in this chapter.

Table 16-2	New HTML Tags	
Tag	**Close Tag**	**Meaning**
`<INPUT`		
`TYPE=button`		General Purpose Button
`onClick=s`		Script to execute when button is clicked (usually JavaScript).
`<LABEL`	`</LABEL>`	Label associated with a specific element.
`FOR=s`		Specify the element associated with the label (use ID=s in the element).
`<FIELDSET>`	`</FIELDSET>`	Divide form into logical parts.
`<LEGEND`	`</LEGEND>`	Name associated with fieldset.
`ALIGN=s`		Specify alignment of legend in display (top, bottom, left, right).
`TABINDEX=x`		Specify the order of elements when user pressed the Tab key.
`ACCESSKEY=c`		Specific key to allow keyboard shortcuts to specific elements.
`DISABLED`		Element is disabled, but displayed onscreen.
`READONLY`		Element is displayed onscreen but not editable.

Summary

This chapter expanded your knowledge of additional form capabilities added in the HTML 4.0 specification, including the very useful `TABINDEX` and `ACCESSKEY` attributes. Chapter 17 will continue the theme with an exploration of the other new additions introduced in the Cougar specification.

Additional HTML 4.0 Capabilities

In This Chapter

New HTML tags

The OBJECT tag

Other interesting additions

As should be clear by now, the HTML 4.0 specification doesn't offer a dramatic change in the hypertext language used to create Web pages, but, rather, it's a large set of useful and valuable refinements to improve the Web experience for users, while giving designers and authors greater control over the presentation.

Some of the new elements are quite useful — I like inline frames (<IFRAME>) quite a bit, for example — but there are many elements of HTML 4.0 that seem to have limited value. In the interest of completeness, however, in this chapter, I talk about not only the additional 4.0 tags that are worth knowing, but I also spend some time discussing new features of HTML that I don't think will ever get into widespread use.

As with the rest of HTML, you should make your own decisions regarding which elements you use and which you skip. I vary what tags I use based on the type of site I'm developing; if it's a cutting-edge site and I can really go wild, I'll use very advanced tags in sophisticated ways. If it's a general public site, then I'll avoid tags that don't gracefully degrade for older browsers or text-only users, because they'll always be an important part of the online public.

A New HTML Tag: Q

Three HTML tags have been added in the HTML 4.0 specification that haven't been discussed yet in the book. The first tag, `<Q>`, is an alternative to `<BLOCKQUOTE>`, and is intended to be used for shorter quotes that don't require a paragraph break.

Here's how that might be used:

```
The move into the new home went well, though, as our
daughter said,
<Q>Are we really here now?</Q>
which seemed to sum everything up neatly.
```

Mark Your Edits with INS and DEL

A more interesting pair of tags are `<INS>` and `<DEL>`, which enable you to mark specific edit changes that you've made to the document. You don't know how the text is going to be formatted, of course, but presumably there'll be some color change, a strikethrough, or some similar treatment when it's displayed to the user.

The tags can accept two attributes: `CITE=url` should point to a document that explains why the current page was modified. It could be a copy of a memorandum explaining the rationale for the modifications. `DATETIME=value` should specify the exact date and time of the modification to the document, enabling users — eventually — to obtain further information on the evolution of a document without necessarily having to jump to the rationale document.

The format of the `DATETIME` argument is:

```
YYYY-MM-DDThh:mm:ssTZD
```

And the individual elements are shown in Table 17-1.

Table 17-1	Format of the DATETIME value string
Mnemonic	**Meaning**
YYYY	Year
MM	Month
DD	Day
hh	Hour
mm	Minute
ss	Second
TZD	Time zone designator

Here's an example of some HTML that includes both insertion and deletion markup:

```
<H1>Corporate Mission</H1>
Acme Widgets focuses on making the <INS CITE=edit3-dt.html
DATETIME=1997-11-05T13:15:30PST>highest-quality</INS>
<DEL CITE=edit3-dt.html DATETIME=1997-11-
05T13:15:30PST>best</DEL>
possible doodads for the manufacturing trade. We've been
in business since
1907 and we're <DEL>darn</DEL> proud of our position as
<DEL DATETIME=1997-11-15T13:08:30PST >#1</DEL>
<INS DATETIME=1997-11-15T13:08:30PST >a top company</INS>
in the industry.
```

In this example, the original text was "Acme Widgets focuses on making the best possible doodads for the manufacturing trade. We've been in business since 1907 and we're darn proud of our position as #1 in the industry." On November 5, 1997 at 1:15, pm the word "best" was replaced by "highest-quality"; at an unspecified time, the word "darn" was deleted; and on November 15th of the same year, "#1" was replaced with "a top company." The first change was also documented in an associated page called "edit3-dt.html," but the other changes have no citations associated with them.

Obviously, <INS> and <DEL> aren't intended for normal human use: I think it'd drive me completely batty to try and enter the date and time correctly by hand. Using sophisticated programs that can offer an edit audit trail within an HTML document, however, is an intriguing possibility and one that I expect will arrive, albeit for very specialized uses.

The OBJECT Tag

An important tag that I haven't talked about much at all is the ⟨OBJECT⟩ tag. If you have been exploring the different facets of Web page design, you might have already bumped into the ⟨APPLET⟩ tag, to include Java programs. The ⟨APPLET⟩ tag is going away, replaced by the ⟨OBJECT⟩ tag. But there's more to ⟨OBJECT⟩ than just including Java applets. In fact, you can include just about any type of Web page information with the ⟨OBJECT⟩ tag, from graphics to programs, even to other HTML Web pages.

There are an amazing number of different possible attributes that can be specified in this super tag, including all the attributes of an IMG tag (align, height, width, border, hspace, vspace, usemap, and name), and lots more, too. At its most basic, ⟨OBJECT⟩ requires a CLASSID attribute. Here's an example:

```
<OBJECT CLASSID=someURL></OBJECT>
```

Actually, there are types of information that browsers might not be able to execute, display, or render — for example, an MPEG image on a system without graphics. In that case, instead of using the ⟨ALT⟩ tag, objects can have an alternative text value by tucking it between the ⟨OBJECT⟩ and ⟨/OBJECT⟩ tags.

What's cool about the way they've created the ⟨OBJECT⟩ tag and its defaults is that you can have a sequence of different object types, and the browser will step from the outermost to the innermost, trying to find something to display on the screen:

```
<OBJECT title="The Earth as seen from space"
classid=someURL.py>
<OBJECT data="Earth.mpeg" type="application/mpeg">
    <OBJECT src="Earth.gif">
        A View of the Earth
    </OBJECT>
  </OBJECT>
</OBJECT>
```

In this case, the browser will try to run a Python program (the ".py" suffix) if possible; and if not, it'll try to display an MPEG movie (if supported), and if that's also not available, it'll display the graphic image "Earth.gif." If it can't do that either, the text "A View of the Earth" is displayed onscreen.

The "title" attribute in the first `<OBJECT>` is for alternative browsers, typically for the visually disabled.

There's an associated HTML tag that enables you to specify run-time parameters to the program you're invoking, as needed, called `<PARAM>`. It must appear within an `<OBJECT>` and usually is of the form `name=` and `value=`, as demonstrated:

```
<OBJECT classid=someURL.py>
  <PARAM NAME="height" VALUE=120 VALUETYPE=data>
  <PARAM NAME="width" VALUE=120 VALUETYPE=data>
  You'd see a bouncing ball if you could display Python
applications.
</OBJECT>
```

You might also specify the type of code directly to ensure that only browsers that can render that type of information spend the time downloading it:

```
<OBJECT classid="java:program.start"
    codetype="application/octet-stream">
</OBJECT>
```

Because codetypes are MIME types, this specifies a generic executable file (an octet-stream). Notice in a previous example that there was an alternative type specified as "application/mpeg." A GIF file is specified as "application/gif," JPEG is "application/jpeg," and so on.

Another spiffy thing you can do with the `<OBJECT>` tag is use the `declare` attribute to detail what and where, without actually loading the program or object itself. Then, later in the code, you could have a reference to the object, at which time it would be loaded. A demonstration:

```
<OBJECT declare
   id="earth"
   data="earth.mpeg"
   type="application/mpeg">
     Watch a wonderful movie about the Earth
</OBJECT>
When you're ready to watch our movie about the Earth,
then you should <a href=#earth>start it up</a>.
```

Including Graphics with OBJECT

Similar to the previous listings, it's worth noting directly that you can replace any `<IMG>` tag with an `<OBJECT>` tag. Here's how that would work:

```
<IMG SRC=sample.gif ALT="A Sample of Our Product"
   HEIGHT=120 WIDTH=120  HSPACE=5 VSPACE=5>
```

That exact same image could be included in your Web page as:

```
<OBJECT DATA=sample.gif TYPE="image/gif" HEIGHT=120
    WIDTH=120 HSPACE=5 VSPACE=5>A Sample of Our
Product</OBJECT>
```

There are some rumblings in the HTML standards community that they'd like to do away with the `<IMG>` tag in favor of this more abstruse `<OBJECT>` usage, but I am quite skeptical. As with the `<LEGEND>` tag in Chapter 16, the greatest problem with the use of the `<OBJECT>` tag is its incompatible way of specifying the alternative text. An older browser will ignore the `<OBJECT>` tag and just render the text itself, which is a frustrating result if you're just specifying a GIF or JPEG.

Include another HTML page in your page

One more interesting trick you can do with the `<OBJECT>` tag is to actually include an additional HTML snippet within your page. It'd look like this:

```
<OBJECT data="header.html"></OBJECT>
```

which can let you easily include shared snippets of HTML across dozens, or hundreds, of different pages. Having header and footer material all neatly tucked into a single file that is included in the other pages could be a great improvement to any site-management strategy. What's more interesting, perhaps, is that you can include the HTML from any Web site as part of your own, which opens up the possibility of the following:

```
<h1>Here's Yahoo:</h1>
<OBJECT data=http://www.yahoo.com/></OBJECT>
<h1>Here's Excite:</h1>
<OBJECT data=http://www.excite.com/></OBJECT>
<h1>And Here's Hotbot:</h1>
<OBJECT data=http://www.hotbot.com/></OBJECT>
```

which has serious potential legal implications: if you can easily wrap your material around another Web site, then what about having adverts that you're profiting by surrounding a different site? That is, what would happen if I were to have something like this:

```
<a href=http://www.advertiser.com/><img
src=advert.gif></a>
<OBJECT data=http://www.cnn.com/></OBJECT>
<h3>Learn how to <a href=advertise.html>advertise
here</a></h3>
```

Server-Side Includes

There is, however, another way to include HTML in your page. Server-side includes would enable you to actually have it as part of the page. Typically, you'd have the server-side includes specified as buried within comments:

```
<!--#include file="header.html" -->
```

The server often requires that files with SSI material have a different suffix. The servers I use specify SSI material with ".shtml" instead of ".html."

If your Web server supports SSI, they can be very useful; there is often a wide variety of different SSI instructions you can specify, including time of day, text-based counters, and more. It's not a universal solution, however, because there are also many different types of Web servers that either don't support SSI at all, or support a different version, with different notation.

Ultimately, I think using SSI is better than using the OBJECT tag to include other HTML in your pages if both are on the same server, but if you want to include material from another Web site, OBJECT is the best option available.

Other Interesting Additions

There are two other things that I want to cover before we leave the HTML 4.0 specification — somewhat of a grab bag of attributes.

Soft hyphens

First on the list is an interesting character entity — `&shy;` — which doesn't say that your page won't display for strangers, but instead is a soft hyphen. It is a way for you to specify, if a hyphen is needed for word wrap to look best, where it should be placed. You could use it particularly with long words:

```
        <h1>Mr. Smith Has a Tro&shy;glo&shy;dy&shy;tic
Quality...</h1>
```

which would tell the browser that it could break the word troglodytic between any of its syllables: "tro," "glo," "dy," or "tic." If the browser didn't need to insert any breaks in the word to display it, then the `&shy;` sequences should all be ignored. (Except on some of the older browsers, where `&shy;` is actually shown as a dash; in that case, the word in the example above would be shown as Tro-glo-dy-tic, with all the hyphens visible.)

Easier internal references with ID

All the way back in Chapter 7 you learned that the standard way to have references within a document is to define their places with:

```
<A NAME=word></A>
```

and then reference it with:

```
<A HREF=#word>jump</A>
```

HTML 4.0 extends the `ID` attribute to replace this mechanism. As you saw in the previous chapters, you can name any HTML tag uniquely in a document. The nifty addition is that you can reference any of these ID attributes in a way completely analogous with the above. Here's how it might be used in a small snippet of HTML, a Web page from Romeo and Juliet:

```
<H2 ID=mother>Enter MOTHER</H2>
MOTHER: What noise is here?<BR>
NURSE: O lamentable day! <BR>
MOTHER: What is the matter? <BR>
NURSE: Look, look! O heavy day! <BR>
MOTHER: O me, O me! My child, my only life! <BR>
Revive, look up, or I will die with thee! <BR>
Help, help! Call help.
<H2 ID=father>Enter FATHER</h2>
```

Later in the document, a reference might help people find the right point in the play:

```
<a href=#mother>Mother enters</a> and then just a moment
or two later,
<a href=#father>Father enters the room.
```

You can add these ID attributes to any HTML tag, which makes them tremendously flexible. Even smarter, you can use this in combination with the older `<a name>` tag so that both old and new browsers do something graceful.

In Conclusion

Having now learned about how to do just about anything with your Web pages through the many elements available in HTML, it should be clear that the evolution and improvements in HTML 4.0, like any other update to a language, is a mixed bag. Some of the new attributes are terrific and a valuable extension to the page-layout capabilities, but others seem to be of minimal utility.

The greatest challenge is now, when the least number of HTML 4.0 compatible browsers are in use. As time passes, however, the percentage of people who will be able to render the most sophisticated of pages will increase, which means it'll soon reach critical mass, where more people who visit your page will be able to render it correctly than otherwise.

Summary

This chapter covered all the stray pieces of HTML 4.0 that weren't discussed in earlier chapters. Chapter 18 will talk about the next step: now that you have created a Web site using all these advanced layout capabilities, how do you let people know about it and spread the word?

Needles in
Haystacks

In this chapter, I discuss how Web search engines work and how to design your material so it will be useful when indexed by AltaVista, WebCrawler, Lycos, Yahoo!, and the many other search applications available on the Web. I then talk about where you should announce your new Web site and other things you can do so you can build lots of traffic.

Having your own Web site is definitely worthwhile, but like an exhibit of art in a gallery, the real fun begins when people come to visit. The fundamental puzzle of the World Wide Web — and the Internet as a whole — is *how to find information*. If you can't find other people's stuff, it stands to reason that others will have difficulty finding your stuff, too.

People have applied many different strategies for solving the indexing problem, ranging from creating simple databases of Web sites that accept information about your site to unleashing powerful *crawler* programs that stealthily visit your site and add your information to their massive indexes.

Producing Index-Friendly Pages with META

Before you start to worry about what sites to visit when you're starting to build traffic, it's important to begin building the most search-engine friendly site possible. There are a number of ways to ensure that your site is understandable to the robots that roam the Net and index everything, but the two most important are unquestionably creating well-titled pages and liberal use of the <META> HTML tag to offer information that's specifically for the robots to read.

Create meaningful titles

When someone bookmarks your Web site, the entry that they have from then on in their bookmark list is the exact title of your page. Further, some search systems use the document title as the basis of their indexing, so, in either case, the more meaningful your title is, the more likely your site will be found when people search the Web. To wit, if you're busy creating a site that explores the intricacies of coffee roasting, "Coffee Roasting: The Quest for the Perfect Cup" is much better (and more interesting) than "The Coffee Home Page."

 I recommend against using the words "home page" and "Web" in your page's title at all. Instead, add a few descriptive words, like "Satellite TV and DSS Central."

Again, to reiterate, titles are used not only by search tools; titles are also what users see when they save your URL to their hotlists. A hotlist full of titles such as "The Internet Mall," "All About Starbucks," "Digital Games Review," and "Sony Consumer Electronics" offers a great deal more information with less clutter than "Ray-o-Vac World Wide Web Page" or "Stanford University Web Home Page."

Some wit and verve can help, too. Which of these pages would you rather visit?

➡ Home Page for Pete Nesterenko

➡ Who Is This Pete Nesterenko Guy?

➡ My Home Page

Needless to say, that last one offers no information about the Web page at all and should be avoided like the plague.

Finally, if you aren't going to use the META tag, ensure that the first paragraph of text in your home page contains a meaningful description of the contents therein. Because some of the Web index systems grab the first few sentences, carefully crafting them will help ensure people find your information when they search with the various tools listed in this chapter.

Using the META tag

There's an important HTML tag that can be a great help in ensuring that meaningful information about your site is included in the crawler sites — the <META> tag. It doesn't cause anything to be displayed to the visitor, but all of the "robot" sites highlighted in this chapter will use the contents of the <META> tag as the abstract or summary description of the site and its contents instead of just the first few dozen words on your page. You use the tag like this:

```
<META  NAME=description  CONTENT="The Custer Battlefield
Historical  and Museum Association  is  a  non-profit
educational  and  research  association  for  the  study  of  the
Custer Battlefield.">

<META  NAME=keywords  CONTENT="custer,custer
battlefield,sitting bull,reno,american indians,native
american,little big horn,general custer,general george
custer,plains indians,montana,monument,benteen">
```

The results of a search on a system such as AltaVista will show the description as the summary of the site rather than the first few dozen words. Here's how it might look:

```
The Custer Battlefield Historical  and Museum Association

The Custer Battlefield Historical  and Museum Association
is  a  non-profit  educational  and  research  association  for
the  study  of  the  Custer  Battlefield.
http://www.intuitive.com/custer  —size 6k—15 Nov 97
```

 Search Engine Watch is a great site for learning the latest scoop on how different search engines rate and index pages. Check it out online at www.searchenginewatch.com.

Knowing that, let's poke around on some other sites and see how they use the <META> tags to improve their listings in the search engines:

Apple Computer (http://www.apple.com)

```
<META NAME="Keywords" CONTENT="Apple Computer, Inc.,
Computers, Computer Hardware, Power Macintosh, Software,
Operating Systems, Mac OS, Newton">
<META NAME="Description" CONTENT="Visit www.apple.com for
the latest news, the hottest products, and technical
support resources from Apple Computer, Inc.">
```

Microsoft (http://www.microsoft.com)

```
<META NAME="KEYWORDS" CONTENT="products; headlines;
downloads; news; Web site; what's new; solutions;
services; software; contests; corporate news;">
<META NAME="DESCRIPTION" CONTENT="The entry page to
Microsoft's Web site. Find software, solutions and
answers. Support, and Microsoft news.">
```

IDG Books Worldwide (http://www.idgbooks.com)

```
<meta name="keywords" content="idg books, computer book,
dummies, book,idg, book, technical book, programming book,
pc book, computer, software,idg books online, windows
software, java book, java, office 97 book, office97,
windows book, windows, books online, mac, online bookstore,
mac book,office 97, word 97, excel 97, access 97, windows
95, windows nt, windows97, windows 98, Web publishing,
internet book, java resource center,dummies book, visual
basic, intranet, network, database, novell, yahoo,secrets,
simplified, bible, creating cool, macworld, discover,
programming,book resources, computer program, computer
software, internet">
<META NAME="description" content="IDG Books Worldwide
publishes computerbooks that are popular, well written, and
user-friendly, including the world-famous ...For Dummies
series.">
```

Intuitive Systems (http://www.intuitive.com)

```
<META NAME="keywords" content="interface,interface
design,human factors,web page,web site,human-computer
interface,HCI,UI,GUI">
<META NAME="description" content=" Intuitive Systems helps
companies design and build easier, more understandable
systems, with a focus on software and hardware interface
design and high level site and systems design for
companies plugging into the Internet. Start Making Sense
with Intuitive Systems.">
```

The Oakland Raiders (http://www.raiders.com)

```
<META NAME="description" CONTENT="The Official Web Site of
the Oakland Raiders NFL Football Organization">
<META NAME="keywords" CONTENT="football, NFL, Raiders,
Oakland, Coliseum, team, sports">
```

Other possible META values

There are also other possible values that you can specify with the `<META>` tag. You've already seen one earlier: `<META>` is one way that you can embed sound in your Web page. The `<META>` tag actually turns out to be somewhat of a general-purpose HTML tag that's used for a wide variety of different things. Want to have your page flip to another after a few seconds? The `<META>` tag can do that, as this snippet from the OrderEasy site (`http://www.ordereasy.com`) demonstrates:

```
<META HTTP-EQUIV=REFRESH CONTENT="6; URL=main.html">
```

After six seconds, the page main.html will replace the current page on the screen. There's another way to specify the same functionality that is suggested in the HTML 4.0 documentation too. It would look like:

```
<META name="refresh" content="6,main.html">
```

The new format is nicer in my view because it's more succinct.

Content rating with PICS

Another possible `<META>` value that's worth discussing is used to detail the type of material included on the site using the convoluted PICS rating information. In late 1996, one of the most hotly argued topics was the quality and appropriateness of content on the Internet. Congress passed the Communications Decency Act of 1996, and Web developers added blue ribbon icons on their pages to protest the intrusion of government regulation onto the Net. One side of the debate over this law chanted its mantra of "Free speech über alles," while the other side shouted "Protect our children!" Both sides raised valid and important issues, and the debate was very interesting. The CDA was later challenged in court and overturned. Publication of pornographic or offensive material on the Internet doesn't violate any specific electronic laws (though it might violate basic pornography and lewd conduct laws, but that's an entirely different debate).

What's my take on all this? I think there's a lot of appalling stuff online, things I don't want my daughter to see, things that are distressingly easy to encounter. Free speech is important, but not to the exclusion of common sense and community decency. I supported a modified version of the CDA when the debate raged, and I refused to add a blue ribbon to my sites.

The best news to come from this entire debate is that Paul Resnick of AT&T and James Miller of MIT's Computer Science Lab developed a content rating system and distributed sample programs demonstrating that voluntary ratings for Web sites can be coupled with screening software such as Net Nanny and SurfWatch, and even built into Microsoft's Internet Explorer program to allow free discussion online while also protecting children from stumbling into inappropriate material.

Resnick and Miller's system is called the *Platform for Internet Content Selection* (PICS) and it enables you, as a parent, teacher, or administrator, to block access to particular Internet resources without affecting what's distributed to other sites on the Internet. It's based on two ideas: instantaneous publishing of information on the Web (in this case, the ratings themselves) and access to Internet resources mediated by computers that can manage far more than any human being.

As the two inventors of PICS state in their original paper:

> Appropriateness, however, is neither an objective nor a universal measure. It depends on at least three factors.

➡ The supervisor: Parenting styles differ, as do management styles.

➡ The recipient: What's appropriate for one 15-year-old may not be for an 8-year-old, or even all 15-year-olds.

➡ The context: A game or chat room that is appropriate to access at home may be inappropriate at work or school.

PICS allows complex site content ratings, which is both a strength and a weakness. If I wanted to create a movie stills archive, but wanted to limit access to the archive to match the original ratings of the films, I could use a rating system for sites based on the movie ratings from the *Motion Picture Association of America* (MPAA). Here's how it would look:

```
((PICS-version 1.0)
 (rating-system "http://moviescale.org/Ratings/
Description/")
 (rating-service "http://moviescale.org/v1.0")
 (icon "icons/moviescale.gif")
 (name "The Movies Rating Service")
 (description "A rating service based on the MPAA's movie
rating scale")

 (category
 (transmit-as "r")
 (name "Rating")
 (label (name "G") (value 0) (icon "icons/G.gif"))
 (label (name "PG") (value 1) (icon "icons/PG.gif"))
 (label (name "PG-13") (value 2) (icon "icons/PG-13.gif"))
 (label (name "R") (value 3) (icon "icons/R.gif"))
 (label (name "NC-17") (value 4) (icon "icons/NC-
17.gif"))))
```

Now let's jump to a real example. Here's a PICS tag in use — this `<META>` tag PICS rating is from the CompuServe home page at `http://www.com-puserve.com`:

```
<META  http-equiv="PICS-Label"
content='(PICS-1.1 "http://www.rsac.org/ratingsv01.html" l
gen true
comment "RSACi North America Server" by "tjacoby@csi.
compuserve.com"
for "http://world.compuserve.com" on "1997.07.28T12:43-
0800" r (n 0 s 0 v 0 l 0))'>
```

Clearly, it's ugly and confusing. Is it going to change things? It seems unlikely, but if the PICS system can become much easier to use and to specify, there's a good chance people will start to voluntarily rate their Web sites; but, one way or the other, we're not going to be able to avoid wrestling with the problem of inappropriate and obscene content on the Internet.

There's lots of information on this topic, including the original PICS design documents, available at: `http://www.bilkent.edu.tr/pub/WWW/PICS/` and there's a competing ratings system called the *Voluntary Content Rating* (VCR). Read about it at: `http://www.solidoak.com/vcr.htm`.

Keeping crawlers away

If you're plugged into the Internet, your pages are eventually going to be indexed by one or more of the crawler programs, or "robots," such as AltaVista, WebCrawler, and various others. It's fun and very useful except for when you'd rather have portions of your Web site remain private or separate. To accomplish this, you need to learn about a special file called robots.txt.

The robots.txt file — and it must be called exactly that regardless of what kind of server you're working with, and it must be at the topmost level of your site organization — contains a set of commands that defines the access that a robot program can have to the Web site. Unfortunately, it's a wee bit complex to write, but once you've got it right, you'll never have to touch it again.

Two fields must be present in the robots.txt file: User-agent and Disallow. The first lets you specify either individual robots (maybe you intensely dislike public crawler programs but like one that's part of your own company), and the second is how you specify directories to omit from the automatic indexing. Take a look at a few examples of this to clarify:

```
User-agent: *
Disallow: /
```

This is the simplest method and says that everyone should simply leave this site unindexed. Here, the * for User-agent indicates that it applies to all crawler or robot programs. Now look at another example:

```
User-agent: Scooter
Disallow: /cgi-bin/sources
Disallow: /access_stats
Disallow: /cafeteria/dinner_menus/
```

Scooter isn't allowed to index any of the files in the cgi-bin/sources directory (a smart move), any of the access statistics (because they probably change quite frequently), or any of the cafeteria dinner menus (because they, hopefully, also change quite frequently). Any other indexing program that visits the site can index everything.

Here's an example robots.txt file from the ESPNzone Web site (http://ESPN.SportsZone.com/robots.txt):

```
User-agent: mozilla/4
Disallow: /
User-agent: Mozilla/4.0 (compatible; MSIE 4.0; Windows NT)
Disallow: /
User-agent: Mozilla/4.0 (compatible; MSIE 4.0; Windows 95)
Disallow: /
User-agent: *
Disallow: /cgi
```

Here you can see that the program is trying to avoid user Web browsers that attempt to automatically crawl the site (Navigator 4 — the code name is Mozilla — and Internet Explorer — MSIE). Any other system can index the entire site, except for anything in the CGI directory.

Another simple example: *USA Today* (http://www.usatoday.com):

```
# robots.txt for http://www.usatoday.com
User-agent:*
Disallow:/feedback
Disallow:/cgi-bin
Disallow:/system
Disallow:/inetart
Disallow:/maps
```

Any robot can index anything on the (very nice) *USA Today* site with the exception of the directories feedback, CGI, system, inetart, and maps.

A couple of sites for you to explore on your own that have impressive and complex robots.txt files include CNN Online (http://www.cnn.com), NBC (http://www.nbc.com), and the U.S. Army (http://www.army.mil).

Learn a lot more about robots and the robots.txt file at: http://info. webcrawler.com/mak/projects/robots/norobots.html.

Registering with Web index and search sites

Clearly, the search sites on the net take different approaches to indexing the Web (which means your data). So, with which site should you register? All of them. Why not? All the sites are free, and lots of people will use each service to find information, which may just be your own home page. There are two primary types of Web index sites presented in this overview: directories of information submitted by users (Yahoo!, SNAP) and crawler systems that find actual Web pages and index them automatically (AltaVista, WebCrawler, and Lycos). To join the former, you need to go to the sites and fill in a form with a brief description of your page or site. The latter services are easier — simply pop over to these sites and add your URL to the database.

Joining a directory site

Let's have a look at each type of registration more closely, and then visit with Submit It!, a site that can send the announcement of your site to dozens of these search systems and directories free!

Yahoo! (http://www.yahoo.com)

Of the many sites that offer a comprehensive database of other Web sites, my favorite is Yahoo!, created by then-Stanford grad students David Filo and Jerry Yang. Filo and Yang developed Yahoo! as a mechanism for maintaining their own ever-growing list of cool Web sites, and the site grew so fast that their two UNIX servers couldn't keep up with the load. Today, Yahoo! has spun off as a separate business and has more than 500,000 Web sites indexed and a ton of spin-off businesses.

To join Yahoo!, click the Add URL button at the top right of the banner atop all Yahoo! pages. Yahoo! recommends that you dig around in its categories of information until you find the category that matches your new site, and then click the button, because Yahoo! will automatically add that information to help the service index your site correctly.

The form you need to fill out looks like that shown in Figure 18-1. Fill in all the blanks, and your site will be added after the administrative folks have a glance at your entry to ensure everything is accurate and the site is appropriate to the Yahoo! system.

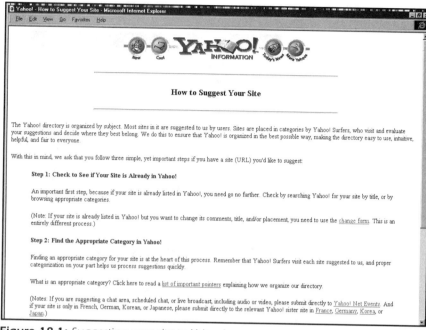

Figure 18-1: Suggesting your site to Yahoo!

SNAP! (http://www.snap.com)

A relative newcomer on the Web, the SNAP! site is designed and maintained by the top-notch team who also maintains CINet, a terrific spot for computer-related information. SNAP! is a more general-purpose online directory and it's a bit more loosely structured than Yahoo!, particularly because it seeks to have a small number of valuable links, rather than thousands upon thousands of links to pages of every stripe.

To add yourself to SNAP! you simply send e-mail to:

```
submitURL@snap.com
```

Excite (http://www.excite.com)

Somewhat of a hybrid, the Excite site is a terrific place to start any sort of online search, and it's consistently one of the top four Web sites by traffic. It's a good place to be listed! Excite has a team of people who explore the submitted URLs and review many of them, but you can submit your URL for their general-purpose index regardless. Figure 18-2 shows the Excite URL submission page.

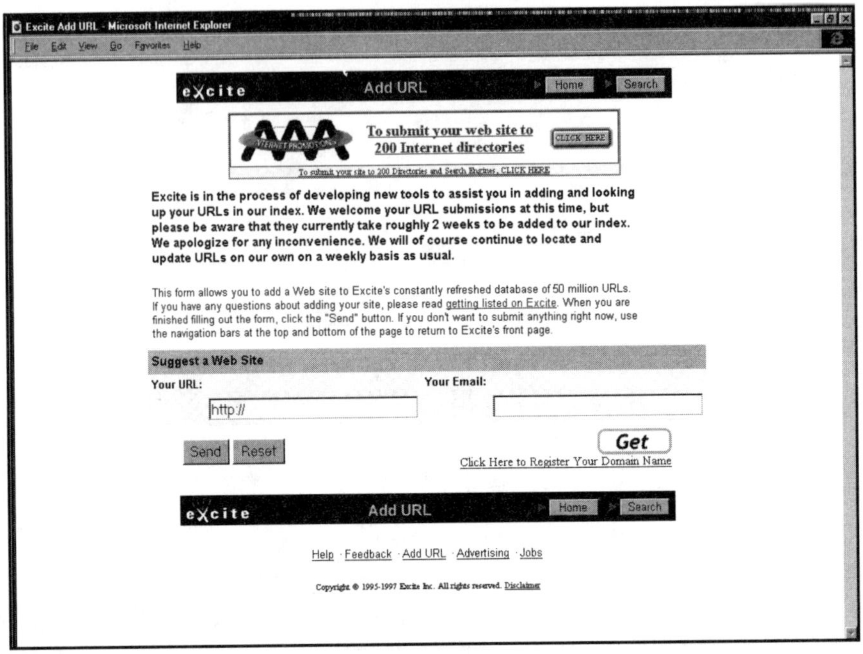

Figure 18-2: Adding your site to Excite

Signing up for a crawler or robot site

The alternative to a site where you go and tell it about your new Web page and how it should be organized and categorized are those sites where you tell them about your URL and they visit your page, read through your META description and keyword information (and you didn't forget to include those, as detailed in this chapter, right?) and then add your pages, one by one, to their massive databases.

The programs that actually index the Web pages are called "robots" and there's not too much difference between them. In fact, you don't really even need to register with these sites; if there's another page on the Web that points to you, they'll eventually find the link and make it to your own Web pages. Of course, it is worth visiting them because letting them know about your URL speeds up their finding and indexing your page.

Lycos (http://www.lycos.com)

Taking a very different approach to the problem from Yahoo!, the Lycos site, first created at Carnegie-Mellon University, indexes more than 50 million Web documents by building a database of URLs and the first few lines of description from each Web page. Minimal textual information is included for the sites in the database, but the results still are surprisingly good. If you check out the site, I'm sure you'll find, as I do, that the home page is incredibly busy, particularly when compared to the sparse simplicity of Yahoo!.

To join the Lycos database, you need to click the Add Your Site to Lycos link almost hidden at the very bottom of the home page. Once you've done so, you'll see a page similar to that shown in Figure 18-3. Enter the information requested and click Submit. It will probably take a week or two before the robot comes to your site and finds your pages.

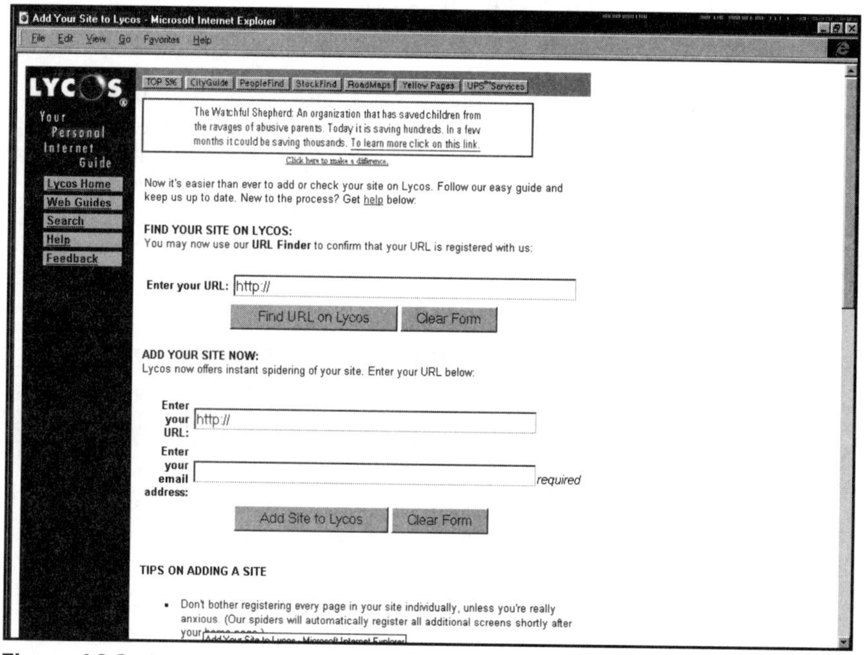

Figure 18-3: Adding your site to Lycos

AltaVista (http://www.altavista.digital.com)

AltaVista is a search system developed by *Digital Equipment Corp.* (DEC) that exploded onto the Web scene in late 1995 and is now one of the busiest search sites. A quick look shows that there's absolutely no way to browse any of the information; it's purely a search-and-see-results design. What's most impressive is the sheer volume of pages it has visited and indexed. As of my writing this chapter, the site has over 50 million Web pages indexed and an additional 5 million Usenet articles in the mix. Billions of words.

On the AltaVista site, you need to choose Add/Remove URL from the list of options on the bottom of the home page. Like Lycos, AltaVista will only ask you for the actual URL of the base page, and it'll take a week or more before Scooter, its crawler program, actually reaches your site.

WebCrawler (http://www.webcrawler.com)

WebCrawler was originally another university-based robot site, quite similar to Lycos. Once the big money companies started to move into the Web, however, many of these simple sites became prime acquisitions, and Intuit finally scooped up WebCrawler. The net result is there is a lot more information on the site than before — lots of articles and features — but it's more difficult to find the Web index thereon, and almost impossible to find out how to request that your own site be added.

Fortunately, I've done the legwork here, so if you'd like to add your site to WebCrawler, your best bet is to get to the right place by way of the help information on the site. When you're in the right spot, you'll be looking at a page similar to Figure 18-4.

Save yourself the digging. It's at `http://www.webcrawler.com/Help/ GetListed/AddURLS.html`.

Figure 18-4: Registering your site at WebCrawler

Using Submit It! (http://www.submit-it.com)

There are a lot of different directories and search sites on the Web — I'm just scratching the surface — and once you've created a Web page, you can easily get trapped in a world where you're spending days entering exactly the same information in a wide variety of different spots. Instead, why not enter it once and have it automatically sent to each of the many search sites? That's the idea behind Submit It!, a terrific utility created by University of Illinois student Scott Banister, and now spun off as its own successful business.

The Submit It! service has over 250,000 Web page designers and publicity specialists signed up, and is a great example of how a simple idea can grow and become its own business, just as Yahoo! started out as a hotlist page for two students. Figure 18-5 shows the Submit It! home page.

Notice the two-column layout. If you peek at the source to this page, you'll see that they've done it with a borderless table.

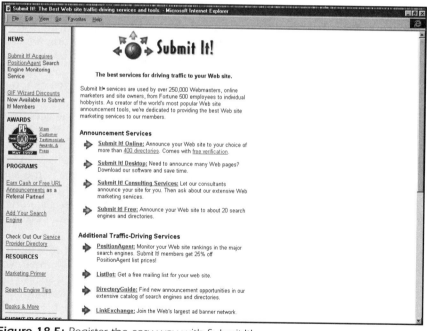

Figure 18-5: *Register the easy way with Submit-It!*

There are two options to Submit It!. The first is a free service that will announce your site to 16 different directories, including: Infoseek, WebCrawler, InfoSpace, Starting Point, ComFind, Yellow Pages Online, LinkStar, Alta Vista, and WebDirect!. The main service that they offer is

Submit It! Online, which, for a small fee, distributes information about your Web site to over 400 different search and category reference sites that are relevant to your topic.

Fee-Based Advertising Spots

Plenty of Web sites charge you money for a listing and/or require you to join their organization in order to get a link from their page to yours. Are these spots worth it? You'll have to decide for yourself. If you're a small entrepreneur, you probably won't be able to ante up the fees for all but the least expensive of them.

Many fee-based sites do, however, offer interesting approaches to Web page design.

If you cast your net a bit wider, you'll also quickly find that there are lots of places where you can buy a banner advertisement for your service or product in order to generate more traffic for your site. Prices for banners can range from the very inexpensive ($50 dollars per month) to amazingly expensive ($10,000 or more for a single month). For the most part, these are sold based on site traffic levels, similar to magazine advertisements. If you want to have a million people see your graphic banner, you'll be paying something on the order of $0.03 per person, or $30,000.00 for that advertisement. I'll explore this topic further later in this chapter.

One important point to make here: The number of viewers isn't the only important criterion, so don't be swayed by thoughts of tons of folks visiting your Web page. The most important criterion is: Who are these people who are seeing your advertisement? I think the demographics and quality of each viewer is critical to an advertising buy decision. Some sites sell you eyeballs, thousands upon thousands of people seeing your advertisement every day, whether it's relevant to them or not. Other sites offer a smarter deal: Everyone who sees your ad banner is already interested in your area.

An example of this is how advertisements are sold in the Internet Mall. If you are a real estate agent in Orlando, Florida, for example, you don't want to pay for people to see your advertisement if they're seeking information on vacation spots in Orlando. If someone's actively looking for real estate agents or real estate in the state of Florida, however, then you're definitely interested in having that person visit your site.

Ultimately, the organization of the site where you're buying an advertising spot is most important, and something you need to examine carefully. If you're selling party T-shirts online, do you really want to pay to display your advert to someone who just searched for "cotton plantation" or is looking for party music?

> **NOTE** One useful place to visit to learn more about banner advertising is Mark Welch's Banner Advertising site at http://www.markwelch.com/bannerad/.

Cooperative Advertising with LinkExchange

http://www.linkexchange.com

Sometimes it seems like there are as many approaches to advertising your site as there are stars in the sky. Most of them are online versions of other media, such as e-zines, which are online versions of newsletters and low-budget magazines, or online yellow pages or other phone directory systems.

Occasionally something new comes along, and the *Internet Link Exchange* (ILE) is just that, with its ingenious approach to advertising sites cooperatively. You can join the Internet Link Exchange for free: All you need to do is be willing to point to an ILE advertising CGI program from within your own Web page. The code you use looks like this:

```
<!-- BEGIN INTERNET LINK EXCHANGE CODE -->
<a href="http://ad.linkexchange.com/X245480/gotoad.map"
target="_top">
<img width=440 height=40 border=1 ismap alt="Internet Link
Exchange"
src="http://ad.linkexchange.com/X228497/logoshowad?free">
</a>
<br>
<font size=1>
<a href="http://www.linkexchange.com/" target="_top">
Member of the Internet Link Exchange</a>
</font>
<br>
<!-- END INTERNET LINK EXCHANGE CODE  -->
```

The idea is deceptively simple: Anyone who comes to your Web page sees a small advertisement for another site in the ILE network (or the exchange itself) as a banner ad on your Web page. Each time you display an advert on your page, you get a credit with ILE. As you accumulate credits, the banner advertisement for your page shows up on other ILE-member sites.

A summary of my LinkExchange account is shown in Figure 18-6.

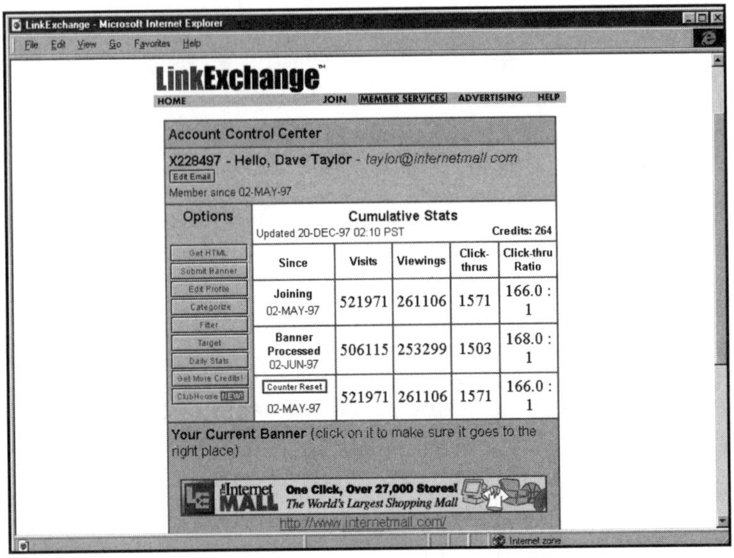

Figure 18-6: Keeping track of banner ads with LinkExchange

If you have a very busy Web site, you could easily build up lots of viewing credits and end up with advertisements for your site throughout the Internet, bringing thousands more directly to you.

If you're looking for easy ways to add traffic to your site, I encourage you to check out the Internet Link Exchange and some of the imitators online.

Tying in with Related Sites Using a Web Ring

Visit a site focused on the *X-Files*, Magic the Gathering, or even a site covering pregnancy and birth resources and you're likely to find that it points to other, similar Web sites. This collection of Web sites pointing to each other, all focused on a single theme, are called Web rings. There's even an organization focused on these loose, cooperative groups of like-minded sites at `http://www.webring.org`. There are over 15,000 different active Web rings hosted at that site.

It's a logical outgrowth of the ubiquitous "favorite links" area of a Web site with a bit of LinkExchange thrown in: a collection of a half-dozen or more sites that the creator of the site feels are related and also of interest to the visitor. Instead of having them all listed on your own page, why not have a central collection of these related links and simply include a "next" link on your site to take visitors to the next site on the list?

Now, you can imagine how these work: a central Web server maintains a list of sites tied to a specific theme or interest, and each site indicates it's part of the ring and includes a pointer to the central ring server. Simple rings include a "next" and "previous" button allowing visitors to travel linearly through the list of links. More sophisticated ones offer subset list views — "show five ring sites" — and a random link that takes the visitor to one of the sites in the ring.

One site that I've developed is hooked into a Web ring: The Peninsula Birth Connection. It's part of the pregnancy and childbirth resources Web ring, and here's the HTML code that's at the bottom of the Peninsula Birth Connection home page:

```
<a href="http://www.fensende.com/Users/swnymph/RingC.html">
<IMG SRC="images/pregc-logo.gif" target=_top align=left
border=0> </a>
<a href="http://www.webring.org/cgi-bin/webring?
ring=pregc&id=5&next"
target=_top ><IMG SRC="images/pregc-next.gif" align=right
border=0></a>

<center>
Member of the
<a href="http://www.fensende.com/Users/swnymph/RingC.html"
target=_top>
Pregnancy Services and Products WebRing</a>
<P>

<a href="http://www.webring.org/cgi-bin/webring?
ring=pregc&random"
target=_top>Visit Another Ring Site</a>
<br>
or learn how to
<a href="http://www.fensende.com/Users/swnymph/RingC.html"
target=_top>Join Our Web Ring</a>
```

Figure 18-7 shows what the Web Ring section looks like on the page.

Figure 18-7: Joining a Web ring

Visit the Peninsula Birth Connection for yourself at `http://www.birthconnect.org`.

It's complex, but there are only two different links in the previous HTML code: RingC.html, the informational page about the pregnancy ring, is listed three times, and the Web ring script at www.webring.org is listed twice: once for the "next in ring" button (with arguments `"ring=pregc&next"`) and once for a random site from the list of different sites in the ring (arguments `"ring=pregc&random"`).

You can join an existing Web ring to gain more exposure for your site, but I must admit I have somewhat mixed feelings about using Web rings for building traffic; if I can get someone to come to my site, why would I want to have them easily pop over to other, similar, sites and possibly not come back? You'll have to make your own choice, but I would encourage you to think this through carefully.

The Basics of Banner Advertising

As I said earlier, one way that you can build traffic to your Web site is to pay for banner advertisements. These are typically 468 pixels wide and 60 pixels high, and a typical banner advert might look like Figure 18-8. Notice that it's small enough to be a minor part of an overall Web page, but large enough that it certainly attracts attention if well designed.

Figure 18-8: A typical banner advertisement

The majority of sites where you'd be able to have your own banner charge a fee for the advertisement, exactly akin to paying for an advert in a print publication. The costs for advertisements online are most often calculated in CPM, which is actually the *cost per thousand* impressions.

The "M" in CPM is actually the Latin "mil" which is "thousand." Think of a millimeter being a thousandth of a meter and you'll be able to remember the acronym meaning.

"What's an impression?" you're probably wondering. Here's where you can see how the Web has grown far beyond just a hobbyist space: the Madison Avenue advertising people brought their jargon to the Internet and now there's a whole language of banner ads to learn.

The most important are that a "hit" represents a request received by the Web server, a "page view" is the number of times an HTML document was requested, an "impression" (or, sometimes, "eyeball") is the number of times that the banner advert was displayed on screen, and a "click through" counts the number of times someone saw the banner advert and clicked it.

Now you can look at a Web page with a more experienced eye: each graphic on the page produces its own "hit" on the server, so while a simple page such as Yahoo! only produces four hits for each visit to the home page, a complex page such as Compaq Computers' (`http://www.compaq.com`) actually has 23 separate graphical elements, producing 24 hits for each viewing of the page. That's how you can hear about Web sites that have millions of "hits" each month, and why you shouldn't care. It's the number of visitors or the number of page views that tell you the real traffic story.

Banner ads are going to cost between $12–$30 for each thousand impressions, and the number of people who click your banner ad is really more in your control than that of the site where your advert is being shown. To create effective banner advertisements, there are three rules of thumb:

1. Offer the viewer a special bargain or deal. An advert that just mentions your company isn't going to be very successful, particularly if no one knows who you are.

2. Keep it simple and uncluttered: it's competing for attention with the rest of the page, so you need to have it be elegant and effective.

3. Have a call to action. The best: "click here" or a mock button as part of the banner.

Advertisements that offer a bargain and tell the viewer how to get that product (for example, a button labeled "buy now!") are the most successful of all.

There are also a standard set of sizes for advertising banners on the Web, set by the *Internet Advertising Bureau* (IAB).

Visit the IAB online at `http://www.edelman.com/IAB`.

The standard banner sizes are enumerated in Table 18-1.

Table 18-1	Standard Banner Advert Sizes
Size	**Typical Use**
468 x 60	Full banner
392 x72	Full banner with vertical navigation bar
234 x 60	Half banner
125 x 125	Square button
120 x 90	Button #1
120 x 60	Button #2
88 x 31	Micro button
120 x 240	Vertical banner

If you opt to try banner advertising, be skeptical of the claims of different Web sites and test out your banner for click-through rates. An effective banner might only have a 2 or 3 percent click-through rate (which means that if 1,000 people saw the banner, only 30 clicked it to reach your site). One good strategy is to try a couple of different banner adverts for a small number of impressions and try to identify which one is the most effective, then focus your campaign on that banner and its style.

The Best Way to Publicize Your Site

The best way to publicize your new Web site is to become active in the Internet community and to be sure to include your site URL in all your documents, advertisements, and in any other materials you use to interact with your peers, friends, and customers. Find the cool Web sites in your area of interest and ask them to include pointers to your information. Almost all sites will do that for free, particularly if you agree to list them at your site, too.

There are a million different destinations on the Web, and many of them might be of interest to you and your business. I have offered you a set of valuable starting points in this chapter, but it doesn't replace the need to explore and find sites that exactly match your own interests and field. Chapter 19 gives you an overview of a dramatic new technology, called dynamic HTML, and wraps up with some musings about the future of the Web.

Dynamic HTML and The Future

In This Chapter

Dynamic HTML with Layers and JavaScript

Dynamic Font Technologies

Page Counters

A Musical Alternative: MIDI

The Future of the Web

The first eighteen chapters of this book covered the entire HTML language, from its beginnings as HTML 1.0 through the latest version — the 4.0 specification. Along the way you've seen a few snippets that only work in Navigator or Internet Explorer, but for the most part, it's the same language displayed the same way with both.

In this final chapter I'm going to delve into some interesting new Web page capabilities that have the potential to dramatically change the way pages interact with users through layers of information, the most interesting part of what people call *Dynamic HTML*. The frustrating part is that there are two different versions of dynamic HTML: there's the Netscape version (that only works for Communicator 4.0 and above) and there's the different version that Internet Explorer supports (again, only the 4.0 release and higher). The Netscape version is easier to learn, so that's what I'll focus on, but I'll also give you a pointer to a great Web site to learn all about Microsoft's view of Dynamic HTML.

I'll also touch on what's happening with typefaces (a particularly weak area with Web page design), show you some page counter tricks, and then wrap up with some thoughts on the future of the Web.

Dynamic HTML with Layers and JavaScript

The combination of tables, frames, and the many other parts of HTML give you a wide range of layout capabilities, but they're all constrained to working within a single dimension: It's all a flat piece of paper and the tags enable you to create sophisticated layouts on that paper, but you can't put elements on top of other elements, or overlap material.

Well, that's not entirely true: Using style sheets, you can control the relative positioning of material and actually have things overlap, but it's not particularly graceful.

To extend Web pages to include multiple layers, Netscape introduced the <LAYER> tag in the 4.0 release of its Navigator Web browser (Communicator is Navigator plus a bunch of other stuff), and this new tag offers a ton of really interesting capabilities, particularly when combined with some simple JavaScript scripting additions.

The <LAYER> tag has a wide variety of different attributes, so let's delve into it by starting with the basics that you must have: a WIDTH and an ID. The most basic layer would look something like this:

```
<LAYER ID=layer1 WIDTH=300>
```

which would define a 300-pixel-wide layer called "layer1." The contents of the layer is specified between the <LAYER> and </LAYER> tag, so the above would be more likely to show up on the page as:

```
<LAYER ID=layer1 WIDTH=300>
Thanks for visiting our site and checking out our product
line.
Please stop by again.
</LAYER>
```

This isn't much to look at yet, so let's add a few more attributes.

Background colors for layers can be specified with the BGCOLOR tag (and background graphics, if you'd prefer that, can be specified with BACKGROUND=url). The location of the layer within the overall window can be specified with the TOP and LEFT attributes, which define an exact location relative to 0,0, the top-left corner.

To extend my example, I could move the layer closer to center of the screen and give it a cheery background with:

```
<LAYER ID=layer1 WIDTH=300 TOP=100 LEFT=100 BGCOLOR=magenta>
This is some information that will appear against a magenta
background, in its own small box on the screen.
</LAYER>
```

Figure 19-1 shows how this displays in Netscape Communicator 4.0, albeit without the background color itself.

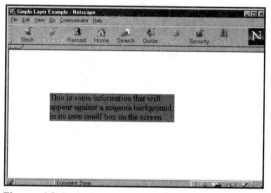

Figure 19-1: A simple LAYER demonstration

So far, this is something you could accomplish with tables, if you were so inclined, so I'll add a second layer to the page for you to really see what's so cool about layers:

```
<LAYER ID=layer1 WIDTH=300 TOP=100 LEFT=100 BGCOLOR=magenta>
This is some information that will appear against a
magenta background, in its own small box on the screen.
</LAYER>

<LAYER ID=layer2 WIDTH=50 TOP=90 LEFT=200 BGCOLOR=white>
<CENTER>
a small, skinny layer atop the other
</CENTER>
</LAYER>
```

Look at the TOP coordinate of the second layer, 90, versus the top of the first layer of 100: If you guessed that they're going to overlap, you're exactly right. Figure 19-2 shows how the white layer overlaps the magenta layer on the screen.

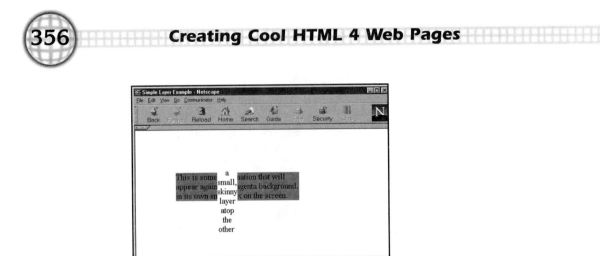

Figure 19-2: Layers can be atop other layers.

This ability for layers to be atop one another is a very important concept for developing layers-based page design. Just like computer graphics, layers on Web pages reference the so-called Z-axis, an imaginary third dimension that shoots straight out of your computer screen and into your eyes.

 The first two dimensions are height and width, of course.

Layers that have a higher z axis value are going to be on top of layers with smaller Z-axis values. By default, the layers on your page increase in Z value as the page is rendered, which is why layer2 in the above example was occluding layer1.

You can specify the Z-axis values for layers directly within the HTML if you want to have them displayed in a different order, in either of two different ways: the Z-INDEX attribute or the ABOVE and BELOW attributes. The Z-INDEX attribute lets you specify numerically which layers should be above which other layers; higher numbered Z-indexes are always above lower-numbered Z-indexes.

To have the previous example shown with layer2 below layer1, simply change the two <LAYER> tags to specify a Z-index:

```
<LAYER ID=layer1 Z-INDEX=2 WIDTH=300 TOP=100 LEFT=100
BGCOLOR=magenta>
This is some information that will appear against a
magenta background, in its own small box on the screen.
</LAYER>

<LAYER ID=layer2 Z-INDEX=1 WIDTH=50 TOP=90 LEFT=200
BGCOLOR=white>
<CENTER>
```

```
a small, skinny layer atop the other
</CENTER>
</LAYER>
```

The second way to affect the order of layers is to explicitly state which layers should be ABOVE or BELOW which other layers. With this approach —
and you can't mix Z-INDEX and ABOVE/BELOW specifications — you only
need to change one of the <LAYER> tags, rather than both. The following
would suffice to have layer1 above layer2:

```
<LAYER ID=layer1 ABOVE=layer2 WIDTH=300 ...
```

You can't specify that two layers should each be above the other, and you
really don't want to have multiple layers with the same Z-index value. In
both cases, the results are undefined and might vary from browser to
browser.

One thing that I should point out is that you can have anything within a
layer, including graphics, tables, and so on.

These layers might not seem too valuable right now because they're always
displayed on the screen, so at best they're offering a way to have overlapping colors. But what if you could actually turn them on and off based on
user events?

The attribute that controls whether a layer is displayed or not is VISIBILITY,
and it has three possible values: "show," "hidden," and "inherit." The first is
the default; the layer is visible. Hidden layers are not visible to the user, but
are rendered and "ready to go" as needed. An inherited visibility means that
the layer inherits the visibility status of its parent layer (because you can
have layers within other layers).

Being able to turn layer visibility on and off is exactly where JavaScript
comes into the picture, as shown in this listing:

```
<BODY BGCOLOR=white>
<CENTER>
<h2>Welcome to the Layer Factory</h2>

<LAYER ID=layer1 WIDTH=50% TOP=25% LEFT=25% BGCOLOR=yellow>
<font size=+1>This is the first, always visible background.
<P>
Do you like
the background color?</font>
```

(continued)

```
(continued)
</LAYER>

<LAYER ID=mystery top=25% LEFT=35% VISIBILITY=hidden>
<IMG SRC=subliminal.gif ALT="subliminal image">
</LAYER>

<FORM>
<INPUT TYPE=BUTTON OnClick="document.mystery.visibility=
'show'; return false;" VALUE="Show Mystery Layer">
 
<INPUT TYPE=BUTTON OnClick="document.mystery.visibility=
'hidden'; return false;" VALUE="Hide Mystery Layer">
</FORM>
</CENTER>
<P>
</BODY>
```

You can see in this listing that the second layer has become a graphical image, and that its default state is to be invisible (`visibility=hidden`). I create two buttons on the base layer of the page that will enable the user to switch the mystery layer to visible, and then back to hidden, as they wish. Figure 19-3 shows what the page looks like upon being first loaded, and Figure 19-4 shows the same page with the mystery window made visible.

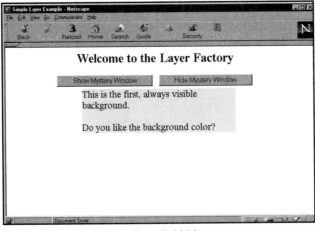

Figure 19-3: The mystery layer is hidden.

Figure 19-4: The mystery layer is visible.

If you're willing to delve further into JavaScript as a way to learn how to make these layers jump through hoops, then there's quite a lot you can do with layers. Here's an example of a graphic that's included as its own layer so I can bounce it around on the screen, using JavaScript:

```
<HTML>
<TITLE>Scripted Layer Example</TITLE>
<SCRIPT LANGUAGE="JavaScript">
var incrementx = 5;
var incrementy = 5;
var continue_bouncing = 1;

function bounce() {
    document.box.top += incrementx;
    if (document.box.top > 300) incrementx = -5;    // past
the bottom edge
    if (document.box.top < 60)  incrementx =  5;   //
past the top edge

    document.box.left += incrementy;
    if (document.box.left > 400) incrementy = -5;  // past
the right edge
    if (document.box.left < 50)  incrementy =  5;   //
past the left edge

    if (continue_bouncing == 1)         // only continue
bouncing if var set
            setTimeout(bounce, 10);
```

(continued)

```
(continued)
}

function startBounce() {
    continue_bouncing = 1;        // turn on the keep
bouncing status var and go!
    bounce();
}

function stopBounce() {
    continue_bouncing = 0;        // stop bouncing by
changing the status var.
}

</SCRIPT>

<BODY BGCOLOR=white>

<CENTER>
<h2>Acme Rubber Ball Testing Facility</h2>

<LAYER ID=box TOP=100 LEFT=100>
<IMG SRC=ball.gif>
</LAYER>

<FORM>
<INPUT TYPE=BUTTON OnClick="startBounce(); return false;"
VALUE="start bouncing">
 
<INPUT TYPE=BUTTON OnClick="stopBounce(); return false;"
VALUE="stop bouncing">
</FORM>
</CENTER>
<P>

</BODY>
</HTML>
```

This is a very complex example, I admit. The basic logic of the page, however, is simple: The initial location of the layer is defined by the <LAYER> statement (TOP=100 and LEFT=100), then the location is successively changed by adding incrementx to the horizontal location and incrementy to the vertical position and redisplaying the page. If the left edge of the graphic goes beyond a certain point, then flip the incrementx variable to be a negative number, which has the loop subtract the value, rather than add it, to the current location; same with the top (vertical) location of the graphic.

There are three routines at work here: `startBounce()` is called to get the ball rolling (quite literally!), while `stopBounce()` stops it moving. The real work is done by the `bounce()` routine itself, which increments the location as detailed above, then checks the status of the `continue_bouncing` variable: if it's set to 1, then it loops, with a $^{10}/_{100}$ ths-of-a-second delay:

```
if (continue_bouncing == 1)                    // only continue
bouncing if var set
        setTimeout(bounce, 10);
```

If it's not set to 1, then the `bounce()` routine just ends and the layer stops moving.

Figure 19-5 shows how the page is displayed, but to really get the full impact, you'll want to jump onto the included CD-ROM and actually experiment with the page; make sure you're using the very latest browser from Netscape, or your results will be pretty boring!

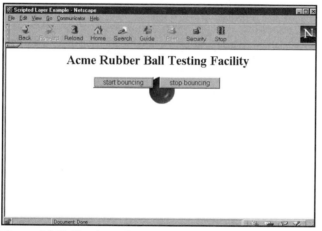

Figure 19-5: The Acme Rubber Ball Testing Facility

Table 19-1 shows you a list of all the possible attributes for the `<LAYER>` tag:

Table 19-1	Attributes for the Netscape Layer Tag
Attribute	**Meaning**
ABOVE	Specifies which layer the current should be above on the display.
BACKGROUND	The background graphics file for the layer.
BELOW	Specifies which layer the current should be below on the display.
BGCOLOR	The background color of the layer.
CLIP	Clipping region for the layer (the material in the layer could be bigger than the actual size of the layer you want to display: the smaller "window" into the larger material is the clipping region).
HEIGHT	The height of the layer on the display.
ID	The name of the layer (also useful for <TARGET> with HREFs).
LEFT	The location of the left edge of the layer border, relative to the parent layer.
PAGEX	The location of the left edge of the layer, relative to the browser window.
PAGEY	The location of the top edge of the layer, relative to the browser window.
SRC	The HTML document that should be displayed in the layer.
TOP	The location of the top edge of the layer, relative to the parent layer.
VISIBILITY	Whether the layer is visible. Possible values: "show," "hidden," and "inherit."
WIDTH	The width of the layer on the display.
Z-INDEX	For defining which layers overlap which other layers (higher number overlaps lower).

A good spot to learn more about layers is on the Netscape site at http://developer.netscape.com/library/documentation/communicator/dynhtml/layers32.htm.

Dynamic HTML According to Microsoft

Microsoft has a different implementation of Dynamic HTML that's similar in how you script it, but different in what you have within your actual HTML. It's probably more robust, but it's quite a bit harder to learn, in my opinion. One plus for Microsoft: its model fits with the object-oriented *Document Object Model* (DOM) as proposed by the W3 HTML standards committee.

 The best online reference for Microsoft Dynamic HTML is at `http://www.microsoft.com/workshop/author/dhtml/`.

Dynamic Font and Printing Technologies

If you have fancy style sheets, what else could you possibly want for Web page design in the future?

An area that continues to need lots of improvement is the management of typefaces. If you've tried to specify typefaces by name so that they'll work on both a Macintosh and PC, you know what I mean. On the Mac it's Times, but on a Windows machine it's Times New Roman. On the Mac it's Courier, but on the PC it's Courier New. The Mac has Helvetica as a standard typeface, but Windows 95 includes Arial instead. And we haven't even started to consider the further complications of typefaces on a UNIX system or a PDA like a Newton or Windows CE device.

Adobe and Microsoft, as a result, announced a new extension to TrueType and PostScript Type 1 called TrueType Open Version 2, or, succinctly, OpenType. Simultaneously, Bitstream and Netscape announced their own version of Web-based typeface control called Dynamic Type (and a related technology called TrueDoc).

The OpenType design is pretty darn smart. Because it's based on TrueType and PostScript Type 1 type, just about all existing fonts will work without any effort on the part of the user. OpenType will make it possible for you to include high-quality, onscreen fonts as part of your pages. If a client doesn't have Arial, you'll be able to send it along with the document — compressed — and the Web page will display the text in the appropriate typeface automatically.

Microsoft and Adobe have submitted a proposal to the World Wide Web Consortium, the group that now manages the growth of HTML, for a standard way to embed OpenType fonts in Web pages. If you're very interested in using specific typefaces, stay tuned for developments in this area.

There's an OpenType FAQ to read: `http://www.microsoft.com/truetype/faq/faq9.htm`.

The Netscape and Bitstream solution is very different, and it's built around having what are called *Portable Font Resources* (PFR) files on your server, that you include in your pages with:

```
<LINK REL="fontdef" SRC="mypage.pfr">
```

This specifies that the PFR file mypage.pfr should be referenced as a font definition if required to render the page (if the user already has all the typefaces on their PC, it doesn't do anything). The typeface is referenced as usual:

```
<FONT FACE="Cataneo" SIZE=4>Fancy Text</FONT>
```

The catch here is that you need to get a special Web development tool to create these portable font reference files called a *Character Shape Recorder* (CSR) (I kid you not). There are a number of CSR programs available, but it's an extra step that might be more trouble than it's worth for you.

Learn more about Dynamic Fonts at `http://www.bitstream.com/world/dynamic.htm`.

Page Counters

Let's switch from serious to fun Web page additions. Topping that list are visitor or page counters. Counters are a popular addition to Web pages that can be done in a variety of different ways. Counters appear as either graphics or text; if you go to my home page, for example, you'll find that it's a text counter. Graphical counters are implemented by using an `<IMG>` tag to include a graphic that's actually a program that computes the counter value and then creates a graphic with the numbers in question.

To use a text counter, you'll need to talk with your system administrator about whether your server supports server-side includes and what kind of changes you need to make to your page to have a text counter work. On my server, I simply rename the filename suffix .shtml rather than .html, and it works like magic. The actual HTML sequence I use on the page to count is:

```
<font size=4><B>Hey! You're the</B></font>
<font size=5><B><!--#counter file="mycounter" --></B></font>
<font size=4><B>visitor!</B></font>
```

If you want a graphic counter, you specify a regular image include that happens to point to the program in question:

```
<img src="apps/Counter.cgi">
```

There's a third option — you can have a third-party site keep track of your hits and produce the counter graphic on the fly for you. There are a number of sites offering just such a service — some free, some for a nominal fee. My favorite is Web Counter, which you can visit at `http://www.digits.com`.

There are lots of fun counters and digit styles available, and it's neat to see that people are actually visiting your pages and exploring your ideas and design. You can help confirm this for me; visit my home page right now and increment my counter: `http://www.intuitive.com/taylor/`.

Looking for more information on page counters? Check out Digit Mania's amazing collection of different digit styles and general info at `http://www.digitmania.com`.

A Musical Alternative: MIDI

Another fun addition to your site sound-wise: If you're really plugged in to the music world, you already know about the fabulous *Musical Instrument Digital Interface* (MIDI) and how it enables you to define a musical passage in terms of triggers — sequences of notes to play in specific voices. It turns out that there are two very cool plug-ins that let you actually play MIDI files while within your Web browser: Yamaha's MIDplug and LiveUpdate's Crescendo. I use both on my site — they're both very cool, and free!

You can get the Yamaha MIDplug at `http://www.cyber-bp.or.jp/yamaha/index_e.html` and Crescendo's available at `http://www.liveupdate.com/get.html`.

The biggest advantage of MIDI is that the files can be tiny and can still offer five to ten minutes — or more — of music. Check out the accompanying CD-ROM: I've included a couple of files for you to enjoy, and they work just as well as a `BGSOUND` or sound player control in Navigator as a standard WAV or AU sound file.

Visit an amazing MIDI archive called MidiFarm if you're even the tiniest bit interested in adding sound or music to your pages. You can find it at `http://www.midifarm.com`.

The Future of the Web

Phew

You've made it to the end of the book. You've learned an amazing variety of different ways to translate the picture in your head to the display on the screen. From tables to frames, style sheets to layers, there are a million and one different ways that you can create the Web site of your dreams. Good job!

But what does the future of the Web hold? As is obvious by the spotty implementation of the latest HTML 4.0 tags and capabilities, and the divergence on the dynamic HTML and typeface models, it's still Internet business as usual: things developing at a breakneck pace but no one talking to anyone else.

Actually, the two big players in this market, Microsoft and Netscape, have a new version of this approach: each claims that it's heavily involved with the standards bodies and that, in the meantime, it wants to ensure that developers can get the best possible pages by using its own capabilities.

But they're both missing the boat. It's important for the HTML language and Web browsers to evolve, but when there are new capabilities added that break older browser presentation (like <LEGEND> and the <LAYERS> additions in Navigator), the companies are foisting a huge mess onto us as developers. It all continues to revolve around the question that was the number-one puzzle to solve for Web designers two years ago: Do you develop your sites for people with the latest tools, do you develop them for people who have even the oldest, most primitive browsers, or do you try to find a happy spot in the middle?

Even the *World Wide Web consortium* (W3) has fallen prey to this inability to standardize, endorse, and help clean up this mess. The most notable missing piece of the HTML 4.0 specification, for example, was a statement that showed W3 was endorsing JavaScript as the official scripting language for future Web browsers. They didn't. Instead, they retained the <SCRIPT> tag and noted that a wide variety of different languages might be used as they become popular.

It's exactly the same with the plug-in architecture. The ability to extend the capabilities of a Web browser is a tremendous boon, but when the user wants to do so, not when the designer forces the user in order for the user to have a good visit. There are too many sites that are "ShockWave enabled" and the like, requiring people to download and add additional software to their computer before they can truly visit and explore the site.

That's a strange message to send someone, in my view. I don't use *any* plug-in-required material on any of the Web sites I develop.

And so, we're at the end of the book, but it's by no means the end of the development of the Web, of the HTML language or of your own Web sites!

I'm not kidding about the continued evolution of HTML: There are already talks starting about the HTML 5.0 specification, and a competing group arguing that the language should just evolve back into its parent language SGML, the standard generalized markup language.

Stay in touch; the home site for this book is at

```
http://www.intuitive.com/coolweb/
```

and you can always reach me via electronic mail at taylor@intuitive.com.

Building Your First Page: A Primer

In This Chapter

Entering and editing HTML with Notepad

Downloading a copy of Paint Shop Pro or Graphic Converter

Building graphics with Paint Shop Pro

Testing your page with Internet Explorer

Uploading with FTP Explorer

A final check

Now that your knowledge and understanding of the HTML language and the capabilities of various Web browsers put you into the top one percent of the Internet community, you're ready to rock and roll, right? Hopefully, you've already been experimenting with some of the ideas in the book, but to make sure you get off to a good start, this appendix will show you, step by step, exactly how I create a simple Web page and upload it to a remote Web server for everyone to enjoy.

If you have an HTML editor or a Web-compatible graphics editor already, you may want to skip those sections. You might, however, find reading along with what I'm doing quite helpful.

Entering and Editing HTML with Notepad

Recently, I was asked by a magazine for my top three tips for people interested in creating slick Web sites, and in this appendix I'm going to lead you through all the steps I took to translate the simple text file for these tips into a cool Web page. Figure A-1 shows the basic text in Notepad, a simple and useful editor included with Windows 95.

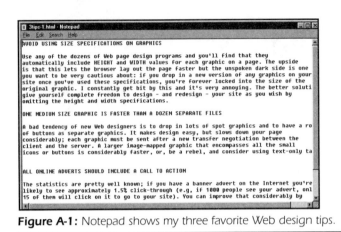

Figure A-1: Notepad shows my three favorite Web design tips.

As you can see, the text is there, but the presentation isn't very exciting. The first step, therefore, is to add some HTML tags to spice up the final presentation. You can do this with some relatively simple additions: `<BLOCKQUOTE>` indents the explanations, `<HR SIZE=1 NOSHADE WIDTH=50%>` adds a fine rule between the title and the first tip, and the `<FONT>` tag emphasizes the tips themselves. The results are shown in Figure A-2.

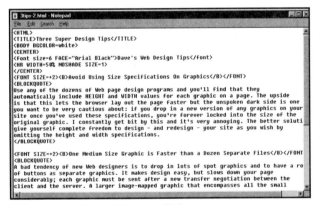

Figure A-2: Design tips with HTML tags

Before I go any further, you should save this file as an HTML document. Choose Save As from the File menu, which displays the dialog box shown in Figure A-3.

Figure A-3: Save the working file as tips.html

By default, Notepad wants to save files as .txt files, which isn't good for a Web page. Use your mouse to click the File name box, then replace "txt" with "html," as shown in Figure A-3.

Having safely saved this file, leave the HTML document alone for a minute and try adding a nice opening graphic with Paint Shop Pro if you're on a PC, or with GraphicConverter if you're a Macintosh user.

Downloading a Copy of Paint Shop Pro

To grab a copy of Paint Shop Pro, launch your Web browser. Then go to the JASC Software Web site at `http://www.jasc.com` (see Figure A-4).

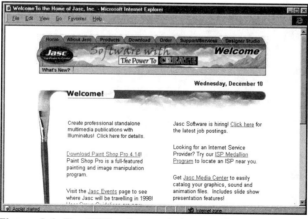

Figure A-4: The JASC web page in Internet Explorer.

Depending on what type of computer you have, you'll want to choose either the Windows 95/Windows NT version or the older Windows 3.1 version of the program. Once you've made your choice, click the "Download Paint Shop Pro shareware" link.

Choose one of the different download links. When you start the file transfer (it's a URL to an FTP site, actually), your browser may ask you if you want to download a file that might be infected by a virus or otherwise dangerous and unknown. If so, click Yes with the understanding that you should run a virus check on all outside files you transfer to your computer. Then specify where you want the file saved and relax for a few minutes while the file downloads to your computer.

Next thing you know, you've got a terrific new shareware application from the Net on your computer. Pretty darn easy, eh?

TIP   If you like Paint Shop Pro, please don't forget to register your shareware!

Downloading Graphic Converter

If you're a Macintosh user, there's a terrific Mac alternative to Paint Shop Pro, which is a Windows-only application. Graphic Converter is a great shareware application written by the talented team at Lemke Software in Germany. To download your own copy, start by going to the Lemke Web site at `http://www.lemkesoft.de/`, as shown in Figure A-5.

Figure A-5: The Lemke Software Web site

Once you're there, choose the "Download" option, and then choose whether you need a PowerPC or 680x0-based system. Choose the right option and let the software download onto your computer. A few minutes of data transfer later, and you'll have a terrific new application on your Macintosh.

One quick note: The examples later in this appendix are done with Paint Shop Pro, but the basics of using "New" to create a new graphic, ensuring that you save the image in GIF or JPEG format, and then referencing it on your Web page are exactly identical in Graphic Converter. Also, if you like Graphic Converter, don't forget to register it and support the author of the program.

Building Graphics with Paint Shop Pro

Armed with your new graphics editor, you launch it and specify that you want a new blank document with which to work. It looks like Figure A-6.

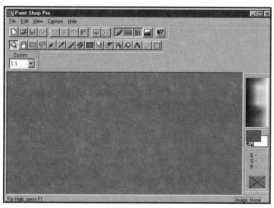

Figure A-6: Paint Shop Pro with a blank page

From here you first need to pick a few colors, which can be done by double-clicking the two overlapping boxes on the right. The left box, which slightly overlaps the other, is the foreground color, and clicking it presents you with a palette of 256 colors from which to choose. I opted for a bright red foreground in this example. Click the other box, the background, and choose white.

Now to enter the text. Choose the text edit tool (the "A" button on the toolbar), which brings up a complex dialog box offering a choice of typeface, style, size, special effects, and more. You can type the text you want to see in the Enter text here box at the bottom of the dialog box, which you can see I've done in Figure A-7.

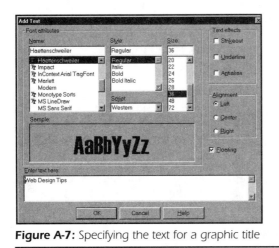

Figure A-7: Specifying the text for a graphic title

Click OK, and now it's just about done and looks pretty slick, as you can see in Figure A-8.

Figure A-8: The graphic title for my new Web page

All that's left is to crop the graphics file to the minimum size that contains the material desired and save it as a GIF-format graphic so that Web browsers can read it.

You accomplish the first by choosing the dashed rectangular box tool on the toolbar and drawing a box that just barely surrounds the text. You can see that in Figure A-9.

Figure A-9: Selecting the region of the graphic to save

With that selected, go to the Image menu and choose Crop. Instantly, the big graphics space will be chopped down to a small window that just contains the graphic. Perfect!

Now use the Save As option on the File menu to save this graphic as a GIF file, as shown in Figure A-10.

Figure A-10: Save the graphic as a GIF file on the desktop

Fabulous! You've created a nice graphic and saved it in a format that works perfectly on the Web. Now take a quick pop back to the HTML document in Notepad to add a couple of lines of HTML at the very top of the document:

```
<CENTER>
<IMG SRC=spiffo.gif>
</CENTER>
```

Now you can preview the document in a Web browser. (Don't forget to save the modifications!)

Testing Your Page with Internet Explorer

The new page and graphic must be in the same folder for this to work — because the URL specified with the `<IMG>` tag above doesn't have any directory information — so just drop them both onto the desktop itself. You can open the page from your hard drive as you would a URL; just type in the path to tips.html.

The page should look just like Figure A-11: a nice, simple, attractive Web page.

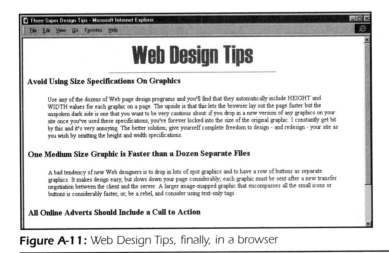

Figure A-11: Web Design Tips, finally, in a browser

Here's where you can really spend hours going back and forth, fine-tuning your graphics and layout, and generally exploring different ways to present information to the user. For this particular example, however, I'll fight my natural urges and leave this as is. Okay with you?

Uploading with FTP Explorer

Because my PC isn't a live Internet Web server, but I want to be able to offer this page to the Web traveling public at large, I need to have an account on a server somewhere on the Net. Fortunately, I do! My base Web account is on Best Internet Communications, Inc., of Mountain View, California (`http://www.best.com`), on a machine called `commerce.best.com`. My account name is `dtaylor`, and my password is, well, wait a second. You don't really want to know my password, do you? Anyway, suffice it to say I have a password!

I want to upload both the HTML file tips.html and the graphics file spiffo.gif to the server. To do this, I use a great utility called FTP Explorer, included on the CD-ROM in this book.

 If you don't have the CD-ROM, get a copy of FTP Explorer at `http://www.ftpx.com`. My favorite Macintosh FTP alternative is the classic Fetch application from Dartmouth, which you can get at `http://www.dartmouth.edu/pages/softdev/fetch.html`

After the program starts, I choose Connect from the Tools menu and enter the information shown in Figure A-12 (note that I used FTP Explorer frequently, so some of the entries on the left side of the screen shot will differ from what you'll see on your screen).

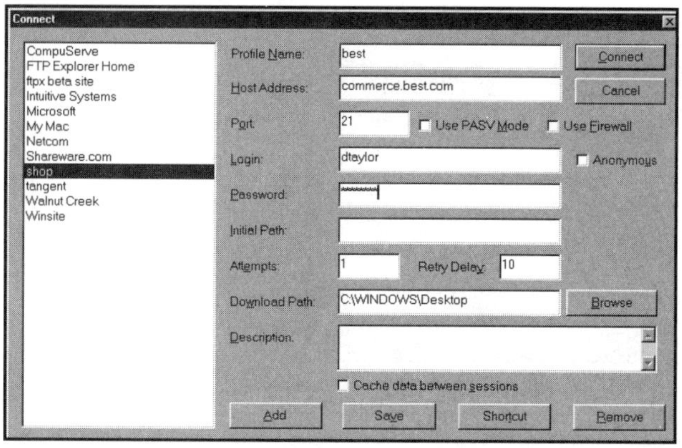

Figure A-12: Specifying the information to connect to Best

Within a few seconds, FTP Explorer connects to the remote site via the file transfer protocol and shows me the files and folders on the remote machine in a form that's quite familiar; it looks just like the Windows 95 Explorer file management program.

You'll need to substitute information as appropriate for your account — and if you don't have one, check out Appendix C, which lists a variety of ways you can find a good Web space provider for your pages.

Figure A-13 shows how things look when I connect to my account. You can see lots of directories and files already there.

Figure A-13: Lots of files in FTP Explorer

From this point, I simply click the up arrow on the toolbar to choose the HTML and graphic files I want to upload to the Web server.

A little trick: Click on a file, then shift-click on a second file, and FTP Explorer can send both files with a single transaction, as you can see is ready to go in Figure A-14.

Figure A-14: Sending files up to the server

That's all you need to send the completed Web page to the server and have it available to the general public.

One Last Check

The files are on the server, and I already know that my domain name on the Best server is www.intuitive.com, so I can put it all together and find that the URL of the new page I've just created is

```
http://www.intuitive.com/tips.html
```

Sure enough, I go to that URL and see the Web page shown here as Figure A-15.

Figure A-15: The final public Web page

Try viewing this page yourself if you're connected to the Net!

As you can see, creating a Web page, adding some graphics, and uploading it to a Web server are straightforward with some good tools, and I'm sure that with a bit of practice you can quickly create some fabulous Web sites of your own.

Step-by-Step Web Site Planning Guide

When you design a simple one-page Web site for personal use, you can probably get away with just letting the page evolve as you experiment. When you design a complex set of interconnecting Web documents or a commercial home page, you need to go about the process more systematically. Here's a guide to planning the process step by step.

Stage One: Conceptualization

A lot of your HTML choices and design decisions follow from overall decisions about the goal of the Web pages and the people you hope to reach with them. Thinking through those questions early in the process will save you a lot of time in the end if you're working on a complex venture.

Step 1: Establish the goal

As with any other project, you can expect the best results if you figure out up front exactly what you want the Web pages to do for you, your company, or your client. It's sometimes a challenge to clearly articulate the purpose, but making sure you know what you're doing and why before you plunge into the design will save a lot of time you'd otherwise lose to unnecessary revisions.

Part of setting the goal for your Web pages is identifying as clearly as possible your intended audience. The tools for identifying who visits a Web page are limited, and so far, there's no accepted standard for how to count the number of users to establish a return on investment or the number of people in the target audience who have received your message. If you spend some time thinking about what kind of people you want to reach, however, during design, you can focus on including things that will attract those people, you can judge which external links to incorporate, and you can zero in on the sites you most want to point to your site. You can also do some contingency planning for what to do if your site turns out to be so intriguing that it's swamped by loads of browsers who aren't in the target audience.

Your target audience will play a big role in determining how you design your pages. For example, if you're preparing a site for Macintosh multimedia developers, you can assume that all targeted users will be able to play QuickTime movies; but that might not be the case for a site directed toward a more general audience. Or, if you're creating a site directed toward Netscape users, you could go ahead and use the Netscape extensions to HTML, but you might want to stick to the standard HTML tags for a broader audience.

Do you want a lot of repeat visitors? If so, you need to plan to change elements of the page frequently to keep the site interesting to the real Web zealots. Some commercial sites are designed to change many times each day, for example.

When considering the audience, think about which browser software you plan to support (and, therefore, test with). And remember, if you want to reach everyone, you'll need to include text alternatives to graphics for Lynx users.

Another factor that may control your design, especially in a corporate setting, is: Who's going to maintain the site, and how much time do they have to do it?

Many companies find that managing and maintaining Web sites and responding to all the inquiries they generate takes more time and money than originally anticipated. If a company goes on the Web, but can't keep up with the visitors' demands for information or follow-up, the company seems unresponsive, so make sure those issues are part of any discussion about a commercial Web site plan. (Interestingly enough, even if a commercial Web site doesn't include a company's Internet address, launching a Web site often leads to more e-mail from the outside world, sometimes radically more e-mail — something else to factor in.)

Remember that it's called the World Wide Web for a reason. Whether you mean to or not, you'll have a global audience; so if your client or company or content has international aspects, be sure to include that in the Web page plan. For example, if you are planning to publish product information for a company that distributes its products worldwide, make sure to include international sales office contact information as well as U.S. contact info. If you don't distribute worldwide, say so. Some Web home pages offer the users a choice of languages; click on your native language and link to a set of pages that you can read without translating.

Step 2: Outline the content

Once you have a goal in mind, it helps to outline what content you want to include in the Web page or set of pages. As you outline, keep track of what content you merely need to collect, which you need to create, and which you need to retool for the online medium. Remember that some of the content may be links to information that's not part of your site — include that in your outline, too. The outline serves as a starting point for mapping out how the parts will interact.

Which of the information is simply text? Which text should be scrollable? Which text should be in short chunks that fit easily within a window of the browser?

What kind of interactivity do you need to build in? Do you need to collect any information about the visitors to the page? Are you going to try to qualify visitors by having them register their addresses or other information in a form? (That creates two tiers of visitors, browsers and users, whom you can attempt to contact in the future through the URLs they leave for you.)

Will the Web site link to any other pages on the same Web server or to external Web documents? Will you make internal links relative (all files in the same subdirectory or folder on the server, so only the unique part of the path name appears in each link address) or absolute (with complete path and file name for each link)?

Step 3: Choose a structure for the Web site

Once you have the big picture of what the Web pages need to cover and what external links you're likely to want, you can settle on a basic organization of the pages. Do you want a linear structure so users switch from screen to screen like a slideshow, using Next and Back navigation buttons? How about a branching structure, with a choice of major topics on the home page that link to content or a choice of subtopics? If a branching hierarchy would be too rigid, how about a more organic web structure with many links that interconnect the parts of the content? What about a hybrid structure that combines a formal hierarchy with some linear slide shows and a complex web as appropriate for the different parts of the site?

Whatever structure seems right for the purpose and content, if it's a complex site, it's a good idea to sketch out a map or storyboard for the pages, using lines to indicate links. You can make your map with pencil and paper, index cards and yarn on a bulletin board, a drawing program, or any other tool that works for you. (There's one program, NaviPress, that helps visualize the relationships in a set of Web pages.) Make sure the home page reflects the organization you choose; that really helps to orient users.

Stage Two: Building Pages

Once you have a plan for the pages, you can roll up your sleeves and get your hands into HTML. You can start with the home page and then move on to the other pages within a set, adjusting the home page design as necessary as you go along. You might feel more comfortable designing the linked pages first and finishing up with the home page; it doesn't really matter, so choose which approach fits your style and remember that it's a process.

Step 4: Code, preview, and revise

You'll find that you work in cycles: coding, placing graphics and links, and then previewing what you've done, changing the code, and previewing again in the browser software (that is, unless you're working with one of those HTML editing tools that offers "what you see is what you get"). As you become accustomed to the effect of the HTML formatting tags, you'll have fewer cycles of coding, previewing, and revising the code, but even experienced HTML tamers expect to go through many revisions.

Fortunately, finding mistakes in the code is relatively simple: Usually the flaw in the page points you to the part of the HTML that's not quite right.

Remember to format your HTML so that it's easy to revise and debug, and include comments about the code if someone else might maintain the HTML files later.

Step 5: Add internal and external links

Once you have the basic framework for your pages, you can add the relevant links and check whether they make sense. Obviously, you'll need to check and recheck links as you develop the material that links back and forth internally.

If you've planned carefully, you'll be able to add links to external pages as you go along. Or you can add external links later. Some pages have sections set aside for a changing set of links to external pages — you can arrange to change the links every week or every day or several times a day, depending on your target audience and the purpose of the page.

Step 6: Optimize for the slowest members of your target audience

Once the pages have all the elements in place, make sure they work for the slowest connections you expect your target audience to use. Remember that a lot of people who use online systems such as CompuServe, America Online, and Prodigy still have 28.8 Kbps or even 14.4 Kbps modems. If you want to reach the lowest common denominator, you need to test your pages at that speed over the online systems and make design changes or offer low-speed alternatives to accommodate these slower connections.

Stage Three: Testing

Just in case you didn't get the message yet: For great Web pages, plan to test, and test, and test your work.

Step 7: Test and revise the site yourself

Even when you think you've worked out all the kinks, it's not yet time to pat yourself on the back and celebrate. If you're serious about Web page design, you need to test the pages with all the browsers you intend to support, at the slowest speeds you expect in your target audience, and on different computer systems your target audience might have. For example, what happens to graphics when they're viewed on a monitor that shows fewer colors than yours?

Step 8: Have other testers check your work

You can only go so far in testing your own work. The same way you tend to overlook your own typos, someone else may find obvious flaws that you're blind to in your own Web pages. As much as is practical, have people in-house test your Web pages if you're creating a site at work or in an organization, or load it all on the Web server as a pilot project and ask a trusted few testers to use the pages and report back any problems or suggestions for improving your Web pages.

Stage Four: Loading the Files on the Web

When you have finished testing the files locally, you're ready to put them on the Web for a live test drive. You may need to do some preparation if you're sending the files to someone else's Web server for publishing.

Step 9: Prepare files for the server

Make sure your files are ready to go on the server. Put all the files for your pages in one folder (or one directory) on the hard disk of the Web server for your own site. Within that folder (or directory) you can name the file you mean to be the home page index.html — that's the file that's loaded as the home page by default by most Web server software.

If you're using someone else's server, find out if there are any file-naming conventions you need to follow — for example, you may need to limit file names to eight characters, plus a three-character extension, such as webpp.htm, for DOS-based servers.

If you're using someone else's server, you'll probably send your Web page files there via FTP, Zmodem file transfer, or some other electronic file transfer. Be careful to save Mac files in binary format, not MacBinary format, if you're sending them to a site that's not running a Mac server. If you're moving referenced text files to a server that's not a Mac server, maybe you can save them in the right format for that platform; check the file format options in your text editor's Save As dialog box.

Step 10: Double-check your URL

If you're not sure of the URL for your pages, check with the administrator for the Web site. Try out the URL to make sure it's correct before passing it around to testers or printing it on business cards.

Step 11: Test drive some more

This is the true test of your Web pages. Can you find and use them? What about the other testers you've lined up? Test, revise, reload, and retest. It may take a while to iron out the wrinkles in a complex set of pages, but hang in there.

If you've transferred your files to an alien system, you may see unexpected results such as line breaks in your Web page text where you didn't intend them, particularly in text formatted with the <PRE> tag. You may have double-spaced text where you meant to show single-spaced text, for example. If you can't easily solve the problem, you may need to use a UNIX filter to fix line break problems; consult the Web site administrator if you're stuck.

Last Stage: Announcing Your Web Page

Finally it's time to let the world know your Web page exists! Use the techniques in Chapter 18 to publicize your Web pages. And take a moment to celebrate your World Wide Web publishing debut.

Finding a Home for Your Web Page

Now that you've built a cool Web page or two, the natural question is, "Now what? Where can I put my pages so that everyone else on the World Wide Web can find and enjoy them?" That's an important question, but it's not as easy to answer as you might think. Why? Because there are seemingly a million different solutions, ranging from sites that advertise their willingness to host your Web pages for free (if they're not too big), to sites that charge a very small amount annually, to those that offer very fast connectivity, but bill you based on megabytes transferred (which means you definitely don't want to have lots of huge graphics!), and finally to sites that will host a reasonable set of Web pages for a small monthly fee.

If you're seeking a commercial presence, even more choices are available because now there are thousands of so-called *cybermalls* eager to offer disk space and access to their *commercial servers* in return for an often-steep monthly fee or a percentage of your online sales. A commercial server is one that can process credit card or other customer transactions — securely — over the Internet.

Regardless of what you choose, the most important factor, in my opinion, is to be able to match your realistic expectations for your page with the capabilities of the *presence provider* (as they're called in the biz). For example, if you want to create a page that will be viewed by thousands each day because you're going to include it in your print advertising or your mom can plug it on her nationally syndicated radio show, then you certainly need to put your page on a fast machine with a fast, reliable network connection. If you're just having fun and want your friends to visit, then a simpler setup with fewer capabilities at less cost should work just dandy.

Key Capabilities

The questions to ask when assessing key capabilities of presence providers, regardless of your performance demands, are

➡ What speed is the connection between the system where your pages will reside and the Internet?

Good answers to this question are T1 and T3. Bad answers are ISDN or a fast dialup.

➡ How many other sites are hosted on the same system?

The more Web sites on the system, the more likely you could be squeezed out in the crush of Web-related traffic.

➡ What guarantee of up-time and availability is offered?

A great site that's offline one day each week is worse than a slower system that guarantees 99 percent up-time.

➡ Can you access your pages online to make changes or add something new?

Because you've read this far and are now an expert at creating cool Web pages, you will also want some sort of easy access to your pages online, rather than having to mail in your changes and updates. If you have something new to add to your Web pages, you want to do it *now!*

Here's a run-down of some of the possibilities for free, inexpensive, and commercial Web page hosting. Which kind you choose is up to you, of course, and I don't necessarily vouch for the quality of any of these sites. They're just fast and seem to feature well-designed and — yes — cool Web pages.

Free Sites

I wouldn't be surprised to find a lot more options than the few I list here, but these should get you started. If you want to find more, there's a page on the Web that, although a bit out-of-date, does seem to list a number of places that offer free or cheap Web page space. It's on Turnpike Metropolis at

```
http://members.tripod.com/~jpsp1/sites.html
```

Geocities

The space isn't unlimited, and it's a bit tricky to get an account, but the Geocities concept is a brilliant one: It offers space for hundreds of thousands of different home pages, divided into virtual cities. Pick, for example, Rodeo Drive, and you'll be able to pick a "street address" and have it for your home page. A very fun concept, and there are some wild pages hosted on this terrific system.

```
http://www.geocities.com/
```

Phrantics Public Housing Project

This is a cooperative venture among five or so different Web sites. Each of the members of the Public Housing Project offers free Web space, with a few caveats. Your best bet is to pop straight over to the list of landlords at the URL shown below and read the details for yourself.

```
http://www.phrantic.com/
```

Tripod

Like Geocities, Tripod is a huge online community offering free Web space to anyone who would like to join the more than 750,000 members. The Tripod site is divided into 28 different "pods," or areas, and lots of fun sites reside on this collection of high-speed server systems.

```
http://www.tripod.com/
```

Inexpensive Presence Providers

The prices for Web presence can range all over the map, and it's astonishing how many different firms now offer some sort of Web site service. The majority of them, though, are clearly geared to grabbing a slice of the business market, as thousands of companies worldwide come onto the Internet. If you're looking for somewhere to keep your personal home page, you might want to carefully consider which of these spots has the aura you seek. They definitely differ quite a bit!

The following listing doesn't even scratch the surface of all the available options. Hundreds, if not thousands, of firms offer relatively low-cost Web space. This is a sampling of different-sized firms so you can get an idea of what's available.

Best Internet Communications

Based in the Silicon Valley, Best offers a wide variety of different Web hosting packages, including one that'd work just fine for your new pages. For $30/month, you get 25MB of disk space, although they do charge for excessive network traffic. The Web pages for my consulting firm, Intuitive Systems, are hosted on a Best system machine, and I recommend Best to all my clients. *Tell 'em I sent you!*

```
http://www.best.com/
```

Di's Online Cafe

A nicely done site that offers you the chance to have your home page as part of the site, though it's not very easy to find. Based in Mobile, Alabama. Contact them for fee structure.

```
http://www.dibbs.net/cafe/
```

Digital Landlords

Only $28/month to host your home page (three-month minimum), although there's no indication of how much they may limit your disk space or bandwidth use. Digital Landlords hosts both personal and business information at this Atlanta-based Internet system.

```
http://home.clever.net/
```

Netcom Communications

Netcom is one of the largest Internet-only companies and has a good track record of growing its business by offering national accessibility at low cost. If you sign up as a NetCruiser user, you also get 1MB of Web space for free.

```
http://www.netcom.com/
```

Northcoast Internet

The group that runs this Northern California company is really cool and fun to work with. In fact, my "Embot" program lives on this system. Check out this site for its inexpensive Web hosting prices too: fees start at $25/month.

```
http://www.northcoast.com/
```

The Well

If you're looking for a funky and fun online community with lots of writers, musicians, and even a few members of the Grateful Dead, then the Well, created by the Whole Earth Access team, is the spot for you. Web page hosting is inexpensive here, too, starting at $5/month for each 2MB of storage space if you have an account on the Well, which starts at $15/month.

```
http://www.well.com/
```

Commercial Hosts / Cybermalls

If you think that a lot of new companies have popped up offering Web space, you haven't seen the absolutely frantic explosion of commercial hosts and so-called cybermalls! It's astounding. A year ago there were perhaps a dozen or so, and now there are thousands of these, ranging from large, complex, well-funded systems to a PC in someone's basement. If you're hoping to gain a new income stream for your business from the online community, you'll want to make doubly sure that the company you sign up with has the speed and reliability that you need and that the other shops in the mall are acceptable to you and your customers.

Don't forget about security and the possibility of digital, online commerce, with secure transactions that let you take credit card orders directly online. For more information about these topics, I recommend you pick up a copy of the book *The Internet Business Guide* by Rosalind Resnick and me (SAMS.NET, 1994).

Best Internet Communications

The same firm I listed earlier as an inexpensive presence provider also has a complete commerce package available and hosts a large number of commercial sites, including the Oakland As' baseball team, the Internet Mall, and more!

```
http://www.best.com/bizcomm.html
```

Branch Mall

With hundreds of stores, one of the largest and most established of the electronic shopping malls is Branch Mall, from Branch Internet Systems. Branch Mall offers your customers access not only through the Web, but through Gopher and e-mail too, all as part of one price package.

```
http://www.branch.com/
```

CyberHouse

This firm will build a Web presence for you, but it's also happy to work with you on installing custom lines, hosting your Web information on its server, and using its secure server for online transactions.

```
http://www.cyberhouse.com/
```

Downtown Anywhere

This is one of the few firms that's been around longer than a few months, and it's always had a terrific vision of how to help build a compelling site. It also offers you space for whatever cool Web information you'd like to make available yourself.

```
http://www.awa.com/
```

ViaWeb

This is an example of a different kind of Web site, one that lets you focus on the products you're selling and not worry so much about the Web page design. Of course, if you've just finished reading this book, you probably want to design your own pages, but a combination of professional pages for online ordering of your products and your own custom pages for other parts of your site might prove a good solution.

```
http://www.viaweb.com/
```

The Virtual Village

The Virtual Village, based in Hawaii, offers a small-town metaphor for its commercial space. The Village includes a variety of shops and will rent you space for your commercial presence.

```
http://www.interpac.net/village/
```

Not Enough Choices?

You can also dig around in the ever-fun Yahoo! online directory to find a wide variety of Web presence providers. And remember that if the provider can't even publicize itself, it's not likely to help you publicize your site. Pop over to http://www.yahoo.com and search for Web presence, or perhaps web, and your city or state.

Nationally distributed Internet-related magazines can be a good place to find presence provider advertisements, too. A few magazines immediately come to mind: *PC World, Internet World, Internet Life,* and *Boardwatch*. Finally, don't forget to check with your local computer magazines or newspapers. Most of the major cities in the United States now have one or more computer-related publications, and the advertisements in these are a terrific place to learn about local Internet companies and their capabilities. If you have access, I'd particularly recommend *Computer Currents*, which is available in at least eight U.S. cities.

Also remember that there's absolutely no reason you have to work with a company in your own city. After you have some sort of access to the Internet (perhaps through school or work), you can easily work with a presence provider located anywhere.

Glossary

To achieve precision in communication, experts and amateurs alike speak in what sounds an awful lot like a secret code. This Glossary is a decoder ring of sorts that should help you understand the various mystery words surrounding HTML and the World Wide Web.

anchor

A spot in a document that actually links to either another place in the document or another document (a hypertext link). Also, the spot elsewhere in the document that can be quickly reached through a hypertext link.

anonymous FTP

A scheme by which users can retrieve files over the Internet without having an account on the remote system. Usually, the user logs in as anonymous and leaves his or her e-mail address as the password.

attribute

An addition to an HTML tag that qualifies or extends the meaning of the tag. For example, in `<body BGCOLOR=blue>`, the underlined text is the attribute.

boldface

To set text off with a heavier font; **this text is boldface**.

bookmark

A Web URL that's automatically stored by the browser software for easy access later (also see *hot list*).

browser

Software program such as winWeb, MacWeb, or Netscape that can read and navigate HTML documents. Browsers are the client application that you run on your PC or Mac.

data

The never-ending stream of stuff that appears on the Internet, as differentiated from *information*, which is data that has some meaning or value to the user.

e-mail

Electronic mail — a convenient way to send messages to other users or groups without the hassle of paper or postage stamps.

Ethernet

A low-level protocol for high-speed networks. The Internet runs on Ethernet connections. Ethernet was invented a few decades ago by my friend Bob Metcalfe.

Explorer, Internet Explorer

A powerful and feature-laden Web browser available for free from Microsoft Corporation.

font

A particular use of a typeface. Bodoni Poster is a typeface, but Bodoni Poster 12-point italic is a font.

frame

An advanced Web browser feature that allows you to have multiple individual pages displayed simultaneously, one in each *pane* of the viewer's browser window.

FTP (File Transfer Protocol)

The way files are sent and received over the Internet. Typically, a user needs an account on the remote system unless it allows anonymous FTP access (see *anonymous FTP*).

Gopher

A popular information-distribution service based on a hierarchical menu system; often overshadowed by the more sophisticated World Wide Web. The main Gopher site is at the University of Minnesota.

home page

The central or initial document seen by visitors to your Web site. You can have many other Web pages connected to your home page.

hostname

The unique combination of computer and domain name that describes a particular computer on the Internet. For example, `sage.cc.purdue.edu` is a hostname in the Purdue University Computer Center domain. On the other hand, some people believe just the name of the computer itself is its hostname, with all additional information the domain name. That would mean the same computer would have a hostname of `sage` and a domain name of `cc.purdue.edu`. There's no consensus.

hot list

A Web URL that is automatically stored by the browser software for easy access later; also known as a collection of *bookmarks*.

HTML (HyperText Markup Language)

The language that is used to define and describe the page layout of documents displayed in a World Wide Web browser. HTML is an application of SGML (Standard Generalized Markup Language).

HTML tag

A specific formatting instruction within an HTML document. Tags are usually contained within angle brackets, as in `<HTML>`.

HTTP (HyperText Transfer Protocol)

The underlying system whereby Web documents are transferred over the Internet.

hypermedia

Any combination of hypertext and graphics, video, audio, and other media. The World Wide Web is a hypermedia environment because it allows multiple types of media to be used simultaneously in a document.

hypertext

An interconnected web of text information, wherein any given word or phrase may link to another point in the document or to another document.

information

The small subset of data that is actually useful and meaningful to you at the current moment.

inline graphics

Graphics that appear beside the text in a Web page when viewed via a browser (as opposed to graphics that require separate viewer programs).

the Internet

The global network of networks that enables some or all of the following: exchange of e-mail messages, files, Usenet newsgroups, and World Wide Web pages. Also known as the Net.

italics

A typographic convention typically used for emphasis or citations; *this text is italicized.*

link

A word, picture, or other area of a Web page that users can click to move to another spot in the document or to another document.

markup language

A special type of programming language that allows users to describe the desired appearance and structural features of a document.

Mosaic

The original graphical World Wide Web browser program developed at the National Center for Supercomputing Applications at the University of Illinois. Its release in 1993 sparked the explosive growth of the Web and helped boost interest in the Internet. Many software programs similar to Mosaic — commercial, shareware, and freeware versions for almost any platform — have been developed since Mosaic's release.

Navigator

A World Wide Web browser developed by Netscape Communications, created by some of the original NCSA Mosaic programmers. Navigator is the most popular browser on the Net.

the Net

Another term for the *Internet*, and an amusing movie with Sandra Bullock as a programmer who never leaves the house, eats pizza she orders online, yet looks great in a bikini.

ordered list

A list of items, often numbered, that describe steps in a process (steps 1, 2, 3, and so on).

pointer

A word, picture, or other area that users can click to move to another spot in the document or to another document; same as *link*.

port

A particular "frequency" used to transfer a particular type of information between Internet computers; FTP uses one specific port, whereas HTTP uses another. Somewhat analogous to television channels.

SGML (Standard Generalized Markup Language)

The markup language that is the parent of HTML. SGML provides a means of defining markup for any number of document types (such as HTML). You don't mark up text in SGML, per se — you mark up text using an application or instance of SGML. HTML is one of those applications.

TCP/IP (Transmission Control Protocol/ Internet Protocol)

A system networks use to communicate with each other over the Internet.

telnet

An Internet service that enables users to log on to a remote system and work on it as though they were directly connected to the system on-site.

typeface

A particular design of a set of characters and symbols. Times and Courier are common typefaces. A specific size and style of a typeface — Courier 12 point, for example — is known as a *font*.

UNIX

A very powerful operating system that is the object of a lot of criticism and adoration. Probably the most common operating system on the Internet, UNIX has some Internet features built right into it.

unordered list

A list of items that have no implied order; commonly, a set of bulleted items.

URL (Uniform Resource Locator)

The standardized way in which any resource is identified within a Web document or to a Web browser. Most URLs consist of the service, host name, and directory path. An example of a URL: `http://www.timeinc.com/ time/daily/time/latest.html`.

World Wide Web

A massive, distributed hypermedia environment that is part of the Internet. Consisting of millions of documents, thousands of sites, and dozens of indexes, the Web is a fluid and often surprising hive of information and activity.

HTML
Quick
Reference

Appendix E

When you've learned how to create documents in HyperText Markup Language, it's inevitable that you'll need to quickly double-check the form of a particular option, the spelling of a tag, or some other detailed information. That's why I include this helpful quick reference material.

Adding Images (Chapter 8)

`<IMG`	Image inclusion tag
`SRC=url`	Source to the graphic file
`ALT=text`	Text alternative to display, if needed
`ALIGN=alignment`	Image alignment on page / alignment of material surrounding the image. Possible values: top, middle, bottom, left, right
`HEIGHT=x`	Height of graphic (in pixels)
`WIDTH=x`	Width of graphic (in pixels)
`BORDER=x`	Border around graphic when used as hyperlink
`HSPACE=x`	Additional horizontal space around graphic (in pixels)
`VSPACE=x`	Additional vertical space around graphic (in pixels)

Basic HTML (Chapter 3 and elsewhere)

\<ADDRESS\>	\</ADDRESS\>	Address and creator information
\<BODY\>	\</BODY\>	Body of the HTML page
\<BR		Line break
CLEAR=*opt*		Force break to specified margin. Possible values: left, right, all.
\<HEAD\>	\</HEAD\>	HTML formatting information
\<H*n*\>	\</H*n*\>	Document header level (*n* = 1-6)
\<HR\>		Horizontal rule
\<HTML\>	\</HTML\>	Define a Web-formatted file
\<P\>	\</P\>	Paragraph breaks
\<PRE\>	\</PRE\>	Preformatted information
\<!--	--\>	Comments within HTML

Advanced HTML (Chapter 10 and elsewhere)

\<CENTER\>	\</CENTER\>	Center material on the page
\<HR		Horizontal rule
SIZE=*x*		Height of rule (in pixels)
WIDTH=*x*		Width of rule (in pixels or percentage)
NOSHADE		Turn off shading in horizontal rule
ALIGN=*align*		Alignment of horizontal rule on page (left, center, right)
COLOR=*color*		Color of horizontal rule (RGB or name) (IE only)

`<BODY`	Body of the document
`BGCOLOR=color`	Background color for page (RGB or color name)
`TEXT=color`	Color of text on page (RGB or color name)
`LINK=color`	Color of unvisited links on page (RGB or color name)
`VLINK=color`	Color of visited links on page (RGB or color name)
`ALINK=color`	Color of links during user click (RGB or color name)
`BACKGROUND=url`	Background graphic for page
`<EMBED`	Embed audio on a Web page
`SRC=url`	Source of the audio file
`WIDTH=x`	Width of the displayed control, if any
`HEIGHT=x`	Height of the displayed control, if any
`HIDDEN=value`	If "true", then control is hidden from view
`CONTROLS=opt`	Type of display: "console" or "smallconsole"
`VOLUME=x`	Specify volume of the playback (0-255)
`LOOP=x`	Number of times to loop the audio
`<STYLE    </STYLE>`	Style sheet information specified
`TYPE=val`	Type of style sheet. Usually "text/css".

Internet Explorer-Only (Chapter 10)

`<MARQUEE`	Scrolling marquee
`BEHAVIOR=opt`	Behavior of the marquee
`DIRECTION=opt`	Direction from which the marquee scrolls (left, right)

HEIGHT=x	Height of marquee
WIDTH=x	Width of marquee
HSPACE=x	Additional horizontal space around marquee
VSPACE=x	Additional vertical space around marquee
BGCOLOR=color	Background color of marquee (RGB or color name)
SCROLLAMOUNT=x	Amount of material to scroll (in pixels) per unit time
SCROLLDELAY=x	Delay between refreshes in marquee (in milliseconds)
<BGSOUND	Background sound
SRC=url	Source of the audio file
LOOP=x	Number of times to loop the audio

Building Forms (Chapter 12)

<FORM	</FORM>	Interactive HTML form
ACTION=url		CGI program on server that receives data
METHOD=method		How data is transmitted to server (GET or POST)
<LABEL	</LABEL>	Label associated with a specific element
FOR=s		Specify the element associated with the label (use ID=s in the element)
<FIELDSET>	</FIELDSET>	Divide form into logical parts
<LEGEND	</LEGEND>	Name associated with fieldset
ALIGN=s		Specify alignment of legend in display (top, bottom, left, right)
TABINDEX=x		Specify the order of elements when user pressed the Tab key

ACCESSKEY=*c*	Specific key to allow keyboard shortcuts to specific elements
DISABLED	Element is disabled, but displayed on screen
READONLY	Element is displayed on screen but not editable
<INPUT	Text or other data-input field
TYPE=*opt*	Type of <INPUT> entry field. Possible values: text, button, password, checkbox, hidden, file, radio, submit, reset, image.
NAME=*name*	Symbolic name of field value
VALUE=*value*	Default content of text field
CHECKED=*opt*	Button/box checked by default
SIZE=*x*	Number of characters in text field
MAXLENGTH=*x*	Maximum characters accepted
onClick=*s*	Name of script to execute when button is clicked (usually JavaScript)
<SELECT </SELECT>	Grouped check boxes
NAME=*name*	Symbolic name of field value
SIZE=*x*	Number of items to show at once (default = 1)
MULTIPLE	Allow multiple items to be selected
<OPTION	Specific choice within a <SELECT> range
VALUE=*value*	Resultant value of this menu choice
<TEXTAREA </TEXTAREA>	Multiline text-entry field
NAME=*name*	Symbolic name of field value
ROWS=*x*	Number of rows in <TEXTAREA> box
COLS=*x*	Number of columns (characters) on a line within the box

Character Formatting (Chapter 4)

`<B>`	`</B>`	Display text in bold
`<I>`	`</I>`	Display text in italic
`<U>`	`</U>`	Underline specified text
`<TT>`	`</TT>`	Monospace text
`<CITE>`	`</CITE>`	Bibliographic citation
`<CODE>`	`</CODE>`	Code listing
`<DFN>`	`</DFN>`	Word definition
`<EM>`	`</EM>`	Logical emphasis style
`<KBD>`	`</KBD>`	Keyboard text (similar to `<CODE>`)
`<SAMP>`	`</SAMP>`	Sample user input
`<STRONG>`	`</STRONG>`	Logical stronger emphasis
`<VAR>`	`</VAR>`	Program or other variable
`<BASEFONT`		Specify the default font size for the page
`SIZE=n>`		(range 1-7, 7 being largest. Default: 3)
`<FONT`	`</FONT>`	Specify attributes for subsequent text
`SIZE=n`		Size of text: range is 1-7, 7 being largest
`FACE="a,b"`		Specify typeface to use: a, if available, or b
`COLOR=s`		Color of text, either as color name or RGB value

Image Maps (Chapter 11)

`<IMG`	Image inclusion tag
`ISMAP`	Specify that it's a server-side image map
`USEMAP=mapname`	Use the specified client-side image map

LOWSRC=*url*	Lower-resolution image to load first (Navigator only)
<MAP </MAP>	Specify regions of a client-side image map
NAME=*mapname*	Name of image map (corresponds to USEMAP in <IMG> tag)
<AREA	Define a specific region in an image map
SHAPE=*shape*	Shape of region. Possible values: rect, circ, point, poly.
COORDS=*coords*	Coordinates on image. Value varies by region shape.
HREF=*url*	URL associated with the specified region

Frames (Chapters 9 and 15)

<FRAMESET </FRAMESET>	Frame-based page layout defined
COLS=*x*	Number of, and relative sizes of, column frames
ROWS=*x*	Number of, and relative sizes of, column rows
BORDER=*x*	Specify border on or off for the FRAMESET (0 or 1)
FRAMEBORDER=*x*	Specify size of frame border
FRAMESPACING=*x*	Amount of spacing between frame panes
<FRAME	Definition of a specific frame
SRC=*url*	Source URL for the frame
NAME=*name*	Name of the pane (used with TARGET=name as a part of the <A> anchor tag)
SCROLLING=*scrl*	Set scrollbar options. Possible values: on, off, auto.
FRAMEBORDER=*x*	Size of border around the frame

MARGINHEIGHT=x		Additional spacing above and below specific pane
MARGINWIDTH=x		Additional spacing to the left and right of the pane
<NOFRAMES>	</NOFRAMES>	Section of page displayed for users who can't see a frame
<IFRAME		Inline frame (IE only)
SRC=url		Source for the frame
NAME=s		Name of the window (for TARGET usage)
HEIGHT=x		Height of the embedded frame (pixels or percentage)
WIDTH=x		Width of the embedded frame (pixels or percentage)

Hypertext References (Chapters 6 & 7)

<A	</A>	Anchor tag
HREF=url		Pointer to hypertext reference
HREF=#name		Reference to internal anchor name
NAME=name		Defining an internal anchor

Lists (Chapter 5)

<DD>		Definition description
<DL>	</DL>	Definition list
<DT>		Definition term

`<LI>`	List item
`<OL`	Ordered list
`TYPE=type`	Type of numbering. Possible values: A, a, I, i, 1
`START=x`	Starting number of ordered list
`<UL`	Unordered list
`TYPE=shape`	Shape of bullet to use. Possible values: circle, square, disc.

Scripting Your Page (Chapter 11)

`<SCRIPT` `</SCRIPT>`	Include a script, usually JavaScript, in Web page
`LANGUAGE=lang`	Language used for script
`EVENT=event`	Event that triggers specified script
`FOR=objectname`	Name of object on page that script acts upon
`<OBJECT` `</OBJECT>`	Include an arbitrary object on the page
`CODETYPE=opt`	MIME type of object (ex: application/octet-stream)
`CLASSID=url`	Identify the object or class of object (Java only)
`WIDTH=x`	Width of space needed for object on page
`HEIGHT=x`	Height of object on page
`<PARAM`	Parameters to send to OBJECT
`NAME=name`	Name of parameter
`VALUE=str`	Value of named parameter

Special Character Codes for HTML Documents (Chapter 5)

Character	HTML Code	Common Meaning
&	&	Ampersand
<	<	Less than
>	>	Greater than
©	©	Copyright symbol
®	®	Registered trademark symbol

See Chapter 5 and Chapter 15 for a more extensive list of special character codes within HTML.

Tables (Chapter 9)

`<TABLE>    </TABLE>`	Web-based table
`BORDER=x`	Border around table (pixels or percentage)
`CELLPADDING=x`	Additional space within table cells (in pixels)
`CELLSPACING=x`	Additional space between table cells (in pixels)
`WIDTH=x`	Forced table width (in pixels or percentage)
`FRAME=val`	Fine tuning the frames within the table (see Table 9-2)
`RULES=val`	Fine tuning the rules of the table (see Table 9-3)
`BORDERCOLOR=color`	Specify color of table border (RGB or color name)
`BORDERCOLORLIGHT=color`	Lighter of the two colors specified (RGB or color name)
`BORDERCOLORDARK=color`	Darker of the two colors specified (RGB or color name)
`ALIGN=left`	Align table on the left side of the page, with text flowing around the right

ALIGN=right		Align table on the right side of the page, with text flowing to left
HSPACE=x		Additional horizontal space around table (pixels)
VSPACE=x		Additional vertical space around table (pixels)
COLS=x		Specify the number of columns in the table
<COLGROUP>	</COLGROUP>	Define a set of column definitions with <COL> tags
<COL		A specific column width defined
WIDTH=x		Width of the column, in pixels, percentage or '*' notation
<THEAD>	</THEAD>	Organization for tables: this denotes table head material
<TBODY>	</TBODY>	Organization for tables: this denotes the body of the table
<TR	</TR>	Table row
BGCOLOR=color		Specify the background color for the entire row (RGB or color name)
ALIGN=align		Alignment of cells in this row (left, center, right)
<TD	</TD>	Table data cell
BGCOLOR=color		Background color for data cell (RGB or color name)
COLSPAN=x		Number of columns for this data cell to span
ROWSPAN=x		Number of rows for this data cell to span
ALIGN=align		Alignment of material within the data cell. Possible values: left, center, right.
VALIGN=align		Vertical alignment of material within the data cell. Possible values: top, middle, bottom.
BACKGROUND=url		Specify the background picture for the cell
NOWRAP		Prevent word wrap within a data cell (be careful with this tag)

ALIGN=baseline	Align data cell with the baseline of adjacent text
ALIGN=char	Align a column on a specific character (default ".")
ALIGN=justify	Line up both the left and right margin for the text.

What's a URL? (Chapter 2)

service :// hostname (:port) / directory (and *filename*)

service can be:

http	HyperText Transfer Protocol — Web pages
mailto	E-mail address
telnet	telnet to a remote system
ftp	FTP file archive
news	Usenet news server

What's on the CD-ROM

Appendix F

As part of my efforts to make *Creating Cool HTML 4 Web Pages* a truly cool book, I've arranged for you to have lots of fun and useful shareware and freeware on this CD-ROM. This appendix (or should I call this a spleen and get it over with?) describes what's on the disk, including the home page for the software on the Internet and directions for installing from the CD-ROM. Because this is a cross-platform CD-ROM, there are some packages that are just for Windows users and others that are just for the Macintosh users. Please pay attention to the platform specified, so that you don't get frustrated when the coolest sounding program isn't, in fact, available for your computer!

A quick, nagging, reminder: The vast majority of the software included on this CD-ROM is shareware. Shareware means that the developer has spent hundreds of hours creating a professional-quality program, but instead of forcing you to buy it and then decide whether it really meets your needs, they're letting you get it for free. Their hope is that if you like it, you'll send in your shareware registration fee, which is usually quite small. So that we continue to have these great programs available directly without having the middlemen of all the software stores and distributors, it's very important that you *register your shareware* if you're going to use it! Besides, if you use the program and don't register it by sending in the shareware fee, I predict that you'll gradually feel more and more guilty about it.

Web Browsers

There's not much you can do with Web page design without a Web browser to view your creations, and because it's so important to test your page designs on both major environments (Netscape and Microsoft) and both operating systems (Mac and Windows 95), I've included four different Web browsers with this book. Count'em: both Netscape Navigator and Microsoft Internet Explorer, each for both Macintosh and Windows 95. Whichever is your favorite, remember again that really great Web pages look cool in all programs.

Internet Explorer (Macintosh and Windows)

Internet Explorer, as you no doubt know, is Microsoft's Web browser software, which Microsoft is integrating into the functionality of Windows 98. I've included the latest version, 4.0, on this CD-ROM for both Macintosh and Windows.

Home page: http://www.microsoft.com/products/prodref/206_ov.htm

To install Internet Explorer for the Macintosh, look in the Internet Explorer folder under Shareware/Mac Software. Then double-click the installer that corresponds to your platform: PowerPC or 68k.

To install Internet Explorer for Windows, double-click setup.exe in the Internet Explorer folder, and then follow the prompts onscreen.

Navigator (Macintosh and Windows)

Navigator is Netscape's Web browser software, and it currently has the greatest market share. I've included both Macintosh and Windows versions on the CD-ROM; for the Macintosh, I've included versions for both PowerPC and 68K. Navigator comes as part of Netscape's integrated Internet package, Communicator, or as a stand-alone product.

Home page: http://home.netscape.com/

To install Navigator for Windows, double-click n32e404.exe in the Navigator folder under Win 95 on the CD-ROM; then follow the prompts onscreen.

To install Navigator for Macintosh, first choose the appropriate folder under Mac Software for your platform: PowerPC or 68K. Then open the Netscape Installer folder and double-click Netscape Installer; then follow the prompts onscreen.

Web Tools

You've gotten this far, so you're already a complete Web design expert. You can code in raw HTML and do everything to your site including making it jump through various hoops, but it'd still be nice to have some tools to help see what's going on and develop your pages faster. That's the focus of this section.

Coffee Cup Image Editor (Windows)

Don't be confused by the weird name. The Coffee Cup Image Editor is a straightforward tool that helps you create your own sophisticated image maps quickly. The program supports both client-side and server-side output, too.

Home page: `http://www.coffeecup.com/`

To install, simply double-click the setup.exe icon within the Coffee Cup Image Editor folder on the CD-ROM. It will prompt you for where you'd like to install the program on your PC.

Cookie Commander (Macintosh)

A lot of people will tell you cookies are evil creatures. I hope, however, that your reading this book and exploring how cookies actually work has saved you from such muddled thinking. Anyway, it's certainly interesting to know what's going on with the cookies on your computer, seeing what different systems are storing on your hard disk, and whether it's at all comprehensible. That's why I'm including this simple program, Cookie Commander.

Home page: `http://www.chelmsford.com/home/star/liquid/welcome.html`

To install, just drag the CCommander application and the readme file onto your own hard disk, and then double-click the application to start it and see what cookies you've got stored on your system.

FTP Explorer (Windows)

One of my favorite Windows 95 programs, FTP Explorer, from the talented Alan Chavis, is a great file-transfer application that makes keeping your local files and the copies of your Web files on your ISP system a snap.

Home page: http://www.ftpx.com/

To install FTP Explorer, double-click setup.exe and follow the directions in the Install Wizard to place it in your preferred directory on your PC.

 I really wanted to include the great Fetch FTP client for Mac users, but Dartmouth University, owner of the program, has some weird and unfathomable restrictions, so instead I will simply encourage Mac users to download the program from your favorite shareware archive (I always use http://www.shareware.com/).

Image Mapper (Macintosh)

There are a number of different image map helpers available for the Macintosh, but I think that Image Mapper is hands-down one of the best you can get. It supports a wide variety of graphics formats and can output client-side or server-side maps. There's also support — albeit kind of limited — for JavaScript and Java-based rollover events and more.

Home page:
http://www.dcs.gla.ac.uk/~snaddosg/help/updates.html

To install Image Mapper, drag all the files in the ImageMapper folder from the CD-ROM into a folder on your own hard disk and you're ready to try the program.

Quid Pro Quo (Macintosh)

An elegant and simple Web server for your Macintosh, Quid Pro Quo will enable you to explore what it's like to not only have pages on your computer, but to actually run a server. Hook it up to the Net 24 hours a day and you can be your own Internet Service Provider!

Home page: http://www.socialeng.com/

To install Quid Pro Quo, click the Install Quid Pro Quo icon in the Finder. The installer will then ask you to specify where you'd like to have the program installed on your hard disk and unpack all the pieces necessary.

Text Editors

If you have a computer to read the CD-ROM, then you already have some text editors available on your system. On a PC, you've definitely got NotePad and WordPad, both of which are included with the Windows 95 operating system, and if you're on a Macintosh, TeachText and SimpleText are the equivalent programs. But more sophisticated tools can definitely make your life better, and that's why I've included a small selection of different, alternative editors for your perusal.

ApplePie (Windows)

As a general rule, I don't like to use HTML editors because I think their view of clean and correct HTML code is different from my own. I do, nonetheless, occasionally delve into one of these tools to get started quickly. ApplePie is a good example of a simple program that offers you the ability to speed up the development of your HTML pages.

To install ApplePie, double-click setup.exe and follow the directions in the installer.

BBEdit Lite (Macintosh)

If you're on a Macintosh, you already know that BBEdit is the #1 HTML source and programmer's text editor available. Surprisingly, BBEdit is rather expensive (about $200), so it's good news that the developers, Bare Bones Software, also have a shareware version of the program that offers the majority of the useful features available. That's what BBEdit Lite is, and it's a great part of your Web designer toolbox.

Home Page: http://www.barebones.com/

To install BBEdit Lite, copy the BBEdit Lite 4.01 folder to your hard drive, and then double-click BBEdit Lite 4.0. For configuration options, read the BBEdit Lite QuickStart and About BBEdit Lite.

NotePad Plus (Windows)

NotePad is actually a very useful editor that's included with Windows 95, but there are a number of quirky things about the program that make it less than ideal as a Web page editor. That's where the slick NotePad Plus by Rogier Meurs is a great alternative. The ability to open multiple files simultaneously is the best reason for the switch, but there are lots of nice bells and whistles you'll find in the program, too.

Home page: `http://lelystad.flnet.nl/~Omeurs01/`

To install NotePad Plus, drag and drop the NotePad+ application onto your hard disk. If you want to change Windows 95 to use NotePad Plus instead of NotePad when it needs an editor, follow the directions in the "README" file included.

Tex-Edit Plus (Macintosh)

BBEdit is a great text editor, but it's really a programmer's editor. Tex-Edit is a good replacement for the general-purpose TeachText and SimpleText editors. In fact, I wish Apple would just license and include Tex-Edit instead of their tools, since it's such an improvement, yet just as small and just as fast to use. I think you'll like it too.

Home Page: `http://members.aol.com/tombb/`

To install Tex-Edit Plus, simply drag all the files in the Tex-Edit Plus folder onto your hard disk, then start the program by double-clicking the icon that looks like the state of Texas (Tex-Edit, Texas, get it?).

WebWeaver (Windows)

As I noted for ApplePie, I am not a huge fan of HTML-producing programs and editors, but occasionally will find something that can help get you rolling with your Web site development quickly. WebWeaver has been around for a while and is a good example of a useful HTML development tool. Try it and see if you think it helps speed up your page development.

Home page: `http://www.mcwebsoftware.com/`

To install WebWeaver, double-click setup.exe and follow the directions in the installer wizard.

Graphics

Text-only Web pages can look nice, but there's no question that to really make your pages cool, you'll want to add graphics. But, as discussed in Chapter 8, how do you get graphics? One solution is to create your own, and that's what the tools in this area of the CD-ROM enable you to do; from creating GIF animations to building your own images from scratch, these should get you started developing an attractive veneer on your site!

GraphicConverter (Macintosh)

This is one of my favorite examples of a great shareware program. I've enjoyed watching GraphicConverter grow and improve year after year as it's become the absolute best choice for any sort of translation from one graphics format to another. It's also a capable editor, and you'll find you can do some very attractive work in this application.

Home page: `http://www.lemkesoft.de/`

To install GraphicConverter, double-click the Install GraphicConverter icon.

GIF Builder (Macintosh)

This is an older program but is still my favorite for building animated GIF images. Simply drop all the images you want to use onto the program, then you can easily alter the speed of switching images, the transition effects, and much more. A must-have for building effective banner adverts.

Home page: `http://iawww.epfl.ch/Staff/Yves.Piguet/clip2gif-home/GifBuilder.html`

To install this program, simply drag all the files in the GIF Builder folder onto your hard disk in the location of your choice.

Animagic (Windows)

This is a nice program for creating animated GIF images on your Windows machine without much fuss. It supports a variety of graphic formats and has some very cool capabilities that you'll find useful if you spend some time experimenting.

Home page: `http://www.rtlsoft.com/animagic/`

Installation of Animagic is easy: just double-click setup.exe.

Paint Shop Pro (Windows)

This is unquestionably the best graphics editor I've included on the CD-ROM because, not only does it do almost everything that the Mac GraphicConverter does, but it's also a very powerful and full-featured graphics editor and composition program, too. Spend some time reading the documentation included with this program and you'll find that you can get some terrific results with it quickly.

Home page: `http://www.jasc.com/`

To install Paint Shop Pro, double-click paintshoppro.exe on the CD-ROM. It will then lead you through all the steps to unpack and install the program on your Windows system.

Fun and Games

I admit it: Sometimes when I'm starting to go bug-eyed looking at the computer I take some time off and play a computer game! I looked and looked for fun and entertaining games that didn't involve knee-jerk killing and was surprised that I didn't find anything I thought was really good on the Windows platform. If you have suggestions of great Windows shareware, I'd love to hear about it!

For this CD-ROM, I have therefore included three terrific Mac shareware games: Hearts Deluxe, Enigma, and the amazing Escape Velocity. They're all easy to install and I think you'll find them quite enjoyable.

Wrap-Up

I hope all this software is valuable and fun for you. If there are programs here that you think aren't up to snuff, or other programs that you think would be a great addition to the CD-ROM, let me know!

Dave Taylor

`taylor@intuitive.com`

Symbols

<SAMP> </SAMP> (sample user input) tag, 60
sans-serif font family, 280
scanning images for use in Web pages, 140-142
 copyright laws pertaining to, 142
 FAQ online Web site, 142
<SCRIPT> </SCRIPT> tag, 215
scripts, for receiving information from forms, 268
scrolling attribute, frames, 174
scrolling messages, JavaScript, 220-222
scrolling text, in Explorer marquees, 194-196
Search button, Netscape Navigator version 4.0 toolbar, 13
Search Engine Watch, Web site address, 333
search sites, registering with, 339-346
searching other sites from your page, 246-249
section-block notation, 34, 39
section heads, defining, 43-46
sections, breaking your documents into, 38-40
Security button, Netscape Navigator version 4.0 toolbar, 13
sed command in UNIX, using to decode URLs, 267
<SELECT> </SELECT> FORM tag, 232-234
 SIZE option in, 234
semicolon (;), in HTML code, 73
serif font family, 280
server-side image maps, 204-207
server-side includes versus the <OBJECT> tag, 327
SGML (Standard Generalized Markup Language), 31, 204
shades, specifying for horizontal rules, 183-184
shareware graphics packages, 137-138
Shift-Reload, forcing a new copy of a page with, 13
Shockwave plug-in, Macromedia Web site address, 229
signature information, formatting in HTML, 37
Silencing Critical Voices Web site, 129-132
SIZE attribute, in <HR> tag, 183
SIZE option, <SELECT> tag, 234
SNAP!, joining directory site, 341

soft hyphens (­), HTML 4.0, 328
sound
 adding to Web pages, 146-147
 recording your own for Web pages, 147
spaces, nonbreaking, 75
<SPAN> </SPAN> tag, 289
special characters, in HTML documents, 73-75, *73*
SRC=*filename* attribute, <IMG> tag, 111-115
START extension, ordered lists, 186-188
start page, changing your default, 17-18, *18*
Stephens, Chris, 143
Stop button, Netscape Navigator version 4.0 toolbar, 13
streaming audio and video, 148
<STRIKE> </STRIKE> tag, 52-55
strikethrough (<STRIKE> </STRIKE>) tag, 52-55
<STRONG> </STRONG> tag, 59-60
style sheets, 273-289
 attributes, *277-279*
 changing size of links, 287
 cool tricks, 287-289
 external, 286-287
 generic font families, *280*
 header styles, 284-286
 inline, 276-283
 line-height attribute, 278
 margin attributes, 278
 saving as documents, 286-287
 superimposing and overlapping text, 288-289
 text-align attribute, 279
 text-decoration attribute, 279
 text-indent attribute, 279
 units of measurement to use with, 279
 using classes within to create your own types of HTML tags, 284-286
<STYLE> </STYLE> tag, 275-276
 (subscript) tag, 52-54
SUBMIT <INPUT> type, 233
Submit It! Online, 346
Submit It! service, for sending Web pages to sites, 345-346
Submit It! utility, developer of, 345
subscript () tag, 52-54
summary lines, creating at top of

Web pages, 97-98
 (superscript) tag, 52-54
superimposing or overlapping text, using style sheets, 288-289
superscript () tag, 52-54
SurfWatch, Web content rating program, 336

Tab key controls on input, 315-317
TABINDEX attribute, 315-317
TABLE attributes, *154, 161,* 305
table data (<TD> </TD>) tag, 152-157, 292, *305*
<TABLE FRAME= attributes, 161-162
table header <TH> tag, 292-293
table of contents, adding to large Web documents, 93-105
table row <TR> </TR> tag, 152-157
<TABLE RULES= attributes, 161-162
<TABLE> </TABLE> tag, 152-157
 advanced, 292-295, *305*
 new HTML 4.0 elements, 295-298
tables
 advanced, 292-295
 advanced formatting of, 158-159
 and frames, 151-178
 basic formatting of, 152-157
 COLSPAN option, 157
 forms, 164
 FRAME attribute, 161-162
 improvements in with HTML 4.0, 291-292
 Internet Explorer capabilities for, 159-160
 modifying edges and grid lines, 161-162
 new HTML 4.0 elements, 295-298
 organizing information in, 152-157
 ROWSPAN option for, 159
 RULES attribute, 161-162
 spanning multiple table columns for header, 157
 spanning multiple lines of a table, 159

(continued)

IDG BOOKS WORLDWIDE, INC.
END-USER LICENSE AGREEMENT

4. **Restrictions on Use of Individual Programs.** You must follow the individual requirements and restrictions detailed for each individual program in Appendix F of this Book. These limitations are also contained in the individual license agreements recorded on the Software Media. These limitations may include a requirement that after using the program for a specified period of time, the user must pay a registration fee or discontinue use. By opening the Software packet, you will be agreeing to abide by the licenses and restrictions for these individual programs that are detailed in Appendix F and on the Software Media. None of the material on this Software Media or listed in this Book may ever be redistributed, in original or modified form, for commercial purposes.

5. **Limited Warranty.**

(a) IDGB warrants that the Software and Software Media are free from defects in materials and workmanship under normal use for a period of sixty (60) days from the date of purchase of this Book. If IDGB receives notification within the warranty period of defects in materials or workmanship, IDGB will replace the defective Software Media.

(b) **IDGB AND THE AUTHOR OF THE BOOK DISCLAIM ALL OTHER WARRANTIES, EXPRESS OR IMPLIED, INCLUDING WITHOUT LIMITATION IMPLIED WARRANTIES OF MERCHANTABILITY AND FITNESS FOR A PARTICULAR PURPOSE, WITH RESPECT TO THE SOFTWARE, THE PROGRAMS, THE SOURCE CODE CONTAINED THEREIN, AND/OR THE TECHNIQUES DESCRIBED IN THIS BOOK. IDGB DOES NOT WARRANT THAT THE FUNCTIONS CONTAINED IN THE SOFTWARE WILL MEET YOUR REQUIREMENTS OR THAT THE OPERATION OF THE SOFTWARE WILL BE ERROR FREE.**

(c) This limited warranty gives you specific legal rights, and you may have other rights that vary from jurisdiction to jurisdiction.

6. **Remedies.**

(a) IDGB's entire liability and your exclusive remedy for defects in materials and workmanship shall be limited to replacement of the Software Media, which may be returned to IDGB with a copy of your receipt at the following address: Software Media Fulfillment Department, Attn.: *Creating Cool HTML 4 Web Pages*, IDG Books Worldwide, Inc., 7260 Shadeland Station, Ste. 100, Indianapolis, IN 46256, or call 1-800-762-2974. Please allow three to four weeks for delivery. This Limited Warranty is void if failure of the Software Media has resulted from accident, abuse, or misapplication. Any replacement Software Media will be warranted for the remainder of the original warranty period or thirty (30) days, whichever is longer.

(b) In no event shall IDGB or the author be liable for any damages what-soever (including without limitation damages for loss of business prof-its, business interruption, loss of business information, or any other pecuniary loss) arising from the use of or inability to use the Book or the Software, even if IDGB has been advised of the possibility of such damages.

(c) Because some jurisdictions do not allow the exclusion or limitation of liability for consequential or incidental damages, the above limitation or exclusion may not apply to you.

7. **U.S. Government Restricted Rights.** Use, duplication, or disclosure of the Software by the U.S. Government is subject to restrictions stated in paragraph (c)(1)(ii) of the Rights in Technical Data and Computer Software clause of DFARS 252.227-7013, and in subparagraphs (a) through (d) of the Commercial Computer — Restricted Rights clause at FAR 52.227-19, and in similar clauses in the NASA FAR supple-ment, when applicable.

8. **General.** This Agreement constitutes the entire understanding of the parties and revokes and supersedes all prior agreements, oral or writ-ten, between them and may not be modified or amended except in a writing signed by both parties hereto that specifically refers to this Agreement. This Agreement shall take precedence over any other documents that may be in conflict herewith. If any one or more provi-sions contained in this Agreement are held by any court or tribunal to be invalid, illegal, or otherwise unenforceable, each and every other provision shall remain in full force and effect.

my2cents.idgbooks.com

Register This Book — And Win!

Visit **http://my2cents.idgbooks.com** to register this book and we'll automatically enter you in our fantastic monthly prize giveaway. It's also your opportunity to give us feedback: let us know what you thought of this book and how you would like to see other topics covered.

Discover IDG Books Online!

The IDG Books Online Web site is your online resource for tackling technology — at home and at the office. Frequently updated, the IDG Books Online Web site features exclusive software, insider information, online books, and live events!

10 Productive & Career-Enhancing Things You Can Do at www.idgbooks.com

- Nab source code for your own programming projects.

- Download software.

- Read Web exclusives: special articles and book excerpts by IDG Books Worldwide authors.

- Take advantage of resources to help you advance your career as a Novell or Microsoft professional.

- Buy IDG Books Worldwide titles or find a convenient bookstore that carries them.

- Register your book and win a prize.

- Chat live online with authors.

- Sign up for regular e-mail updates about our latest books.

- Suggest a book you'd like to read or write.

- Give us your 2¢ about our books and about our Web site.

You say you're not on the Web yet? It's easy to get started with IDG Books' *Discover the Internet,* available at local retailers everywhere.

CD-ROM Installation Instructions

The accompanying CD-ROM contains example files from the text and a great selection of shareware for both Macintosh and Windows. For a description of the shareware and instructions for how to install each application, see Appendix F or the file readme.txt on the CD-ROM. To see the example files, open the file coolweb.html in your Web browser; you'll be able to navigate through all the examples in the book.